PUBLIC RELATIONS LEADERS AS SENSEMAKERS

Public Relations Leaders as Sensemakers presents foundational research on the public relations profession, providing a current and compelling picture of expanding global practice. Utilizing data from one of the largest studies ever conducted in the field, and representing the perspectives of 4,500 practitioners, private and state-run companies, communication agencies, government agencies, and nonprofits, this work advances a theory of integrated leadership in public relations and highlights future research needs and educational implications.

This volume is appropriate for graduate and advanced undergraduate students in international public relations and communication management, as well as scholars in global public relations, communication management, and business. It is also intended to supplement courses in public relations theory, strategic communication, business management, and leadership development.

Bruce K. Berger, PhD, is professor emeritus of advertising and public relations at the University of Alabama. He was the co-principal investigator for the global leadership study. He serves as research director for the Plank Center for Leadership in Public Relations at the University of Alabama and as editor of the Organizational Communication Research Center online site for the Institute for Public Relations. Previously, Berger was a public relations professional and executive for The Upjohn Company and Whirlpool Corporation for 20 years. He worked on communication projects in more than 30 countries. His research focuses on communication management and leadership, employee communications and power relations inside organizations. He has authored or edited four books and more than 80 book chapters and scholarly and professional articles.

Juan Meng, PhD, is Assistant Professor of Advertising and Public Relations in the Grady College of Journalism and Mass Communication at the University of Georgia. She was the co-principal investigator for the global leadership study. She is a Fellow of the Plank Center for Leadership in Public Relations at the University of Alabama. Her research focuses on the quantitative measurement of public relations leadership, leadership development in a global context, strategic stakeholder engagement, and corporate reputation management in evolving markets. Her research on public relations leadership has been published in *The SAGE Handbook of Public Relations, Journal of Public Relations Research, Public Relations Review, Public Relations Journal,* and *Journal of Communication Management,* among others.

PUBLIC RELATIONS LEADERS AS SENSEMAKERS

A Global Study of Leadership in Public Relations and Communication Management

Edited by
Bruce K. Berger and Juan Meng

Routledge
Taylor & Francis Group

NEW YORK AND LONDON

First published 2014
by Routledge
711 Third Avenue, New York, NY 10017

and by Routledge
2 Park Square, Milton Park, Abingdon, Oxon OX14 4RN

Routledge is an imprint of the Taylor & Francis Group, an informa business

© 2014 Taylor & Francis

Library of Congress Cataloging-in-Publication Data
A catalog record has been requested for this book.

ISBN: 978-0-415-71091-6 (hbk)
ISBN: 978-0-415-71092-3 (pbk)
ISBN: 978-1-315-85893-7 (ebk)

Typeset in Bembo
by Apex CoVantage, LLC

Printed and bound in the United States of America by Publishers Graphics, LLC on sustainably sourced paper.

Dedicated to Betsy Ann Plank (1924–2010)
Leader, mentor, teacher, counselor and, above all,
friend and kindred spirit to thousands
of public relations practitioners, educators and students.
Godspeed, Betsy.

CONTENTS

SECTION IV
Creating the Future   **295**

FIGURES

TABLES

CONTRIBUTORS

Andréia S. Athaydes is professor of advertising and public relations at the Lutheran University of Brazil (ULBRA) and Integrated College of Taquara (Faccat). Currently, she manages the Directorate of Community Affairs of ULBRA and is Chairman of the Federal Council of Public Relations Professionals (Conferp). Athaydes holds a master's degree in business administration and marketing and is a PhD candidate in organizational communication. Her research focuses on memory and practice of public relations in Brazil and Ibero-America. She has authored several scholarly articles, and she has joined the executive board of several entities in the public relations field. She has done advisory consulting in public and private organizations in the education, culture, and health sectors in addition to managing undergraduate programs in social communication.

Mark Bain, in 2012, founded upper 90 consulting LLC, which helps leaders and their teams improve performance. The firm provides professional development and leadership support to companies of varying sizes. Prior to forming upper 90, Mark was Global Director of Communications for Baker & McKenzie, the world's largest law firm, and Vice President, Corporate Communications worldwide for Alticor Inc., the corporate parent of Amway Corp., the world's largest direct-selling company. Mark started his career with Burson-Marsteller, working for nearly 16 years in the firm's New York, Los Angeles, Hong Kong, and Tokyo offices. He graduated with a degree in advertising and public relations from the University of Utah, where, as a distinguished lecturer and adjunct professor, he taught the school's first course on corporate reputation management.

Nilanjana R. Bardhan, PhD, is Associate Professor of public relations and intercultural communication at Southern Illinois University, Carbondale (SIUC). Her research focuses on public relations in India and in global cultural contexts. In the area of intercultural communication, she researches the relationship between globalization and postcoloniality and the construction of culture, communication, and identity. She has coedited two books and coauthored one and has published several scholarly journal articles and book chapters. She also serves as director for graduate studies for the Department of Speech Communication at SIUC.

Gustavo Becker is professor of Public Relations and Corporate Education Programs at the Lutheran University of Brazil (ULBRA). Currently he is director of University Extension at ULBRA. He holds a master's degree in social communication from the Pontifical Catholic University of Rio Grande do Sul, a Marketing Specialist degree at Federal University of Rio Grande do Sul and a degree in Public Relations from the University of Vale do Rio dos Sinos. He is a board member at the Federal Council of Public Relations Professionals (Conferp). His research focuses on organizational communication, teaching public relations, scientific dissemination, and event management.

Rodrigo Silveira Cogo is professor in the MBA program in Management in Corporate Communications at the Brazilian Association for Business Communication/Aberje, where he is also Content Manager, working on digital interfaces. He is a researcher of the Research Group of New Narratives/GENN-ECA-USP and a member of the Association of Researchers in Organizational Communication and Public Relations/Abrapcorp. He holds a master's in communication sciences from the School of Communication and Arts of the University of São Paulo/ECA-USP and expert qualification in strategic organizational communication and public relations from the same institution. His research focuses on corporate memory and storytelling. He has a degree in public relations from the Federal University of Santa Maria. He has done consulting on corporate communication for clients such as Rhodia, HP, Telefonica, Goodyear, Embraer, and Mapfre.

Elina Erzikova, PhD, is Associate Professor of public relations at Central Michigan University. She was a country investigator (Russia) for the global leadership study. Erzikova is a fellow of the Plank Center for Leadership in Public Relations at the University of Alabama. She was recognized as one of the top women professors in Michigan in 2013. Erzikova won two university-wide Excellence in Teaching awards in 2012–2013. The Association for Education in Journalism and Mass Communication named her an Emerging Scholar in 2012. Her research interests are located at the intersection of journalism, public relations, and political communication. In her native country, Russia, Erzikova was the editor in chief of a regional newspaper, and she worked as a public relations manager for a political party.

Mateus Furlanetto is Executive Director of Aberje, the Brazilian Association for Business Communication, and professor in the Public Relations program at Casper Libero College. He is a board member of the Global Alliance for Public Relations and Communication Management. He holds a master's in communications science from the School of Communications and Arts of the University of São Paulo/ECA-USP. His research focuses on crisis communication and public relations for the performing arts. He is a researcher of the Research Group of New Narratives/GENN-ECA-USP.

Mark Harris is Vice President of Communications for IBM Global Business Services, the $20-billion unit that provides business consulting and applications management services to IBM clients around the world. He is responsible for the competitive positioning of IBM's business advisory services with media, analysts and via social platforms, and leads executive support and communications to a global workforce of more than 100,000. During the 1990s turnaround of IBM, Mark was a senior communications advisor and speechwriter for IBM Chairman and CEO Lou Gerstner. Prior to joining IBM, he was a reporter for United Press International. He is a member of the board of advisors at the Plank Center for Leadership in Public Relations at the University of Alabama, and holds BA and MA degrees in journalism from the same university.

Marco V. Herrera is Founder of Grupo Public, a communications agency established in Mexico in 1996. He was the principal researcher for the study in his country. He is a member of the Commission on Global Public Relations Research in the Institute for Public Relations and a member of the advisory board in the Center for Global Public Relations of the University of North Carolina. Marco was president of the Mexican Association of Public Relations Professionals, where he achieved the signing of the Mexico Accord for Public Relations. He participated in the advisory committee for the Stockholm Accords in the Global Alliance. Previously Marco was a public relations professional for 15 years in banking institutions. He has published over 200 professional articles in Mexico.

William Heyman is President and CEO of Heyman Associates, an executive search firm that places senior-level communications professionals in leading corporations, foundations, academic institutions, and professional associations. He is a founding board member of the Plank Center for Leadership in Public Relations at the University of Alabama and co-chairs the Milestones in Mentoring Dinner. With the university, he has also been involved with three groundbreaking public relations leadership studies. A *PRWeek* Power List Supporting Power Player,

Bill serves on the committee of The Seminar, the Arthur W. Page Society, the Institute for Public Relations, and the College of Charleston's Department of Communication Advisory Council. He graduated from Gettysburg College and serves on the school's Communications and Marketing Advisory Council. He earned his MBA from Adelphi University.

Chun-ju Flora Hung-Baesecke, PhD, is Assistant Professor and Option Coordinator of the Public Relations & Advertising Option in the Department of Communication Studies at Hong Kong Baptist University. Her research interests are relationship management, strategic management, corporate social responsibility, reputation management, crisis communication, and conflict resolution. Dr. Hung has published her research in book chapters and in international refereed journals, such as the *Journal of Public Relations Research*, the *Journal of Communication Management, Public Relations Review*, and the *International Journal of Strategic Communication*, and has presented research papers in international conferences. She is active in the public relations academy and industry in the Greater China region and a member of the Academic Committee in China International Public Relations Association, and was named one of the Top 100 PR People in China in 2009.

Yan Jin, PhD, is Associate Professor of Public Relations at the Virginia Commonwealth University (VCU). She serves as Associate Director for Research and Outreach at the VCU School of Mass Communications, and as Executive Director of the Center for Media+Health at VCU. Her research interest is in the areas of crisis communication and strategic conflict management, as well as how emotions influence public relations leadership and strategic communication decision-making processes. Her work has been published in *The Handbook of Crisis Communication, Communication Research*, the *Journal of Applied Communication Research*, the *Journal of Public Relations Research, Public Relations Review, Corporate Communication: An International Journal*, the *Journal of Contingency and Crisis Management*, and *Newspaper Research Journal*, among others.

Kwang Hee Kim, PhD, is Adjunct Professor of Integrative Health Science at Inha University, Inchon, South Korea. She serves as the chief of Healing Communication Center. She is very active on Twitter, with more than 32,000 followers on various communication topics (twitter.com/Comm_Love). Her early study focused on the teaching methods in media education. She is now interested in developing Self Esteem Development Programs through intrapersonal communication. She has authored five books.

Jaesub Lee, PhD, is Associate Professor of Communication in the Valenti School of Communication, University of Houston. His research focuses on relationship development and maintenance, leadership communication, media and information processing, risk communication, and intercultural communication. His research has appeared in variety of academic and professional journals, including the *Journal of Public Relations Research, Public Relations Review, Human Communication Research, Management Communication Quarterly,* and others. He has been also associated with a number of consulting and research projects, including Dresser, Schlumberger, Shell, Baker Oil, Texaco, TCI, Veritas, Sterling Bank, Sysco, and Local Emergency Planning Committees in Houston suburbs.

Anne Linke, MA, is a research associate at the institute of communication and media studies at the University of Leipzig, Germany. She has worked in the professional field of corporate communications and measurement and was a visiting lecturer at the University of Technology Sydney, Australia. Her postgraduate degree in communication and media studies and sociology, obtained at the University of Leipzig and Universitat de Valencia, Spain, was a starting point for her doctoral research in the fields of social media and communication management. She has published on online communications, innovation and communication, and strategic communication in academic journals and received best paper awards from major international conferences.

Rebeca I. Arévalo Martínez, Master in Communications, is professor of corporate communication, advertising, and public relations at the Universidad Anáhuac in Mexico. She was the co-researcher of the Cross-Cultural Study of Leadership in Public Relations and Communication Management for Mexico. She is a researcher at the Center for Applied Communication Research (CICA) of the School of Communication at the Universidad Anáhuac. Previously, Arévalo was a corporate communication professional and executive for Grupo DESC for 13 years. She has worked on corporate communication and public relations projects as consultant for more than 5 years. Her researches focus on corporate communication, public relations, digital communication, and media ethics. She has participated nationally and internationally in more than 15 academic events and authored more than 8 scholarly articles.

Ángeles Moreno is Titular Professor at the Universidad Rey Juan Carlos of Madrid, Spain, where she has occupied diverse managerial positions as current Director of the Postgraduate Expert Title in Online Strategic Communication. She is an active member of the Group of Advanced Studies in Communication (GEAC) and participates in research projects of this institution and the Science and Innovation Spanish Department, EUPRERA or the European Union. Her work is currently published in indexed journals and has received three nominated top papers in recent years. She also belongs to the executive board of the Public Relations Researcher Association, the scientific board and core of reviewers of diverse international congresses and journals, and the Science and Innovation Spanish Department.

Paulo Nassar, PhD, is president of Aberje, the Brazilian Association for Business Communications, and also professor in the Public Relations Program at the School of Communications and Arts of the University of São Paulo (ECA/USP). He is currently doing post doctorate research at IULM-Italy. He is the author of numerous books, including *What is Business Communication* and *Using Public Relations to Combine Organizational History and Narrative to Strengthen Corporate Reputation*. He also is editorial director of the magazines *Business Communication*, *MSG and BR*, and *PR*, which is the first global publication of business communication and public relations in Brazil. He has a degree in journalism from the Pontific Catholic University of São Paulo, and an MA and a PhD in communications science at USP. In 2012, he won the Atlas Award for Lifetime Achievement in International Public Relations, awarded by the Public Relations Society of America.

Jongmin Park, PhD, is professor and department chair of journalism and communication at Kyung Hee University, Seoul, Korea. He earned his PhD at the Missouri School of Journalism and served as research director for the Communication Research Center at Kyung Hee University. Previously, Jongmin Park was an advisory committee member of National Crisis Management Center at the Blue House (the Korean presidential residence) and is a board member of directors at the Independence Hall of Korea. His research focuses on governmental and corporate public relations studies such as issue and crisis management, conflict management, corporate social responsibility and leadership and organizational communication. He has authored 20 scholarly articles in the United States and three books, six book chapters, and 80 scholarly articles in Korea.

Padmini Patwardhan, PhD, is professor of mass communication at Winthrop University with research interests in international advertising and public relations, integrated marketing communication, media dependency and global learning strategies. She was India co–project director on the global leadership study. She is author/coauthor of 22 journal articles or book chapters and more than 30 conference papers. She has won multiple conference awards and research grants from the Plank Center, the American Academy of Advertising, National Association of Broadcasters, and the Winthrop Research Council, among others. A copywriter/creative consultant by training, she worked for leading agencies in India. She is a 2011 Winthrop Thompson Scholar, a 2006 Advertising Educational Foundation Fellow-Visiting Professor Program and 2008 and 2009 chair of the International Advertising Education Committee of the American Academy of Advertising.

Baiba Pētersone, PhD, is a senior lecturer at Middlesex University in London. Her research focuses on international public relations and communication management. She has taught in the United States, Europe, Central Asia, and the

Middle East. Her industry experience includes working for various Washington, D.C.–based international affairs and culture organizations, including U.S. Civilian Research and Development Foundation, John Hopkins University's American Institute for Contemporary German Studies, the John F. Kennedy Center for the Performing Arts, and the Smithsonian Institution. Her professional affiliations include the International Communication Association, Middle East Public Relations Association, and European Public Relations Education and Research Association, where she also is an internal auditor. She holds a doctoral degree from the University of Georgia and a master's degree from the University of Maryland.

Bryan H. Reber, PhD, is Professor of Public Relations and Assistant Head of the Department of Advertising and Public Relations at the Grady College of Journalism and Mass Media, University of Georgia. He is a member of the board of directors for the Plank Center for Leadership in Public Relations. He has conducted research and consulted for the Sierra Club, Ketchum, Missouri Public Service Commission, Georgia Hospital Association and others. Prior to joining the academic ranks, he worked in public relations at Bethel College, Kansas, for 15 years. His research focuses on public relations, crisis communication, and health communication. He is coauthor of three top-selling public relations textbooks. He has published about 50 journal articles, book chapters, and encyclopedia entries on public relations topics.

Ulrike Röttger, PhD, is Professor for public relations and Managing Director of the Department of Communication at the University of Münster, Germany. She has been the president of the German Communication Association (DGPuK), the professional organisation of scholars and researchers in communication science, and a member of the association's executive board for several years. She holds a graduate degree in journalism from the University of Dortmund, Germany, and a doctorate in communication science from the University of Zurich, Switzerland. She has published widely, including 17 books and more than 100 articles in several languages. Her research fields include public relations and organizational communication, corporate communications, campaigns, issues management, internal communication, and public relations consulting.

Cristina Navarro Ruiz, PhD, is professor at the Rey Juan Carlos University (Madrid, Spain) where she teaches courses in public relations and journalism at both the BA and MA levels. She has participated in national and international research projects focused on media effects, professionalism, and leadership in public relations and communication management. She is an active member of GEAC (Group of Advanced Studies in Communication) and is author and coauthor of several papers in Spanish and international journals. Previously, she has worked in print and online media and has been a consultant in public relations agencies for almost 20 years. Her research is on a range of topics in public relations, with a particular focus on social media strategy and digital communications.

Jae-Hwa Shin, PhD, MPH, is Associate Professor of Public Relations at the University of Southern Mississippi. She worked as Public Relations Director for Korea Economic Research Institute and Center for Free Enterprise of the Federation of Korea Industries, which was founded in 1961 by multinational corporate members such as Samsung, LG, SK, and other industry leaders. She was responsible for a wide range of integrated communication activities designed to build relationships with media, government, opinion leaders, interest groups, employees, and the community. Her research areas include public relations theories, strategic conflict management cycle, agenda-building process, and health communication. She has published dozens of articles in major journals and recently coauthored *Public Relations Today: Managing Competition and Conflict* and *Think Public Relations.*

Janne Stahl, MA, is a research associate at the Department of Communication at the University of Münster, Germany. She holds a doctoral research stipend from the Academic Society of Corporate Leadership and Communication and works in the field of leadership in communication management. She graduated in communication studies, politics and philosophy in Münster, worked for the state-funded research project "Organisation and Publics of Universities," and gained practical experiences in public relations, marketing, and event management.

Ansgar Zerfass, PhD, is Professor of Communication Management and Vice Dean of the School for Social Sciences at the University of Leipzig, Germany, as well as Adjunct Professor in communication and leadership at BI Norwegian Business School, Oslo, Norway. He serves the research community as president of the European Public Relations Education and Research Association, Brussels; editor of the International Journal of Strategic Communication (Routledge); and lead researcher of the annual European Communication Monitor survey covering more than 40 countries. He holds a doctorate in business administration, a habilitation in communication science and has worked in management positions in business for 10 years. His publications (29 books and more than 200 journal articles and chapters) cover corporate communications, online communication, measurement and international communication.

PREFACE

This book takes a deep dive into the concept of leadership in public relations and communication management. We believe that excellent leadership in and of the practice is an extraordinarily valuable asset—a difference maker. The quality of public relations leaders and their day-to-day performance in organizations and in the profession has a great deal to do with the success, reputation, and future of those organizations and the profession itself, especially in a dynamic and fast-changing world in which the only certainty of the future is uncertainty.

Thousands of managerial leadership studies have been conducted in a number of fields during the past century. Above all, they confirm that the leadership concept is complex, as evidenced in the diverse perspectives through which the topic has been explored. Curiously, however, the concept of leadership in public relations has not been widely researched or systemically or strategically addressed by professional associations and educational institutions. Although many agree that leadership in public relations and communication management is a valuable form of human capital, studies carried out by the Plank Center for Leadership in Public Relations suggest that leadership in the field is largely under-examined, underdeveloped, and unmeasured.

We are not sure why this is so, but we produced this book to try to address this important present and future issue, along with some related questions. What, for example, constitutes excellent leadership in public relations? What are the crucial dimensions, and can we theorize and assess them? Is excellent leadership a local or global phenomenon? Who is responsible for the cultivation and development of leaders in communication management? What roles do individuals, organizations, and professional associations play in improving leadership for the future? Why don't we do more to systematically cultivate leadership and manage it like a precious asset, rather than a cost?

To address such questions, and under the auspices of the Plank Center, we developed and carried out a global study of leadership in public relations and communication management in 2011–2012. This book presents the results of that comprehensive study, makes the case for greater understanding of leadership in the profession, and calls for more informed and systematic development of future leaders to increase their skills, capabilities, and overall capacity to lead.

The Global Study

The book is thoroughly grounded on a rich empirical foundation—the largest study of leadership ever conducted in our field. In 2012, an international team of 28 researchers conducted survey and interview research regarding leadership in public relations. In the first phase, nearly 4,500 practitioners in 23 countries completed a 58-question online survey in nine languages. The survey examined key issues in the field, how leaders manage them, how the issues affect leaders' roles and practices, and what might be done to improve the development of communication leaders for an uncertain and complex future. The survey also captured individual perceptions about leaders, organizational culture, gender, and the profession.

In the second phase, the researchers used an 18-question interview guide to conduct 45-minute interviews with 137 communication leaders in 10 countries and regions. The interviews (a) provided deeper insights about managing issues in a turbulent environment, (b) examined how organizational culture and structure influence leadership practices and decisions, and (c) explored crucial qualities and characteristics of excellent leaders and what future leaders might require. Findings from both research projects are presented in the book and provide the essential basis for the arguments herein. All 29 authors served as country investigators or carried out other support activities for this major research project, and collectively they represent a tremendous cross section of countries, academic institutions, and organizations.

Outline of the Book

The book includes four sections. Section I focuses on the background for the study and provides a framework for the global project. Chapter 1 introduces five assumptions on which the book is based, defines some key terms, and explains how "sensemaker" is an appropriate metaphor for leadership in public relations in our dynamic, high-speed world of information flow. Chapter 2 reviews the vast managerial leadership literature and underscores the many diverse perspectives that have characterized theorizing in the area for the last century. The chapter concludes with five research questions that guided the global study. In Chapter 3, we describe the survey and interview methods used in the global study. One of the study's central purposes was to test an integrated model of excellent leadership in public relations, and this is discussed in the chapter, as well. Chapter 4 briefly profiles the communication professionals who participated in the online survey and in the interviews.

Section II is a comprehensive report of the results of the online survey, which involved 4,484 participants in 23 countries. Chapter 5 sets the stage by reviewing the top 10 issues in the field, which are crucial to leadership because they provide the context in which practice occurs. Issues influence what leaders do and how they do it. Chapter 6 reviews the strategies and tactics leaders use to manage the 10 issues. Chapter 7 explores in depth the seven dimensions of the integrated model of excellent leadership in communication management. Survey results suggest the model may have application in a number of countries, which bears implications for the training and development of future leaders in the field.

Chapter 8 explores 12 approaches that might be used to better develop leaders for the future. In some of the most consistent survey findings, practitioners emphasized the importance of developing greater soft skills—better listening skills and change and conflict management capabilities. Participants also responded to a set of questions that captured their perceptions about leadership and gender, organizational culture and the overall profession, and these results are examined in Chapter 9. A Summated Leadership Index, which indicates the extent to which an organization's environment is conducive to excellent leadership in communication, is also presented. The descriptive index suggests there's a great deal of room for improvement in leadership in all of the countries in the study.

Section III provides a close-up look at public relations leadership in 10 countries and regions in the study, in this order: the Chinese-speaking countries, India, South Korea, the German-speaking countries, Latvia, Russia, Spain, Brazil, Mexico, and the United States. Each chapter in this section explores the key issues in the country or region, how these issues affect leadership roles and practices, and organizational cultural and structural factors that facilitate or impede excellent practice. The 10 chapters are heavily grounded in the depth interviews conducted with senior leaders in each country or region. Overall, these chapters provide rich cultural perspectives on the leadership concept.

The concluding Section IV summarizes the research findings and discusses their implications for practice, education, and additional research. A profile of future leaders is also presented, based on the insights of the leaders we interviewed. We argue that the profession needs to systemically research and discuss the topic of leadership and then address leadership development and assessment needs.

ACKNOWLEDGMENTS

We want to thank the many organizations and individuals who helped us conceptualize and carry out our global study and produce this book. We are especially grateful to the Plank Center for Leadership in Public Relations at the University of Alabama, Heyman Associates, and IBM Corporation for sponsoring and funding the global study. They were excited about the project from our first discussions of it. We also want to thank three research allies that were vital to completing the project successfully: the Academic Society for Corporate Leadership and Communication in Germany, the Brazilian Association for Business Communication (Aberje), and the Hong Kong Public Relations Professionals' Association.

Julia Sammaritano and Linda Bathgate at Routledge provided helpful suggestions and excellent support throughout the writing and preparation process. Many colleagues at the University of Alabama, University of Georgia, and University of Leipzig provided intellectual stimulation, technical assistance, and enthusiastic support, including Karla Gower, Kaitlyn Honnold, Joe Phelps, Holley Reeves, Katharina Simon, Sophia Charlotte Volk, and Franziska Weber. Working with the team of international researchers was an exhilarating experience, and we thank all of them for their hard work and invaluable contributions. Their voices and rich insights illuminate this book.

Finally, we want to thank our spouses—Joan and Po-Lin—for their unqualified love and support throughout this lengthy 3-year project. Their enthusiasm and encouragement were crucial to the successful completion of this project.

SECTION I

Shining a Light on Leadership in Public Relations

This section provides background and a framework for the global study.

Chapter 1 introduces five assumptions on which the book is based, defines some key terms, and argues that *sensemaker* is an appropriate metaphor for leadership in public relations. Chapter 2 reviews the vast literature regarding managerial leadership and presents five research questions that guided the study. The survey and interview methods used in the global study are explained in Chapter 3, and communication professionals who participated in the online survey and depth interviews are profiled in Chapter 4.

1

MAKING SENSE OF LEADERS AND LEADERSHIP IN PUBLIC RELATIONS

Bruce K. Berger and Juan Meng

Several years ago in Miami we presented a conference paper regarding the importance of leadership and role modeling. During the discussion session, Professor Don Wright of Boston University observed, "I'm glad to see some research about leadership in public relations. Leadership is one of the two most overlooked 'L's' in the field; listening is the other." We couldn't agree more. Leadership in public relations is little researched, is often overlooked, or is simply taken for granted, which raises important questions about this vital form of human capital:

- Beyond the annual glamour parades of awards for public relations projects, programs, and people, why don't we pay more attention to the concept and development of leadership in public relations?
- Why isn't the cultivation of excellent leadership a national or international priority for a profession that remains ill defined even to its own members and subject to ongoing cynicism and distrust among diverse publics?
- What constitutes excellent leadership in public relations? How do we know? How would we measure it?
- Why do some leaders succeed beautifully, while others fail miserably?
- What are the implications of our dynamic and fast-moving world for the preparation and development of leaders for an uncertain future?
- How much better would public relations leaders be if their leadership capacities and capabilities were intentionally and systematically developed and cultivated over time?

These and related questions are the framework for this book, which is the first in-depth examination of leadership in communication management. General leadership studies, and there are thousands of them, document that leaders play crucial roles in groups, organizations, and nations. Leaders make strategic decisions, allocate key resources, and influence organizational culture. They are key influencers of employee perceptions, attitudes, trust levels, and job- and organization-related outcomes (Shaffer, 2000). Leaders are literally and symbolically *the* organization to many internal and external stakeholders (Pincus, Rayfield, & Debonis, 1991). The performance of leaders good and bad is linked to the success, image and future of their groups, organizations, and nations (Berger & Meng, 2010), and we believe the same is true for public relations leaders.

Until recently, however, few research studies have directly explored leadership in communication management. Perhaps one reason is that the topic isn't sexy enough. Even a cursory examination of the scholarly or trade literatures reveals that far more attention is devoted to more seductive issues such as big data, social media, personal branding, crisis communications, best practices, and so forth. Another reason might be that leadership is a complex and cumbersome research topic, as demonstrated in a century of diverse studies and theoretical perspectives. Yet, as the world and the practice spin rapidly into an uncertain future, the need for better understanding leadership in public relations, and improving the preparation of leaders for this future, may be more crucial than ever.

The primary purpose of this book, then, is to focus attention on leaders and leadership in our field—we want to pull leadership from the margins of our reflections into the foreground of our thinking. We bring the topic to life by grounding it in rich quantitative and qualitative data that were gathered in 2012 in our global study of communication leadership, the largest study of its kind in our field. Nearly 4,500 public relations professionals in 23 countries participated in an online survey in nine languages in the first phase of the study. Carried out by a 28-member international research team, the survey examined key issues in the field, the strategies and tactics leaders use to deal with the issues, how the issues affect leadership roles and practices, and what might be done to better prepare leaders for the future.

A second study phase in 2012–2013 involved depth interviews with 137 leaders in 10 countries and regions that were included in the survey. These conversations examined more deeply how leaders deal with crucial issues in their daily work, and the influences of the digital age on their roles. The leaders also discussed the relative influences of organizational culture and structure on their work and described some ways in which future public relations leaders will and must be different. Findings from the survey and the interviews provide most of the content for Section II and Section III in the book, respectively.

By way of laying a foundation for theory, we present an integrated model of excellent leadership in public relations that helps us understand the crucial dimensions of communication leadership and may help us better prepare future leaders. The model highlights six dimensions of excellent leadership in public relations: self-dynamics, ethical orientation, relationship-building skills, strategic decision-making capability, team collaboration, and communication knowledge management. An important seventh dimension, organizational culture and structure, influences the extent to which public relations leaders may be effective.

Some Definitions

Researchers have defined *leaders* and *leadership* in diverse ways. Rost (1991) identified more than 200 definitions of leadership in his analysis of articles and books on the topic in the 20th century. We imagine more have appeared in recent years, for example, the current focus on "authentic" leadership. Rather than review this vast literature of definitions, we draw from several sources that reflect our view of leaders and leadership in public relations. First, from Northouse's (2007) comprehensive overview of leadership theory and practice, we adopt the definition of *leaders* as "the people who engage in leadership" (p. 3) and who are responsible for others or for influencing others to achieve a common goal. We enrich this definition when we define *excellent leadership in public relations* later in the book.

An *assigned leader* has positional or structural power based on organizational hierarchy. An *emergent leader* has personal power based on the actual influence one has regardless of title or position. This individual is perceived by others to be a leader, and often gains this support through positive communication behaviors, for example, listening skills and being engaged in dialogue (Northouse, 2007, pp. 5–7). We are interested in both types of leaders in this book.

According to Northouse (2007), *leadership* is "a process whereby an individual influences a group of individuals to achieve a common goal" (p. 3). This simple definition emphasizes that leadership is an interactive and ongoing process, not just a set of traits or characteristics. It also reflects four key elements that are often present in lengthier definitions of the term, that is, relationships between leaders and followers, the importance of context, the use of influence, and goal achievement.

Second, Hackman and Johnson (2009) argue compellingly that leadership is best understood from a communication perspective: At its core, leadership is communication. They claim that leadership is and always has been a universal concept—an integral part of human life in tribal, industrial, and informational societies—and language is the powerful tool of effective leadership. They define *leadership* as "human (symbolic) communication, which modifies the attitudes and behaviors of others in order to meet shared group goals and needs" (p. 11). This perspective underscores the crucial roles of public relations leaders who assist other leaders and followers in their organizations in (1) making sense of a complex and dynamic world and (2) then communicating and interacting more effectively, transparently, and ethically with others in the world.

Finally, we are interested in leaders at all levels in the function, and the term *dispersed leadership* (Gardner, 1990) captures this idea—leaders can be found at all levels in diverse nations, organizations, professional associations, and groups, and functions. This is important because local or lower level leaders are often closer to problems and opportunities and may be able to more quickly and efficiently resolve them. This directly benefits organizations and may provide a road map for dealing with related issues or stimulating needed change.

Our focus in the book, then, is primarily *on* leaders of the public relations function and leaders at various levels *within* the function in diverse organizations in many countries. We believe that excellent and effective functional leaders are more likely to be involved in strategic decision making at high levels in their organizations and thereby able to also be "business" leaders who help their organizations achieve goals.

Public Relations Leaders as Sensemakers

One useful approach to studying the complex topic of leadership is by using metaphor. A metaphor is a *trope*, an overall term for a figure of speech in which a word is used in a nonliteral way to depict some similarity (e.g., analogy, metaphor, and simile) or some dissimilarity (e.g., anomaly, irony, and paradox). Metaphors force us to see things in new or unusual ways. They create images or pictures in our minds that help us see, feel, and remember them (Morgan, 1986). They convey meaning in efficient ways, energize us, and can transcend diverse audiences (Parry, 2008). They also can be catalysts for purposeful reflection and meaningful action (Fuda, 2012). Metaphors are used in everyday life to describe organizations, jobs, experiences, and human characteristics. Life, for example, is sometimes described as a *rat race* or a *journey*. Brave and courageous individuals are *lionhearted*. Organizations have been described as *cultures*, *machines*, *mazes*, and *psychic prisons* (Morgan, 1986).

Metaphors for leaders have been used widely in popular books and trade journals. George (2004) and George and Sims (2007) used a compass metaphor to describe "authentic" leadership. In *True North* they discussed that "internal compass" that guides one successfully through life and helps one become an authentic leader, which emphasizes values, self-knowledge, relationships, and "doing the right thing" (George & Sims, 2007). Fuda (2012) argued that the use of metaphor is the best way to drive deep discussion and analysis of leadership. Focused on leader development, he highlighted seven metaphors for leadership transformation, for example, fire, snowball, coach, chef, and so forth, each of which represents a portal through which to see and discuss key dimensions of leadership. McKergow (2013) provided a long list of metaphors for leaders that were generated at the World Open Space forum; these include fire starter, visionary, lighthouse, guardian, storyteller, and many more.

In the scholarly literature, Parry (2008) argued that leadership is fundamentally about *sensemaking* and that leaders are *sensemakers*. He is referring to leaders in general, not to communication leaders. This sensemaker metaphor may be rooted in the work of Smircich and Morgan (1982), who claimed that leaders are concerned with managing (influencing) meaning among followers. Leaders attempt to manage the meaning of issues, events, and experiences so that followers understand those issues and events within the preferred interpretation of the leader. In doing so, followers may better understand their role in dealing with these issues and experiences, identify more closely with their organization, and increase contributions to goal achievement. This is important because leaders spend most of their time gathering, processing, and distributing information about issues, problems, and opportunities confronting their organizations (Walsh, 1995).

Karl Weick (1995) has been a leading theorist for group sensemaking, or how people work together to try to make sense of their experiences and issues. The basic idea of sensemaking is that "reality is an ongoing accomplishment that emerges from efforts to create order and make retrospective sense of what occurs" (Weick, 1993, p. 635). In this constructivist approach, "organizational sensemaking is first and foremost about the question: How does something come to be event for organizational members? Second, sensemaking is about the question, "What does the event mean?" (Weick, Sutcliffe, & Obstfeld, 2005, p. 410). How people see things, and think about them, become valuable resources.

Gioia and Chittipeddi (1991) described three cognitive processes for considering the sensemaking work of leaders. Though they focused on strategic change management in a case study, the processes apply to other events and issues, and they provide a framework for our consideration of public relations leaders. The first process is *sensemaking*, which gives meaning to experiences and events. This involves (1) information seeking or scanning wherein leaders search their organization's environment for issues that may have an impact on the organization and (2) then constructing meaning to provide a framework or structure for decision making and action.

Sensegiving is the second process. Here, leaders interpret and explain to others what the issue means for the organization, in their view. They attempt to influence meaning construction to gain followers' support, and they may use a variety of tactics or approaches to do so, including rites, rituals, metaphors, storytelling, rewards, and internal systems and processes to support their favored interpretations (Schein, 1992). The use of stories, metaphors, and rites and rituals can add an affective dimension to the cognitive process and enhance memory (Parry, 2008).

The third process is *sensenegotiating*, which refers to the interplay of the leader's preferred meanings, and the views of other organizational members who have their own interpretations of the issue, as they attempt to negotiate some collective understanding as the basis for subsequent decisions and actions. These three processes play out continuously in organizations because the global political-economic-social environment is dynamic and fast moving, and organizations must successfully adapt to external changes and integrate them internally. Organizational history, past practices, and structure and culture also bear on the three processes and render them more complex (Bartunek, Krim, Necochea, & Humphries, 1999).

This metaphor seems particularly appropriate for communication leaders. J. E. Grunig (1992) didn't use the term *sensemaker* in excellence theory, so far as we know, but he essentially outlined the process 20 years ago:

> Public relations managers who are part of the dominant coalition communicate the views of publics to other senior managers, and they must communicate with publics to be able to do so. They also communicate to other senior managers the likely consequences of policy decisions after communicating with publics affected by the potential policy. (pp. 4–5)

Today, these managerial communication responsibilities and professional requirements involve multidimensional sensemaking, sensegiving, and sensenegotiating. Like all leaders, communication managers try to make sense of experiences, events, and issues inside and outside of their organizations. They then adopt preferred meanings for those issues and convey them to their team members and followers, who make their own sense of the issues and how they affect them. This leads to negotiation of preferred meanings among communication leaders and their followers.

For public relations leaders, however, sensemaking goes beyond this traditional leader–follower interaction. Public relations leaders today must process a vast, high-speed flow of information and data to (a) determine what seems most relevant to the organization, (b) evaluate the relevant information strategically and tactically, and (c) identify what corresponding worthwhile opportunities for engagement and interaction are presented in the information flow. Communication leaders then try to make sense of these things in their interactions and negotiations with organizational leaders and employees. They add more to these processes when they prepare or facilitate communications between other organizational leaders and their work teams or followers, or with other stakeholders. In short, leaders effectively write, edit, produce, and deliver a variety of sensemaking scripts.

Further, through boundary-spanning activities, public relations leaders try to make sense of their organization's world of stakeholders and their issues and demands. They gather information from groups and stakeholders and translate it tactically and strategically to organizational leaders and decision makers. They engage in sensenegotiations and decision making about what to do, and especially how and what to communicate about what they decide to do, in an increasingly transparent world. In the data and digital age, then, sensemaking, sensegiving, and sensenegotiating are increasingly complex and difficult, but ever more crucial due to the volume, velocity, and tremendous variety of global information.

Two examples from the professional world illustrate this metaphor in action. First, GolinHarris redesigned its public relations agency structure in 2011, and in doing so it created "The Bridge," which is a high-tech room, or electronic listening and observing post, that tracks conversations and information globally about its clients in real time—blogs, traditional media, websites, Facebook posts, tweets, and so forth. The Bridge is thus a super-environmental scanner that facilitates and expedites sensemaking of client matters by reducing the amount of time needed to discover potential problems, opportunities, and issues.

Second, in one of our interviews with U.S. executives, the communication leader in a large energy company described how her work has been radically altered by social media—how the sensemaking, sensegiving, and sensenegotiating processes have changed:

> Social media has redefined everything we do, and here's how we are managing now. We outsourced some information gathering and preparation of briefing documents. They troll information all the time. Then we [the communication team] have a really solid briefing first thing every morning. I have a team that has a pretty good sense of what to bubble up, and I have a sense of what to bubble out, down, up, which means we are tethered 24/7. I've had to learn to manage when to focus on information and when to be thoughtful about what to do with it. How we changed from three years ago is there are a lot more face-to-face meetings— a lot more communication among executives to make sure that everybody is fully informed and participating in problem solving.

Processing and reflecting on information that has been strategically selected out of the vast data flow by a third-party partner; bubbling it up, down, and out; negotiating meanings with and among senior leaders; engaging in decision making—these are some of crucial requirements for public relations leaders, the multidimensional sensemakers. We explore this metaphor further in the book and use the term to conceptualize leadership in the field today.

Self-Disclosures: Our Assumptions and Sponsors of the Leadership Study

Our views in this book are grounded in five assumptions about leaders and leadership in public relations. They are important frameworks for our thinking, and we share them here along with our specific relations to the research project through the Plank Center for Leadership in Public Relations at the University of Alabama. The Plank Center, the executive search firm Heyman Associates, and IBM Corporation sponsored and funded the study. All funding was used to support direct research costs, which included translations of surveys; data processing, cleaning, and testing; transcriptions of interviews and coding interview transcripts; production of country research reports; and fees for use of the global Unipark survey site and data collection center in Germany.

Assumptions About Leaders and Leadership in Public Relations

1. Public relations leaders can be difference makers, especially in a digital and information-bursting world. It's long been recognized that public relations leaders possess communication knowledge and expertise that assist organizations in making appropriate decisions about what to communicate, how, and when with diverse groups. In doing so, leaders help organizations build relationships with others and achieve organizational objectives (Berger & Reber, 2006). More recently, communication is growing in strategic importance due to increasing global competition, newly empowered stakeholders, the rapid diffusion of new information and communication technologies, and the corresponding torrent of data and information that organizations must manage (Meng, 2009).

Today, public relations leaders are often valued members of the management team because they help organizations deal successfully with two pressing and ongoing challenges that all organizations confront: adaptation to the external world, and internal integration of change (House, Hanges, Javidan, Dorfman, & Gupta, 2004). Communication leaders are crucial sensemakers who help organizations assess and select strategic choices before they act, based on their close analysis of issues or the "dynamics within and without the organization" (Pang, Jin, & Cameron, 2010, p. 21). Through this process, public relations moves the organization "to be outer directed and to have a participative organizational culture" (Heath, 2006, p. 76). All of this suggests that the demand for excellent public relations leaders will rise as their perceived difference-making capabilities are increasingly recognized in an information-turned-digital age that valorizes sensemaking.

2. Leadership is a complex and dynamic process that will become even more challenging in the future. We agree with Northouse (2007), Hackman and Johnson (2009), and others that leadership is a process, not simply a set of characteristics or qualities. However, the process requires individuals with some core leadership skills and qualities who are capable of acquiring, and are willing to acquire, new knowledge; developing new skills; being authentic and empathetic; and continually growing as leaders into the future. With so many major changes in the world today—growing demands for transparency, instant communication, Twitter-driven demonstrations and revolutions, global awareness—it seems inevitable that some aspects of leadership must change, too, or that new qualities and skills become far more crucial. It also seems likely that the development of leaders, and even the conceptualization of leadership, must change (Middlebrooks & Allen, 2008).

Our interviews with 137 communication leaders in the global study support this notion. The executives we interviewed said future leaders will think digital first, and they must possess greater business acumen, heightened cultural awareness and sensitivity, greater listening skills and conflict management capabilities, and the ability to transform communication teams into elite talent forces that can be quickly mobilized to engage problems and opportunities—anywhere and anytime.

3. In terms of performance, leaders are normally distributed, like many things in life, across the population. A few leaders are truly excellent, a few are awful, but most are somewhere between the extremes and trending one direction or another. This assumption is not supported by direct empirical evidence about public relations leaders, but rather by our own experiences and a number of large-scale studies that suggest great variation in the quality and performance of leaders in general and in the field. Our global study, for example, revealed a very deep divide between communication leaders and their followers regarding leadership performance. Leaders may often rate themselves higher than do their followers, but the difference in our study is Grand Canyon–sized across most of the countries and regions (Berger, 2012).

Ketchum's study of leadership in 12 countries underscored the public's dissatisfaction with leaders in business, government, and institutions; key issues for future leaders are gaining trust and closing the "say–do" gap (Ketchum, 2013). At the same time, inadequate communication and interaction by senior executives and frontline managers with employees were seen to substantially impede employee engagement and to have an adverse impact on trust (BlessingWhite, 2011; Maritz Research, 2011). In short, there is room, and perhaps a great deal of room, to improve the performance of public relations leaders and leaders in general in most organizations in most countries.

4. Leadership in the field can be systematically improved over time. We agree with Van Velsor and McCauley (2003) that leadership qualities and capabilities can be developed and improved over time. We view leadership development as a continuous journey or process that can increase a person's leadership capacity and capability. Avolio (2005) examined 100 years of leadership development programs and concluded that most programs do produce modest change in individuals. Sometimes the scope and scale of change are substantial, often based on crucial events or experiences. For most, however, leadership development is an incremental and long-term process of filling in knowledge gaps, developing new skills or strengthening existing ones, honing capabilities and qualities, and continuously learning and applying that learning from experiences and self-reflection about them.

Fallows (2012) made a similar point in his discussion of U.S. presidents. He argued that we often hold unrealistic expectations for what presidents might achieve because, in fact, presidents enter the office and take on responsibilities that they are always in some way unprepared, unsuited, or unable to successfully perform. They may lack essential communication skills, emotional intelligence, self-awareness, listening skills, or other qualities and capabilities. We believe this notion applies to leaders of all kinds, but we view it from a different perspective: We see the lack of certain public relations leadership capacities or capabilities as future *assets* to be enriched and used in the field: The potential to improve leadership in communication management is real and substantial.

Van Velsor and McCauley (2003) distinguish between *leader* development and *leadership* development. *Leader development* refers to individual growth and skill advancement that expand one's leadership capacity and improve performance. *Leadership development* refers to an organization's attempt to enhance its team of leaders to strengthen their overall organization and performance. Organizations may also include professional associations and centers that might coordinate a national or systemic effort to maximize the development of leaders over time. Both types of development programs are likely rooted deeply in cultural values and beliefs (Hoppe, 2003).

Any systemic development of leaders in public relations, however, requires careful deliberation. As Middlebrooks and Allen (2008) note, leadership development is complicated. The content and quality of existing training and development programs vary dramatically. Training and development are also expensive, and perhaps the biggest issue is measurement. How do we measure individual development, let alone measure the extent to which leadership in and of the field improves?

5. Meaningful and valid comparisons of national data sets and diverse cultures are problematic and difficult, at best.

We are excited that our global study includes data from 23 countries because no other large-scale studies of leadership in public relations exist. Such studies may help us better understand how to manage organizations and functions with diverse employees, how national and cultural variations affect the perceptions and communications of leaders and leadership performance, and whether leadership competencies and qualities cross national boundaries, among other possible benefits (Northouse, 2007). In fact, globalization drives the need for more global knowledge and greater cultural awareness and sensitivity. We fully agree with Sriramesh (2006) that more public relations studies need to focus on, or incorporate culture—a crucial and complex environmental variable.

Our excitement, however, is tempered by a number of difficulties. We know from studies in other disciplines that the roles, practices, and styles of public relations leaders are likely to differ based on their value system and culture (Hofstede, 1980, 1983, 1993; House et al., 2004). In fact, Dorfman and House (2004) declared that "leader attributes, behaviors, status, and influence vary considerably as a result of centrally unique forces in the countries or regions in which the leaders function" (p. 53). Culture also affects the "amount of influence, prestige, and privilege given to leaders" (House et al., 2004, p. 10). These differences make survey and other data comparisons difficult.

Ethnocentrism is another issue. Our global survey questionnaire was largely constructed based on North American and Western European leadership literature and theories. We also encountered methodological difficulties because we found it necessary to use different sampling approaches in countries given the extent to which professional e-mail databases are available and accessible. As a result, our sample sizes vary substantially in the surveyed countries, which increases the difficulty of comparing national data sets.

To reduce the impact of these issues, we took a number of steps. For example, our international 28-member research team included natives from each of the countries we surveyed, so they provided crucial cultural awareness. In addition, these researchers helped create the survey and interview questions, and the corresponding translations of them, and they were responsible for all data analysis and interpretation in their countries. We also conducted depth interviews with public relations leaders in 15 countries to deepen our collective knowledge about national and cultural specific phenomena and leadership in communication management.

Given these and other issues, we are very sensitive to cultural and methodological complexities inherent in large-scale, multicountry studies. Thus, we carefully report respondent perceptions in each country/region and indicate some national variations; we do not make strong claims about causation, meaning, or evaluation of these variations.

The Plank Center for Leadership in Public Relations

The global study of leadership in public relations was carried out under the auspices of the Plank Center for Leadership in Public Relations at the University of Alabama (UA). The UA board of trustees established the center in 2005 in the name of public relations legend Betsy Plank, a UA graduate who was a pioneer in the field and a lifelong champion of public relations practice, education, and research. The center's mission is to recognize and help develop outstanding leaders and role models in public relations practice and education and to bridge the gap between the practice field and the classroom.

Led by a national advisory board of 24 leading public relations executives and educators, the center pursues its mission through scholarships, speaker programs, publications, meetings and conferences, an educator fellowship program, a national mentorship recognition event, and other programs. Since its inception, the center has focused on research support activities that will help build a research-based body of knowledge about leadership in the field. From 2006 to 2013, the center carried out or funded 22 research projects that examined various aspects of leadership: the qualities and dimensions of excellent leaders, leadership styles, leadership education in university public relations programs, ethics in leadership, and the influences of organizational structure and culture on leadership practices, among others (Berger & Meng, 2010). The global study described in this book is to date the largest center-sponsored study and the first to examine the public relations leadership phenomenon globally.

References

Avolio, B. J. (2005). 100-year review of leadership intervention research: Briefings Report 2004–01, Gallup Leadership Institute, Kravis Leadership Institute. *Leadership Review, 5,* 7–13.

Bartunek, J. M., Krim, R. M., Necochea, R., & Humphries, M. (1999). Sensemaking, sensegiving, and leadership in strategic organizational development. *Advances in Qualitative Organizational Research, 2,* 37–71.

Berger, B. (2012). *Key themes and findings: The cross-cultural study of leadership in public relations and communication management.* Available online at http://plankcenter.ua.edu/wp-content/uploads/2012/10/Summary-of-Themes-and-Findings-Leader-Survey.pdf

Berger, B., & Meng, J. (2010). Public relations practitioners and the leadership challenge. In. R. L. Heath (Ed.), *The SAGE handbook of public relations* (pp. 421–434). Thousand Oaks, CA: Sage.

Berger, B. K., & Reber, B. H. (2006). *Gaining influence in public relations.* Mahwah, NJ: Erlbaum.

BlessingWhite. (2011). *Employee engagement report—2011.* Princeton, NJ: Author.

Dorfman, P. W., & House, R. J. (2004). Cultural influences on organizational leadership: Literature review, theoretical rationale, and GLOBE project goals. In R. J. House, P. J. Hanges, M. Javidan, P. W. Dorfman, & V. Gupta (Eds.), *Culture, leadership and organizations: The GLOBE study of 62 societies* (pp. 51–73). Thousand Oaks, CA: Sage.

Fallows, J. (2012, March). Obama, explained. *The Atlantic,* pp. 54–70.

Fuda, P. (2012, November 1). 7 metaphors for leadership transformation [Blog entry]. Available online at www.peterfuda.com/2012/11/01/7-metaphors-for-leadership-transformation/

Gardner, J. (1990). *On leadership.* New York, NY: The Free Press.

George, B., (2004). *Authentic leadership.* San Francisco, CA: Jossey-Bass.

George, B., & Sims, P. (2007). *True north: Discover your authentic leadership.* San Francisco, CA: Jossey-Bass.

Gioia, D. A., & Chittipeddi, K. (1991). Sensemaking and sensegiving in strategic change initiation. *Strategic Management Journal, 12,* 433–448.

Grunig, J. E. (1992). *Excellence in public relations and communication management.* Hillsdale, NJ: Lawrence Erlbaum Associates.

Hackman, M. Z., & Johnson, C. E. (2009). *Leadership: A communication perspective* (5th ed.). Long Grove, IL: Waveland Press.

Heath, R. L. (2006). A rhetorical theory approach to issues management. In C. Botan & V. Hazelton (Eds.), *Public relations theory II* (pp. 63–100). Mahwah, NJ: Erlbaum.

Hofstede, G. (1980). *Culture's consequences: International differences in work-related values.* Beverly Hills, CA: Sage

Hofstede, G. (1983). The cultural reliability of organizational practices and theories. *Journal of International Business Studies, 14,* 75–89.

Hofstede, G. (1993). Cultural constraints in management theories. *Academy of Management Executive, 7,* 81–94.

Hoppe, M. H. (2003). Cross-cultural issues in the development of leaders. In C. D. McCauley & E. Van Velsor (Eds.), *The Center for Creative Leadership handbook of leadership development* (2nd ed., pp. 331–360). San Francisco, CA: Jossey-Bass.

House, R. J., Henges, P. J., Javidan, M., Dorfman, P. W., & Gupta, V. (Eds.). (2004). *Culture, leadership and organizations: The GLOBE study of 62 societies.* Thousand Oaks, CA: Sage.

Ketchum. (2013, March). *Ketchum leadership communication monitor.* Available online at www. ketchum.com/sites/default/files/2013_klcm.pdf

Maritz Research. (2011, June). *Maritz Research Hospitality Group 2011 employee engagement Poll* (Maritz Research White Paper). St. Louis, MO: Maritz Research.

McKergow, M. (2013). Leadership metaphors from the World Open Space [Blog entry]. Available online at http://hostleadership.wordpress.com/2013/01/09/92/

Meng, J. (2009). *Excellent leadership in public relations: An application of multiple-group confirmatory factor analysis models in assessing cross-national measurement in variance* (Unpublished doctoral dissertation). University of Alabama, Tuscaloosa.

Middlebrooks, A., & Allen, S. J. (2008). Leadership education: New challenges, continuing issues. *International Leadership Journal, 1*(1), 77–85.

Morgan, G. (1986). *Images of organization.* Newbury Park, CA: Sage.

Northouse, P. (2007). *Leadership: Theory and practice* (4th ed.). Thousand Oaks, CA: Sage.

Pang, A., Jin, Y., Cameron, G. T. (2010). Strategic management of communication. In R. L. Heath (Ed.), *SAGE handbook of public relations* (pp. 17–34). Thousand Oaks, CA: Sage.

Parry, K. W. (2008). The thing about metaphors and leadership. *International Leadership Journal, 1*(1), 6–23.

Pincus, J. D., Rayfield, R. E., & Debonis, J. N. (1991). Transforming CEOs into chief communication officers. *Public Relations Journal, 47*(11), 22–27.

Rost, J. C. (1991). *Leadership for the twenty-first century.* New York, NY: Praeger.

Schein, E. H. (1992). *Organizational culture and leadership* (2nd ed.). San Francisco, CA: Jossey-Bass.

Shaffer, J. (2000). *The leadership solution.* New York, NY: McGraw-Hill.

Smircich, L., & Morgan, G. (1982). Leadership as the management of meaning. *Journal of Applied Behavioral Science, 18,* 257–273.

Sriramesh, K. (2006). The relationship between culture and public relations. In E. L. Toth (Ed.), *The future of excellence in public relations and communication management* (pp. 507–527). Mahwah, NJ: Erlbaum.

Van Velsor, E., & McCauley, C. D. (2003). Introduction: Our view of leadership development. In C. D. McCauley & E. Van Velsor (Eds.), *The Center for Creative Leadership handbook of leadership development* (2nd ed., pp. 1–22). San Francisco, CA: Jossey-Bass.

Walsh, J. P. (1995). Managerial and organizational cognition: Notes from a trip down memory lane. *Organization Science, 6,* 280–321.

Weick, K. E. (1993). The collapse of sensemaking in organizations: The Mann Gulch disaster. *Administrative Science Quarterly, 38,* 628–652.

Weick, K. E. (1995). *Sensemaking in organizations.* Thousand Oaks, CA: Sage.

Weick, K. E., Sutcliffe, K. M., & Obstfeld, D. (2005). Organizing and the process of sensemaking. *Organization Science, 16*(4), 400–415.

2
REVIEW OF THE LEADERSHIP LITERATURE

Bruce K. Berger and Juan Meng

Given the importance we attribute to leadership in many realms of life, it's not surprising that leadership research is pervasive in psychology, sociology, management, and organization studies, among other fields. More than two decades ago, Yukl (1989) claimed that research articles about leadership numbered in the thousands, and the volume has continued to grow. Broadly, this vast body of research suggests that managerial leadership takes many forms, that its definitions are myriad, that its dynamics are complicated, and that context counts a great deal. Leaders speak and act in specific situations within distinct organizational and societal cultures, and they are embedded within networks of dynamic relationships with followers, stakeholders, and others inside and outside the organization. Leaders also bring to the task varying skill sets, traits, styles, values, beliefs, and experiences.

Researchers have developed many approaches and theories to explain and predict leadership effectiveness and organizational performance. These approaches encompass leader traits, styles, skills, behaviors, and activities; leader power and influence; situational determinants of leader behavior; and leadership as an attributional process (e.g., Bass, 1985, 1990; Conger, 1999; Dansereau, Graen, & Haga, 1975; Fiedler, 1978; House, 1971, 1999; Kouzes & Posner, 2002; Northouse, 2007; Stogdill, 1948, 1974; Yukl, 1989).

Despite this considerable body of work regarding leadership in general, there's great value in exploring leadership in public relations (PR) in depth. Doing so may help us strengthen current leadership in the field and better prepare future leaders. It also may provide answers to some important questions. For example, do the general theories and concepts apply to leaders in communication management, or do the communicative aspects of our professional role make leadership somehow different? What are the crucial qualities and dimensions of leaders in public relations? Have the roles and responsibilities of communication leaders somehow changed in an information–turned–digital world? Can the development of leadership theory in our field inform practice and help us better prepare leaders for an uncertain future?

In this chapter we first review and summarize this vast body of managerial leadership studies. We then review research studies and perspectives in public relations that have directly or indirectly explored leadership in the field, and we briefly introduce an integrated model of excellent leadership in public relations developed by Meng and colleagues (Meng, 2009; Meng & Berger, 2013; Meng, Berger, & Heyman, 2011). We define the construct "excellent leadership" in public relations and conclude the literature review with five research questions that framed our global study of leadership in communication management.

An Overview of Managerial Leadership

Traditional discussion of leadership traces to philosophies and narratives early in recorded civilization (Clemens & Mayer, 1987). Bass (1997a) argued that the study of leadership rivals in age the emergence of civilization, which shaped its leaders as much as it was shaped by them (p. 3). This early work focused on identifying what leaders did and why they did it to try to ascertain the best methods of organizing societies and political life (Bass, 1990, 1997b). Corresponding theorizing was often based on personal opinions and experiences. As a consequence, the definitions of leaders, their behaviors, and their expected outcomes were general and broad.

In the 1950s, theories of leadership became more narrowly focused on specific dimensions of the concept. A *dimension* refers to a fundamental unit or element of the leadership construct. This focus has distinguished contemporary leadership studies from the early works (Bass, 1990; Clemens & Mayer, 1987; Stogdill, 1974; Yukl, 1989). However, these newer perspectives were accompanied by disagreements over the meaning of leadership so that there is no universal definition of the concept. Bass (1990), in *Bass and Stogdill's Handbook of Leadership*, devoted the entire opening chapter to discussing numerous definitions of leadership that have been used by various researchers. His conclusion was that

> Leadership has been conceived as the focus of group processes, as a matter of personality, as a matter of inducing compliance, as the exercise of influence, as particular behaviors, as a form of persuasion, as a power relation, as an instrument to achieve goals, as an effect of interaction, as a differentiated role, as initiation of structure, and as many combinations of these definitions. (Bass, 1990, p. 17)

Clearly, leadership is a "complex, multifaceted phenomenon" (Yukl, 1989, p. 253), and the literature of managerial leadership research reflects this complexity with its wide range of theoretical perspectives and approaches. A number of comprehensive reviews of this literature are available, and we do not duplicate this extensive work here. For example, Northouse (2007) reviewed and analyzed more than 10 leadership approaches and theories over the past century, including the trait, skills, style, situational, behavioral, and psychodynamic approaches. Yukl's (2002) well-known survey of leadership research and theory over the past 50 years detailed five approaches: trait, behavior, power–influence, situational, and integrative.

From an organizational studies perspective, Parry and Bryman (2006) organized the history of leadership research into five broad stages: (a) trait approach, (b) style approach, (c) contingency approach, (d) new leadership approach, and (e) post-charismatic and post-transformational leadership. In their leadership-is-communication perspective, Hackman and Johnson (2009) recounted the evolution of five primary perspectives for explaining managerial leadership: the trait, situational, functional, relational, and transformational approaches.

Drawing from these works and original studies, we review and critique four major approaches that have consistently been seen to represent major areas of research and theorizing: the trait, behavioral, situational, and transformational approaches. Collectively these approaches and perspectives provide a rich lens through which to examine leadership in public relations.

The Trait Approach

One of the earliest research areas in leadership, the trait approach refers to leaders' attributes such as personality characteristics, intelligence, motives, values, and skills (Stogdill, 1948, 1974). This research focused on identifying personal attributes or superior qualities deemed essential to effective leadership. Traits were the basis for so-called great man theories of leadership, which argued that an individual was born with certain leadership skills, or they weren't: Leaders were born, not made. Studies often compared such traits exhibited by leaders with those exhibited by non-leaders (Bratton, Grint, & Nelson, 2005; Yukl, 1989).

However, researchers found it difficult to identify consistent patterns of traits that differentiated leaders from non-leaders, and they began to question whether traits should be the sole or primary dimension of leadership. Other researchers argued that the situational nature of leadership also was important in determining effectiveness (Lord, DeVader, & Alliger, 1986; Mann, 1959; Stogdill, 1948, 1974). Trait research presented other limitations, too. For example, the massive research effort identified dozens of key traits, but failed to identify or to agree on specific traits that would guarantee effective leadership and succession. Stogdill (1948, 1976) reviewed hundreds of trait studies in two landmark research projects and found no consistent patterns that differentiated leaders from non-leaders.

Another criticism is that the trait approach did not recognize the importance of followers in the leadership process. Such factors as the followers' personality traits, behaviors, and learning processes in the workplace also affect the leadership process and its outcomes (Dansereau, Graen, & Haga, 1975; Graen, 1976; Graen & Cashman, 1975). Acknowledging this, research in this area shifted to the interaction of traits, situations, and the impact of followers' behaviors on leadership.

Despite its limitations, trait research continues, and many still believe that certain traits are essential to effective leadership. In his essay about modern business leaders, for example, Manfredi (2008) argued that successful leaders today must be intelligent, possess high energy, think conceptually, and be able to communicate effectively and connect with others. Research by the Plank Center also highlights the importance of high energy, passion for the profession, and the power of relationships (Berger & Meng, 2010).

The Behavioral Approach

The behavioral approach emphasizes what leaders actually do on the job and the consequences of their behaviors on managerial effectiveness (Fleishman, 1953). Although behavioral theorists have used diverse terms to classify leadership styles, two types of behaviors are most often studied: task-oriented and relationship-oriented behaviors (Bratton et al., 2005). The *task-oriented* approach is concerned with discovering what activities are typical of managerial work and the processes of managerial decision making and problem solving (McCall & Kaplan, 1985; Yukl, 1989). The *relationship-oriented* approach has focused more on leader–follower relationships during the work process, such as showing respect and support for followers (Kotter, 1982; Mintzberg, 1973, 1979).

Two studies in the 1950s provided the foundation for contemporary behavior theories of leadership: The University of Michigan studies and the Ohio State studies. Researchers in both studies were interested in defining the frequency with which leaders engaged in certain behaviors, believing they would then be able to describe what effective leaders do in various situations versus ineffective leaders.

Researchers at the University of Michigan focused on the effects of the leader's behavior on the performance of small groups and identified two discrete types of behaviors: a production orientation and an employee orientation (e.g., Katz & Kahn, 1951, 1978; Likert, 1961). Having a *production orientation* emphasizes the production and technical aspects of work in small groups. Leaders having an *employee orientation*, however, focus more on subordinates' personal needs and their individuality. As more research was conducted, evidence mounted that a leader who emphasized high levels of productivity might also be employee oriented. In later work, the University of Michigan researchers found that leaders who showed high concern for both production and employees were associated with higher group performance (Kahn & Katz, 1960).

The Ohio State researchers investigated how leaders behaved when they were in charge of a work group (Stogdill & Coons, 1957). The research findings suggested that two important dimensions underlie leader behaviors: initiating structure and consideration. *Initiating structure* refers to how a leader's behavior helps support clear patterns of communication and ways to complete tasks. *Consideration* gives special attention to working relationships and the development of mutual respect between leader and subordinates. An effective leader could increase both initiating structure and consideration and maintain a balance between the two (Stogdill & Coons, 1957).

In the 1960s, Blake and Mouton (1964) developed their influential model, the Leadership Grid, which highlighted two dimensions of effective leadership: a production focus and a people focus. Blake and Mouton then plotted five major leadership styles in the grid, that is, authority-compliance, team management, country club management, middle-of-the-road management, and impoverished management. This more refined way of designating leadership styles has provided practical value to organizational training and development efforts over the years.

Despite its practical application, the behavioral approach has limitations. First, researchers using this approach have been unable to describe a universal style of leader behavior that is effective in the vast majority of situations. Second, although many of the identified behaviors are relevant to leadership effectiveness, their predictive power varies across situations (Yukl, 1989). Third, methodology is another criticism, as the earlier behavioral approach relied mostly on descriptive methods such as direct observation, diaries, and anecdotes obtained from interviews, which limit the approach's predictive power (Bratton, Grint, & Nelson, 2005). Despite these issues, leader behaviors continue to be a central area of study because "walking the talk" and "show it, don't tell it" remain important to organizational members.

The Situational Approach

The situational approach emphasizes the importance of the leader's attributes and behaviors within a complex mix of contextual factors such as issues that mark dynamic external environments, the various attributes of subordinates, and diverse internal issues and affairs. The development of this approach is based on the assumption that different behavioral patterns will be effective in different situations or contexts, and the same behavioral pattern cannot be applied effectively to all situations. The inherently situational nature of leadership has produced a variety of theories that try to establish the relevance of, and interrelationships among, behavioral patterns and situations.

Overall, situational theories can be classified into two major categories: one category treats leader behavior as a dependent variable, and corresponding research has focused on discovering (a) how the situation influences leader behavior and (b) how much variation occurs in behavior across diverse situations. The other category seeks to discover how the variable of situation moderates the relationship between leader behavior and leadership effectiveness (Dansereau et al., 1975; Fiedler, 1978; House, 1971; Kerr & Jermier, 1978).

Due to the prominence of situational theories, three are briefly reviewed here: path-goal theory, least preferred coworker (LPC) contingency theory, and leader–member exchange (LMX) theory.

According to *path-goal* theory (House, 1971; House & Mitchell, 1974), the leader's main task is to use the appropriate behavioral style to help followers clarify their paths to achieve both work and personal goals. House (1971) specified four behavior styles: directive, supportive, participative, and achievement oriented. Leaders use different behavior styles to motivate subordinates to enhance performance to encourage them to believe that valued outcomes can be attained with greater effort (House & Mitchell, 1974). Aspects of the situation such as the nature of the task, the working environment, and subordinate attributes determine which behavior style is best for improving subordinate satisfaction and performance.

However, other explanatory processes such as a leader's influence on task organization, resource levels, and skill levels are missing in this theoretical approach (Yukl, 1981). In addition, the four leadership styles were formulated in terms of broad behavior categories, thereby reducing the likelihood of finding strong relationships to criterion variables (Yukl, 2002).

Fiedler's (1978) *LPC contingency theory* proposes that the fit between the leader's orientation and the favorableness of the situation determines the team's effectiveness in accomplishing a task. Leader effectiveness is assessed in terms of the leader's position power, task structure, and leader–member relationships. Fiedler used a semantic differential scale called the LPC to classify a leader's orientation: high LPC (relationship oriented) or low LPC (task oriented). The model specifies that high LPC leaders are more effective in relationship-oriented situations, and low LPC leaders are more effective in task-oriented situations.

However, there is considerable debate concerning the reliability and validity of the LPC model. Different studies have generated varying LPC scores, and the interpretation of the scores has changed several times (Peters, Hartke, & Pohlmann, 1985; Strube & Garcia, 1981). Measurement biases and low measurement reliability, as well as ambiguity about what the LPC scale really measures, have further limited the explanatory power of this approach (Vecchino, 1983; Yukl, 1989).

LMX theory (Dansereau et al., 1975; Graen & Cashman, 1975; Graen & Uhl-Bien, 1995) describes how leaders develop different exchange relationships over time with subordinates. The basic idea is that leaders form two groups of followers: in-groups and out-groups. *In-group* members tend to have characteristics similar to those of the leader and are generally given greater responsibilities, more rewards, and more attention. In contrast, *out-group* members work outside the leader's inner circle and receive less attention and fewer rewards. Research also has confirmed that in-group members are more likely to engage in organizational citizenship behavior, whereas out-group members are more likely to retaliate against the organization (Townsend, Phillips, & Elkins, 2000).

At present, LMX theory is more descriptive than prescriptive. It delineates a typical process of role making by leaders, but it does not specify what pattern of downward exchange relationship is better for leadership effectiveness (Yukl, 1989). In addition, measurement of effect is missing due to the nature of the descriptive method (Graen, Novak, & Summerkamp, 1982; Wakabayashi & Graen, 1984). Another conceptual weakness is that research on the basis for selecting in-group members is still very limited, and it is not clear how this selection occurs (Duchon, Green, & Taber, 1984; Kim & Organ, 1982).

In short, situational theories of leadership effectiveness have contributed significantly to managerial workshops and training programs. The approaches are easy to understand and can be applied in a variety of practical settings (Northouse, 2007). Moreover, the situational approach recognizes the flexibility of leaders (Yukl, 1989) and the importance of context. An effective leader must adapt his or her behavior to cope with different situations. However, despite the practical value of this approach, its contribution to the large body of theoretical research is limited, because few of the theories have been tested and evaluated.

The Transformational Approach

During the late 1970s and early 1980s, leadership research shifted from what is now frequently termed "traditional leadership" to the "new leadership" with the advent of charismatic and transformational approaches (Northouse, 2007). Traditional leadership theories and approaches emphasized rational processes, but the new approaches are more concerned with emotions, values, ethics, and long-term relationships, as well as followers' motives, needs, and satisfaction (Bass, 1985; Burns, 1978; Conger, 1989; Conger & Kanungo, 1987; House, 1977; Shamir, House, & Arthur, 1993).

In addition, theories of charismatic and transformational leadership are broader in scope: They simultaneously involve leader traits, power, behaviors, and situational variables in a dynamic model. Moreover, charismatic and transformational leaders articulate a realistic vision of the future that can be shared by subordinates. Organizational behaviorists in this area have demonstrated that the benefits of charismatic and transformational leadership include broadening and elevating the interests of followers, generating awareness and acceptance among the followers of the mission of the organization, and motivating followers to go beyond their self-interests for the good of the organization (Bass, 1985, 1997b; Beyer, 1999; Conger, 1999; House, 1977, 1999).

This research trend represents an important step toward greater integration in the leadership literature, and this has heavily influenced the field in general. When leadership is examined as a more dynamic interactional phenomenon, its effectiveness is dependent on the reactions of followers. Thus, leadership becomes a matter of mutually reinforcing exchange relationships (Conger, 1999).

Early transformational leadership theory was developed mostly from descriptive research on political leaders (Burns, 1978). Among many theorists in this area, Bass (1985, 1990, 1997b) has contributed a great deal to transformational leadership theory. He regards the idealization of the leader by his or her followers as the most important feature of charisma (Bass, 1985), and he devotes more attention to followers' rather than leaders' needs, as well as to emotional elements and origins of charisma (Northouse, 2007). Bass's leadership model places transformational, transactional, and laissez-faire leadership on an active–passive leadership continuum and describes how these types of leadership are related (e.g., Bass, 1985, 1990; Bass & Avolio, 1993; Yammarino, 1993).

Bass uses four factors in his model to illustrate transformational leadership: idealized influence charisma, inspirational motivation, intellectual stimulation, and individualized consideration. The emphasis of his transformational leadership is to improve the performance of followers and develop them to their full potential (Bass, 1985). Therefore, transformational leadership is defined in terms of the leader's effect on followers: Leaders transform followers by making them more aware of the importance and values of task outcomes and by activating their higher order needs.

To measure the behaviors involved in transformational leadership, Bass (1985) developed the Multifactor Leadership Questionnaire (MLQ), which has become the most well-known survey instrument in transformational research. Bass designed the MLQ to capture the essential behaviors of transformational and transactional leadership. Although most factor analyses supported the proposed distinction between transformational and transactional behaviors, a number of discrepancies and weak discriminant validity of the constructs have been identified (Bass, 1990; Yukl, 1999). The high, positive factor loadings and high interfactor correlations indicated weak discriminant validity of the factor structure.

Although most theories of transformational and charismatic leadership have been criticized for weak capacity to explain leadership effectiveness because of this conceptual weaknesses (Yukl, 1999), the new leadership school has sharply accelerated the development of leadership research (Hunt, 1999). For instance, the visionary aspects of the theories have extended the traditional leader's role into a transformational process; the recognition of the emotional reactions of followers in response to a shared vision has increased the importance of followers in the leader–follower relationship (Hunt, 1999). Overall, the increasing range of topics introduced by the new leadership school has enriched the study of leadership.

Summary of Managerial Leadership Research

The past two decades have witnessed real progress in contemporary managerial leadership research. Increases in the scope of conceptualization and a greater variety of research methods have accelerated our understanding of leadership as a complex and dynamic process. Each of the four areas of research reviewed here remains an active research arena. However, the criticisms of, and challenges for, each major approach and its corresponding theories and methods present problems. Although the majority of theories and models have led to practical applications, only a few have been tested, and the test methods remain open to debate.

Based on this review of the managerial leadership literature, we are left with two thoughts. First, defining the construct of leadership seems crucial, and we imagine this construct must include multiple dimensions. Leadership is not just traits, or certain behaviors, or a particular style, or a set of shifting contexts and situations to which leaders react. Rather, leadership includes and integrates some or most of these various dimensions in some complex set of interrelationships.

Second, measuring the construct appropriately is both necessary and difficult. One major controversy, for example, concerns the advantages of quantitative, hypothesis-testing leadership research versus descriptive-qualitative leadership research. Researchers argue that questionnaires and rating forms that use fixed-response items are susceptible to a variety of biases, especially when the items do not involve specific, observable behaviors (House & Aditya, 1997; Trice & Beyer, 1986). Meanwhile, proponents of quantitative methods argue that the data collection methods in qualitative-descriptive research are also susceptible to biases and distortions, based on subjective interpretation of the data (e.g., Conger & Kanungo, 1987, 1998). To advance leadership research, then, we must resolve these two root problems: lack of a clearly defined construct and appropriate methods to measure and validate the construct. We revisit these thoughts in the next chapter.

Public Relations Research and Leadership

Until recently, few research projects directly explored leaders and the practice of leadership in public relations (Aldoory & Toth, 2004). However, the concept of leadership has been addressed in several essays and is implicit in at least four theoretical perspectives in the field. For example, Thayer (1986) argued that practitioners should take on a strategic communication leadership role in their organizations. Neff (2002) advocated for integrating leadership processes and service into the basic public relations principles course in universities. Other scholars have recognized the importance of applying leadership skills to enhance practice and to help practitioners participate successfully in strategic decision-making arenas (Berger & Reber, 2006; Berger, Reber, & Heyman, 2007; L. A. Grunig, Grunig, & Dozier, 2002; Werder & Holtzhausen, 2009). In this section, we briefly review four theoretical perspectives and highlight their contributions to leadership research in the field.

Excellence and Role Theories

One of the most comprehensive research projects in the field, the International Association of Business Communicators IABC Excellence Study identified key characteristics of excellence in public relations as general principles (J. E. Grunig, 1992;

L. A. Grunig et al., 2002). The well-known principles reflect characteristics and values that a public relations unit could (and should) have at the program, departmental, organizational, and economic levels. We can view these universal principles as a conceptual framework for leadership. Applying some of the principles to leadership, for example, we might conclude that public relations leaders should (a) be involved in strategic management of the organization, (b) be empowered as members of the dominant coalition, (c) possess a managerial worldview and requisite professional knowledge and experience, and (d) use and model two-way symmetrical communication (Broom & Dozier, 1986; Dozier & Broom, 1995; J. E. Grunig, 1992; L. A. Grunig et al., 2002).

Excellence theorists also concluded that an organization's structure and culture influence both the role and effectiveness of public relations. They advocated for a "culture for communication," which is characterized as follows:

> Excellent public relations will thrive in an organization with an organic structure, participative culture, and symmetrical system of communication and in which opportunities exist for women and racial-cultural minorities. Although these conditions alone cannot produce excellent public relations, they do establish a hospitable environment for excellent public relations. Most important, these conditions provide a favorable context in which all employees work most effectively—but especially women and minorities. Within such an organization employees are empowered to participate in decision-making. As a result, they are more satisfied with the organization and are more likely to support than to oppose the goals of the organization. (L. A. Grunig et al., 2002, pp. 533–534)

Excellence theory and role theory, then, highlight certain traits (visionary, managerial view), skills (communication knowledge and expertise), and behaviors (model two-way communication) of public relations leaders. The theories also underscore the influence of organizational culture and structure (power, hierarchy, dominant coalition) on practice and leadership, and the need for diversity and equal opportunities for women and minorities.

Contingency Theory

Cameron and colleagues (e.g., Cameron, Cropp, & Reber, 2001; Reber & Cameron, 2003; Shin, Cameron, & Cropp, 2006) developed contingency theory, which focuses on strategic and conflictual relationships between an organization and its publics. Public relations leaders help strategically manage their organizations by scanning the external environment, identifying crucial issues and interpreting what they mean, and then making appropriate strategic choices based on those issues and actors. These choices fall within an organization–public relationship continuum that ranges from an organization's pure advocacy of its own position on an issue (adversarial) to pure acceptance of the public's position on another issue (accommodative).

This view suggests that "leadership is best not conceived as a universal trait, but as situationally-sensitive management and strategic (even tactical) options" (Shin et al., 2011, p. 172). Public relations leaders must be able to assess external threats and opportunities, make strategic choices, and advocate for those situationally sensitive choices with organizational leaders, based on their close analysis of the issue and the strategic choice continuum (Pang, Jin, & Cameron, 2010). Through this process, public relations moves the organization "to be outer directed and to have a participative organizational culture" (Heath, 2006, p. 76).

Shin, Heath, and Lee (2011) applied contingency theory in a study of U.S. and Korean practitioners that examined preferred leadership styles in routine and nonroutine situations. They were especially interested in situational and cultural variations. They found that U.S. professionals see little difference in leadership activities and behaviors across the two situations, but the Korean practitioners regarded enactment competency as far more relevant to conflict situations than to routine situations (Shin et al., 2011, p. 185). The study also supported the idea that certain basic leadership actions and behaviors may be universally important, but that enactment of actions and behaviors are greatly influenced by cultural variation.

Contingency theory in public relations research reflects the situational approach in leadership theory (Waller, Smith, & Warnock, 1989): Context affects what leaders pay attention to and what they do. This approach also enriches the meaning of context by recognizing the rich and complex diversity of issues with which organizations must deal—internal employee issues, stakeholder activities, public policy matters, organizational cultural and structural factors, societal culture and political-economic realities, and so forth.

Power Relations Theory

L. A. Grunig (1992) linked the power-control perspective with public relations, arguing that public relations executives needed to be part of the dominant coalition—that insider group of key influencers and strategic decision makers in organizations. To gain admission into this group, and to exert influence on the group's decisions, suggests that public relations leaders must possess abundant professional expertise and experience and the ability to obtain, understand, and articulate a variety of stakeholder information that bears on the organization. In addition, it seems apparent that public relations leaders must have the persuasive ability to be an effective advocate and counselor within the dominant coalitions.

Berger and Reber (2006) built on this power-control perspective and explored how power can make public relations units more active, effective, and ethical in organizational decision making. They claimed that public relations practice is inherently political, and networks and relationships built through practice are inherently strategic: The practice exists and occurs within strategic relationships marked by power. As a result, leaders who lack professional expertise and organizational knowledge, and/or who are inexperienced in organizational politics and power relations will be less effective (Berger & Reber, 2006; L. A. Grunig, Grunig, & Dozier, 2002; L. A. Grunig, 1992). To be an effective leader, then, one must increase her or his power and influence, "become more politically astute, employ more diverse influence resources and tactics, and exert greater political will in organizational arenas where decisions are shaped through power relations" (Berger & Reber, 2006, p. 2).

Through interviews with public relations executives, Berger, Reber, and Heyman (2007) further explored factors that help public relations leaders achieve professional success and maintain their leadership positions. They found a complex set of factors and patterns linked to success, including strong communication and rhetorical skills; diverse experiences and assignments; a proactive nature; strong coalition building, networking, and interpersonal skills; and the willingness to take risks on the job.

Power relations research highlights organizational structural and cultural dimensions of leadership and valorizes certain traits and skills (e.g., vision of power, political willpower, and political knowledge of the organization).

Leadership and Gender

Aldoory (1998) interviewed female leaders in public relations to examine their leadership style and found that they exhibited transformational and interactive styles, grounded in a situational context. Aldoory and Toth (2004) examined which leadership styles are the most effective for public relations and how leadership perceptions vary by gender. They found that practitioners strongly favored transformational leadership style over transactional style. Overall, the survey revealed few differences between female and male participants and their preference for style. Focus group participants in the research project, however, generally agreed that women had fewer opportunities for leadership positions in public relations, although they believed that women made better leaders due to their perceived empathy and collaborative efforts.

A comprehensive study of gender and public relations documented a longtime pay gap between women and men in the field and examined why women find it more difficult to ascend to leadership roles (L. A. Grunig, Toth, & Hon, 2001). Gender stereotyping is one of the key drivers. The researchers argued that issues of gender bias are essentially issues of perceptions of women created by both men and women. Although women today represent about 70% of the professional workforce, the pay gap is still an issue. This has been attributed to "years of professional experience, manager role enactment, participation in management decision-making, income suppressing career interruptions, and career specialization" (Dozier, Sha, & Shen, 2012).

Gender studies have highlighted income disparities between male and female professionals and documented that the journey to leadership is more difficult for women due to a variety of historical societal factors as well as organizational cultural and structural barriers. Gender approaches, such as excellence theory, point to the need for equal opportunities for men, women, and minorities to ascend to leadership roles to enhance practice and create an organizational environment for employee participation and job satisfaction.

The Plank Center Studies in Leadership

In 2006 the Plank Center for Leadership in Public Relations at the University of Alabama (UA) launched a research support program to enrich the body of knowledge about leadership in the field. Research grants have been provided to scholars at a number of universities, and the work of these researchers, along with those at UA, has yielded 22 studies, some of which are briefly described here. The studies explore diverse aspects of leadership, including behaviors, styles, dimensions, ethics, emotional intelligence, and education:

- Choi and Choi (2009) identified six leadership behaviors that influence the value of public relations in organizations, including providing employees with a clear vision about public relations policies and strategies, exerting upward influence, acting as a change agent, and creating alliances inside and outside of the organization.
- Werder and Holtzhausen (2009) found that transformational and inclusive leadership styles were most prevalent among practice leaders. The two styles are related: Transformational leaders focus on inspiring followers through communication, while inclusive leaders engage in more participative practices. Both styles were seen to increase the effectiveness of public relations strategies.
- Jin (2010) examined core emotional traits and skills for effective public relations leaders. She found that public relations leaders preferred a transformational leadership style, and empathy played an essential role in this type of leadership. Both leadership style and empathy were significant predictors of public relations leaders' competency in gaining employee trust, managing employee hopes and frustrations, and taking successful stances toward employees and top management in decision-making conflicts.
- Lee and Cheng (2011) used depth interviews with high-level communication executives to examine the ethical dimension of leadership. They found that ethical leadership was grounded more strongly in personal rather than in professional ethics. They also found that advocating for ethical standards and modeling appropriate behaviors facilitated the transfer of ethics knowledge and behaviors in the organization far more effectively than did communicating ethics codes and conducting workshops and training programs.

- Erzikova and Berger (2011, 2012) surveyed university educators to learn how and to what extent leadership is incorporated in public relations education. The teachers said they are advocates for leadership and they help develop future leaders. However, few universities offered actual leadership courses or content. Educators indicated the most important leadership skills and values for students were communication knowledge and skills, a strong ethical orientation, and problem-solving ability.

- Meng and colleagues (Meng, 2009; Meng & Berger, 2013; Meng, Berger, Gower, & Heyman, 2012; Meng et al., 2011) have been carrying out a research program to build theory about leadership in public relations. They have developed and tested an integrated model of excellent leadership in two samples in the United States and one in Singapore. Briefly, the model depicts excellent leadership in public relations as a complex mix of six interrelated dimensions: self-dynamics, team collaboration, ethical orientation, relationship-building skills, strategic decision-making capability, and communication knowledge and expertise. A seventh dimension—organizational culture and structure—influences the extent to which public relations leaders can be excellent. This model is described in detail in Chapter 3, and it was tested further in the global study.

Summary of Leadership Research in Public Relations

A handful of theoretical perspectives in the field, and a small but growing body of leadership studies, suggest that effective public relations leaders can increase the value of communication to organizations and help organizations make sound strategic choices and achieve their goals. In addition, principles of excellence in public relations practice appear linked with some qualities of excellent leaders, for example, participation in strategic decision making, possession of a managerial worldview, and use of two-way communication. Other perspectives call attention to the contingent nature of leadership and the importance of context, the presence of power relations and gender issues, and the preference of many practitioners for transformational and inclusive styles of leadership. Research at the Plank Center has focused on developing and testing a model of excellent leadership in global practice.

Defining Excellent Leadership in Public Relations

Building on this foundation, and to advance theoretical development of leadership, we first provide a definition of excellent leadership in public relations. Drawing from the extensive managerial leadership literature, we conclude that leadership is complex and multidimensional. Therefore, we synthesize diverse perspectives on leadership and adopt an integrative approach to conceptualize the construct of "excellent leadership" in public relations. We use the term *excellent* in the sense of an ideal type (Weber, 1969) rather than in the sense of excellence theory.

The work of J.E. Grunig and colleagues in formulating excellence theory has certainly informed some of the qualities and requirements of public relations leaders, but we use the term *excellent* to refer to what might be the best or most outstanding leadership in communication management, according to practitioners:

> Excellent leadership in public relations is a dynamic process that encompasses a complex mix of individual skills and personal attributes, values, and behaviors that consistently produces ethical and effective communication practice. Such practice fuels and guides successful communication teams, helps organizations achieve their goals, and legitimizes organizations in society.

This definition highlights the process nature of leadership and integrates leader traits, behaviors, and styles with leader–follower relationships and goal achievement at several levels. This definition, along with the seven dimensions of leadership mentioned earlier, underscores the dynamism and complexity of the leadership process in communication management.

Summary of Research and Research Questions

Drawing from the managerial leadership research and the public relations leadership literature, we propose and then examine five research questions in the global study. Because global scholarship about leadership in communication management is limited, research questions are an appropriate approach. The research questions were first explored through an online survey in nine languages of public relations practitioners in 23 countries. In addition, depth interviews with 137 communication executives in the countries/regions were conducted to answer these questions and to explore cultural and structural factors in greater depth.

Research Question 1: What Do Practitioners Believe Are the Most Important Issues Affecting Practice?

Issues are important because they provide the context for practice. Dynamic internal and external issues spur situationally sensitive decision making and the selection of appropriate strategies and tactics (Shin et al., 2011). Examining key issues helps us understand some of the forces that bear on leadership because sensemaking is about understanding how issues affect the organization and translating that knowledge into organizational meaning and purposeful action (Pang et al., 2010).

Rosebush (2012) argued that there are fewer great leaders today because the context for organizations has changed dramatically. Newly empowered stakeholders, globalization, and the digital revolution have radically altered the world and the organizational context. As a result, leaders and their institutions and organizations no longer enjoy privileged access to, and control of information, and trust in institutions and their leaders has sharply declined. At the same time, the pace of these and other changes has increased sharply. Durham (2013) claimed that organizational context now is "so dynamic that many business leaders have accepted the military term *VUCA* (Volatility, Uncertainty, Complexity, and Ambiguity) to describe the unprecedented challenges and opportunities in the global marketplace today."

Research Question 2: What Strategies and Tactics do Public Relations Leaders Use to Try to Manage Key Issues?

Once leaders make sense of an issue, how do they deal with it? What approaches do they employ to try to resolve the issue or capitalize on it? Examining strategies and tactics may help us better understand the strategic thinking of leaders in the field and how their sensemaking translates into local or global actions. It may also shed light on whether strategic choices to deal with key issues differ by culture, geography, organizational type, or other demographic variations.

Research Question 3: Does the Relative Importance of Each of the Seven Dimensions of Leadership Vary According to Specific Issues?

Through this question we explore whether our integrated model of excellent leadership in public relations might have application in other countries. More specifically, we examine whether the relative value of each of the six leadership dimensions, and the influence of organizational culture and structure, is perceived by professionals to change as issues change. Just as contingency theorists suggest that decision making about issues is situationally sensitive, we imagine that some dimensions of leadership will be more crucial than others in managing specific issues.

The capability for team collaboration, for example, might be a more crucial leadership dimension for dealing with the employee engagement issue than with the issue of the profession's image. Ethical orientation might be the strongest dimension for dealing with the image issue. Similarly, crisis decision making might draw more heavily from the strategic decision making dimension of leadership than from other dimensions. This seems intuitive, but as far as we know, it hasn't been demonstrated.

Research Question 4: What Do Practitioners Believe Can Be Done to Improve the Development of Public Relations Leaders in the Future?

Middlebrooks and Allen (2008) contend that the dynamic changes in the world today require that we reconceptualize leadership and develop leaders differently for the future. Development can increase leadership capacity and capabilities

(Avolio, 2005). It also may enhance a leader's ability to better deal with and manage change (Hackman & Johnson, 2008), which seems a crucial capability for future leaders.

Conger and Benjamin (1999) identified three approaches to developing individual leaders: (a) individual skills-based and personal growth programs, (b) socialization activities for company vision and culture, and (c) strategic leadership initiatives that engage individuals in team projects to solve real problems in the organization. Van Velsor and McCauley (2004) differentiate leader and leadership development programs. *Leader development* refers to individual growth and skill advancement that expand an individual's capacity and performance. *Leadership development* refers to an organization's or an association's planned attempts and programs to systematically develop its leadership team over time.

We want to capture the perceptions of diverse practitioners regarding their ideas about the future development needs of both individual leaders and the profession's leadership.

Research Question 5: What Demographic Variations Do Practitioners Present Regarding Perceptions and Beliefs About Leaders and Leadership?

Our study sample represents a diverse set of practitioners working in 23 countries in Europe, Asia, and North and South America. We want to examine to what extent views about key issues, strategies and tactics, and leadership development reflect demographic variations such as culture, organization type, gender, age, hierarchical position, and so forth.

A number of studies have examined cultural variations regarding leader behaviors, preferences, motivations, and styles (Meng, 2009). Most studies, however, have been conducted in North America and Western Europe (Yukl, 2002), and many of the prevailing theories of leadership are North American in character (House, 1995).

The extensive GLOBE research program examined leadership, culture, and organizations in 62 countries (House, Hanges, Javidan, Dorfman, & Gupta, 2004). The research program found that many leader attributes and behaviors, and individual perceptions about leaders, are culturally contingent. Some leadership characteristics and behaviors, however, are more universally linked to effective leadership, for example, team orientation, participative style, and charismatic and value-based approaches.

Generational differences are also of interest. A great deal has been written about the millennial generation and the differing values, beliefs, and practices these individuals bring to the workplace and their communities. They represent a "new breed" of worker and global citizen (Alsop, 2008). We use our large data set from the global survey, as well as the interview transcripts, to carefully examine these and other demographic variations. An online survey was used to gather data to help answer all five of the research questions. Depth interviews with selected leaders in the countries/regions were conducted to deepen and enrich answers to research Questions 1 through 4.

References

Aldoory, L. (1998). The language of leadership for female public relations professionals. *Journal of Public Relations Research, 10*(2), 73–101.

Aldoory, L., & Toth, E. (2004). Leadership and gender in public relations: Perceived effectiveness of transformational and transactional leadership styles. *Journal of Public Relations Research, 16*(2), 157–183.

Alsop, R. (2008). *The trophy kids grow up.* San Francisco, CA: Jossey-Bass.

Avolio, B. J. (2005). 100-year review of leadership intervention research: Briefings Report 2004–01, Gallup Leadership Institute, Kravis Leadership Institute. *Leadership Review, 5,* 7–13.

Bass, B. M. (1985). *Leadership and performance beyond expectations.* New York, NY: Free Press.

Bass, B. M. (1990). *Bass and Stogdill's handbook of leadership: Theory, research, and managerial applications* (3rd ed.). New York, NY: Free Press.

Bass, B. M. (1997a). Concepts of leadership. In R. P. Vecchio (Ed.), *Leadership: Understanding of power and influence in organizations* (pp. 3–23). Notre Dame, IN: University of Notre Dame Press.

Bass, B. M. (1997b). Does the transactional-transformational leadership paradigm transcend organizational and national boundaries? *American Psychologist, 52*(2), 130–139.

Bass, B. M., & Avolio, B. J. (1993). Transformational leadership: A response to critiques. In M. M. Chemers & R. Ayman (Eds.), *Leadership theory and research: Perspectives and directions* (pp. 49–80). San Diego, CA: Academic Press.

Berger, B., & Meng, J. (2010). Public relations practitioners and the leadership challenge. In. R. L. Heath (Ed.), *The SAGE handbook of public relations* (pp. 421–434). Thousand Oaks, CA: Sage.

Berger, B. K., & Reber, B. H. (2006). *Gaining influence in public relations: The role of resistance in practice.* Mahwah, NJ: Erlbaum.

Berger, B. K., Reber, B. H., & Heyman, W. C. (2007). You can't homogenize success in communication management: PR leaders take diverse paths to top. *International Journal of Strategic Communication, 1*(1), 53–71.

Blake, R. R., & Mouton, J. S. (1964). *The managerial grid.* Houston, TX: Gulf Publishing.

Bratton, J., Grint, K., & Nelson, D. L. (2005). *Organizational leadership.* Mason, OH: South-Western.

Broom, G. M., & Dozier, D. M. (1986). Advancement for public relations role models. *Public Relations Review, 12*(1), 37–56.

Burns, J. M. (1978). *Leadership.* New York, NY: Harper & Row.

Cameron, G. T., Cropp, F., & Reber, B. H. (2001). Getting past platitudes: Factors limiting accommodation in public relations. *Journal of Communication Management, 5*(3), 242–261.

Choi, Y., & Choi, J. (2009). Behavioral dimensions of public relations leadership in organizations. *Journal of Communication Management, 13*(4), 292–309.

Clemens, J. K., & Mayer, D. F. (1987). *The classic touch: Lessons in leadership-Homer to Hemingway.* Homewood, IL: Business One Irwin.

Conger, J. A. (1999). Charismatic and transformational leadership in organizations: An insider's perspective on these developing streams of research. *Leadership Quarterly, 10*(2), 145–179.

Conger, J. A. (1989). *The charismatic leader; Behind the mystique of exceptional leadership.* San Francisco: Jossey-Bass.

Conger, J. A., & Benjamin, B. (1999). *Building leaders: How successful companies develop the next generation.* San Francisco, CA: Jossey-Bass.

Conger, J. A., & Kanungo, R. N. (1987). Toward a behavioral theory of charismatic leadership in organizational settings. *Academy of Management Review, 12,* 637–647.

Conger, J. A., & Kanungo, R. N. (1998). *Charismatic leadership in organizations.* Thousand Oaks, CA: Sage.

Dansereau, F., Graen, G., & Haga, W. J. (1975). A vertical Dyad linkage approach to leadership in formal organizations. *Organizational Behavior and Human Performance, 13,* 46–78.

Dozier, D. M., & Broom, G. M. (1995). Evolution of the manager role in public relations practice. *Journal of Public Relations Research, 7*(1), 3–26.

Dozier, D. M., Sha, B-L, & Shen, H. (2012). Why women earn less than men: The cost of gender discrimination in U.S. public relations. *Public Relations Journal, 7*(1), 1–24. Available online at www.prsa.org/Intelligence/PRJournal/Documents/2013DozierShaShen.pdf

Duchon, D., Green, S. G., & Taber, T. D. (1986). Vertical dyad linkage: A longitudinal assessment of antecedents, measures, and consequences. *Journal of Applied Psychology, 71,* 56–60.

Durham, T. (2013, July 23). A fresh approach for leading change [Blog entry]. Available online at http://blog.ketchum.com/four-key-capabilities-for-success/

Erzikova, E., & Berger, B. K. (2011). Creativity vs. ethics: Russian and U.S. public relations students' perceptions of professional leadership and leaders. *Public Relations Journal, 5*(3), 25–49. Available online at www.prsa.org/Intelligence/PRJournal/Documents/2011ErzikovaBerger.pdf

Erzikova, E., & Berger, B. K. (2012). Leadership education in the public relations curriculum: Reality, opportunities, and benefits. *Public Relations Journal, 6*(3), 1–24. Available online at www.prsa.org/Intelligence/PRJournal/Documents/2012ErzikovaBerger.pdf

Fiedler, F. E. (1978). The contingency model and the dynamics of the leadership process. In L. Berkowitz (Ed.), *Advances in experimental social psychology* (pp. 59–112). New York, NY: Academic Press.

Fleishman, E. A. (1953). The description of supervisory behavior. *Journal of Applied Psychology, 37,* 1–6.

Graen, G. (1976). Role-making processes within complex organizations. In M. D. Dunnette (Ed.), *Handbook of Industrial and Organizational Psychology* (pp. 1202–1245). Chicago, IL: Rand McNally.

Graen, G., & Cashman, J. F. (1975). A role-making model of leadership in formal organizations: A developmental approach. In J. G. Hunt & L. L. Larson (Eds.), *Leadership frontiers* (pp. 143–165). Kent, OH: Kent State University Press.

Graen, G., Novak, M., & Sommerkamp, P. (1982). The effects of leader-member exchange and job design on productivity and satisfaction: Testing a dual attachment model. *Organizational Behavior and Human Performance, 30,* 109–131.

Graen, G., & Uhl-Bien, M. (1995). Relationship-based approach to leadership: Development of leader-member exchange (LMX) theory of leadership over 25 years: Applying a multi-level, multi-domain perspective. *Leadership Quarterly, 6*(2), 219–247.

Grunig, J. E. (1992a). Communication, public relations, and effective organizations: An overview of the book. In J. E. Grunig (Ed.), *Excellence in public relations and communication management* (pp. 1–28). Hillsdale, NJ: Erlbaum.

Grunig, J. E. (Ed.). (1992b). *Excellence in public relations and communication management: Contributions to effective organizations.* Hillsdale, NJ: Erlbaum.

Grunig, L. A. (1992). Power in the public relations department. In J. E. Grunig (Ed.), *Excellence in public relations and communication management: Contributions to effective organizations* (pp. 483–502). Hillsdale, NJ: Erlbaum.

Grunig, L. A., Grunig, J. E., & Dozier, D. M. (2002). *Excellent public relations and effective organizations: A study of communication management in three countries.* Mahwah, NJ: Erlbaum.

Grunig, L. A., Toth, E. L., & Hon, L. C. (2001). *Women in public relations: How gender influences practice.* New York, NY: Guilford.

Hackman, M. Z., & Johnson, C. E. (2009). *Leadership: A communication perspective* (5th ed.). Long Grove, IL: Waveland Press, Inc.

Heath, R. L. (2006). A rhetorical theory approach to issues management. In C. Botan & V. Hazelton (Eds.), *Public relations theory II* (pp. 63–100). Mahwah, NJ: Erlbaum.

House, R. J. (1971). A path-goal theory of leader effectiveness. *Administrative Science Quarterly, 16,* 321–339.

House, R. J. (1977). A theory of charismatic leadership. In J. G. Hunt & L. L. Larson (Eds.), *Leadership: The cutting edge* (pp. 189–207). Carbondale: Southern Illinois University Press.

House, R. J. (1999). Weber and neo-charismatic leadership paradigm: A reply to Beyer. *Leadership Quarterly, 10*(4), 563–574.

House, R. J., & Aditya, R. (1997). The social scientific study of leadership: quo vadis? *Journal of Management, 23*(4), 409–474.

House, R. J., Hanges, P. J., Javidan, M., Dorfman, P. W., & Gupta, V. (Eds.). (2004). *Culture, Leadership, and Organizations: The GLOBE Study of 62 Societies.* Thousand Oaks, CA: Sage.

House, R. J., & Mitchell, T. R. (1974). Path-goal theory of leadership. *Contemporary Business, 3,* 81–98.

Hunt, J. G. (1999). Transformational/Charismatic leadership's transformation of the field: An historical essay. *Leadership Quarterly, 10*(2), 129–144.

Jin, Y. (2010). Emotional leadership as a key dimension of public relations leadership: A national survey of public relations leaders. *Journal of Public Relations Research, 22*(2), 159–181.

Kahn, R. L., & Katz, D. (1960). Leadership practices in relation to productivity and morale. In D. Cartwright & A. Zander (Eds.), *Group dynamics: Research and theory.* Elmsford, NY: Paterson.

Katz, D., & Kahn, R. L. (1951). Human organization and worker motivation. In L. R. Tripp (Ed.), *Industrial productivity* (pp. 146–171). Madison, WI: Industrial Relations Research Association.

Katz, D., & Kahn, R. L. (1978). *The Social Psychology of Organizations* (2nd ed.). New York, NY: Wiley.

Kerr, S., & Jermier, J. M. (1978). Substitutes for leadership: Their meaning and measurement. *Organizational Behavior and Human Performance, 22,* 375–403.

Kim, K. I., & Organ, D. W. (1982). Determinants of leader-subordinate exchange relationships. *Group and Organization Studies, 7,* 77–89.

Kotter, J. P. (1982). *The general manager.* New York, NY: Free Press.

Kouzes, J. M., & Posner, B. Z. (2002). *The leadership challenge* (3rd ed.). San Francisco, CA: Jossey-Bass.

Lee, S. T., & Cheng, I.-H. (2011). Characteristics and dimensions of ethical leadership in public relations. *Journal of Public Relations Research, 23*(1), 46–74.

Likert, R. (1961). *New Patterns of Management.* New York, NY: McGraw-Hill.

Lord, R. G., DeVader, C. L., & Alliger, G. M. (1986). A meta-analysis of the relation between personality traits and leadership perceptions: An application of validity generalization procedures. *Journal of Applied Psychology, 71,* 402–410.

Manfredi, J. F. (2008). Selecting leaders who make a difference. *International Leadership Journal, 1*(1), 91–94.

Mann, R. D. (1959). A review of the relationship between personality and performance in small groups. *Psychological Bulletin, 56,* 241–270.

McCall, M. W., & Kaplan, R. E. (1985). *Whatever it takes: Decision makers at work.* Englewood Cliffs, NJ: Prentice Hall.

Meng, J. (2009). *Excellent leadership in public relations: An application of multiple-group confirmatory factor analysis models in assessing cross-national measurement in variance* (Unpublished dissertation). University of Alabama, Tuscaloosa.

Meng, J., & Berger, B. (2013). An integrated model of excellent leadership in public relations: Dimensions, measurement, and validation. *Journal of Public Relations Research, 25*(2), 141–167.

Meng, J., Berger, B. K., Gower, K. K., & Heyman, W. C. (2012). A test of excellent leadership in public relations: Key qualities, valuable sources, and distinctive leadership perceptions. *Journal of Public Relations Research, 24*(1), 18–36.

Meng, J., Berger, B. K., & Heyman W. C. (2011). Measuring public relations leadership in the trait approach: A second-order factor model in the dimension of self-dynamics. *Public Relations Journal, 5*(1), 1–24. Available online at www.prsa.org/Intelligence/PRJournal/Documents/2011WinterMengBergerHeyman.pdf

Middlebrooks, A., & Allen, S. J. (2008). Leadership education: New challenges, continuing issues. *International Leadership Journal, 1*(1), 77–85.

Mintzberg, H. (1973). *The nature of managerial work.* New York, NY: Harper & Row.

Mintzberg, H. (1979). *The structure of the organization.* Englewood Cliffs, NJ: Prentice Hall.

Neff, B. D. (2002). Integrating leadership processes: Redefining the principles course. *Public Relations Review, 28*(2), 137–147.

Northouse, P. G. (2007). *Leadership: Theory and practice.* Thousand Oaks, CA: Sage.

Pang, A., Jin, Y., & Cameron, G. T. (2010). Strategic management of communication. In R. L. Heath (Ed.), The *Sage handbook of public relations* (pp. 17–34). Thousand Oaks, CA: Sage.

Parry, K. W., & Bryman, A. (2006). Leadership in organizations. In S. R. Clegg, C. Hardy, T. B. Lawrence, & W. R. Nord (Eds.), The Sage handbook of organization studies (2nd ed.). London: Sage.

Peters, L. H., Hartke, D. D., & Pohlmann, J. T. (1985). Fiedler's contingency theory of leadership: An application of the meta-analysis procedures of Schmidt and Hunter. *Psychological Bulletin, 97,* 274–285.

Reber, B. H., & Cameron, G. T. (2003). Measuring contingencies: Using scales to measure public relations practitioner limits to accommodation. *Journalism & Mass Communication Quarterly, 80*(2), 431–446.

Rosebush, J. S. (2012). Why great leaders are in short supply [Blog entry]. Available online at http://blogs.hbr.org/cs/2012/03/why_great_leaders_are_in_short.html

Shamir, B., House, R. J., & Arthur, M. B. (1993). The motivational effects of charismatic leadership: A self-concept theory. *Organization Science, 4,* 1–17.

Shin, J.-H., Heath, R. L., & Lee, J. (2011). A contingency explanation of public relations practitioner leadership styles: Situation and culture. *Journal of Public Relations Research, 23*(2), 167–190.

Stogdill, R. M. (1948). Personal factors associated with leadership: A survey of the literature. *Journal of Psychology, 25*, 35–71.

Stogdill, R. M. (1974). *Handbook of leadership: A survey of the literature.* New York, NY: Free Press.

Stogdill, R. M., & Coons, A. E. (Eds.). (1957). *Leader behavior: Its description and measurement* (Research Monograph No. 88). Columbus: Bureau of Business Research, The Ohio State University.

Strube, M. J., & Garcia, J. E. (1981). A meta-analytic investigation of Fiedler's contingency model of leadership effectiveness. *Psychological Bulletin, 90*, 307–321.

Thayer, L. (1986). Rethinking leadership for public relations. *Public Relations Review, 12*(1), 3–12.

Townsend, J., Phillips, J. S., & Elkins, T. J. (2000). Employee retaliation: the neglected consequence of poor leader-member exchange relations. *Journal of Occupational Health Psychology, 5*(4), 457–463.

Trice, H. M., & Beyer, J. M. (1986). Charisma and its routinization in two social movement organizations. *Research in Organizational Behavior, 8*, 113–164.

Van Velsor, E., & McCauley, C. D. (2004). Introduction: Our view of leadership development. In *The Center for Creative Leadership handbook of leadership development* (2nd ed., pp. 1–22). San Francisco, CA: Jossey-Bass.

Wakabayashi, M., & Graen, G. B. (1984). The Japanese career progress study: A seven-year followup. *Journal of Applied Psychology, 69*, 603–614.

Waller, D. J., Smith, S. R., & Warnack, J. T. (1989). Situational theory of leadership. *American Journal of Health System Pharmacy, 46*(11), 2335–2341.

Weber, M. (1969). *Basic concepts in sociology* (H. P. Secher, Trans.). New York, NY: Greenwood Press.

Werder, K. P., & Holtzhausen, D. (2009). An analysis of the influence of public relations department leadership style on public relations strategy use and effectiveness. *Journal of Public Relations Research, 21*(4), 404–427.

Yammarino, F. J. (1993). Transforming leadership studies: Bernard Bass's leadership and performance beyond expectations. *Leadership Quarterly, 4*(3), 379–382.

Yukl, G. (1971). Toward a behavioral theory of leadership. *Organizational Behavior and Human Performance, 6*, 414–440.

Yukl, G. (1989). Managerial leadership: A review of theory and research. *Journal of Management, 15*(2), 251–289.

Yukl, G. (1999). An evaluation of conceptual weaknesses in transformational and charismatic leadership theories. *Leadership Quarterly, 10*(2), 285–305.

Yukl, G. (2002). *Leadership in organizations* (5th ed.) Upper Saddle River, NJ: Prentice Hall.

3

RESEARCH DESIGN AND METHODS

Juan Meng and Bruce K. Berger

This chapter explains the research design, methods, and theoretical background of constructs defined in the global project. These constructs include critical issues in the field and issue management, public relations leadership, and leader and leadership development. To measure the constructs, and help us answer the five research questions, we used both quantitative (online survey) and qualitative (in-depth interviews) research methods to collect responses from targeted populations globally. The detailed description of both research methods is first presented in the following sections. The second half of the chapter elaborates the key constructs.

Research Design

The research for this global project was designed to focus on how dynamic changes—globalization, the rise of powerful social media, empowered stakeholders, and other diverse social changes—affect organizational communications, and especially the roles, strategies, and daily practices of public relations leaders. In addition, the global nature of the project lends itself to a long-term and multi-method research program. The time range for the completion of the entire project ran from the summer of 2011 until the end of 2012.

This global research project is the largest, most comprehensive study of leadership ever conducted in our discipline: a global team of 26 country/region co-investigators, together with the two principle investigators, carried out the study in 23 countries and regions (see Table 3.1). The 23 countries/regions were selected purposively to provide variations in geography, history, economic development, demographics, and sociocultural characteristics (based on House, Hanges, Javidan, Dorfman, & Gupta, 2004) and to represent a suitable context for investigating the

TABLE 3.1 Countries and Regions Participating in the Global Leadership Project

Cultural Clusters*	Country/Region
Confucian Asia	Mainland China, Hong Kong, Singapore, South Korea, and Taiwan
Southern Asia	India
Eastern Europe	Estonia, Latvia, and Russia
Germanic Europe	Austria, Germany, and Switzerland
Latin Europe	Spain
Anglo	United Kingdom and United States
Latin America	Brazil, Chile, and Mexico

* We used the cultural clusters that were developed and tested in the GLOBE Project (House, Henges, Javidan, Dorman, & Gupta, 2004) as a guide to ensure some diversity in our sample. Our list of participating countries did not represent the complete list of cultural clusters (e.g., the Nordic Europe, the sub-Saharan Africa, and the Middle East clusters) and countries (e.g., Japan, the Netherlands, Canada, Australia, etc.). We did conduct the survey in the Middle East cluster (i.e., Egypt, Jordan, Lebanon, Qatar, and United Arab Emirates) as well. However, due to the limited access to the professionals and the lack of an accurate and updated database of public relations professionals in the regions, we were unable to collect sufficient data for comparative purposes. However, data from this region were included in the overall results.

different levels of development in the communication profession round the world. Although we were unable to include all societies or cultures, the countries and regions we investigated represent some major geographical regions in the world (i.e., Confucian Asia, Southern Asia, Eastern and Western Europe, North America, and Latin America). Those geographical regions reflect diverse societal cultures, powerful economies, and varying stages of development of the communication profession.

Phases of Research

The global project consists of three relevant phases: (1) construct conceptualization, measurement development, and pilot tests; (2) the administration of an online global survey; and (3) the completion of in-depth interviews with selected communication leaders in researched countries and regions.

Phase 1: Defining the Constructs to Be Measured and Pilot Testing

The first phase involved conceptualizing the constructs and developing relevant measurement scales for the testing purpose. The constructs tested include critical issues in current communication practice, responsive strategies used to manage the issues, the role of leadership dimensions in managing the issues, approaches in leadership development, and practitioners' perceptions regarding leadership and self, gender, organization, and profession. Items used to measure the defined constructs were largely adapted from previous research in public relations, leadership development, issue management, and other critical research subjects in the field (e.g., crisis management, ethics, transparency, and employee engagement) to ensure the reliability of the measurement itself. A detailed description of the measurement development for defined constructs is addressed in the section "Theoretical Background and Final Measures in the Global Questionnaire" in this chapter.

All measures were assessed in two pilot tests with two small groups of practitioners. Before conducting the first pilot test, the constructs were defined by the two principal investigators and subsequently were discussed within the global research team via a conference call in June 2011 and in a series of subsequent communications. The communications focused on the appropriateness and accuracy of the constructs to be tested. Questions and concerns regarding the list of critical issues in public relations practice, development approaches in public relations leadership, and leadership perceptions were first addressed. The researchers then reviewed the scope of the defined constructs and suggested several revisions for the measurement statements. As a result, several constructs, survey questions, and measurement items were modified.

Sampling strategies and concerns also were discussed, and the research team agreed that a mixed sampling strategy (i.e., mixed random and convenience sampling) was the best way to recruit participants in the diverse countries. Though random sampling is the ideal approach, we recognized early on that cost constraints and limited or no access to professional e-mail databases in many countries made random sampling impossible. Thus, a convenience (i.e., snowball) sampling procedure was used in a number of countries—for example, China, India, Latvia, Russia and so forth—to obtain a reasonably diffuse sample and a better response rate.

Once the global research team agreed on the defined constructs and their related measures, we carried out the first pilot test by sending the sample questionnaire to 92 purposively selected senior communication executives who possessed diverse backgrounds in practice and rich experience in management. The first test assessed the definition of "leader" in public relations and communication management, a list of critical issues in the field, and perceptions about leadership regarding (a) self as the leader, (b) gender and leaders, (c) organizational support for the practice, and (d) the profession in the future.

We invited participants to evaluate the listed issues in terms of their importance in affecting practice and asked them to write down potential critical issues that were not on the list. The pilot test essentially confirmed the list of issues, although we revised some of the issue statements and the four perceptual areas of questions to better reflect professional terminology. The first pilot test was carried out in July and August 2011.

We conducted a second pilot test in October 2011 that focused on the other two major constructs in the questionnaire: (a) responsive strategies and actions toward critical issues and (b) approaches that might be taken to better develop and prepare leaders for the future. After confirming the list of 10 critical issues based on the first pilot test, we developed five relevant responsive strategies and actions for each issue, as well as 12 leadership development approaches. These strategies, actions, and development approaches were largely adapted from existing literature regarding the issue itself, related case studies, and extensive leadership development studies. We invited a different group of 65 senior public relations executives to evaluate the developed measures of responsive strategies and leadership development approaches. As a result, we eliminated several strategies and approaches and replaced them with new ones. We also replaced two developmental approaches with new ones; that is, developing emotional IQ and improving stress management were added.

Overall, discussions and communications within the global research team and the two pilot tests helped us finalize the defined constructs of interest, improve the statement of description for each issue, and confirm the appropriateness of their measurement in terms of face validity.

Phase 2: The Global Online Survey

The second phase of the project focused on empirically testing constructs and measures developed in Phase 1 by conducting an online survey in all participating countries. (See Appendix A for the questionnaire). As explained, due to the difficulty of obtaining professional directories in most countries, a mixed sampling strategy was employed to increase the final completion rate for the online survey. We used a comprehensive online survey software service, the Unipark system in Germany, to implement the survey itself. This system supported multiple languages.

The original survey questionnaire was developed in English, and the pilot tests were carried out in English. To accommodate varied levels of English proficiency in participating countries, and to ensure the validity of defined constructs in each investigated country, the research partners in each country/region translated the questionnaire into their home language. We recognize that language is a major concern in global research, so we made sure that the survey items were translated into the target country's official language using back translation procedures (Brislin, 1970) by the research team or partners of bilingual proficiency (i.e., English and their home language). In addition, the research partners in each country were scholars or senior practitioners in communication and public relations disciplines. With this approach, it is implicitly assumed that the defined constructs are appropriately understood and translated to adequately measure the same constructs across different countries.

We compared the translated version with the initial English version and revised it until it was very close to the original. As many as three revisions were undertaken for several translations. After modifications based on these procedures, the final translation in nine languages was judged as displaying satisfactory translation and calibration equivalence (Douglas & Craig, 2009) by using the testing link. However, the respondents still had the flexibility to choose the language (English or their native language) to answer the final online survey when they clicked the survey link. Finally, the online survey was implemented in nine languages, including Arabic, Chinese (both simplified and traditional), English, Estonian,

German, Korean, Portuguese, Russian, and Spanish. The researchers in each country were responsible for developing their sample of participants and communicating with them, following requirements of institutional review boards or other relevant research governing bodies.

The global online survey was launched in different countries at different times, and the survey site itself was opened in November 2011 and closed in May 2012. During that time, more than 10,000 professionals visited the survey link. Nearly 4,500 public relations and communication professionals worldwide completed the survey, and 4,483 were retained for analysis after data cleaning and discarding incomplete responses. This represented satisfactory response rates among site visitors (45% total, 44% usable). Comprehensive demographics for the survey are included in Chapter 4.

As the demographics suggest, the respondents are communication professionals who fit the general characteristics of communication leaders or potential leaders, a desirable quality because they influence the views of others in the communication team and may be involved in the decision-making process in their organizations. They are of particular interest to the global project as they represent practitioners working in different cultural contexts. Therefore, the overall sample meets the key properties of adequacy and relevance in light of the global study's objectives (Craig & Douglas, 2006).

Phase 3: In-Depth Interviews With Executives

The third phase focused on collecting a deeper understanding of developed constructs through in-depth interviews with senior executives in participating countries. (See Appendix B for the Interview Guide). We used the qualitative method to learn more about culture-specific interpretations of critical issues, about how the issues influence leadership roles and practices, and about leadership development approaches. Country co-investigators conducted the interviews in each designated country/region. Similarly, a mixed sampling strategy was employed for the third phase of research as well. A snowball sampling approach was used in most countries to locate potential participants for the interviews. The same back-translation procedures were employed for the Interview Guide to ensure the meaning of each defined construct was appropriately understood and translated. Participants were given the option to conduct the interview in English or in their home language.

Major questions and topics discussed during the in-depth interviews focused on participants' perceptions of critical issues in communication; we were especially interested in how issues affect leaders' practices, roles, and decision making. In addition, the interviews sought to discover what types of cultural or structural factors in the organization either facilitated or impeded successful communication practice. A third area of questioning probed for qualities of excellent leadership in public relations and for requirements for future public relations leaders.

Overall, 137 in-depth interviews were completed in 10 countries/regions, or about 14 interviews for each. The number of interviews ranged from 8 (Latvia) to 22 (Chinese-speaking countries); however, 12 to 15 interviews were completed in most countries. Participants included 68 women and 69 men who were high-level communication executives, most representing companies or agencies. The vast majority of interviews were conducted via telephone, although a few were completed via Skype or in person. The shortest interview lasted 30 minutes; the longest, more than 2 hours. On average, the interviews lasted about 52 minutes.

All interviews were recorded, transcribed, and then subjected to data analysis using the constant comparative method (Glaser & Strauss, 1967; Lincoln & Guba, 1985). More details about the sample and analysis, as well as the results for each country/region, are included in Section III of this book.

Theoretical Background and Final Measures in the Global Questionnaire

Critical Issues and Issue Management

The first key construct defined in our global study is *issue and responsive strategies in issue management*. Successful communication management ultimately depends on properly recognizing the critical issues and the drivers of these issues. Issues are important to organizations because they provide the context for decision-making and action. According to Dutton and Ottensmeyer (1987), issues are developments or trends that emerge from an organization's internal or external environment and have the potential to affect an organization's performance (p. 355). Therefore, identifying and monitoring issues is a crucial part of strategic planning.

Issues management (IM) refers to how and to what extent organizations may try to deal with and resolve issues they deem important. IM is thus the "organized activity of identifying emerging trends, concerns or issues likely to affect an organization in the next few years and developing a wider and more positive range of responses toward that future" (Coates, Coates, Jarratt, & Heinz, 1996, p. ix). This is important because the comprehensive GLOBE studies in 62 countries demonstrated that external forces or issues in society do affect organizational culture and practices (House et al., 2004).

Often, IM is considered in the public policy arena where organizations engage in discussion and influence attempts to shape governmental legislation and regulation (Heath, 2006). In this regard, IM can play an important role in linking "the PR function and the management function to help the organization be outer directed and to have a participative organizational culture" (Heath, 2006, p. 76). Doing so may help organizations resolve issues in ways that produce favorable outcomes, strengthen relationships, or yield other benefits.

Clearly, understanding, analyzing, and interpreting issues are crucial to communication leaders and leaders of all kinds. Rosebush (2012) suggested that one of the reasons we may seem to have fewer great leaders today is because the context for leadership is changing dramatically—new issues have changed some important requirements for leaders. He argues that leaders today no longer have privileged

TABLE 3.2 The Final List of 10 Critical Issues Used in the Global Survey

Ten Issues

1. Dealing with the speed and volume of information flow
2. Being prepared to deal effectively with crises that may arise
3. Managing the digital revolution and rise of social media
4. Improving the measurement of communication effectiveness
5. Improving employee engagement and commitment in the workplace
6. Dealing with growing demands for transparency of communications
7. Finding, developing and retaining highly talented communication professionals
8. Meeting increasing demands for corporate social responsibility
9. Meeting communication needs in diverse cultures and globalizing markets
10. Improving the image of the profession

access to information (it's widely dispersed, thanks to technology); institutions are no longer as revered as they were in previous generations; and trust in leaders has sharply declined. In this world, the abilities to understand vast flows of information, to crystalize that information into inspiring narratives, and to display integrity in all behaviors become ever more vital.

Thus, in our global study we wanted to first examine what public relations professionals and leaders believe are the most important issues affecting their organizations today—we wanted to understand the context for practice. We cast a wide net to assemble an eventual list of 10 issues for professionals to evaluate. To assemble the list, we first carried out a comprehensive review of issues discussed in professional and academic conferences. These included conferences of the Public Relations Society of America and the Arthur W. Page Society, among others. The websites of these and other organizations, along with various trade publications, also were examined to create an exhaustive list of issues.

In addition, we reviewed findings from the *European Communication Monitor* 2010 (Zerfass, Tench, Verhoeven, Vercic, & Moreno, 2010) as it captured perceptions of public relations professionals in 40 countries regarding the most important issues in the field for communication managers. Then, the list of issues were compiled and finalized through the two pilot tests as previously described. All 10 issues were measured with 7-point Likert scales (1 = *a little bit of importance*, 7 = *a great deal of importance*). Table 3.2 displays the final list of 10 issues we measured in the global survey.

Public Relations Leadership as an Integrated Construct

The second key construct defined in our global project is *public relations leadership*. To measure this defined construct, we adapted Meng's (2010a) integrated model of public relations leadership as the subject of leadership is relatively understudied in public relations. As described in Chapter 2, the literature of contemporary leadership has exhibited a broad range of theories from personal attributes, to behavior, to situational factors, to transformational style, and to authentic leadership development (Nohria & Khurana, 2010). We assert that the complexity and multidimensionality of the leadership construct eliminate the possibility of generating a simple definition, even within our profession.

Leadership cannot mean only one thing in excellent public relations practice because it takes on multiple meanings and approaches as the issue or the situation evolves. The process of achieving leadership effectiveness in communication management presents the dynamic nature of the construct itself by mapping the relationships across multiple factors such as individual traits, leader behaviors, team collaboration, relationship management, communication management capabilities, and the realities of organizational structure and culture.

Based on a comprehensive literature review of relevant leadership theories, Meng (2010a) proposed a theoretical model of leadership in public relations by identifying six key dimensions and a major environmental moderator of the leadership effectiveness in the context of communication practice. The six key dimensions include *self-dynamics, team collaboration, ethical orientation, relationship building, strategic decision-making capability*, and *communication knowledge management*. The major environmental moderator, which serves as the seventh dimension, is the *organizational structure and culture* in which the team and leaders practice communication. Figure 3.1 is the graphic presentation of the relationships of

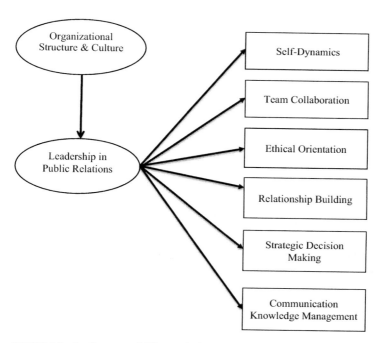

FIGURE 3.1 An Integrated Theoretical Model of Public Relations Leadership

such dimensions to the leadership construct, which has been tested and confirmed by empirical research (Meng, 2010b, 2012; Meng & Berger, 2013).

Measurement and Validation of the Integrated Leadership Model

As described before, the proposed theoretical model suggests seven major dimensions as good candidates for describing the complexity of the leadership construct itself in public relations and communication management. All seven dimensions appear to be highly relevant to effective public relations practice and could possibly offer public relations leaders some distinct advantages in initiating communication efforts. This model has been tested through empirical research (Meng, 2010a, 2010b, 2012; Meng & Berger, 2013; Meng, Berger, & Heyman, 2011), and it is described in greater detail in Chapter 7.

A rigorous measurement approach was used to assess the validity of the proposed theoretical model and concepts of leadership dimensions. A brief summarization of the testing process includes the following steps:

1. We conducted an intensive search of existing literature and theories in leadership and public relations to specify the theoretical domain of interest and identify the necessity for developing new measures and models in public relations leadership.
2. We developed multiple-item measures (more than 70) of all seven dimensions of public relations leadership based on relevant theoretical statements in the literature of public relations, managerial leadership, and organizational behavior research.
3. Two pilot tests were carried out with two small groups of purposively selected senior public relations practitioners to reevaluate the multiple-item measures we have suggested and to reduce the number of measurement items for each dimension.
4. Based on the results of pretests, we reformatted the statements of the multiple-item measures (45 in total) into 7-point rating scales for the final survey instrument.
5. We conducted an online survey via zoomerang.com and distributed the survey to multiple groups of public relations practitioners nationwide and internationally. The final usable sample included three groups of respondents: a group of senior public relations executives in the United States ($n = 222$), a group of mid-level public relations practitioners in the United States ($n = 162$), and a group of international public relations practitioners ($n = 110$).
6. A series of statistical tests (e.g., internal consistency analysis, item aggregation, and correlation analysis) and a multilevel modeling process (e.g., confirmatory factor analysis on first- and second-order models, model specification and refinement, composite reliability assessment, and multi-group–measurement invariance assessment) were applied to the three groups of respondents for empirical testing.

TABLE 3.3 The Final List of Seven Leadership Dimensions Used in the Global Survey

Leadership Dimensions
Possessing communication knowledge to develop appropriate strategies, plans and messages
Participating in your organization's strategic decision making regarding the issue
Possessing a strong ethical orientation and set of values to guide actions
Having the ability to build and manage professional work teams to address the issue
Providing a compelling vision for how communication can help the organization
Having the ability to develop coalitions in and outside the organization to deal with the issue
Working in an organization that supports two-way communication and shared power

Overall, the measures of all proposed leadership dimensions possessed solid psychometric properties and demonstrated significant reliability of response consistency. The validity of the theoretical model was confirmed through repeated tests and measurement invariance evaluation across groups (Meng, 2010b, 2012; Meng & Berger, 2013; Meng et al., 2011, 2012). For a more detailed description of the measurement scale development and psychometric tests of the theoretical model, please see Meng's (2010a) and Meng and Berger's (2013) studies.

To be able to test the functions of leadership dimensions in issue management in this global study, we adapted the original measurement scales of all seven leadership dimensions into a short version: we treat each individual dimension as a composite indicator and adapted the multi-item measures of each dimension into a single statement. All seven leadership dimensions were measured with 7-point Likert scales (1 = *a little bit of importance*, 7 = *a great deal of importance*). Table 3.3 displays the final measures of the leadership dimensions used in this global study. Again, Chapter 7 explains the process in greater detail.

Leader and Leadership Development

Another key construct defined in our global study is *leader and leadership development*. We defined this construct based on research in leadership development. We agree that to facilitate the advancement of the public relations profession is to enable the development of highly qualified professionals who will become future leaders not only in the organization but also for the profession. Are leaders born or made? This is an age-old question that has been argued by leadership scholars (e.g., Mumford, Zaccaro, Connelly, & Marks, 2000). We fully acknowledge that people may start with different levels of inherited leadership capabilities, especially at the individual level of personal attributes or psychological perspectives (e.g., Chatman & Kennedy, 2010). However, we strongly believe that leaders can be developed and improved, especially in a dynamic profession that is experiencing rapid development under the influence of media, cultural, and social changes (Servaes, 2012).

Leadership development can be defined as "the expansion of the organization's capacity to enact the basic leadership tasks needed for collective work: setting direction, creating alignment, and maintaining commitment" (Van Velsor & McCauley, 2004, p. 18). Thus, leadership development should be seen as a continuous journey or as a process that can improve a person's leadership capacity and capability. This is a contrasting view to *management development*, which aims at helping managers to acquire the specific knowledge and skills needed to enhance task performance in the management role (Day, 2000).

Van Velsor and McCauley (2004) also distinguished between *leader* development and *leadership* development. Leader development refers to individual growth and skill advancement that expand one's leadership capacity and improve performance; leadership development focuses more on an organization's attempt to enhance its team of leaders to strengthen their overall organizational performance. Rather than focusing on technical job skills, leadership development initiatives usually pay more attention to broader capabilities and competencies in an interpersonal context, such as flexibility, conflict management, team building, change management, self-awareness, and/or interpersonal skills (e.g., Day & Harrison, 2007). Such initiatives see leadership development as a process involving cultivating and leveraging strengths while understanding and minimizing weaknesses (Hernez-Broome & Hughes, 2004).

Previous research on leadership development has focused on three major categories: the "knowing," the "doing," and the "being" dimensions of becoming a leader. The knowing dimensions highlight the cognitive capabilities and multiple intelligences such as analytical intelligence, social intelligence, and emotional intelligence the leader requires (e.g., Riggio, 2001). The doing dimensions highlight the behavioral components or skills such as problem solving skills, conflict management, or adaptive skills a leader should be able to demonstrate to followers in varied contexts (e.g., Mumford et al., 2000). The being dimensions address a unique perspective of looking into leadership development from the concept of self-identity, which enables someone to think of him- or herself as a leader and to interact with the team from that identity (e.g., Ibarra, Snook, & Guillén Ramo, 2010). Such self-perception will generate an identity-based model of leader development to enlist the followers.

The leadership development literature also suggests the importance of actual experience in developing leadership talent. Although an individual's naturally occurring life experiences, and what he or she learns from the experiences, have been found to generate a significant impact on a leader's development (Bennis, 2009), organizations also are crucial in helping talented employees gain the right experiences at the right time to accelerate their development as leaders (e.g., McCall, 2010; McCauley, Ruderman, Ohlott, & Morrow, 1994).

McCall (2010) identified five leveraging points organizations can use to create a supportive institutional context for leadership learning and development: (a) identifying developmental experiences, (b) identifying people with potential to be leaders, (c) developing processes for getting the right learning experience, (d) increasing the odds that learning will occur, and (e) taking a career-long perspective with a focus on critical career transitions.

Research on formal leadership development initiatives generated similar results with a heavy focus on the role of organizations in such efforts. For example, Conger (2010) has argued that it is important for organizations to not only create formal leadership development initiatives that not only focus on individual skill development but also to integrate corporate vision and values, add strategic interventions to promote major changes, and design active learning approaches to address organizational challenges and opportunities.

Avolio (2010) also argued that to develop authentic leadership, organizations should accelerate the development of positive leadership for sustainable impact not only on individuals but also on groups, communities, and nations. Kegan and Lahey (2010) apply adult development theories to the concept of leadership development and argue that the focus should be placed on the process of *development*, instead of on the concept of *leadership*.

Overall, the broad literature in the field has suggested that best-practice organizations view leadership development programs as a way to increase competitive advantage and support corporate strategy (e.g., Fulmer & Goldsmith, 2001). The literature on leadership development also confirms that leaders develop through multiple approaches: their individual experiences, formal or structured leadership development programs, educational programs or other types of interventions, formal training developed by organizations, and the influence of role models, mentors, and coaches (e.g., Conger & Fulmer, 2003). The importance of such leadership development initiatives presents the complicated nature of leadership itself. So the central question in our field becomes *How can we develop effective leaders in public relations and communication management when the context for leadership is changing dramatically?*

Given the global nature and the uniqueness of our study, which focuses on the discussion of leader and leadership development for the public relations profession, we were particularly interested in identifying (a) diverse types of development approaches for public relations professionals, (b) the relative prevalence of such approaches in our profession, and (c) development approaches that might be applied effectively across cultures.

Therefore, we constructed a list of 12 possible development approaches for both individual (leader) and organizational (leadership) development actions, which were based on existing leader and leadership development literature (e.g., Conger, 2010; Hackman & Johnson, 2009; Van Velsor, McCauley, & Ruderman, 2010). The list of 12 development approaches was refined and finalized through the two pilot tests previously described. Table 3.4 displays the 12 developmental

TABLE 3.4 The Final List of 12 Leader and Leadership Development Approaches

Leader and Leadership Development Approaches
Increase cultural understanding and sensitivity
Improve the listening skills of professionals
Develop training to enhance emotional intelligence
Urge professional associations to work together to develop leaders
Strengthen the business/economic component of communication education programs
Enhance conflict management skills
Develop better measures to document the value and contribution of public relations
Require professional accreditation or licensing
Impose tough penalties on ethical violators
Develop a core global education curriculum
Enhance professional skills in coping with work-related stress
Strengthen change management skills and capabilities

approaches. All leadership development approaches were measured by using the 7-point Likert scales (1 = *strongly disagree*, 7 = *strongly agree*).

Leadership Perceptions

We also tested leadership perceptions in the global survey from four different perspectives: (a) self as the leader, (b) gender and leaders, (c) organizational support for the practice, and (d) the profession in the future. Leadership can be conceived in terms of the criteria used to decide appropriate strategies and relevant processes for attaining desired outcomes (House et al., 2004). Either implicitly or explicitly, managerial leadership theories provide statements about preferred means or outcomes (Yukl, 1989).

A number of current leadership theories emphasize the interaction between leaders' behaviors and followers' perceptions to explain the leadership process (e.g., Lord & Maher, 1991). Implicit leadership theory suggests the leadership creation process is revealed by looking into how an executive's values translate into followers' perceptions. From this point of view, followers' perceptions and interpretation of leaders' actual behaviors might have a direct effect on the followers' level of motivation (Lord & Brown, 2001).

The GLOBE research project addressed the importance of having a culturally endorsed, implicit leadership theory (House et al., 2004). Although the results from the GLOBE research showed that some leadership qualities or prototypes vary across societal cultures, several leadership prototypes are universally endorsed. For example, visionary leadership, a critical component of the broader transformational leadership concepts, has been confirmed to have universal appeal as an effective leadership prototype (House, Wright, & Aditya, 1997).

Although we didn't directly measure leader–follower interaction in the global project to test how perceptions of leadership dimensions may be related to followers' motivation and effort, we argue that it is still important to see how leaders in communication management perceive their own leadership style, which may also be related to their executive decision-making process. Therefore, we tested individual leaders' perceptions about self-leadership, gender equality in leadership, organizational conditions for public relations leadership, and emerging leadership in the profession. The reason for assessing leadership perceptions in this manner stems from the public relations literature in effective individual traits (e.g., Berger, Reber, & Heyman, 2007), gender issues in the profession (e.g., Aldoory, 1998), organizational support (e.g., Deetz, Tracy, & Simpson, 2000), and the image of the profession (e.g., Heath & Bowen, 2002).

Therefore, we constructed a list of 12 statements to describe leadership perceptions in the four subjects explained (three statements for each subject defined) from existing public relations literature (e.g., Aldoory, 1998; Berger et al., 2007; Deetz et al., 2000; Heath & Bowen, 2002). The list of 12 statements of leadership perceptions was refined and finalized in the first pilot test. Table 3.5 displays the 12 leadership perception statements. All perception statements were measured by using the 7-point Likert scales (1 = *strongly disagree*, 7 = *strongly agree*).

TABLE 3.5 The Final List of 12 Leadership Perceptions

Leadership Perceptions
Individual perceptions
I consider myself to be a leader in communication management.
I want to be a leader in communication management.★
I learn more about excellent leadership from role models and/or mentors on the job than from university education or management development programs.
Gender perceptions
Males and females can be equally capable leaders in public relations.
I prefer to work for a male leader on the job.★
Females have better interpersonal communication skills than males.★
Organization perceptions
The highest ranking PR professional in my organization is an excellent leader.
My organization encourages and practices two-way communication.
The CEO or top executive in my organization understands the value of PR.★
Profession perceptions
Leadership in public relations is different from leadership in other fields.
Leadership skills are more important than communication skills in leading a public relations unit or department.
I am optimistic about the future of the public relations profession in my country.

Note: ★ indicates items that were reverse-coded.

Overall, the nature of our global project, and our five research questions, required that we employ multiple research methods (a mixed design with both quantitative and qualitative methods) to best capture the meaning of leadership in current communication practice and the role of leadership in effective issue management. We used multiple measurement approaches, either adapting existing measures from previous research or developing new measures based on core public relations research on the subject, to empirically validate defined constructs. Chapters in Section II of the book present the detailed findings on each key defined construct.

References

Aldoory, L. (1998). The language of leadership for female public relations professionals. *Journal of Public Relations Research, 10,* 73–101.

Avolio, B. J. (2010). Pursuing authentic leadership development. In Nitin Nohria & Rakesh Khurana (eds.), *Handbook of leadership theory and practice* (pp. 739–768). Boston, MA: Harvard Business Press.

Bennis, W. G. (2009). *On becoming a leader* (4th ed.). Philadelphia: Basic Books.

Berger, B. K., Reber, B. H., & Heyman, W. C. (2007). You can't homogenize success in communication management: PR leaders take diverse paths to top. *International Journal of Strategic Communication, 1,* 53–71.

Brislin, R. W. (1970). Back translation of cross-cultural research. *Journal of Cross-Culture Psychology, 1,* 185–216.

Chatman, J. A., & Kennedy, J. A. (2010). Psychological perspectives on leadership. In N. Nohria & R. Khurana (Eds.), *Handbook of leadership theory and practice* (pp. 159–182). Boston, MA: Harvard Business Press.

Coates, J. F., Coates, V. T., Jarratt, J., & Heinz, L. (1986). *Issues management: How you can plan, organize and manage for the future.* Mt. Airy, MD: Lomond.

Conger, J. A. (2010). Leadership development interventions: Ensuring a return on the investment. In N. Nohria & R. Khurana (Eds.), *Handbook of leadership theory and practice* (pp. 709–738). Boston, MA: Harvard Business Press.

Conger, J. A., & Fulmer, R. M. (2003). Developing your leadership pipeline. *Harvard Business Review, 81*(12), 76–84.

Craig, C. S., & Douglas, S. P. (2006). Beyond national culture: Implications of cultural dynamics for consumer research. *International Marketing Review, 23,* 322–342.

Day, D. V. (2000). Leadership development: A review in context. *Leadership Quarterly, 11,* 581–613.

Day, D. V., & Harrison, M. M. (2007). A multilevel, identity-based approach to leadership development. *Human Resource Management Review, 17,* 360–373.

Deetz, S. A., Tracy, S. J., & Simpson, J. L. (2000). *Leading organizations through transition: Communication and cultural change.* Thousand Oaks, CA: Sage.

Douglas, S. P., & Craig, C. S. (2009). *International Marketing Research* (3rd ed.). Hoboken, NJ: Wiley.

Dutton, J. E., & Ottensmeyer, E. (1987). Strategic issue management systems: Forms, functions, and contexts. *Academy of Management Review, 12,* 355–365.

Fulmer, R. M., & Goldsmith, M. (2001). *The leadership investment: How the world's best organizations gain strategic advantage through leadership development.* New York, NY: AMA.

Glaser, B., & Strauss, A. (1967). *The discovery of grounded theory: Strategies for qualitative research*. Thousand Oaks, CA: Sage.

Hackman, M. Z., & Johnson, C. E. (Eds.). (2009). *Leadership: A communication perspective* (5th ed.). Long Grove, IL: Waveland Press.

Heath, R. L. (2006). A rhetorical theory approach to issues management. In C. Botan & V. Hazelton (Eds.), *Public relations theory II* (pp. 63–100). Mahwah, NJ: Erlbaum.

Heath, R. L., & Bowen, S. A. (2002). Public relations' role in defining corporate social responsibility. *Journal of Mass Media Ethics, 4*, 21–38.

Hernez-Broome, G., & Hughes, R. L. (2004). Leadership development: Past, present, and future. *Human Resource Planning, 27*, 24–32.

House, R. J., Henges, P. J., Javidan, M., Dorfman, P. W., & Gupta, V. (Eds.). (2004). *Culture, Leadership and Organizations: The GLOBE Study of 62 Societies*. Thousand Oaks, CA:

House, R. J., Wright, N., & Aditya, R. N. (1997). Cross cultural research on organizational leadership: A critical analysis and a proposed theory. In P. C. Earley & M. Erez (Eds.), *New perspectives on international industrial and organizational psychology* (pp. 535–625). San Francisco, CA: Jossey-Bass.

Ibarra, H., Snook, S., & Guillén Ramo, L. (2010). Identity-based leader development. In N. Nohria & R. Khurana (Eds.), *Handbook of leadership theory and practice* (pp. 657–678). Boston, MA: Harvard Business Press.

Kegan, R., & Lahey, L. (2010). Adult development and organizational leadership. In N. Nohria & R. Khurana (Eds.), *Handbook of leadership theory and practice* (pp. 769–787). Boston, MA: Harvard Business Press.

Lincoln, Y., & Guba, E. (1985). *Naturalistic inquiry*. Thousand Oaks, CA: Sage.

Lord, R. G., & Brown, D. J. (2001). Leadership, values, and subordinate self-concepts. *Leadership Quarterly, 12*, 133–152.

Lord, R. G., & Maher, K. J. (1991). *Leadership and information processing: Linking perceptions and performance*. Boston, MA: Unwin Hyman.

McCall, M. W. Jr. (2010). The experience conundrum. In N. Nohria & R. Khurana (Eds.), *Handbook of leadership theory and practice* (pp. 679–708). Boston, MA: Harvard Business Press.

McCauley, C., Ruderman, M., Ohlott, P., & Morrow, J. (1994). Assessing the developmental components of managerial jobs. *Journal of Applied Psychology, 79*, 544–560.

Meng, J. (2010a). Excellent leadership in public relations: An application of multiple-group confirmatory factor analysis models in assessing cross-national measurement invariance. *Dissertation Abstracts International Section A, 70*(8-A), 3086.

Meng, J. (2010b, June). *The generalization and universality of public relations leadership: An application of multiple-group assessment in measurement invariance*. Paper presented at the 60th annual convention of the International Communication Association, Singapore.

Meng, J. (2012). Strategic leadership in public relations: An integrated conceptual framework. *Public Relations Review, 38*, 336–338.

Meng, J., Berger, B. K., Gower, K. K., & Heyman, W. C. (2012). A test of excellent leadership in public relations: Key qualities, valuable sources, and distinctive leadership perceptions. *Journal of Public Relations Research, 24*, 18–36.

Meng, J., & Berger, B. K. (2013). An integrated model of excellent leadership in public relations: Dimensions, measurement, and validation. *Journal of Public Relations Research, 25*, 141–167.

Meng, J., Berger, B. K., & Heyman W. (2011). Measuring public relations leadership in the trait approach: A second-order factor model in the dimension of self-dynamics.

Public Relations Journal, 5(1). Available online at www.prsa.org/Intelligence/PRJournal/Documents/2011WinterMengBergerHeyman.pdf

Mumford, M. D., Zaccaro, S. J., Connelly, M., & Marks, M. A. (2000). Leadership skills: Conclusions and future directions. *Leadership Quarterly*, *11*, 155–170.

Nohria, N., & Khurana, R. (2010). Advancing leadership theory and practice. In N. Nohria & R. Khurana (Eds.), *Handbook of leadership theory and practice* (pp. 3–25). Boston, MA: Harvard Business Press.

Riggio, R. Murphy, S., & Pirozzolo, F. (Eds.) (2001). *Multiple intelligences and leadership.* Mahwah, NJ: Erlbaum.

Rosebush, J. S. (2012, March 30). Why great leaders are in short supply [Blog entry]. Available online at http://blogs.hbr.org/cs/2012/03/why_great_leaders_are_in_short.html

Servaes, J. (2012). Soft power and public diplomacy: The new frontier for public relations and international communication between the US and China. *Public Relations Review*, *38*, 643–651.

Van Velsor, E., & McCauley, C. D. (2004). Our view of leadership development. In C. D. McCauley & E. Van Velsor (Eds.), *The Center for Creative Leadership handbook of leadership development* (2nd ed., pp. 1–22). San Francisco, CA: Jossey-Bass.

Van Velsor, E., McCauley, C. D., & Ruderman, M. N. (Eds.). (2010). *The Center for Creative Leadership handbook of leadership development* (3rd ed.). San Francisco, CA: Jossey-Bass.

Yukl, G. (1989). Managerial leadership: A review of theory and research. *Journal of Management*, *15*, 251–289.

Zerfass, A., Tench, R., Verhoeven, P., Vercic, D., & Moreno, A. (2010). *European Communication Monitor 2010: Status quo and challenges for public relations in Europe. Results of an empirical survey in 46 countries.* Brussels, Belgium: EACD/EUPRERA, Helios Media.

4

PROFILE OF SURVEY AND INTERVIEW PARTICIPANTS

Bruce K. Berger and Juan Meng

Survey Demographics

Nearly 4,500 (4,484) public relations and communication professionals in 23 countries completed the online global leadership survey. This chapter provides simple descriptive statistics for the global survey sample. Section II in the book provides a depth report on the survey findings.

Gender

More women (2,318 or 51.7%) than men (2,165 or 48.3%) completed the survey. However, the gender mix varied greatly among countries, ranging from more than 70% female participants in Brazil, Russia, and Latvia/Estonia to fewer than 50% female participants in Germany, the United Kingdom, and United States.

Years of Experience

Many participants were seasoned practitioners; nearly two thirds (64.6%) of those surveyed possessed more than 11 years of professional experience (see Table 4.1).

TABLE 4.1 Participants' Years of Experience

	Frequency (*n*)	Percentage
<11 years	1,585	35.3
11–20 years	1,772	39.5
>20 years	1,126	25.1

Type Organization

The sample included a reasonably balanced mix of organizational types, as shown in Table 4.2. Private and state-run companies are more common in Europe and South America. The nonprofit category also includes practitioners who work in educational institutions, government agencies, and political organizations.

Reporting Level

As shown in Table 4.3, nearly three quarters (74.1%) of participants served as the top-unit or functional leader, or they reported directly to the unit or functional leader.

Age

The percentages of participants in the designated age ranges were roughly equal, although a smaller number were older than 55. Communication professionals in South American and Asian countries tended to be younger than were practitioners in other countries and regions (see Table 4.4).

TABLE 4.2 Organization Types of Participants

	Frequency (n)	Percentage
Public company	887	19.8
Private/state-run company	1,048	23.4
Nonprofit organization	1,095	24.4
Communication agency	918	20.5
Self-employed, other	556	11.9

TABLE 4.3 Participants' Reporting Levels

	Frequency (n)	Percentage
Level 0 (top leader)	1,779	39.7
Level 1	1,541	34.4
Levels 2–5	1,161	25.9

TABLE 4.4 Participants' Ages

	Frequency (n)	Percentage
<36 years	1,207	26.9
36–45 years	1,435	32.0
46–55 years	1,261	28.1
>55 years	580	12.9

TABLE 4.5 Participants' Unit Sizes

	Frequency (n)	Percentage
Fewer than 5 professionals	1,697	37.8
5–15 professionals	1,606	35.8
16–25 professionals	385	8.6
More than 25 professionals	794	17.7

TABLE 4.6 Participants' Education Levels

	Frequency (n)	Percentage
High school degree or equivalent	184	4.1
Bachelor's degree	1,364	30.4
Master's degree	2,263	50.5
Doctoral degree	381	8.5
Other	290	6.5

Work Unit Size

Nearly three quarters (73.6%) of those surveyed worked in small or medium-sized units in their organizations (see Table 4.5). This may reflect the large number of participants who worked in nonprofits or who were self-employed.

Education

As shown in Table 4.6, participants were largely well educated; more than half (59%) possessed graduate degrees.

Major Area of Study

The areas of education specialization, or major fields of study, were wide ranging (see Table 4.7). Men majored significantly more often in business, natural sciences, and social sciences than did women. Women majored significantly more often in public relations (one in five females) and humanities. In Brazil, nearly 60 percent of female participants majored in public relations.

Participants by Countries and Regions

The number of survey participants varied greatly from one country to another, which makes national comparisons difficult. The number of respondents in Brazil, the German-speaking countries, and the United States were sufficient to generalize results to their survey populations, which, in Germany and the United States, there were more than 20,000 practitioners. The number of participants is modest

TABLE 4.7 Participants' Major Areas of Study

	Frequency (n)	Percentage
Humanities	739	16.5
PR, Corporate Communications	734	16.4
Journalism	542	12.1
Business	536	12.0
Communication/Media Studies	495	11.0
Social Sciences	419	9.1
Advertising, Marketing	253	5.6
Other	785	17.3

TABLE 4.8 Participants' Regions/Countries

	Frequency (n)
Austria	222
Brazil	303
Chile	156
Chinese-speaking countries	143
Estonia	30
Germany	1,405
India	140
Latvia	112
Mexico	213
Russia	215
South Korea	205
Spain	210
Switzerland	146
United Kingdom	139
United States	828
Others	20
Total participants	4,484

in Chile, the Chinese-speaking countries, India, and Latvia and Estonia, but seems quite acceptable when compared with the numbers of public relations survey participants from those countries in previous published scholarly studies. The small number of completed surveys in the Middle East was included in the overall results, but the region was not included in comparative assessments. In Table 4.8, China includes mainland China, Hong Kong, Singapore, and Taiwan.

The Interviews With Public Relations Leaders

Overall, 137 in-depth interviews were completed in 10 countries/regions, including the Chinese-speaking countries, India, South Korea, the German-speaking countries, Latvia, Russia, Spain, Brazil, Mexico, and the U.S. The number of interviews ranged from 8 (Latvia) to 22 (Chinese-speaking countries); 12 to 15 interviews were completed in most countries. All of the researchers used the Interview Guide (see Appendix B), which was translated into the relevant local language.

Participants were high-level communication executives, most with 20 years or more of experience. Men and women were equally represented in the interviews (68 women and 69 men), and they were leaders in three types of organizations: public or private companies (64), communication agencies (38), and nonprofit organizations (35), which included government agencies, universities, and political groups and organizations.

The vast majority of interviews were conducted via telephone, although a few were completed via Skype or in person. The shortest interview lasted 30 minutes; the longest, more than 2 hours. On average, each interview lasted about 52 minutes.

All interviews were recorded, transcribed, and then subjected to data analysis, which was grounded in the constant comparative method. More details about the sample and analysis, as well as the results for each country/region, are included in Section III of this book.

SECTION II

Results and Implications of the Global Leadership Survey

This section reports the results of the online survey, which involved 4,484 participants in 23 countries. Chapter 5 examines findings for the top 10 issues in the field, and Chapter 6 reviews the strategies and tactics leaders use to manage these issues. Chapter 7 explores the seven dimensions of our integrated model of excellent leadership in communication management; survey results suggest the model may be applicable in a number of countries. Chapter 8 presents findings regarding 12 approaches that may be used to improve the development of future leaders, and Chapter 9 reveals participants' perceptions about leadership and organizational culture, gender, and the overall profession.

5

THE CONTEXT FOR LEADERSHIP IN PUBLIC RELATIONS

Key Issues in the Field

Ansgar Zerfass, Anne Linke, and Ulrike Röttger

Communication management in the 21st century exists within a dynamic environment, which makes leadership in the field simultaneously more complicated and more important (Berger & Meng, 2010; Hackman & Johnson, 2009). To learn more about the current context of leadership in public relations (PR), it helps to know what practitioners consider the most important issues in the field. These perceptions shape discussions in the profession and mark areas where actions by leaders can make a difference.

For example, because the limits of a purely economic rationality became apparent in many developed countries, leaders are more preoccupied with the effects corporate action has on the environment and how this is perceived by key stakeholders. Accordingly, corporate social responsibility (CSR) has flourished and has led to new communicative challenges, extending the scope of action for public relations leaders. A deeper understanding of relevant issues enables leaders to consider future developments or alternative options, and consequently, it helps with strategic decisions (e.g., Northouse, 2013). In the example given, leaders can benchmark their organization's performance in CSR communications and make decisions on investing or disinvesting in this field.

When referring to issues that influence today's public relations practice, concepts such as the digital revolution , stakeholder emancipation, or globalization are often named. However, statements about trends are often based on poor data and are seldom analyzed in a scientific manner. The global study of leadership in public relations was therefore useful in capturing the perceptions and insights of nearly 4,500 practitioners in 23 countries in an online survey (see Chapter 3 for details). More than 70% of the professionals interviewed throughout the year 2012 held the top or second-most position in their organization's communication management function. Hence, their opinion is relevant for the communication function, they are well informed about it, and they decide on the organization's strategy regarding important issues. This chapter focuses on the data of the overarching project regarding the most important issues. The results are described and are discussed with reference to additional insights and future developments.

Assessment of Key Issues

Participants in the global leadership survey were asked to indicate the relative importance of 10 issues in the field, which had been identified through previous international studies (Zerfass, Verhoeven, Tench, Moreno, & Vercic, 2011) and professional reports (Table 5.1). A 7-point scale was used, ranging from 1 = *a little bit important* to 7 = *a great deal of importance*. For comparative purposes, ratings of 5.0 or higher indicate that the issue is important. The three highest rated issues in the survey are addressing the speed and volume of information flow (M = 5.88), dealing with crises (M = 5.76), and managing social media and the digital revolution (M = 5.75).

A detailed analysis of the data shows that women rate all 10 issues higher than do men, and 8 of them significantly higher. The greatest variance relates to the image of the public relations profession: Female respondents state quite

TABLE 5.1 Importance of Relevant Issues in the Field of Communication Management (N = 4,483)

Issues	Mean	Standard Deviation
Dealing with the speed and volume of information flow	5.88	1.24
Meeting increasing demands for corporate social responsibility	5.10	1.45
Managing the digital revolution and rise of social media	5.75	1.22
Improving the measurement of communication effectiveness to demonstrate value	5.49	1.36
Being prepared to deal effectively with crises that may arise	5.76	1.35
Dealing with growing demands for transparency of communications and operations	5.34	1.36
Meeting communication needs in diverse cultures and globalizing markets	4.83	1.70
Improving the image of the public relations/ communication management profession	4.47	1.81
Finding, developing, and retaining highly talented communication professionals	5.25	1.59
Improving employee engagement and commitment in the workplace	5.49	1.44

clearly that improvements are important ($M = 4.70$, $n = 2,218$), whereas men agree less strongly ($M = 4.21$, $n = 2,146$, $p < .1$). Female leaders might be more critical because the public perception of the field has been shaped by "old boys" such as Edward Bernays in the United States or Albert Oeckl in Germany and their networks, or because the predominant female workforce is still underrepresented among industry leaders in public relations in most countries.

Corresponding with other parts of the survey, Brazilian professionals generally tend to give stronger approvals to statements than their peers in Germany and the United Kingdom. This is a general effect, which has to be taken into account when interpreting single data. It can be argued that the public relations field is less developed in Brazil and that leaders see more need to advance. However, the differences might also simply be based on various cultures of showing support or criticism—Europeans are known to be more reluctant to give maximum ratings, which can be observed in schools and universities as well in professional assessments.

More interestingly, leaders at the highest hierarchical level rank all issues linked to the digital world (information flow, managing social media, demands for transparency) significantly higher than those at other levels. However, cross-cultural approaches and globalization are evaluated lower on the first level ($M = 4.69$, $n = 1,778$) and second level of leadership ($M = 4.71$, $n = 1,541$) compared to professionals working on all lower levels ($M = 5.23$, $n = 1,161$, $p < .01$). Top leaders might be more experienced in tackling these challenges in their daily work, which makes the issue less important to them compared with other professionals.

When comparing the feedback from various regions, it becomes apparent that the digital media issue is ranked highest in Brazil, China, India, and Mexico and lowest in East European countries. This is no surprise, because most former communist countries in Europe still have a strong infrastructure of traditional mass media, whereas the dynamic influence of the Internet is very visible in emerging countries with a much younger population. CSR is very challenging for public relations professionals in Latin America, whereas their peers in the United States and the United Kingdom rate this issue of lower importance.

Both these countries and South Korea rate employee engagement the lowest. This issue is most important in the BRIC countries (Brazil, Russia, India, China), as well as in Mexico. Many fast-growing regions struggle to find and motivate a skilled and loyal workforce. This challenge might be less relevant in an environment with free-labor markets and an oversupply of labor. European countries hold a middle position with established systems of long-term employer–employee relationships shaped by strong commitments to corporate culture, vocational education, and career development on all hierarchical levels. Obviously, more research is needed to explore these and other variations in detail. Quantitative surveys are limited in this respect, especially because the basic understandings of some concepts might differ from country to country.

TABLE 5.2 The Most Important Issues Selected by Public Relations Leaders Globally

Issues	Frequency (n)	Percentage
1. Dealing with the speed and volume of information flow	1,029	23.0
2. Managing the digital revolution and rise of social media	684	15.3
3. Improving the measurement of communication effectiveness to demonstrate value	547	12.2
4. Being prepared to deal effectively with crises that may arise	532	11.9
5. Dealing with growing demands for transparency of communications and operations	375	8.4
6. Improving employee engagement and commitment in the workplace	354	7.9
7. Finding, developing and retaining highly talented communication professionals	337	7.5
8. Meeting communication needs in diverse cultures and globalizing markets	274	6.1
9. Meeting increasing demands for corporate social responsibility	239	5.3
10. Improving the image of the public relations/ communication management profession	112	2.5

When forced to pick the most important issue for their organizations, almost one quarter of the respondents in the global study selected the challenge of dealing with the growing speed and volume of information (Table 5.2). This is most relevant as information flow cross-fertilizes every other issue listed here. For example, managing social media is so challenging because there are myriads of online channels and potential partners for dialogue, analyzing communication content is difficult if opinion building is based on real-time information, and developing a long-term approach to social responsibility might be impaired by the continuous flow of new demands articulated by stakeholders on a global scale.

Based on those empirical insights, the following sections delve deeper into the most important issues by discussing relevant developments and future challenges for those who are responsible for strategic communication in today's organizations. We focus on the top issues of social media, measurement, crisis communication, employee engagement, and corporate social responsibility (CSR).

Building Organizational Infrastructures for Social Media Communication

Three of the five top-rated issues are linked to the growing relevance of digital media and online communications. Communication leaders are confronted with more and more information, increasing both in speed and in volume. At the same time, stakeholders demand more transparency in communications, as well as in core business processes. Ultimately, the question is not only what happens online and why it happens, but also how corporations can manage social media communications. Kaplan and Haenlein (2010) define social media as "a group of Internet-based applications that build on the ideological and technological foundations of Web 2.0, and that allow the creation and exchange of User Generated Content" (p. 61). Social media can no longer be categorized as "new media," as those platforms have been around since the beginning of the 21st century (Macnamara, 2010, p. 5). Nonetheless, their integration into existing organizational structures and communication processes remains a challenge.

Communication leaders have to find a way of dealing with this, subject to the organization's internal and external environment, because the social media situation for a consumer goods company cannot be compared to that of a public administration entity. Nonetheless, the experiences of peers and case studies might offer valuable insights. By way of illustration, the so-called Dell Hell crisis of the computer manufacturer Dell spurred many organizations to take influential bloggers more seriously. From a more positive aspect, organizations can learn from Starbucks and from other companies that engage stakeholders online, who profit from their feedback and crowd intelligence.

The literature review on this topic reveals a step-by-step process of adopting social media for strategic communication. In the early days of social media, many organizations merely experimented with interactive technologies, mainly because they didn't want to miss out while their competitors reaped the benefits. Early research (Kaplan & Haenlein, 2010; Li & Bernoff, 2008) criticized this approach, suggesting the focus should be on strategies and overarching organizational structures instead. However, the potentials of social media communication are still not fully exploited and lag behind expectations. This is partly caused by poor development of prerequisites such as governance structures, especially rules and resources guiding the application of interactive media in organizational settings. Research has shown that this diagnosis can be applied to public relations in Asia, Australia, and New Zealand, as well as in Europe (Macnamara & Zerfass, 2012).

Besides these organizational aspects, leaders have to deal with personnel challenges, predominantly the development of social media skills (e.g. Breakenridge, 2008; Linke & Zerfass, 2013; Tench et al., 2013). Despite ongoing debates in the profession, a 2013 survey of communication managers in 43 countries revealed that European public relations professionals rate their competencies as mostly average or even worse (Table 5.3). However, these skills form the basis for long-term success in social media, because communication instruments need to be designed appropriately and evaluated with new performance indicators (e.g., measures of online engagement). Compared to a similar survey 2 years earlier, skills have increased the most in hands-on areas such as delivering messages via the social web and setting up social media platforms, whereas more advanced

TABLE 5.3 Self-Assessment of Social Media Skills by Public Relations Professionals Across Europe ($N = 2,710$)

Social Media Skills	Percentage With High Capability Ratings (4–5)	Mean	Standard Deviation
Delivering messages via the social web	53.5	3.46	1.14
Knowing about social media trends	50.9	3.45	1.07
Developing social media strategies	44.0	3.25	1.15
Evaluating social media activities	39.1	3.12	1.14
Knowing how to avoid risks and handle crises on the social Web	38.9	3.09	1.17
Setting up social media platforms	36.4	2.99	1.22
Managing online communities	35.4	3.00	1.17
Knowing the legal framework for social media	31.5	2.86	1.21
Initiating web-based dialogues with stakeholders	29.2	2.82	1.16

Note: Items were measured on a 5-point Likert scale (1 = *very low*, 5 = *very high*).

and strategic skills, such as initiating web-based dialogues, are still underdeveloped (Zerfass, Moreno, Tench, Verèiè & Verhoeven, 2013, p. 41).

Looking to the future, a Delphi study on the use of social media in corporate communications (Linke & Zerfass, 2012) suggests that dedicated budgets, social media guidelines, and other structural aspects will improve in the near future. But social media evaluation and cooperation across the boundaries of departments and organizational functions are likely to stay underdeveloped. Organizational arrangements that merge decentralized and centralized responsibilities combine the advantages of both flexibility and strategic orientation; they are best suited for the practical challenges of leading dynamic social media initiatives. Prospectively, more organizations will establish these models of cooperation (Linke & Zerfass, 2012), and communication leaders must pave the way for long-term processes of organizational change that are linked to those developments.

Aligning Strategic Objectives and Establishing Measurement Routines

Improving the measurement of effective communication and demonstrating its value has been identified as the third most important issue for public relations leaders in the global study. This is no surprise, because the topic is known as one of the weakest points in communication management in general. The possibility of measuring the effects of communication for organizations is critically discussed in the literature, particularly regarding complex environments (Likely & Watson, 2013; Röttger & Preusse, 2009; Van Ruler, Tkalac Verèiè, & Verèiè, 2008).

Research in this field is confronted with two defining problems. First, the organizational function responsible for measuring processes and effects has several names: "evaluation," "accounting," "management accounting," "financial accounting," or "controlling." Second, the underlying connotations of these terms are often too narrowly associated with examination or supervision (Garrison, Noreen, & Brewer, 2011). Noble (1999) characterizes an appropriate measurement or evaluation strategy for public relations with seven principles:

1. Evaluation is research, meaning rigorous and logic.
2. Evaluation looks proactively forward and reviewingly backward.
3. Evaluation is user and situation dependent.
4. Evaluation is short term.
5. Evaluation is long term.
6. Evaluation is comparative.
7. Evaluation is multifaceted. (pp. 19–20)

The literature describes many measures and tools to fulfill these demands. To plan effective public relations, Michaelson, Wright, and Stacks (2012) suggest a generic model that includes a degree of standardization against which to compare. On the other hand, Watson and Zerfass (2011) gave an overview on the diverse views regarding return on investment (ROI) in public relations literature, and the concepts used by agencies and measurement service providers. The authors argued against simple ROI concepts and concluded that "PR practitioners have alternatives that can bring them 'inside the tent' with organisational management by adopting a more planned approach" (Watson & Zerfass, 2011, p. 11).

A comprehensive concept for aligning communication goals and organizational objectives, as well as measuring communication processes in detail, has been created by the German Public Relations Association (DPRG) and the International Controller Association (ICV). The interdisciplinary framework has been adopted by many blue-chip corporations and service providers in the region. The concept (Figure 5.1) standardizes the dimensions of communication effects, and classifies the most important levels of steering and evaluation. It is supplemented by generic value links and key performance indicators for the main areas of corporate communications (Zerfass, 2010).

The framework should not be misunderstood as a mathematical model to calculate communication effects; rather, it can be used by public relations leaders to discuss shared perceptions of communication processes with top management, team members, and supporting agencies. It helps to make sense of this complex issue, and focuses on evaluation criteria that are useful for managing strategic communication.

Watson and Noble (2007) found a vast gap between the scholarly description of evaluation and what is put into action by practitioners: "Although some researchers claim that practitioners are becoming more sophisticated, the evidence

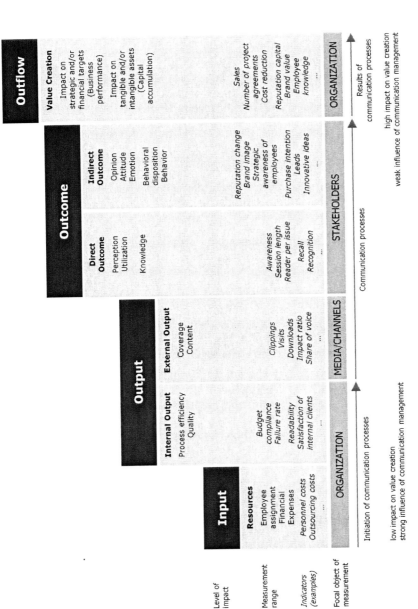

FIGURE 5.1 The DPRG/ICV Framework for Communication Controlling

Source: Zerfass (2010, p. 958).

Note: DPRG = German Public Relations Association; ICV = International Controller Association.

is that there are barriers to widespread acceptance of systematic evaluation" (p. 28). For example, communication professionals in Europe demonstrate a narrow view on evaluation, mainly relying on monitoring press clippings and media response (82.3%), Internet or Intranet usage (69.7%), and the satisfaction of (internal) clients (57.2%; Zerfass, Tench, Verhoeven, Verčič, & Moreno, 2010, p. 98). All those measures are linked to the output level of communication in the framework mentioned earlier (Figure 5.1). Consequently, the researchers state, "a predominance of external output evaluation is obvious, followed by exploring the direct outcome on stakeholders' perception or knowledge. Measures that catch the far ends of the overall process . . . are utilized at a significantly lower rate" (Zerfass et al., 2010, p. 97).

These insights were supported by findings in the global leadership study for other regions of the world. Monitoring and analyzing media coverage of the organization and its competitors are the most common approaches to measuring communication effectiveness and demonstrating value ($M = 5.48, n = 547$), whereas evaluating business outcomes at the performance level ($M = 4.82, n = 547$) and nonfinancial performance indicators ($M = 4.64, n = 547$) are less popular. Public relations leaders should try to overcome these limitations. They have the potential to affect their organizations by establishing a broader approach to measurement, which will thus provide a fuller picture of the communications needed for reaching strategic goals.

Mastering Different Phases of Crisis Communication

Being prepared to deal with crises is named as the second most important issue by professionals in the global study on public relations leadership. Coombs (2012) defines a crisis as "the perception of an unpredictable event that threatens important expectancies of stakeholders and can seriously impact an organization's performance and generate negative outcomes" (p. 2). As part of strategic crisis management, crisis communication is considered one factor "to combat crises and to lessen the actual damage inflicted" (Coombs, 2012, p. 5).

Coombs (2012) also divides crisis processes into the general cyclic phases of prevention, preparation, response, and revision, which require different communication needs. Leadership plays an important role in all crisis phases, and public relations leaders must implement communicative prevention measures across the whole organization. During the acute response phase, public relations leaders help top management to steer through difficult situations (mostly with high costs and risks), and their messages are perceived by the media and key stakeholders. Often, communication leaders function as the face of the crisis and have to ensure knowledge transformation throughout the revision stage (Hackman & Johnson, 2009, p. 406).

In general, it is important to know how response strategies are aligned to the specific needs of different crisis types (Sellnow & Seeger, 2013). This requires knowledge about the types of crises that are most likely to occur, and this obviously depends on corporate strategies, industry characteristics, stakeholder power, and cultural aspects. Yet, empirical data are rare. In Europe, public relations professionals mostly report on facing institutional crises such as adverse campaigns by critics (21.1%), performance crises (18.7%), and management or leadership crises (17.5%; Zerfass et al., 2013, p. 75). Despite the different situations, the majority use information strategies to deal with crises (82.7%), meaning that they provide stakeholders with facts and figures. Expressing sympathy for those affected was less common; only 26.8% employ such a strategy (Zerfass et al., 2013, p. 77).

Ulmer (2012, p. 523) found evidence that the majority of organizations struggle to communicate effectively during crises. Because of this, he sees the need to turn from a positive scientific perspective to a more normative one:

> I believe that to make a larger impact on society we need to move toward developing and testing interdisciplinary normative theories on crisis communication. [. . .] I believe that our normative theories in crisis communication must emphasize open, honest, and collaborative communication processes and outcomes. To be anything but forthcoming about the information that the organization has about the crisis cannot be advised. (Ulmer 2012, pp. 537–538)

Yang, Kang, and Johnson (2010) studied individual interpretations of crisis communication messages in an experiment. They found that

> The openness to dialogic communication is essential to creating and enhancing audience engagement in crisis communication, which, in turn, leads to positive postcrisis perceptions. Among several dimensions of audience engagement, reduction of negative emotions was a critical mediator that connected the impact of openness to dialogic communication with positive postcrisis perceptions. (Yang et al., 2010, p. 473)

Altogether, an understanding that crises are varied processes with specific subprocesses can help public relations leaders address them more appropriately.

Improving Employee Engagement Through Internal Communication

Interacting effectively with potential and actual employees represents another important pillar in the global leadership study. The topic relates to three of the top 10 issues in the global leadership survey: improving employee engagement and commitment; finding, developing, and retaining top talent; and meeting communication needs in diverse cultures in global organizations (e.g., Owyang, 2011; Scholes, 1997). Internal communication can be defined as the "strategic management of interactions and relationships between stakeholders at all levels within organizations across a number of interrelated dimensions" (Welch & Jackson, 2007, p. 183). Recognition of internal communication's importance began to increase in the 1990s in the United States, and spread to Europe around the beginning of the new millennium (Tkalac Verèiè, Verèiè, & Sriramesh, 2012, p. 223).

Many authors emphasize how internal communication supports value creation (Tench & Yeomans, 2006, p. 337; Welch & Jackson, 2007, p. 178). It is seen as helping to strengthen employees' commitment to, and their identification with, the organization, which forms the basis of cooperation. Also, innovation potential can be addressed, which might lead to competitive advantages. However, "internal and external workplace diversity and the technology-induced time constraints of multinational competition make the challenge of improving organizational communication bigger than ever" (Barker & Gower, 2010, p. 395). Welch (2012) sums up the underlying crux as follows:

> Internal communication underpins organisational effectiveness since it contributes to positive internal relationships by enabling communication between senior managers and employees. Paradoxically, internal communication can also pose a threat to organizational relationships, as poor communication can be counter-productive. (p. 246)

Despite the obvious relevance, the field is still understudied by communication scholars, which makes it hard for leaders to find criteria to form comparisons or from which to learn. In general, this is hindered by the many different conditions required for internal communication in varying organizations, which makes it nearly impossible to identify generic success factors. Google, for example, makes a special effort to allow its employees free time for creativity or collaboration. Top managers talk to employees relatively colloquially, encouraging direct feedback via multiple channels. This fits the company's organizational culture and services. Along this line, the global leadership study shows that creating a positive communication climate ($M = 5.78, n = 394$) and increasing the visibility and accessibility of senior leaders ($M = 5.78, n = 394$) are the main strategies used to increase commitment.

Empirically, Welch (2012, p. 253) discovered a hierarchy of preferences for different communication channels among employees: It starts with digital formats, and is then followed by blended approaches (digital and print) and print formats. This knowledge might help to improve cooperation or create innovations, but employees do not share uniform preferences, and consequently must be targeted as a "multi-dimensional set of diverse internal stakeholders rather than a single entity" (Welch, 2012, p. 253).

Many theories and practical guidelines simply differ between "the organization"—represented by top management—and employees at large. The various leaders in all areas of an organization are one group that has long been neglected and deserves specific attention. Communication that is aimed at those leaders needs to accept their position as stakeholders—as employees who will not merely identify themselves by the goals set by top management but who will also act as multipliers towards employees in their respective domain (Voss & Röttger, 2014).

From a more general perspective, Ruck and Welch (2012, p. 294) compared different studies on this topic, and find more management-centric than employee-centric approaches. They concluded that employee satisfaction with internal communication ranges from roughly 50% to 60%: "Internal communication assessment is currently focused on channels used, or volume of information generated (the what); essentially process explanations rather than the content of the communication itself, how well it is provided, or understanding" (Ruck & Welch, 2012, p. 301). Those measures reveal very little about the effects on identification, collaboration, and value creation as the ultimate goals of internal communication.

Further research is needed to develop new approaches to internal communication in the digital age, and public relations leaders should dedicate more time to the topic. Much knowledge about employee communication has been created by disciplines such as human resource management and organizational psychology. Using these insights is as important as establishing a productive working relationship between communications and personnel functions in corporations. Berger (2011) has argued that research has long told us what organizations need to do to create effective internal communication programs around various topics. So neither the challenge nor the solutions are new—public relations leaders need to take the initiative and do what needs to be done.

Making Sense of Corporate Social Responsibility Communication

An often-cited definition of the World Business Council for Sustainable Development (WBCSD) describes corporate social responsibility as "the commitment of business to contribute to sustainable economic development, working with employees, their families, the local community and society at large to improve their quality of life" (WBCSD, 2000, p. 10). With so many complex elements, CSR has to be conceptualized as a dynamic concept, especially as it provokes many moral discussions about how organizations have to deal with the ecological and social consequences of their actions:

> It is unthinkable that a corporation today will declare publicly that its only goal is to make money for its shareholders. Instead, corporations typically claim to balance the need of society and the environment against the need to make a profit. (Ihlen, Bartlett & May, 2011, p. 3)

Communication leaders have to develop strategic plans for communicating their organization's specific needs and contributions to their stakeholders, and to mediate between different interest groups.

Corporations face the challenge of managing communication processes holistically and of rooting their CSR positioning in corporate strategy. However, gaps can often be found between organizations' claims and actions, because CSR activities can range from actual engagements linked to the core processes of value creation to mere impression management (e.g., Crane, Matten, McWilliams, Moon, & Siegel, 2008). Official CSR statements often represent ideals that organizations find hard to fulfill (Frankental, 2001; Ramus & Montiel, 2005). For example, British Petroleum (BP) started to position itself as an environmentally friendly corporation when it claimed to go "Beyond Petroleum" in 1997. However, the main activities of BP are still in the petroleum business, and the company had been punished many times for pollution incidents, the oil spill in the Gulf of Mexico in 2010 being one of the most well-known cases.

Such discrepancies alert the media and influential stakeholders. Organizations have to live up to their promises, and public relations leaders have to balance between communicating high standards they cannot fulfill, which might cause discrepancies and loss of credibility, and not engaging in the public debate at all. However, Christensen, Morsing, and Thyssen (2013) argued that a lack of consistency between CSR talk and action does not have to be "a serious problem that needs to be eliminated" (p. 372). Instead, the differences can inspire further discussions, dialogue, and research. Again, this might improve future practice, particularly if leaders do not back away from critical discussions or taking risks every now and then. Advanced leaders will not limit their focus to superficial image building, but also include the early identification of risks and opportunities.

Empirical data on this topic reveals an ambiguous status quo. More and more companies are managing sustainability to improve processes and enhance business, rather than focusing on reputation alone (Bonini & Görner, 2011). Despite the continuing debates surrounding communication research, a longitudinal study among public relations professionals in Europe shows that the importance of dealing with CSR has been subsiding since 2011 (Zerfass et al., 2013). The authors of that study propose two explanations: "Professionals might have found proper strategies and ways how to communicate in this field, so it is less challenging now, or CSR has been overvalued in the past and a more realistic view is prevailing now" (Zerfass et al., 2013, p. 83). Communication leaders should be aware of alternative routes when dealing with responsibility issues in the future and should refrain from jumping on a bandwagon that loses touch with organizational goals and strategies.

Conclusion

Those in leadership positions in communication management must cope with a variety of different issues. On the whole, this topic is only rarely addressed by academic research. However, the global study of leadership in public relations closes this gap. The data identify the most important issues that shape the thinking and actions of those who are in charge of future developments. The global study also examines the strategies and approaches leaders adopt to manage these top issues, and how and to what extent particular issues affect different dimensions of leadership. These areas are covered in the next two chapters.

The issues mentioned here define important fields that public relations leaders should explore in more detail. In order to make the most of the chances and to minimize the risks associated with social media communication, leaders need to decide on integrating social media into existing organizational structures and strategies. Competent dialogical communication focused on listening and moderating, rather than speaking out, needs to be established within communication teams. Another ongoing challenge for public relations leaders is the field of goal alignment and measurement. Judging evaluation to be important is only the first step; finding the right way to do so in a specific organization needs to follow it. Leaders have to choose between different measures at their disposal. Instead of merely using them as rituals, a strong system of measuring that enables managing should be established.

In addition, CSR communication deserves a closer look. Many studies report on the rising importance of CSR and CSR communication while acknowledging the gap between strategic relevance and theoretical demands, on one hand, and corporate practices, on the other. Other data show a decline in perceived importance in some regions, possibly because leaders know by now how to deal with the issue. Internal communication is considered highly relevant by leaders, but public relations research in this field is still rather weak and insights from other disciplines are seldom used. Leaders should cross these borders. Crisis communication can be defined by a set of typical phases. During these phases, the need for communication and leadership varies. Leaders have to keep the general process and respective tasks in mind, starting long before the acute outbreak of a crisis and continuing thereafter.

The issues spotlighted here help us to understand what communication leaders have to deal with. Excellent leaders in the future will understand these issues and act accordingly. To encourage that development, more research into leadership communication and the development of public relations leaders needs to be done.

References

Barker, R. T., & Gower, K. (2010). Strategic application of storytelling in organizations: Toward effective communication in a diverse world. *Journal of Business Communication*, 47(3), 295–312.

Berger, K. (2011, October). *Employee communication: Let's move from knowing to doing.* The 2011 Grunig Lecture hosted by the Institute of Public Relations, delivered at PRSA International Conference, Orlando, FL. Available online at www.instituteforpr.org/wp-content/uploads/Grunig-Lecture-2011-Berger5.pdf

Berger, B. K., & Meng, J. (2010). Public relations practitioners and the leadership challenge. In R. L. Heath (Ed.), *The SAGE handbook of public relations* (pp. 421–434). Thousand Oaks, CA: Sage.

Bonini, S., & Görner, S. (2011). *The business of sustainability: Putting it into practice* (Sustainability & Resource Productive Practice). New York: McKinsey & Company. Available online at www.mckinsey.com/~/media/mckinsey/dotcom/client_service/sustainability/pdfs/putting_it_into_practice.ashx

Breakenridge, D. (2008). *PR 2.0: New media, new tools, new audiences.* Upper Saddle River, NJ: FT Press.

Christensen, L. T., Morsing, M., & Thyssen, O. (2013). CSR as aspirational talk. *Organization, 20*(3), 372–393.

Coombs, W. T. (2012). *Ongoing crisis communication: Planning, managing, and responding* (3rd ed.). Los Angeles, CA: Sage.

Crane, A., Matten, D., McWilliams, A., Moon, J., & Siegel, D. (Eds.). (2008). *The Oxford handbook of corporate social responsibility.* Oxford, England: Oxford University Press.

Frankental, P. (2001). Corporate social responsibility—a PR invention? *Corporate Communications: An International Journal, 6*(1), 18–23.

Garrison, R., Noreen, E., & Brewer, P. (2011). *Managerial accounting* (14th ed.). New York, NY: McGraw-Hill.

Hackman, M. Z., & Johnson, C. E. (2009). *Leadership: A communication perspective* (5th ed.). Long Grove, IL: Waveland Press.

Ihlen, Ø., Bartlett, J., & May, S. (Eds.). (2011). *The handbook of communication and corporate social responsibility.* Hoboken, NJ: Wiley.

Kaplan, A. M., & Haenlein, M. (2010). Users of the world, unite! The challenges and opportunities of social media. *Business Horizons, 53*(1), 59–68.

Li, C., & Bernoff, J. (2008). *Groundswell: Winning in a world transformed by social technologies.* Boston, MA: Harvard Business School Press.

Likely, F., & Watson, T. (2013). Measuring the edifice: Public relations measurement and evaluation practices over the course of 40 years. In K. Sriramesh, A. Zerfass, & J.-N. Kim (Eds.), *Public relations and communication management: Current trends and emerging topics* (pp. 143–162). New York, NY: Routledge.

Linke, A., & Zerfass, A. (2012). Future trends of social media use in strategic communication: Results of a Delphi study. *Public Communication Review, 2*(2), 17–29.

Linke, A., & Zerfass, A. (2013). Social media governance: Regulatory frameworks for successful online communications. *Journal of Communication Management, 17*(3), 270–286.

Macnamara, J. (2010). "Emergent" media and public communication: Understanding the changing mediascape. *Public Communication Review, 1*(2), 3–17.

Macnamara, J., & Zerfass, A. (2012). Social media communication in organizations: The challenges of balancing openness, strategy and management. *International Journal of Strategic Communication, 6*(4), 287–308.

Michaelson, D., Wright, D. K., & Stacks, D. W. (2012). Evaluating efficacy in public relations/corporate communication programming: Towards establishing standards of campaign performance. *Public Relations Journal, 6*(5), 1–24.

Noble, P. (1999). Towards an inclusive evaluation methodology. *Corporate Communications: An International Journal, 4*(1), 14–23.

Northouse, P. G. (2013). *Leadership: Theory and practice* (6th ed.). Thousand Oaks, CA: Sage.

Owyang, J. K. (2011). *Social business readiness: How advanced companies prepare internally.* San Mateo, CA: Altimeter Group. Available online at www.altimetergroup.com/research/reports/social-business-readiness.

Ramus, C. A., & Montiel, I. (2005). When are corporate environmental policies a form of greenwashing? *Business & Society, 44*(4), 377–414.

Röttger, U., & Preusse, J. (2009). Communication controlling revisited: Annotations to a consolidation of the research agenda on planning and controlling communication management. In A. Rogojinaru & S. Wolstenholme (Eds.), *Current trends in international public relations* (pp. 165–184). Bucharest, Hungary: Tritonic.

Ruck, K., & Welch, M. (2012). Valuing internal communication: Management and employee perspectives. *Public Relations Review, 38*(2), 294–302.

Scholes, E. (Ed.). (1997). *Gower handbook of internal communication.* Brookfield, VT: Gower.

Sellnow, T. L., & Seeger, M. W. (2013). *Theorizing crisis communication: Foundations in communication theory.* Chichester, England: John Wiley & Sons.

Tench, R., & Yeomans, L. (2009). *Exploring public relations* (2nd ed.). Harlow, England: Pearson Education.

Tench, R., Zerfass, A., Verhoeven, P., Verèiè, D., Moreno, A., & Okay, A. (2013). *Competencies and role requirements of communication professionals in Europe: Insights from quantitative and qualitative studies* (ECOPSI Research Project Report). Leeds, England: Leeds Metropolitan University.

Tkalac Verèiè, A., Verèiè, D., & Sriramesh, K. (2012). Internal communication: Definition, parameters, and the future. *Public Relations Review, 38*(2), 223–230.

Ulmer, R. R. (2012). Increasing the impact of thought leadership in crisis communication management. *Communication Quarterly, 26*(4), 523–542.

Van Ruler, B., Tkalac Verèiè, A., & Verèiè, D. (Eds.). (2008). *Public relations metrics: Research and evaluation.* New York, NY: Routledge.

Voss, A., & Röttger, U. (2014). Führungskräftekommunikation: Herausforderung und Umsetzung [Communication addressing leaders: Challenges and implementation]. In A. Zerfass & M. Piwinger (Eds.), *Handbuch Unternehmenskommunikation* (2nd ed., pp. 1129–1147). Wiesbaden, Germany: Springer Gabler.

Watson, T., & Noble, P. (2007). *Evaluating public relations: A best practice guide to public relations planning, research and evaluation* (2nd ed.). London, England: Kogan Page.

Watson, T., & Zerfass, A. (2011). Return on investment in public relations: A critique of concepts used by practitioners from the perspectives of communication and management sciences perspectives. *PRism, 8*(1), 1–14.

Welch, M. (2012). Appropriateness and acceptability: Employee perspectives of internal communication. *Public Relations Review, 38*(2), 246–254.

Welch, M., & Jackson, P. R. (2007). Rethinking internal communication: A stakeholder approach. *Corporate Communications: An International Journal, 12*(2), 177–198.

World Business Council for Sustainable Development. (2000). *Corporate social responsibility: Making good business sense.* Geneva, Switzerland: Author. Available online at http://research.dnv.com/csr/PW_Tools/PWD/1/00/L/1–00-L-2001–01-/lib2001/WBCSD_Making_Good_Business_Sense.pdf

Yang, S., Kang, M., & Johnson, P. (2010). Effects of narratives, openness to dialogic communication, and credibility on engagement in crisis communication through organizational blogs. *Communication Research, 37*(4), 473–497.

Zerfass, A. (2010). Assuring rationality and transparency in corporate communications: Theoretical foundations and empirical findings on communication controlling and communication performance management. In M. D. Dodd & K. Yamamura (Eds.), *Ethical issues for public relations practice in a multicultural world – 13th international public relations research conference* (pp. 947–966), Gainesville, FL: IPR.

Zerfass, A., Moreno, A., Tench, R., Vercic, D., & Verhoeven, P. (2013). *European communication monitor 2013: A changing landscape – managing crises, digital communication and CEO positioning in Europe. Results of a survey in 43 countries.* Brussels, Belgium: EACD/EUPRERA, Helios Media.

Zerfass, A., Tench, R., Verhoeven, P., Verčič, D., & Moreno, A. (2010). *European communication monitor 2010: Status quo and challenges for public relations in Europe. Results of an empirical survey in 46 countries.* Brussels, Belgium: EACD/EUPRERA, Helios Media.

Zerfass, A., Verhoeven, P., Tench, R., Moreno, A., & Verèiè, D. (2011). *European communication monitor 2011: Empirical insights into strategic communication in Europe. Results of a survey in 43 countries.* Brussels, Belgium: EACD/EUPRERA, Helios Media.

6

STRATEGIES AND TACTICS LEADERS USE TO MANAGE ISSUES

Bryan H. Reber

As noted in the preceding chapter, the international survey of about 4,500 public communication professionals in 23 countries identified 10 issues of key importance to public relations leaders. Of course, the rankings of issues varied by country or region, but overall, the 10 issues ranked in importance as follows:

1. Dealing with the speed and volume of information flow
2. Managing the digital revolution and the rise of social media
3. Improving the measurement of communication effectiveness
4. Being prepared to effectively deal with crises that may arise
5. Dealing with growing demands for transparency
6. Improving employee engagement and commitment
7. Finding, developing, and retaining top talent
8. Meeting demands for corporate social responsibility
9. Meeting communication needs in diverse cultures
10. Improving the image of the profession

The next step in the global survey was to identify what leaders believed were the most effective strategies and/or tactics in dealing with the issues they identified as most important. This chapter is devoted to discussing the importance of strategies, goals, objectives, and tactics; insights from the survey about effective issue management; and implications of the findings for professional practice and ongoing scholarship.

Why Strategies and Tactics Are Important

Understanding strategies, goals, objectives, and tactics is essential to grasping the role and actual practice of leaders in today's organization. Strategies and goals are broad, whereas objectives are specific and measurable. Tactics are the means of implementing strategies, goals, and objectives. Public relations leaders must embrace both strategic and tactical thinking (Wilcox & Reber, 2013).

Definitions

Strategy as an organizational concept is relatively nascent. Its roots are found in military nomenclature (Moss, 2005). *Strategy* is a planned course of action to deal with a specific circumstance or a set of circumstances (Mintzberg, 1991). As a concept in public relations specifically, it may be even younger. There is a dearth of literature on the role of strategy in public relations (Moss, 2005). This may be because public relations is often absent from decision making in organizations (White & Dozier, 1992), or because public relations leaders lack experience in dealing with organizational issues that require strategic thinking (Moss, 2005).

Differentiating goals from objectives in public relations is essential (Stacks, 2002). "[A] *goal* is long-term and gives direction," according to Stacks (2002, p. 26). A goal represents a general, desired outcome from a public relations campaign or program. An *objective*, on the other hand, is as specific as possible. Objectives should address a specific audience or public and be measurable (Wilcox, Cameron, Reber, & Shin, 2013). Objectives identify projected outcomes (Stacks, 2002).

Tactics are the means of operationalizing objectives. *Tactics* are what one does to reach objectives. Tactics, and they are numerous, may be press releases or tweets, special events or meetings with stakeholders, blogging or pitching stories to bloggers, and so forth.

Public relations is moving beyond tactical management and increasingly developing as a strategic management profession. According to Smith (2013), "Today's environment—and more importantly, tomorrow's—calls for greater skill on the management side of communication" (p. 2). Strategic public relations leaders need to understand research, strategic planning, effects of tactic choice, the broadening toolbox of tactics, and program evaluation (Smith, 2013). It is, therefore, increasingly important for scholars and practitioners to ask questions related to developing effective leadership skills and effective leaders.

The Role of Public Relations in Organizations

In his seminal work, James Grunig (1992) and his colleagues examined in depth the contributions of public relations to effective organizations. Grunig noted that "excellent organizations have leaders who rely on networking and 'management-by-walking-around' rather than authoritarian systems" (p. 233). He claimed that the "dominant coalition" of leadership within an organization plays a crucial role in developing an organizational climate that embraces public relations outreach. William Ehling (1992) made the argument that public relations contributes directly to the bottom line of organizations.

Larissa Grunig, James Grunig, and David Dozier (2002) wrote that public relations brings value to the organization when it "reconciles the organization's goals with the expectations of its strategic constituencies" (p. 97). They point out that such contributions have direct, financial value to the organization. These contributions develop from public relations leadership within the organization strategically developing, nurturing, and maintaining stakeholder relationships. Leading organizations to build and maintain strong, positive relationships contributes to the organization financially through increased market share, premium product pricing, avoiding overregulation, satisfied and productive employees, positive media coverage and more (L. Grunig et al., 2002, p. 101). The ability to bring such value to organizations is most likely when the public relations manager is a member of (or at a minimum has direct access to) the dominant coalition or the decision-making body within the organization, according the L. Grunig, Grunig, and Dozier (2002, p. 97).

Public relations leadership may require chameleon-like moves within the organization—fitting in among multiple dominant coalitions or decision-making bodies, according to Berger (2005). He proposed that "the existence of a single, all-prevailing dominant coalition is a myth: Power relations occur in multiple dominant coalitions in large organizations" (Berger, 2005, p. 9). Extending and further examining that line of thinking, Berger and Reber (2006) noted from their research that most public relations (PR) professionals argue that influence within an organization requires PR's presence in decision-making circles (i.e., the dominant coalition). Among the most important issues in public relations, according to Berger and Reber's (2006) study, was to "strengthen leadership skills within the profession" (p. 6); named as a most-needed influence resource was "stronger PR leadership" (p. 92).

In summary, to contribute in a positive and useful way to an organization, public relations needs to gain access to the dominant coalition or coalitions. With such access and influence, public relations can directly improve stakeholder relationships, thereby contributing to the organization's financial bottom line in a number of ways. Access to the organization's decision-making circle may not be as easy as serving on the executive board because multiple centers of decision-making power exist in organizations. To finesse membership into dominant coalitions, stronger leadership in public relations is needed. To develop strong leaders, public relations scholars and practitioners need to examine, via voices of current industry leaders, the concerns and the means of addressing concerns within the profession.

Examining Public Relations Leadership Worldwide

The Plank Center for Leadership in Public Relations at the University of Alabama provided conceptual, organizational, logistical, and funding support for a global study of the most important issues in public relations among industry leaders and how they are currently addressing those issues. Many of the findings that follow are gleaned from the study summary (Berger, 2012). The top 10 issues were listed at the opening of this chapter. For each of the 10 categories, five strategies were listed on the leadership survey. Respondents were asked to rank how much their organization was implementing the listed strategy/activity on a scale of 1 = *a little bit* to 7 = *a great deal*. The results are listed in Table 6.1. Here we examine each of those issues and global leaders' responses to them. An examination of the issue and solutions in a larger context within the profession is made when possible.

Dealing With the Speed and Volume of Information Flow

Of respondents, 23% ($N = 1,029$) identified dealing with the speed and volume of information as the most important issue for their organization. When responding to this issue, five strategies and tactics were identified. Strategies and tactics scores on the 1-to-7 scale ranged from 3.28 on the low end to 5.31 on the high end. Thus, the range was notable, but moderate. Practitioners deal with the fire hose of information flow by working on improving skills and processes ($M = 5.31$). They use this flow to both collect and distribute information faster ($M = 5.30$). Addressing the speed and volume through hiring more staff was the least common activity ($M = 3.28$).

The findings suggest that the increased availability of digital information management tools must be embraced by public relations leaders. Mobile technology such as smartphones and tablets with applications that help push and manage pertinent information and notifications may allay such overload. Edelman account executive Deanna Southerling reported in a Council of Public Relations Firms blog:

> Twitter helps me to stay up to speed in what is happening in the public relations industry . . . Fellow PR pros are always sharing information about the campaigns they're working on, the experiences they've encountered in the industry, client challenges and work-arounds, etc., that provide interesting insights into the industry. (Shaw, 2012, para. 6)

Today most global public relations agencies have some sort of digital and social media monitoring operation. GolinHarris provides clients The Bridge, "where employees can monitor traditional and social media in real time on behalf of clients," according to the *New York Times* (Elliott, 2011, p. B7). Similarly, in 2011, Porter Novelli introduced its Radar—a real-time media monitoring operation to help clients deal with the rise of digital and social media (Sullivan, 2011). Brad MacAfee, senior partner and managing director of Porter Novelli's Atlanta office was quoted in a press release:

> Porter Novelli Radar helps our clients understand what is happening *as it happens.* We have all seen a Tweet and/or Facebook comment or traditional

news story explode onto the world stage in a matter of minutes. With these extra capabilities, we can ensure that our clients are rapidly prepared and ready to blunt any challenges to their reputations. (Sullivan, 2011, para. 6)

GolinHarris and Porter Novelli are just two examples of media monitoring operations that help public relations leaders sort out the most important issues among the deluge of information, as well as the most important opportunities in that flow they might choose to engage.

Managing the Digital Revolution and the Rise of Social Media

Slightly more than 15% (15.3%) of respondents ($N = 684$) said that management of digital and social media was the most important issue for their organization, making it the second most cited issue. Responses to the five strategies and tactics alternatives offered to manage digital and social media were all above mid-range on the 1-to-7 scale. Leaders are managing digital and social media by revising strategies for increased use of social media ($M = 5.92$) and training staff to be more proficient in social media ($M = 5.48$). They are least likely to create performance measures for social media ($M = 4.65$), but the measurement metric is still well above the midpoint of 3.50.

One need look no further than the pages of a trade publication such as *PRWeek* to see evidence of increased availability of social media management tools for public relations leaders. A quick search of 2013 articles in the U.S. trade publication described the prospective value of products such as "Sprout Social," "Sprinklr," and "Spredfast." Leaders have access to tools that assist with everything ranging from social media project management to monitoring, measuring, and analyzing social media campaigns. When global public relations leaders say they are revising their strategies and training staff, a cursory glance at one trade publication reinforces such emphases through its coverage of industry trends.

Improving the Measurement of Communication Effectiveness

About 12% (12.2%) of leaders ($N = 547$) cited communication measurement as the biggest issue for their organization. However, leaders said they use the tried and true approach of monitoring and analyzing media content to demonstrate value of the public relations function ($M = 5.48$). The second highest mean score went to linking communication effectiveness to business outcomes ($M = 4.82$). Just as with other categories, they were least inclined, as measured by mean scores, to increase staffing to deal with metrics and measurement ($M = 4.00$).

Concern about meaningful measurement of the communications function is nothing new. It has long been a subject of discussion, even debate. In October

1996, a Public Relations Evaluation Summit was held in New York City. An outcome of the summit was publication of "Guidelines and Standards for Measuring and Evaluating PR Effectiveness," written by Dr. Walter Lindenmann (1997, 2003), then head of the Ketchum Research and Measurement Department. In 2009, the Public Relations Society of America convened a Measurement Working Group, whose charge was to put forth measurement standards for PR's contributions to business outcomes that could be adopted industry-wide.

In 2010 representatives from five global public relations organizations came together in Barcelona to introduce what have become known as the Barcelona Principles for public relations measurement. Today blogs, webinars, books, and workshops are devoted to the subject of effective measurement of the public relations activity. It would be hard to find a public relations leader today who would not give support to the importance of reliable evaluation of the public relations function. Yet, findings from this global study suggest that the old measures are still in place.

Being Prepared to Effectively Deal With Crises That May Arise

Nearly 12% (11.9%) of survey respondents ($n = 532$) identified crisis preparedness as the most important issue in their organization. In fact, 10 of 12 countries or regions ranked dealing effectively with crises above 6.0 on the 1-to-7 scale, indicating particular importance for this issue. Only respondents in Germany ($M = 5.15$) and Spain ($M = 5.84$) ranked crisis management leadership below 6.0. Also in this instance, organizations use all five of the strategies and tactics to deal with crises. Preparation for crises comes from effective crisis communications plans ($M = 5.66$) and proactive programs to address crisis risks ($M = 5.11$). Even the least favored strategy, training employees in crisis management procedures, had a relatively high mean ($M = 4.83$).

Steven Fink (2013) wrote in his book *Crisis Communications: The Definitive Guide to Managing the Message*, "Today, a crisis in business is as inevitable as death and taxes; it is not a question of *if*, but rather *when*" (p. xiii). In addition, public relations leaders have said they are most influential when they are dealing with a crisis in their organization (Berger & Reber, 2006). The inevitability of crises in today's business environment, paired with the importance of the public relations function when an organization is in crisis, leads quite naturally to the finding in this global study: Being prepared is important, and all five strategies and tactics are valuable.

These top four categories account for almost two thirds (62.4%) of respondents. The remaining six categories were all cited as "most important" by fewer than 10 percent of respondents (Table 6.1). These categories are only briefly described here; employee engagement and CSR were dealt with more fully in the previous chapter.

TABLE 6.1 Means of Strategies and Tactics to Manage the Issues

Issues, Strategies, and Tactics	Means*
Dealing with the speed and volume of information flow ($n = 1{,}029$)	
Develop new skills and/or improve work processes in your unit	5.31
Use new technologies to collect, analyze, and distribute info faster	5.30
Assign more work and responsibilities to existing employees	4.96
Increase the use of external consultants or agencies	3.67
Hire additional permanent or part-time employees	3.28
Managing the digital revolution and rise of social media ($n = 684$)	
Revise communication strategies to make greater use of social media	5.92
Train employees in social media use	5.48
Monitor stakeholder communications on the social web	5.19
Hire employees with specialized digital media skills	5.01
Create key performance indicators for measuring social media activities	4.65
Improving measurement of communication to demonstrate value ($n = 547$)	
Monitor and analyze media coverage of the organization and competitors	5.48
Use business outcome metrics to measure performance effectiveness	4.82
Focus on nonfinancial performance indicators more than financial ones	4.64
Attend workshops on measurement to learn best practices	4.10
Hire external experts to provide measurement skills and develop metrics	4.00
Being prepared to deal effectively with crises that may arise ($n = 532$)	
Develop effective crisis communication plans for action	5.66
Implement effective issues management to reduce the risk of crises	5.11
Use issue scanning technologies to identify and track problems	5.05
Educate stakeholders about emergency communication and responses	4.92
Provide employees with training in crisis management procedures	4.83
Meeting demands for more transparency of communications (n = 375)	
Implement a strategy to increase transparency through the organization	5.56
Post more company information on the Internet and/or Intranet	5.42
Provide more two-way communication between employees, leaders	5.36
Communicate directly with external groups to address transparency	5.21
Monitor stakeholder communications to identify transparency concerns	5.03
Increasing employee engagement, commitment in the workplace ($n = 394$)	
Create a positive communication climate to increase commitment	5.78
Increase accessibility to, and visibility of senior organizational leaders	5.48
Facilitate the transfer of knowledge and best practices in the organization	5.28
Train front-line supervisors to improve listening and communication	4.95
Use reward and recognition programs to honor employees	4.38
Finding, developing and retaining highly talented professionals ($n = 337$)	
Provide greater autonomy on the job to highly talented individuals	5.70
Design individualized development plans for high potential professionals	5.20
Provide superior financial incentives and benefits to top talent	4.48
Support the education of future professionals at universities	4.26
Use search firms to help locate and evaluate talent	3.67

Issues, Strategies, and Tactics	Means*
Meeting increasing demands for corporate social responsibility ($n = 274$)	
Convince organizational leaders that CSR programs are important	5.56
Create public awareness of CSR programs	5.24
Interact directly with groups that make CSR demands	5.17
Showcase CSR achievements and employee accomplishments	4.91
Involve more employees in community activities	4.55
Meeting communication needs in diverse cultures ($n = 239$)	
Implement a global communication strategy	5.74
Monitor media coverage in global media	5.35
Use national experts to guide country communication programs	5.12
Hire more employees with international experience	4.82
Provide cultural training for employees	4.44
Improving the image of the profession ($n = 112$)	
Model professional standards and ethical behaviors	5.30
Participate actively in professional association activities	4.93
Support the education of future professionals at universities	4.79
Support research to advance professional knowledge	4.66
Provide ethics training for team members and others	4.40

*Mean indicated on a scale of 1 = *a little bit* to 7 = *a great deal.*

Dealing with Growing Demands for Transparency

Increased demands for transparent communication was cited by 8.4% percent of respondents ($n = 375$) as their organization's most important public relations issue. As with crisis management, public relations leaders are pursuing each of the five strategies to address an increasing need for organizational transparency internally and externally.

Improving Employee Engagement and Commitment

Almost 8% (7.9%) of respondents ($n = 354$) noted that employee relations was their most important issue. Leaders say they increase employee commitment by creating a positive communication environment and by increasing connections with, and the visibility of, senior leadership.

Finding, Developing, and Retaining Top Talent

Linked to employee engagement, employee recruitment and retention was named as the most important issue by 7.5% of respondents ($n = 337$). Practitioners say that high producers should be given more autonomy to attract and retain them.

Meeting Demands for Corporate Social Responsibility

Slightly more than 6% (6.1%, $n = 274$) ranked CSR as the most important issue in their organization. Leaders said they work to convince organization leaders of the importance of CSR and promote CSR projects to the public at large. There appears to be a significant opportunity to more fully engage employees in such efforts.

Meeting Communication Needs in Diverse Cultures

About 5% (5.3%) of respondents ($n = 239$) cited diversity as the most important issue for their organization. Implementation of a global communication strategy was the most common solution for meeting the communication needs of diverse cultures. Providing cultural training for employees was not widely pursued.

Improving the Image of the Profession

The image of public relations was noted by only 2.5% of respondents ($n = 112$) as the most important issue for their organization. Leaders consistently said they try to model professional standards and ethical behavior in order to improve the professional image. Ethics training was employed only modestly in many countries.

How Can We Apply Findings to Practice?

The global study provides some useful findings to help inform both practice and scholarship. This section will discuss implications for practice. What do we learn from the voices of almost 4,500 public relations practitioners in 23 countries? Are regional or cultural differences apparent? How can the findings be applied to practice to improve leadership and management of communication issues for organizations?

Parsing the "Most Important Issue"

Respondents told us the most common and nettling problem worldwide for practitioners is the speed and volume of information flow. Nearly one quarter (23%) of respondents cited information overload as the most important issue facing the profession. Top-level leaders ranked the issue significantly higher than did their lower level counterparts. This suggests that the pressure of dealing with the relentless flow of information is a particular problem at the uppermost levels of the communication function.

We don't know whether this issue is linked to a perceived need to gather every morsel of information before developing a strategic plan or whether it is the combination of information flow and other demands on an executive's time or something else entirely. What we do know is that it may be of particular importance that top-level leaders are able to harness the digital tools available to them, aggregating applications for mobile devices, for example, to manage the speed and volume of information demanding their attention.

As previously noted, reliable measurement of the organizational contribution of the communication function has historically been a problem. More than 1 in 10 (12.2%) respondents in this study cited measurement as the most important issue in public relations. But the issue seemed particularly troublesome in Latin America. Respondents in Brazil ($N = 303$) and Mexico ($N = 213$) collectively named measurement the number one issue facing public relations. In Chile ($N = 156$), respondents ranked it the number two issue. Although it was notable that all three Latin American countries ranked improving measurement of communication effectiveness so highly, the same issue also was as highly problematic in other regions of the world, too; for example, it was the number two issue in India ($N = 140$), South Korea ($N = 205$), and the United Kingdom ($N = 139$).

Because public relations is a relatively more nascent profession in Latin America and the BRIC countries (Brazil, Russia, India, and China) than it is in the United States, for example, it is understandable that justifying its importance to organizations is a special concern. But the emphasis on the issue in South Korea and the United Kingdom is a bit harder to explain. Measurement manifestos such as the 2010 Barcelona Principles (Grupp, 2010) have denigrated long-held and relied-on measures such as advertising equivalency. Perhaps practitioners, even in regions in which public relations is well developed, are struggling for measures that provide impressive bottom-line contributions to make the case to management for investing in the communication function.

Overall, employee recruitment, development, and retention were not highly ranked. Only 7.5% of respondents identified employee recruitment and retention issues as the most important issue in public relations. But the issue was dominant in BRIC countries (i.e., Brazil and Russia: $n = 215$; India and Chinese-speaking countries: $n = 143$), perhaps because of their rapid development in communication professions. Finding, developing, and retaining top public relations talent was the number one issue in Chinese-speaking countries (i.e., China, Hong Kong, Singapore, and Taiwan) and India. It was ranked the second most important issue in Russia and was sixth out of 10 in Brazil. Similarly, employee engagement was rated highest in mean scores (>5.86) in Mexico and the BRIC countries. This hyper-attention to employees may suggest a shortage of public relations talent in these countries, thereby providing opportunity for the profession to grow.

Although issues surrounding Corporate Social Responsibility and transparency were not dominant on the most important issues list, the nations that ranked them high and low are nevertheless interesting. Meeting the increasing demands for CSR (Most Important Issue 8) and dealing the demands for greater transparency (Most Important Issue 5) were more important issues for German-speaking countries (i.e., Austria, Germany, Switzerland; $n = 1,773$) than they were for other countries or regions in the study. Latin American countries (i.e., Brazil, Chile, and Mexico) gave the highest mean scores to the need to meet increasing demands for CSR. CSR scores were lowest among United Kingdom ($M = 4.26$) and the United States ($M = 4.81, n = 827$) respondents. It's possible that industry or organization type may play a role, or perhaps the issue is less important because some leaders feel they have adequately addressed it.

Parsing Strategies and Tactics to Manage the Issues

Following the identification of most important issues, respondents noted strategies and tactics their organizations were using to handle the issues. To deal with the unrelenting speed and volume of information, respondents collectively selected developing their skill set or tweaking work processes ($M = 5.31$) with a close second choice being employing new technology to manage information ($M = 5.30$). South Korea had the highest mean scores for developing new skills ($M = 5.81$) and using new technologies ($M = 6.17$) to manage information. The United States had the highest mean for increasing the workloads of existing employees ($M = 5.29$) as a way to attack information overload, the third most common tactic globally.

When dealing with the flood of information, it might actually be counter-productive to saddle employees with increased workloads. Requiring the use of new technologies might be wise for tech-savvy employees, but it may actually slow the information management process for any employees who are tech-phobic. Leaders should carefully assess the abilities of their subordinates before assuming a new technology will ease and speed the processing of information. Training and employee development may be a prerequisite to simply tossing technology at the problem.

The strategies and tactics to deal with the second most important issue, managing digital and social media, were all ranked high according to global means, ranging from 5.92 to 4.65. Measurement of social media effectiveness rated the lowest among the five strategies and tactics. It was rated particularly low among German-speaking countries ($M = 4.01$). In this category, India stood out as it identified training employees to effectively use social media ($M = 6.20$) as its most common strategy or tactic.

Measurement, as noted in the next paragraph, remains a challenge in public communication. In that light, "Creating key performance indicators for measuring social media activities" was the least used strategy or tactic in managing the evolving medium. Because of the fast-moving development of social media, practitioners may be most focused on staying on top of that development and trying to match the latest medium to particular publics or demographics. Getting our arms around social media use may be perceived as antecedent to evaluation. If this is the case, leaders may need to reconsider the wisdom of such a stance for our profession.

Improvement of measurement of communication effectiveness continues to be a sticky wicket. The survey means for strategies and tactics to improve measurement were among the lowest for all 10 most important issues. Respondents were also provided a space to offer alternative measurement solutions; few did. These findings cross national and cultural boundaries. Although communication evaluation has been at the forefront of the public relations profession for many years, there are still miles to go it seems. This conundrum is only exacerbated by the seemingly daily addition of communication tools, thanks to emerging and evolving media as noted earlier.

Crisis preparedness is addressed by all five strategies and tactics, based on mean responses. Planning was the highest rated approach in all but one country ($M = 5.66$). South Korea had the highest mean average for using technology to track issues ($M = 6.10$). Training employees in crisis management was particularly valued in Brazil ($M = 5.50$) and Mexico ($M = 5.59$). German-speaking countries provided a significantly lower mean ($M = 4.15$) compared to other countries and regions for implementing issues management programs as a way to curb crises. When a crisis occurs, all resources must be brought to bear on its successful resolution. The reported use of all five strategies and tactics reinforces this notion and suggests an understanding worldwide of the role that communications leaders must play in dealing with such challenges.

To meet increasing demands for transparency, as with crisis preparedness, all five strategies and tactics play a role, according to respondents. The rankings were relatively consistent across countries and regions. A notable exception was South Korea, which had the highest mean scores among all countries and regions for making more information available via the Internet ($M = 6.48$) and actively monitoring stakeholders' transparency concerns ($M = 6.45$). South Korea has historically been a country of early adopters. According to the Korea Internet and Security Agency (*Smart device* . . ., 2013), smartphone penetration in South Korea rose from 39.2% in 2011 to 78.5% in 2012 among consumers aged 12 to 59. The country ranks among the top 25 countries worldwide in Internet penetration. In 2013 the International Telecommunication Union (2013) reported an Internet penetration rate in South Korea of 84.1%. While other countries in our sample surpass even that rate, the combination of Internet penetration and technology adoption may explain South Korea's embrace of the Internet to increase organizational transparency.

In response to listed strategies and tactics for increasing employee engagement and commitment, the highest mean globally went to creating a positive communication environment for employees ($M = 5.78$). Whereas trade literature often lauds the value of reward and recognition programs, the public relations leaders in this study ranked such strategies the lowest, with some notable exceptions. Chinese-speaking countries ($M = 5.60$), Estonia/Latvia ($M = 5.63$), and Russia ($M = 5.22$) favor such programs and use them more often than most other countries. In fact the three aforementioned countries/regions use reward and recognition programs significantly more often than do organizations in German-speaking countries (M = 3.82).

Related to employee engagement and commitment is the seventh ranked most important issue: recruitment, development, and retention of top professionals. Respondents from German-speaking countries (M = 6.03), the United Kingdom (M = 6.25), and Mexico (M = 6.25) said their most commonly used strategy for recruiting and retaining talented employees was to provide them autonomy. Autonomy was less favored by respondents from Brazil (M = 4.68), Russia (M = 5.05), and Spain (M = 5.17).

Going Forward

Several takeaways bubble up from the data for both public relations practitioners and scholars. Here are a few:

* Leaders overwhelmingly identified dealing with the speed and volume of information flow as the most important issue that public relations practitioners deal with worldwide. Every indicator suggests this issue will only intensify, and top leaders in the study are particularly troubled by information overload.
* Perhaps predictably, communication leaders found management of the digital revolution and harnessing the rise of social media as particularly challenging. At the same time, they are effectively employing digital media to address a wide range of concerns and top issues.
* The need for uniform and reliable measures of communication effectiveness remains a concern among global public relations leaders.
* Leaders understand that they are expected to step in and defuse crises, and they use a broad toolbox in addressing that expectation.
* BRIC countries noted talent identification, recruitment, and retention as particularly important.
* Training and using existing employees to address important issues—everything from crisis management to curbing information flow to developing social media strategies—is more common than outsourcing such work. Nevertheless, there appears to be a lot of room for more fully engaging employees in issues management, for example, CSR, diversity, and so forth.
* Offering autonomy to top performers is a common way to reward and retain talent, although reward and recognition systems are more common in Eastern Europe and Asia.

Finally, scholarship in public relations benefits in several ways from this groundbreaking study and its findings. This study points toward many more studies for communication scholars worldwide:

* Ongoing mining of the data from the largest global public relations study ever attempted will continue to benefit practice, pedagogy, and scholarship.

- What are social media strategies in South Korea? It appears that valuable lessons could be learned by studying the excellent job South Korean companies have apparently done in using social media to connect with external publics.
- Another series of studies might look at how different types of organizations (e.g., manufacturing versus service, business to customer versus business to business) in select countries have managed to tame the speed and flow of information. Have units been restructured to manage the volume of information? Have new training programs been implemented? If so, what lessons have been learned? Similarly, what can we learn from agencies' innovative approaches to this issue?
- Measurement appeared to be a special concern in Latin America. What sorts of measurement are currently being used? Which indicators are most valued by organization leaders?
- Employee recruitment and retention should be further studied in BRIC countries.
- CSR and transparency were notably important in German-speaking and Latin American countries. What similarities or differences in CSR practice and policies exist in these regions of the Northern and Southern Hemispheres?
- When it comes to crisis communication, South Korea stands out for its use of technology in issues tracking. Case studies to identify best practices would be valuable to crisis communication managers worldwide.
- How is employee communications practiced in China, Estonia/Latvia, and Russia? These countries were identified as embracing employee recognition programs. Why are these programs particularly useful in these countries? What can other internal communicators learn from these practices?
- Finally, the seven dimensions of leadership can be further tested and developed. We imagine this integrated model of leadership can be instructive for education and training programs.

The research programs that can be generated by the findings from this study could be local, regional, or comparative between regions. We urge public relations scholars to look for direction and insights from this study to extend their own work and interests.

References

Berger, B. (2005). Power over, power with, and power to relations: Critical reflections on public relations, the dominant coalition, and activism. *Journal of Public Relations Research*, 17(1), 5–27.

Berger, B. (2012). *Key themes and findings: The cross-cultural study of leadership in public relations and communication management*. Tuscaloosa, AL: The Plank Center for Leadership in Public Relations. Available online at http://plankcenter.ua.edu/wp-content/uploads/2012/10/Summary-of-Themes-and-Findings-Leader-Survey.pdf

Berger, B., & Reber, B. (2006). *Gaining influence in public relations: The role of resistance in practice.* Mahwah, NJ: Erlbaum.

Ehling, W. (1992). Estimating the value of public relations and communication to an organization. In J. E. Grunig (Ed.), *Excellence in public relations and communication management* (pp. 617–638). Hillsdale, NJ: Erlbaum.

Elliott, S. (2011, June 14). Account executive is antiquated. Consider yourself a catalyst. *The New York Times*, p. B7.

Fink, S. (2013). *Crisis communications: The definitive guide to managing the message.* New York, NY: McGraw-Hill.

Grunig, J. (Ed.). (1992). *Excellence in public relations and communication management.* Hillsdale, NJ: Erlbaum.

Grunig, L., Grunig, J., & Dozier, D. (2002). *Excellent public relations and effective organizations: A study of communication management in three countries.* Mahwah, NJ: Erlbaum.

Grupp, R. (2010). *The Barcelona Declaration of Research Principles.* Gainesville, FL: The Institute for Public Relations. Available online at: www.instituteforpr.org/2010/06/the-barcelona-declaration-of-research-principles/

International Telecommunication Union (2013). *Statistics.* Available online at: www.itu.int/en/ITU-D/Statistics/Documents/statistics/2013/Individuals_Internet_2000-2012.xls

Lindenmann, W. (1997, 2003). *Guidelines for measuring the effectiveness of PR programs and activities.* Gainesville, FL: The Institute for Public Relations. Available online at: www.instituteforpr.org/wp-content/uploads/2002_MeasuringPrograms.pdf

Mintzberg, H. (1991). Five P's for strategy. In H. Mintzberg & J. B. Quinn (Eds.), *The strategy process: Concepts, contexts, and cases* (2nd ed., pp. 12–19). Englewood Cliffs, NJ: Prentice Hall.

Moss, D. (2005). Strategies. In R. L. Heath (Ed.), *Encyclopedia of Public Relations, Vol. 2.* Thousand Oaks, CA: Sage.

Shaw, M. (2012, July 11). Channeling the flow: How PR professionals are managing information overload [Blog entry]. Available online at http://prfirms.org/voice/2012/channeling-the-flow-how-pr-professionals-are-managing-information-overload

Smart device user penetration explodes in South Korea (Feb. 27, 2013). Available online at: www.emarketer.com/Article/Smart-Device-User-Penetration-Explodes-South-Korea/1009696

Smith, R. (2013). *Strategic planning for public relations.* New York: Routledge.

Stacks, D. (2002). *Primer of public relations research.* New York, NY: Guilford.

Sullivan, C. (2011, August 16). Porter Novelli Radar: Real-time monitoring [Press release]. Available online at www.porternovelli.com/news-room/porter-novelli-launches-real-time-monitoring-service

White, J. & Dozier, D. (1992). Management decisionmaking. In J. E. Grunig (Ed.), *Excellence in public relations and communication management* (pp. 91–108). Hillsdale, NJ: Erlbaum.

Wilcox, D., Cameron, G., Reber, B. & Shin, J-H (2013). *Think public relations* (2nd ed.). Boston, MA: Pearson.

Wilcox, D. & Reber, B. (2013). *Public relations writing and media tactics* (7th ed.). Boston, MA: Pearson.

7

LEADERSHIP DIMENSIONS AND ISSUE MANAGEMENT

Juan Meng

Our collective understanding of leadership and how it affects practice in communication management continues to evolve in terms of complexity and sophistication, progressing from the most basic (i.e., leader-centric and individual–trait approach) to the most advanced (i.e., leadership as a transformational shared process; Bass, Avolio, Jung, & Berson, 2003). Although both scholars and practitioners have recognized the link between excellent leadership and effective practice, few have attempted to explain the multifaceted nature of the leadership construct in excellent public relations and communication management. A key question remains unanswered in our field: What crucial dimensions help to fully explain the meaning of leadership to effective public relations practice?

As described in Chapter 3, Meng (2010a) first proposed an integrated theoretical framework to define the construct of leadership and conceptualize key dimensions of leadership that can contribute to communication excellence. Meng and associates (e.g., Meng, forthcoming; Meng & Berger, 2013; Meng, Berger, & Heyman, 2011 then tested the model and validated the multidimensionality of the leadership construct. Despite this research, it remains unclear whether this framework of leadership in public relations may be perceived differently in diverse cultures, and, if so, how these perceptual differences may affect the application of effective leadership styles in communication practice.

In this global project, we continued testing and confirming crucial leadership dimensions established in Meng's (2010a) research. We extended the integrated model of excellent leadership in public relations into different cultures and societies to test whether such crucial leadership dimensions might have universal applicability. In addition, we wanted to find out whether the seven leadership dimensions can generate a positive impact on the management of current critical issues and challenges in the field. The complexity of challenges in today's communication practice calls for a comprehensive understanding of the leadership process. More important, the increasing frequency with which communication teams and organizations encounter such challenges underscores the need to leverage the leadership capacity in organizations of all kinds.

Thus, this chapter focuses on testing the universality of the leadership construct and its dimensions. We compare and analyze national, cultural, and other demographic variations that appeared in our global leadership survey. The analysis focuses on the subject of issue management, as the effectiveness of the leadership dimensions in managing critical issues was a major part of our global survey. Leadership is critical in managing complex issues, and our global findings offer insights for implementing relevant leadership skills and capabilities in diverse situations. Accordingly, the chapter concludes with a rethinking of the very concept of leadership in issue management in public relations practice by discussing the implications of global findings for academic researchers and practitioners across regions.

Adapting Leadership Dimensions Into the Global Project

The Single Factor of Public Relations Leadership

To investigate the role of leadership dimensions in helping practitioners deal with current issues and challenges, we used the integrated model of leadership in public relations established by Meng and associates (Meng, 2010a, 2010b, 2012, 2013; Meng & Berger, 2013). We adapted the original measurement scales of all seven leadership dimensions into a shortened version due to the overall length of the survey instrument for the global project. We treated each individual dimension as a composite indicator and adapted the multiple-item measures of that dimension into a single statement.

For instance, in the original measurement, the dimension of ethical orientation has five item measures, which have been tested and confirmed. As the dimension itself has exhibited a very high level of composite reliability (>.70), it confirmed the reliability and validity of the multiple-item measures (see Meng & Berger, 2013, for a detailed report on composite reliability scores for all dimensions). Thus, it is safe for us to aggregate the measures into a single-item measure to represent the dimension in this global study. Therefore, we described the dimension of ethical orientation as "possessing a strong ethical orientation and set of values to guide actions." We implemented the same approach for all seven dimensions, which generated a shortened set of measures for the construct of leadership as exhibited in Table 7.1.

The seven leadership dimensions were hypothesized to either facilitate or impede the management of a selected critical issue in communication

TABLE 7.1 Single-Item Measures of the Seven Leadership Dimensions

Seven Leadership Dimensions	Single-Item Measure (The leader is able to . . .)
Communication knowledge management	Use communication knowledge to develop appropriate strategies, plans, and messages.
Strategic decision-making capabilities	Participate in the organization's strategic decision making regarding the issue.
Ethical orientation	Possess a strong ethical orientation and set of values to guide actions.
Team collaboration	Build and manage professional work teams to address the issue.
Self-dynamics	Provide a compelling vision for how communication can help the organization.
Relationship building	Develop coalitions in and outside the organization to deal with the issue.
Organizational structure and culture	Work in an organization that supports two-way communication and shared power.

Note: The respondents were asked to assess how important each leadership dimension is in helping their communication leader deal successfully with the specific issue based on their selection of the most important issue from a list of 10 current issues. The evaluation of the importance was achieved through 7-point rating scales on all seven single statements, with 1 = a little bit of importance and 7 = a great deal of importance. For more information on the list of the 10 current issues and challenges, see Chapter 5.

management. Respondents in our global survey were asked to assess the importance of all seven leadership dimensions or conditions.[1] Based on the results of the entire global sample ($N = 4,483$), respondents gave all seven leadership dimensions consistently high ratings, which suggests that all seven dimensions were perceived to be important for communication leaders to master and apply to daily practice, as well as to varied challenging issues or situations. The mean scores for the seven leadership dimensions ranged from 5.63 to 6.30 with the scores of standard deviations ranging from .97 to 1.39 across the entire sample.

An exploratory factor analysis was applied to the seven dimensions. The results confirmed that only one factor was extracted and the initial Eigenvalue was 3.48 for the component extracted, explaining 47.16 of the variance in the sample. We named the extracted factor *public relations leadership*. Tables 7.2 and 7.3 display the correlation matrix and the results of factor analysis of the seven leadership dimensions. Such a result is very consistent with what the integrated model of leadership in public relations (Meng & Berger, 2013) has suggested and confirmed: *Leadership in public relations represents a complex and multifaceted phenomenon*. The leadership construct encompasses seven essential dimensions: self-dynamics, team collaboration, ethical orientation, relationship building, strategic decision making, communication knowledge management, and organizational structure and culture.

TABLE 7.2 Interitem Correlation Matrix of the Seven Leadership Dimensions

	CM	DM	EO	TC	SD	RB	OS
Communication knowledge management (CM)	1.00						
Strategic decision-making (DM)	.42	1.00					
Ethical orientation (EO)	.33	.41	1.00				
Team collaboration (TC)	.35	.38	.47	1.00			
Self-dynamics (SD)	.33	.37	.39	.46	1.00		
Relationship building (RB)	.29	.33	.40	.48	.46	1.00	
Organizational structure and culture (OS)	.26	.30	.41	.39	.38	.42	1.00

Note: All correlations were significant at $p < .01$.

TABLE 7.3 Factor Analysis on Leadership Dimensions and Scale Statistics ($N = 4,483$)

Seven Leadership Dimensions	Mean	Standard Deviation (SD)	Item-Total Correlation	The Leadership Factor
				Factor Loadings (standardized)
Communication knowledge management	6.14	1.06	.46	.60
Strategic decision-making capabilities	6.30	.97	.52	.66
Ethical orientation	5.63	1.37	.58	.71
Team collaboration	5.91	1.12	.61	.75
Self-dynamics	6.04	1.13	.58	.71
Relationship building	5.71	1.26	.58	.71
Organizational structure and culture	5.62	1.39	.52	.66
Eigenvalue				3.48
% of variance				47.16
Cronbach's alpha (standardized)				.81

Note: Scale mean = 41.35 (SD = 5.71). Grand mean = 5.91, $F(6, 4,465) = 351.46, p < .01$. Deleting any item will not improve Cronbach's alpha.

Demographic Variances in the Perceptions of Leadership Dimensions

Although we have confirmed that a single leadership factor has been extracted based on the entire sample, we still looked into some possible demographic variations as reflected in respondents' perceptions regarding the importance of the seven leadership dimensions. Some variations are briefly discussed here:

1. Generally, female respondents across the sample rated all seven leadership dimensions significantly higher than male respondents (Table 7.4). Women

TABLE 7.4 Gender Perceptual Differences on the Importance of Leadership Dimensions

Leadership Dimensions	Female (n = 2,318)	Male (n = 2,164)	F Value
	Mean	Mean	(df = 2, 4,480)
Communication knowledge management	6.22	6.05	15.31**
Strategic decision making	6.37	6.23	11.55**
Ethical orientation	5.77	5.49	24.48**
Team collaboration	6.03	5.78	27.65**
Self-dynamics	6.16	5.91	27.81**
Relationship building	5.85	5.57	28.88**
Organizational structure and culture	5.80	5.44	36.48**

Note: df = degrees of freedom.
**p < .01.

showed confidence in all seven leadership dimensions in helping communication leaders manage issues. A slightly larger deviation was shown on the dimension of organizational structure and culture: The mean difference between female and male respondents was .37, $F(2, 4,480) = 36.48$, $p < .01$, indicating that female respondents perceived this as a critical supportive condition for communication leaders to be successful. These results may reflect the feminization of the public relations profession because more than 70% of the junior-level practitioners are female (Aldoory & Toth, 2004). The relationship between leadership and gender has become more significant as female practitioners see leadership as a necessary component in their socialization and empowering processes. A supportive organizational structure and culture are critical for female practitioners to break through the glass ceiling and acquire increasingly responsible leadership positions.

2. Years of working experience in the profession also affected respondents' assessment of the importance of certain leadership dimensions. Generally, respondents with more professional experience (more than 20 years in the profession) rated all seven dimensions higher than did those with fewer years of experiences (fewer than 11 years and between 11–20 years). Specifically, the senior group showed a significantly higher mean on five leadership dimensions: communication knowledge management, strategic decision-making, ethical orientation, team collaboration, and self-dynamics (Table 7.5). The demographic analysis of our sample showed that 25.1% of participants have worked in the profession for more than 20 years, and their direct experiences may reflect the importance of mastering those leadership capabilities in varied communication situations.

3. Public relations leaders and those one level below them perceived the dimension of strategic decision making as the most important leadership capability,

TABLE 7.5 Mean Differences on the Importance of Leadership Dimensions by Years of Experience

Leadership Dimensions	<11 Years (n = 1,584)	11–20 Years (n = 1,772)	>20 Years (n = 1,126)	F Value
Communication knowledge management	6.14	6.07	6.23	8.28**
Strategic decision making	6.22	6.31	6.41	12.62**
Ethical orientation	5.54	5.53	5.92	32.87**
Team collaboration	5.91	5.84	6.01	7.57**
Self-dynamics	6.03	6.00	6.12	4.16**
Relationship building	5.69	5.69	5.79	2.58
Organizational structure and culture	5.61	5.59	5.69	1.94

Note: Degrees of freedom = 2, 4,479.

**$p < .01$.

TABLE 7.6 Mean Differences on the Importance of Leadership Dimensions by Reporting Level

Leadership Dimensions	0 Level (n = 1,779)	1 Level (n = 1,540)	>2 Levels (n = 1,161)	F Value
Communication knowledge management	6.13	6.10	6.20	3.06*
Strategic decision making	6.41	6.28	6.17	22.50**
Ethical orientation	5.65	5.53	5.75	8.92**
Team collaboration	5.90	5.85	5.99	5.17**
Self-dynamics	6.08	6.00	6.04	1.92
Relationship building	5.72	5.65	5.79	3.75*
Organizational structure and culture	5.59	5.59	5.73	4.50**

Note: Degrees of freedom = 2, 4,477.

*$p < .05$. **$p < .01$.

compared to respondents who work at two or more levels below the leader. This may be a result of their likelier greater involvement in strategic decision making. However, those at lower levels rated five leadership dimensions (communication knowledge management, ethical orientation, team collaboration, relationship building, and organizational structure and culture) significantly higher than their leaders (Table 7.6). Lower level professionals also emphasized the importance of a supportive organizational structure and culture.

4. Consistent with the results we found in the demographic category of years of experience, the senior age group in our global sample (older than 55 years) presented perceptual differences on certain leadership dimensions compared

TABLE 7.7 Perceptual Differences on the Importance of Leadership Dimensions by Age

Leadership Dimensions	<36 Years	36–45 Years	46–55 Years	>55 Years	F-Value
	n = 1,206	n = 1,435	n = 385	n = 794	
Communication knowledge management	6.19	6.08	6.12	6.21	3.32*
Strategic decision making	6.24	6.32	6.31	6.38	3.46*
Ethical orientation	5.56	5.55	5.65	5.95	13.29**
Team collaboration	5.96	5.85	5.89	5.96	2.71*
Self-dynamics	6.04	6.02	6.04	6.11	.88
Relationship building	5.73	5.70	5.68	5.77	.88
Organizational structure and culture	5.69	5.57	5.56	5.77	4.51**

Note: Degrees of freedom = 3, 4,478.

$*p < .05.$ $**p < .01.$

to other age groups. Specifically, the senior age group believed that communication knowledge management, strategic decision making, ethical orientation, team collaboration, and organizational structure and culture are of particular importance for communication leaders to learn and apply (Table 7.7). Ethical orientation received the highest rating score by the most senior respondents, which could be a reflection of professional advancement itself, or of the long-time expectation, or at least the claim that public relations practitioners must be ethics counselors in their organizations.

Perceptual Variances in Geographic Locations

We also examined cultural variations, which may be related to a specific culture or the development of the public relations profession in that specific culture/society. Mindful of our assumption that national and cultural comparisons are difficult at best, we looked into the data sets for each of the 12 countries/regions with regard for the similarities and differences in perceptions of the seven leadership dimensions (Table 7.8). We speculate about some of the variations, but more research is required to better explain the variations:

1. Participants from German-speaking countries (Germany, Switzerland, and Austria) generally rated all seven dimensions relatively low compared with other surveyed countries and regions, except for the dimension of strategic decision making. This was true for German-speaking participants' responses in most sections of the surveys, which could mean that the leadership construct is a bit different in these countries. It also could mean that educational systems or approaches to evaluating survey questions are qualitatively or culturally different in those countries.

TABLE 7.8 Mean Differences on Leadership Dimensions by Country/Region

Leadership Dimensions	Country/Region												F Value
	GE $n=1,773$	CL $n=156$	CN $n=143$	EL $n=142$	ME $n=213$	RU $n=215$	SK $n=205$	SP $n=210$	U.K. $n=139$	U.S. $n=827$	BR $n=303$	IN $n=140$	
CK	5.95	6.36	6.01	5.99	6.31	6.16	6.22	6.16	6.03	6.28	6.65	6.18	15.12**
DM	6.25	6.55	5.86	6.27	6.29	6.20	6.10	6.22	6.41	6.45	6.66	6.09	11.93**
EO	5.09	6.34	6.00	5.86	6.24	5.49	5.64	5.83	5.47	6.02	6.58	5.93	64.01**
TC	5.67	6.35	6.03	6.17	6.21	6.05	5.91	5.93	5.83	5.94	6.44	5.98	18.94**
SD	5.87	6.40	5.99	6.06	6.37	5.85	6.01	6.02	5.81	6.14	6.59	6.09	15.30**
RB	5.47	6.31	5.84	5.80	6.23	5.57	6.09	5.76	5.62	5.70	6.21	5.76	19.74**
OS	5.37	6.08	5.72	5.49	6.03	5.20	6.23	5.80	5.16	5.70	6.22	6.01	23.32**

Note: Degrees of freedom = 11, 4,454. For country/region, GE = German-speaking countries; CL = Chile; CN = Chinese-speaking region; EL = Estonia and Latvia; ME = Mexico; RU = Russia; SK = South Korea; SP = Spain; U.K. = United Kingdom; U.S. = United States; BR = Brazil; IN = India. For leadership dimensions, CK = communication knowledge management; DM = strategic decision making; EO = ethical orientation; TC = team collaboration; SD = self-dynamics; RB = relationship building; OS = organizational structure and culture.

** $p < .01$.

2. Participants from eight of the surveyed countries/regions rated the dimension of strategic decision making as the most important leadership dimension. However, practitioners in the Chinese-speaking countries rated team collaboration the highest, Mexican professionals rated self-dynamics the highest, and practitioners in India and South Korea rated communication knowledge management the highest. Such variations could be due to the relatively early development stage of the public relations profession in those countries and regions. In addition, the Chinese-speaking region is experiencing a shortage of highly talented or qualified communication professionals.

3. Respondents in Brazil, Chile, and Mexico gave all seven dimensions relatively higher ratings when compared with other countries and regions. The demographic analysis showed that the Latin American participants were more often women, younger, less experienced, and working at lower levels in their organizations. Perhaps geography influences these higher scores, or a different cultural worldview. Gender may play a role; as we saw earlier, women seem more passionate about the leadership dimensions because they may see them as crucial steps to take on the road to self-advancement.

Although we didn't use previously established cultural dimensions (e.g., Hofstede's cultural dimensions or the GLOBE study's nine cultural dimensions) (Dorfman & House, 2004; Hofstede, 2001) to test specific relationships between cultural dimensions and public relations leadership practice in a given society, we believe that respondents' evaluations of the importance of the seven leadership dimensions in helping them deal with critical issues in daily communication practice tend to reflect the societal orientation and cultural preference in which they practice. Some reasonable perceptual variations (i.e., high in some countries and low in the other) in certain leadership dimensions, such as strategic decision-making, ethical orientation, and organizational structure and culture, could be relevant to the leadership culture of that society. They also could be due to the development of the profession in that society, or the organizational context in which public relations is practiced. Understanding these and other cultural and national variations may help us better prepare leaders to deal with global issues and opportunities in the future.

The Impact of Leadership Dimensions on Top Issues

A major question addressed in our global project concerns the most important issues in today's practice and how communication leaders manage them. From the leadership perspective, we explore the extent to which specific leadership dimensions can be universally applied in effective issue management. As described in the previous chapter, we identified a list of 10 current issues based on topics that have been frequently discussed in both scholarly research and professional publications and at professional conferences, for example, the Public Relations Society of America.

Based on the frequencies of the overall responses from our global sample (N = 4,483), the top four most important issues are (1) dealing with the speed and volume of information flow (n = 1,029, 23.0%), (2) managing the digital revolution and the rise of social media (n = 684, 15.3%), (3) improving the measurement of communication effectiveness to demonstrate value (n = 547, 12.2%), and (4) being prepared to deal effectively with crises that may arise (n = 532, 11.9%). Nearly two thirds of respondents named one of these four issues as the top issue in the field. We then examined the functions of seven leadership dimensions with respect to the top four most important issues. We wanted to learn whether the relative value of each dimension varied as the issue changes.

The results indicated a similar pattern to assess the supportive functions of seven leadership dimensions in managing selected important issues (Figure 7.1). The moving patterns of the lines in Figure 7.1 represent the rating scores respondents gave to each specific leadership dimension as they considered the importance of that specific dimension in dealing with a specific issue. The patterns indicate that strategic decision making and communication knowledge management are the two highest rated leadership dimensions for dealing with all four issues. The mean scores for these two dimensions ranged from 6.10 to 6.44. The dimensions of ethical orientation and organizational structure and culture, although certainly rated as important, received the lowest mean scores, ranging from 5.28 to 5.62.

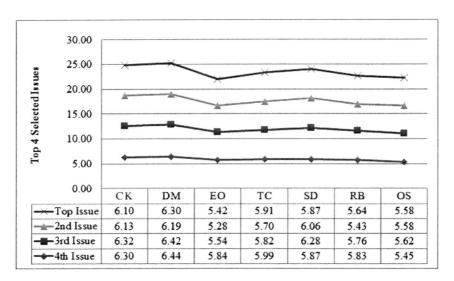

	CK	DM	EO	TC	SD	RB	OS
Top Issue	6.10	6.30	5.42	5.91	5.87	5.64	5.58
2nd Issue	6.13	6.19	5.28	5.70	6.06	5.43	5.58
3rd Issue	6.32	6.42	5.54	5.82	6.28	5.76	5.62
4th Issue	6.30	6.44	5.84	5.99	5.87	5.83	5.45

FIGURE 7.1 The Importance of Leadership Dimensions Varied as Issues Change

Note: CK = communication knowledge management DM = strategic decision making; EO = ethical orientation; TC = team collaboration; SD = self-dynamics; RB = relationship building; OS = organizational structure and culture.

The mean comparisons of the seven leadership dimensions across the top four issues yielded some significant results:

- For the issues of improving measurement efforts (Top Issue 3) and managing crises (Top Issue 4), the dimensions of strategic decision-making, $F(3, 2,787) = 9.00, p < .01$, and communication knowledge management, $F(3, 2,787) = 9.24, p < .01$, in leader behavior were perceived as more effective, or more valuable.
- When dealing with crises (Top Issue 4), possessing a strong ethical orientation and a set of values to guide actions, $F(3, 2,787) = 17.81, p < .01$, is particularly important. Building and managing professional work teams are also a critical leadership condition for crises, as it is for dealing with Top Issue 1—the speed and volume of information flow, $F(3, 2,787) = 8.08, p < .01$.
- It is important for the communication leader to provide a compelling vision for how communication can help the organization, $F (3, 2,787) = 18.57, p < .01$, when there is a need to improve the measurement of communication effectiveness (Top Issue 3).
- Relationship building ability seems to be a natural requirement for communication leaders in most situations; however, this dimension is particularly important when the team needs to be prepared to deal with crises that may arise, $F(3, 2,787) = 12.91, p < .01$.
- The organizational structure and culture dimension appears to contribute more or less equally (means ranging from 5.45–5.62) to managing all of the issues, $F(3, 2,787) = 1.46, p < .01$) as a supportive internal environment generally enhances communication effectiveness (Deetz, Tracy, & Simpson, 2000).

Variances in Leadership Dimensions in Issue Management

To further test the direct impact a given leadership dimension could generate on the management of a selected issue, several multiple linear regression models with a stepwise estimation approach were created. A stepwise estimation is perhaps the best approach to find out the most significant predictors in a multiple linear regression model when multiple predictors have been entered into the model (Hair, Anderson, Tatham, & Black, 1995). This approach is able to examine the contribution of each predictor variable to the regression model. We created a multiple regression model for each of the top four issues, and the results of the regression model suggested some variances in selecting appropriate leadership capabilities and conditions in dealing with the issues:

- For the top issue (dealing with the speed and volume of information flow), the stepwise approach identified five leadership conditions as critical ones in contributing to the issue management. These five leadership dimensions are strategic decision-making, relationship building, team collaboration, communication knowledge management, and ethical orientation; all five identified dimensions demonstrated strong regression coefficients (Table 7.9). However, the stepwise method didn't suggest the dimensions of self-dynamics and organizational structure and culture as significant predictors in dealing with the top issue. This finding supports the idea that managing the speed and flow of information is a complex and demanding challenge for public relations leaders.

- The regression model on the second issue (managing the digital revolution and rise of social media) identified three significant predicting leadership dimensions: communication knowledge management, team collaboration, and strategic decision making (Table 7.10). The stepwise method didn't suggest the dimensions of self-dynamics, ethical orientation, relationship building, and organizational structure and culture as significant predictors in dealing with the second issue.

- For the third issue (improving the measurement of communication effectiveness to demonstrate value), the regression model identified three significant leadership dimensions in issue management: strategic decision making, self-dynamics, and team collaboration (Table 7.11). The stepwise method didn't suggest the dimensions of communication knowledge management, ethical orientation, relationship building, and organizational structure and culture as significant predictors in dealing with the third issue.

- For the fourth issue (being prepared to deal effectively with crises), the regression model identified the dimensions of strategic decision-making, communication knowledge management, and ethical orientation as significant predictors in dealing with this issue (Table 7.12). The stepwise method didn't suggest the dimensions of self-dynamics, team collaboration, relationship building, and organizational structure and culture to be significant in dealing with this issue.

TABLE 7.9 Results of a Stepwise Multiple Regression Analysis on Top Issue ($n = 1,029$)

Predictors: Leadership Dimensions	M	Dependent Variable: Top Issue (Dealing With the Speed and Volume of Information Flow)				
		The Stepwise Model				
		Std. β	t value	R^2	Adjusted R^2	R^2 Change
Constant		4.53	23.82**			
Strategic decision making	6.30	.12	3.47**	.059	.058	.059
Relationship building	5.64	.10	2.83**	.084	.082	.025
Team collaboration	5.91	.09	2.43*	.094	.092	.011
Communication knowledge management	6.10	.08	2.43*	.101	.097	.007
Ethical orientation	5.42	.07	2.06*	.104	.100	.004

Note: $F(5, 1,028) = 23.87$, $p < .01$.

$*p < .05$. $**p < .01$.

TABLE 7.10 Results of a Stepwise Multiple Regression Analysis on Second Issue ($n = 684$)

Predictors: Leadership Dimensions		Dependent Variable: Second Issue (Managing the Digital Revolution and the Rise of Social Media)				
	M		The Stepwise Model			
		Std. β	t value	R^2	Adjusted R^2	R^2 Change
Constant		4.48	22.14**			
Communication knowledge management	6.13	.19	4.74**	.086	.085	.086
Team collaboration	5.70	.18	4.46**	.128	.125	.041
Strategic decision making	6.19	.12	3.00**	.139	.135	.011

Note: $F(3, 683) = 36.63$, $p < .01$.

*$p < .05$. **$p < .01$.

TABLE 7.11 Results of a Stepwise Multiple Regression Analysis on Third Issue ($n = 546$)

Predictors: Leadership Dimensions		Dependent Variable: Third Issue (Improving the Measurement of Communication Effectiveness)				
	M		The Stepwise Model			
		Std. β	t value	R^2	Adjusted R^2	R^2 Change
Constant		3.98	15.79**			
Strategic decision making	6.42	.21	4.85**	.111	.109	.111
Self-dynamics	6.28	.16	3.47**	.148	.145	.037
Team collaboration	5.82	.16	3.37**	.166	.161	.018

Note: $F(5, 545) = 35.93$, $p < .01$.

*$p < .05$. **$p < .01$.

TABLE 7.12 Results of a Stepwise Multiple Regression Analysis on Fourth Issue ($n = 532$)

Predictors: Leadership Dimensions		Dependent Variable: Fourth Issue (Being Prepared to Deal Effectively with Crises)				
	M		The Stepwise Model			
		Std. β	t value	R^2	Adjusted R^2	R^2 Change
Constant		4.24	17.11**			
Strategic decision making	6.44	.21	4.51**	.109	.107	.109
Communication knowledge management	6.30	.17	3.53**	.139	.135	.030
Ethical orientation	5.84	.11	2.40**	.148	.143	.009

Note: $F(3, 531) = 30.55$, $p < .01$.

*$p < .05$. **$p < .01$.

Conclusion

Although we have addressed the uniqueness of each leadership dimension in effective issue management, our global results confirmed that public relations leaders must possess a range of skills and capabilities and then draw from them to varying extents in managing specific issues. Each leadership dimension we tested has some compelling advantages in managing specific issues, whereas all seven leadership dimensions combine to provide a richer capacity and broader range of capabilities for communication leaders to master.

To summarize, the leadership dimensions tested in this global project further confirmed the integrated model of public relations leadership (Meng & Berger, 2013) and should be useful in many practical approaches. First, the dimension of strategic decision making stands out as the most significant leadership condition in various situations and geographic locations. It was the best predicted leadership dimension in dealing with various critical issues and challenging situations in communication practice. Practitioners and some theorists have long argued that public relations leaders need to be involved in strategic decision-making groups in their organizations, and our study confirms that perception in virtually every situation and every country. Perhaps, then, this leadership dimension can be universally endorsed by practitioners in different societies, because it may help practitioners establish culture-free, acceptable, and effective leader behaviors.

Second, the dimension of communication knowledge management appeared to be another critical leadership condition for practitioners to master in managing these four issue and likely many others. Given the nature of the profession, this finding isn't surprising. However, it is crucial for communication leaders to develop relevant cross-cultural training on communication knowledge management and prepare future communication leaders to be able to learn, apply, and convert relevant communication knowledge into effective leader behaviors and practices within a complex and dynamic issue environment globally.

Third, the global results identified the importance of all seven leadership dimensions from the perspective of issue management. Accordingly, effective issue management strategies seem a particularly useful area to integrate leadership skills and capabilities and to concentrate future leadership development efforts in a given organization or culture. A wide range of leadership roles and capabilities must be filled and enacted in different situations. Leadership development efforts in our profession would benefit from a greater focus on leaders' capacity for managing varied challenging issues and influencing strategic decision-making effectively.

Recall that a central theoretical proposition in the integrated model of excellent public relations leadership is that leadership is a complex and multifaceted phenomenon, and it encompasses seven unique, but equally important dimensions (Meng, 2010a, 2010b, 2012, 2013; Meng & Berger, 2013). Although the societal orientation or the cultural preferences might affect whether practitioners select or draw from one leadership dimension over the other in dealing with a specific issue, we suggest that issue-management-based leader behaviors could be universally endorsed and may bear wide implications across cultures.

We also suggest that the different ratings of the seven leadership dimensions in the 12 surveyed countries and regions can be used as a resource guide to those considering (a) more comprehensive leadership preparation for issue management or (b) additional preparation of future communication leaders for assignments in a specific nation. Professionals in a specific situation can select certain leadership dimensions tested in our global study and recombine them into issue management programs that have been specifically tailored to their own circumstances. Each of the dimensions has compelling advantages, and the integrated application of all seven dimensions provides us with a practical set of options for effective issue management.

Note

1. All seven statements were rated on a 7-point scale that ranged from a low of 1 (*this leadership condition or quality contributes little to the successful management of this specific issue*) to a high of 7 (*this leadership condition or quality contributes greatly to the successful management of this specific issue*).

References

Alddory, L., & Toth, E. (2004). Leadership and gender in public relations: Perceived effectiveness of transformational and transactional leadership. *Journal of Public Relations Research, 16*, 157–183.

Bass, B. M., Avolio, B. J., Jung, D. I., & Berson, Y. (2003). Predicting unit performance by assessing transformational and transactional leadership. *Journal of Applied Psychology, 88*, 207–218.

Deetz, S. A., Tracy, S. J., & Simpson, J. L. (2000), *Leading organizations through transition: Communication and cultural change.* Thousand Oaks, CA: Sage.

Dorfman, P. W., & House, R. J. (2004). Cultural influences on organizational leadership. In R. J. House, P. J. Hanges, M. Javidan, P. W. Dorfman, & V. Gupta (Eds.), *Culture, leadership, and organizations: The GLOBE study of 62 countries* (pp. 51–73). Thousands Oak, CA: Sage.

Hair, Jr. J. F., Anderson, R. E., Tatham, R. L., & Black, W. C. (1995). *Multivariate data analysis with readings* (4th ed.). Upper Saddle River, NJ: Prentice Hall.

Hofstede, G. (2001). *Culture's consequences: Comparing values, behaviors, institutions, and organizations across nations* (2nd ed). Thousand Oaks, CA: Sage.

Meng, J. (2010a). Excellent leadership in public relations: An application of multiple-group confirmatory factor analysis models in assessing cross-national measurement invariance. *Dissertation Abstracts International Section A, 70*(8-A), 3086.

Meng, J. (2010b, June). *The generalization and universality of public relations leadership: An application of multiple-group assessment in measurement invariance.* Paper presented at the 60th annual convention of the International Communication Association, Singapore.

Meng, J., Berger, B. K., & Heyman W. (2011). Measuring public relations leadership in the trait approach: A second-order factor model in the dimension of self-dynamics. *Public Relations Journal, 5*(1). Available online at www.prsa.org/Intelligence/PRJournal/Documents/2011WinterMengBergerHeyman.pdf

Meng, J. (2012). Strategic leadership in public relations: An integrated conceptual framework. *Public Relations Review, 38,* 336–338.

Meng, J. (forthcoming). Unpacking the relationship between organizational culture and excellent leadership in public relations: An empirical investigation. *Journal of Communication Management.*

Meng, J., & Berger, B. K. (2013). An integrated model of excellent leadership in public relations: Dimensions, measurement, and validation. *Journal of Public Relations Research, 25,* 141–167.

8

DEVELOPMENT OF FUTURE LEADERS

Yan Jin

The Importance of Developing Future Leaders

Public relations leaders who participated in our global leadership study shared their insights regarding key issues our industry is facing, as well as leadership skills and capabilities that have proved effective in addressing those key issues. One of the emerging top issues is to fully realize the importance of developing future leaders and to identify what leadership skills and capabilities should be carried over to the future needs of our profession.

Numerous leadership books, workshops, and forums have been created to prepare public relations practitioners as PR leaders. Educators have strongly recommended incorporating public relations leadership training in PR curricula, especially at the graduate level. In discussing the standards for a master's degree in public relations, aiming at educating for complexity, the Commission on Public Relations Education (2012) recommended a wide range of strategic public relations management skills. Two leadership related items were ardently advocated (Commission on Public Relations Education, 2012, p. 13):

- Management of an organization's communication functions. This area should include management of people, programs, and resources, as well as communication with an organization's leadership.
- Leadership and entrepreneurship. Leadership topics should include personality types and personality tests, emotional intelligence, creative problem solving, how to influence others, how to inspire a shared vision for the organization, and how to deal with conflict within organizations.

The preceding recommendations touch on at least two facets of public relations leadership: The capability of effective communication with organizational leadership, and the ability as a public relations leader to guide and inspire the communication team. On one hand, a *PR leader* must communicate with *an organization's leader* and/or *leadership team*, such as the CEO and the board, when needed and possible. As Grossman (2013) articulated, public relations practitioners need to know "how to think like a CEO in order to become a better leader" (p. 7). On the other hand, the leadership traits embedded in public relations leadership are distinct from any other types of leadership. For instance, among the six dimensions of leadership (i.e., self-dynamics, ethical orientation, team collaboration, relationship building, strategic decision making, and communication knowledge management) identified by Meng and Berger (2013), the emotional aspect of excellent public relations leadership is implied in the self-dynamics dimension, which is closely related to public relation leaders' self-insight and shared vision (Meng & Berger, 2013).

When the importance of developing future leaders is discussed, Grossman (2013) pointed out its urgency from the organizational leadership perspective:

> Grow leaders, especially future leaders—Today's boards want to know there are a number of possible CEO successors in place; like-wise, one of the CEO's important jobs is to ensure a competent management team across the organization, and to create a solid succession plan. (p. 7)

Grossman (2013) further highlighted General Electric (GE) CEO Jack Welch's emphasis on developing talent and the process of gardening and nourishing future leaders. It is critical for public relations leaders and educators to identify the key ingredients and nutrients most needed for the public relations leadership development mission. Future leaders, with different demographic and cultural backgrounds, might need different training programs for their readiness. For instance, as Luttrell and McLean (2013) pointed out, working with millennials, the new generation of professionals, five steps should be taken: collaboration and innovation, customized jobs and professional development, freedom, mutual respect, and fun at work. Many Public Relations Student Society of America (PRSSA) chapters across the United States have taken agency approaches to immerse students in leadership roles in and outside the classroom.

To fully tackle this important global issue and build on the invaluable insights shared by U.S. practitioners, our global leadership study provides the most recent research-based, empirical evidence regarding (a) 12 approaches that might be used to improve the development of future leaders in different countries and regions, (b) factors underlying these different approaches, (c) demographic differences regarding practitioners' perceptions of the identified approaches, and (d) overall implications for practitioners and educators when it comes to developing future leaders.

Approaches to Improving the Development of Future Leaders

In conducting the global public relations leadership survey, we asked participants to share their insights about developing communication leaders for the future and strengthening the profession. The demand for excellent leaders may be even greater in a dynamic and uncertain future. So we asked participants to indicate to what extent (on a 1–7 scale) they agreed with the relative importance of each of 12 actions that might be taken to improve development of future leaders. The 12 approaches were drawn from the literature and from professional development programs. The mean scores for their responses are indicated throughout the chapter: a mean score of 5 or higher is important; scores approaching 6, or higher, mean it's very important.

Of the 12 approaches, 3 were consistently rated by public relations leaders as most important; indeed, these are among the most consistent findings in the global leadership study. Another five approaches rated as important, whereas the remaining four approached rated as less important.

Most Important Approaches: Top Three People Skills

The most important three approaches are associated with *people skills*:

1.   Strengthen change management skills and capabilities ($M = 5.67$)
2.   Improve the listening skills of professionals ($M = 5.51$)
3.   Enhance conflict management skills ($M = 5.51$)

Strengthening change management capabilities ($M = 5.67$) was rated highest, a strong reflection of the dynamic changes in practice, in organizations, and in the global marketplace. We know that organizational change is driven by internal communication, which affects the cycle time required for change to be processed, understood, and adopted. Thus, managing change in the function to help manage change in organizations to improve performance is a priority that may only become more urgent.

Two other traditionally softer skills—listening and conflict management—were also highly rated (both $M = 5.51$). Listening skills are related to 2 of the 13 ways Grossman (2012) listed as essential to becoming a better leader: "Stop talking and listen now" and "Pick up the phone or walk down the hall to actually talk with someone" (p. 12). Other ways Grossman mentioned, such as "Have the tough conversations that you've been meaning to have" (2012, p. 12), and "communicate bad news in the same way, and with the same zest, as good news" (2012, p. 13) are associated with conflict management skills.

Change often is caused by, involves, and/or leads to conflicts, at smaller or larger scale, within or from outside an organization. In examining programs aimed at preparing managers for their roles at business and management schools in the United States and Europe, White and Verčič (2001) listed a few sources of conflicts in the workplace that challenge the leadership of public relations managers in the United States and Europe such as incomplete information, possibly conflicting objectives, and multiple participants in the decision-making process. According to Moss and Green (2001), making communication policy decisions, counseling management, supervising the work of others, and acting as a catalyst for management decisions were 4 of the 10 key aspects for public relations manager to demonstrate their manager's role and leadership.

For public relations leaders, the daily management function tends to be twofold (Jin, 2010): On one hand, they need to manage their staff and communicate with the employees about the group tasks and connect them with missions and rapport; on the other hand, public relations managers report to the top management, and make recommendations on decisions. Both demand appropriate handling of emotions, constant negotiation, and strategic positioning to accomplish tasks and improve relationships. Therefore, to manage change effectively, future public relations leaders must know and be efficient and ethical in managing conflicts. It's no wonder that public relations leaders across the countries and regions that we surveyed consistently named these three intertwined people skills as the most important approaches for developing future public relations leaders.

Five Other Important Approaches

Five other approaches were rated by our global public relations leadership survey participants as important to developing future leaders:

4. Develop better measures to document value ($M = 5.34$)
5. Strengthen the business component of education ($M = 5.26$)
6. Increase cultural understanding and sensitivity ($M = 5.10$)
7. Enhance skills to cope with stress ($M = 5.06$)
8. Enhance the emotional intelligence of professionals ($M = 5.05$)

As elaborated on in previous chapters, the importance of measurement is emphasized here as an item to be carried over from current public relations leaders to future generations of public relations leaders. Also, the business component of education and increasing cultural understanding are items widely recognized by practitioners and educators as critical for preparing future public relations leaders (Commission on Public Relations Education, 2012).

Bass (1985) suggested the involvement of emotions and their values in the leadership transforming processes. Obtaining insights from public relations practitioners in the United Kingdom, Yeomans (2007) highlighted the role of emotions in rational decision-making and the fact that "[e]motion and emotion management skills tacitly accompany the many activities performed by a public relations executive in delivering a personal service to journalist and clients" (p. 217). Among the six dimensions of leadership (i.e., self-dynamics, ethical orientation, team collaboration, relationship building, strategic decision making, and communication knowledge management) identified by Meng and Berger (2013), the emotional aspect of excellent public relations leadership is inherent in the self-dynamics dimension, which is closely related to public relation leaders' self-insight and shared vision.

Emotional intelligence and the capability of coping with stress are related items, both relatively new to the realm of public relations leadership development practice and research. In terms of emotional intelligence, Jin (2010) posited that emotional leadership is one key dimension of effective public relations leadership. Based on a national survey among U.S. public relations leaders, empathy was identified as one of the significant predictors of public relations leaders' competency in gaining employee's trust, managing employees' frustration and optimism, as well as handling decision-making conflicts (Jin, 2010).

Empathy has been identified as the most important emotion for transformational leadership (Salovey & Mayer, 1990), which is defined as the ability to comprehend another's feelings and to reexperience them oneself. It allows leaders to guide emotional responses of their followers and enhance the emotional consistence between leaders and followers (Salovey & Mayer, 1990). Summarizing the role of empathy in public relations leadership, Jin (2010) noted that strong emotional self-management usually includes the ability to recognize emotion in others compared to just being better at creating and expressing emotions.

In a busy and noisy world, the ability to manage stress and understand the roles of emotions in the work place is also emphasized. This echoes the importance for public relations practitioners to effectively cope with work–life conflict caused by a variety of stressors (Jin, Sha, Shen, & Jiang, 2012), based on the results from a national survey of Public Relations Society of America (PRSA) members. Jin et al. (2012) identified three sources of work–life conflict, as reported by practitioners in the United States: behavior driven, work driven, and life driven. Survey participants also reported strong preferences in using more proactive conflict coping strategies, such as rational action and positive thinking.

Further, it was found that although behavior-driven work-life stressors are associated with proactive coping strategies such as rational action and positive thinking, work-driven stressors tended to trigger more avoidance. Non-work-driven stressors seem to predict more passive coping tendencies, such as denial and avoidance. The tendency and efficiency in using more proactive coping to deal with different types of stressors can be an indicator of both emotional intelligence and the skill level of coping with stress among public relations leaders.

Four Other Less Important Approaches

Four systemic approaches in the profession were rated much lower in terms of the perceived importance among public relations leaders participating in the survey:

9. Impose tough penalties on ethical violators ($M = 4.51$)
10. Urge associations to work together to develop leaders ($M = 4.37$)
11. Develop a global education curriculum ($M = 4.24$)
12. Require professional accreditation or licensing ($M = 3.90$)

Accreditation or licensing ($M = 3.90$), a core global education program ($M = 4.24$), urging professional associations to jointly tackle the leadership issue ($M = 4.37$), and firmly punishing ethical violators ($M = 4.51$) are important professional actions, but survey participants said they are significantly less important to the development of future leaders than the other approaches. The relatively lower level of perceived importance might be because among the surveyed countries and regions, not all of them have an accreditation or licensing body in place. For many countries or regions, the infrastructure and available resources of the professional associations might not allow them to jointly address leadership issues yet. When it comes to ethical matters in public relations practice, cultural, historical, and socio-economic factors play significant roles and make it almost impossible, for now, to have or require a standard ethical rule across the globe or to enforce such a code.

Demographic Variations

Among the 12 leadership development approaches, some significant differences associated with the survey participants' demographics, such as years of experience, country, and gender. For example, the most experienced practitioners (>20 years) rated listening skills and cultural understanding significantly higher than did less experienced groups. The least experienced practitioners gave significantly higher ratings to most other approaches. The three Latin American countries gave the highest mean scores to 7 of the 12 approaches. Of the 12 surveyed countries/ regions, 11 ranked change management skills at the top of the list, whereas Germany ranked it second and just below conflict management skills. Participants two or more levels below the top leader rated all 12 approaches significantly higher than did top leaders or their direct reports. Women rated all 12 approaches significantly higher than did men.

Some of these demographic variations are in line with previous studies. Public relations manager demographics (Moss & Green, 2001), based on a case study of British Telecom, and organizational characteristics (DeSanto, Moss, & Newman, 2007; Moss & Green, 2001; Moss, Newman, & DeSanto, 2005) primarily based on a survey of practitioners in the United Kingdom and the United States, were found to have direct impact on public relations leadership.

Gender-related findings, however, seem to suggest that female public relations leaders place more weight on developing future leaders on all fronts regardless of their nationality or hierarchical position. Interestingly, public relations leadership research has consistently suggested the significant role gender plays in the development of the public relations profession (Aldoory & Toth, 2004). Recently, Jin et al. (2012) examined how public relations practitioners in the United States cope with work–life conflict through a national survey of PRSA members. They found that female practitioners reported more coping behaviors than did male practitioners, everything else being equal. These survey findings in the United States, and now at the global level, seem to indicate that female public relations leaders are keener to coping with stress and more aware of the importance of developing future leaders.

Two Critical Factors Underlay Leadership Development Approaches

We used exploratory factor analysis on the 12 approaches to determine whether any relationships existed among them. Two factors were extracted, which we labeled *self-development approaches* and *systemic development approaches* (see Table 8.1).

TABLE 8.1 Exploratory Factor Analysis with Oblique Rotation on 12 Leadership Development Approaches

12 Leadership Development Approaches	Rotated Factor Loadings	
	Factor 1	Factor 2
Factor 1: Self-Development Approaches		
• Improve the listening skills of professionals	.89	.21
• Develop training to enhance the emotional intelligence of PR professionals	.76	−.03
• Enhance conflict management skills	.69	−.07
• Increase cultural understanding and sensitivity	.59	−.09
• Strengthen change management skills and capabilities	.55	−.15
• Enhance professional skills in coping with work–related stress	.54	−.15
Factor 2: Systematic Development Approaches		
• Require professional accreditation or licensing	−.12	.86
• Develop a core global education curriculum	−.01	.81
• Impose tough penalties on ethical violators	.01	.71
• Develop better measures to document the value and contributions of public relations	.05	.63
• Urge professional associations to work together to develop leaders	.26	.57
• Strengthen the business/economic component of communication education programs	.20	.48
Eigenvalues	5.00	1.18
% of variance	41.70	9.81
Cronbach's alpha (standardized items)	.80	.82

Note: Total variance explained by the two factors is 51.51%. The variables listed in the table by rotated factor loading size (i.e., from large to small).

Factor 1: Self-development approaches. Self-development approaches include six interrelated approach items ($M = 5.32$, $SD = 5.76$):

- Improve listening skills
- Enhance emotional intelligence
- Enhance conflict management skills
- Increase cultural understanding, sensitivity
- Strengthen change management skills
- Enhance skills to cope with stress

Self-development approaches are a strong factor: The Eigenvalue is 5.00; the Cronbach's alpha (standardized items) is .80; and it accounts for 41.70% of variance in the sample. This group of approaches focuses on individual development of what have unfortunately been called "soft skills," as well as the power of self-insight and awareness, which is one of the crucial seven dimensions of leadership.

As an illustration of the importance of self-development approach, we share some quotes from public relations leaders we interviewed in the data collection process; they spoke about the needs and trends of future leaders. For example, one public relations leader in South Korea mentioned the two core issues for future leaders:

> Deep love and understanding of the organization, not the technique or method, but to think about how to make the organization remain as a meaningful entity to the public. Even if the senior managers/members feel uncomfortable, we must do things that would be useful to the entire organization . . . Leadership of harmony between management with experience and employees with creative minds.

In terms of balancing work–life conflict, one public relations leader from the Chinese-speaking areas commented that future leaders must have the following preparation:

> They might find it even harder to separate their personal life from their work life, because communications will evolve to a point where it's essentially instantaneous, it's essentially happening all the time. They're going to be expected to be a lot more mobile than what we are expected to be at the moment.

Factor 2: Systemic development approaches. Systemic development approaches include ($M = 4.60$, $SD = 7.14$):

- Require accreditation, licensing
- Develop a global education curriculum

- Penalize ethical violators
- Develop better measures
- Strengthen the business component of education
- Urge associations to work together to develop leaders

The Eigenvalue for this factor is 1.18; the Cronbach's alpha (standardized items) is .82; and it accounts for 9.81% of variance in the sample. Together, the two factors account for 51.5% of variance, a good outcome. This group of approaches focuses on strengthening the overall profession through improved education (more business and cultural knowledge) and the development and spread of core values and standards (codes of ethics, accreditation, and measurement). Such changes might be best accomplished through the combined efforts of professional associations and educational institutions.

To illustrate the impact of structural factors, Jin et al. (2012) found that organizational factors can determine how practitioners in the United States cope with work–life conflict. As organizational demands increased to separate life from work, more instructions seemed necessary for employees to better cope with work–life conflicts. Positive thinking, as a type of cognitive coping, tends to increase when there is more immediate supervisor support and to decrease when an organization's work–life culture is skewed toward promoting work as the sole priority. Therefore, public relations leaders need to strive for support from organizational leaders and to advocate for an organizational structure that supports a work–life balance for employees working in the communication team.

Implications for Professional Development and Public Relations Education Programs

In the managerial leadership theories overview, Meng (2012) identified the trait approach as one of the predominant leadership frameworks, which focuses on identifying personal attributes or superior qualities that are essential to effective leadership. To better prepare communication leaders for a dynamic and uncertain future, our survey participants point to efforts that focus on (a) the *software or soft skills of individuals* to increase self-insights and reflection, to improve interpersonal skills to manage change and conflict, and to create a greater sense of awareness of other cultures and (b) the *hardware or professional and educational structures* that produce measurement skills and guidelines, ethical frameworks, and knowledge of the practice and the economic and global environments in which they occur.

One interesting observation through our study is that, although measurement is crucial, as are social media skills, the increasing complexity and uncertainty of the world and the practice emphasize the need for improved listening and conflict management skills, increased cultural understanding and better management of new technologies, especially for the next generations of public relations leaders. Systematic changes, such as ethics codes, accreditation and core education curricula, are also important, but far less so than soft skills in most countries.

The Software or the Soft Skills of People

The software includes the following:

- Increase reflection and self-insights
- Improve interpersonal skills for conflict, change management
- Create greater awareness of others, cultures

As Berger (2012) pointed out, "soft skills are the future" (p. 9), the importance of which has been one of the most consistent findings across cultures when it comes to developing future leaders. One of the most important leadership skills, yet the least studied one in public relations literature, is the role of emotion in public relations management and leadership (Jin, 2010). Humphrey (2002) called for more research on emotional leadership linking emotions to conflict and coping, because conflict has always been seen as an emotionally arousing process that can lead to feelings of hostility (Fox & Spector, 1999) and that is a very stressful process for both leaders and followers (Humphrey, 2002). As Dasborough and Ashkanasy (2002) posited, leadership is intrinsically an emotional process, where leaders display emotion and attempt to evoke emotion in their members, which echoed the call from Moss and Green (2001) for mounting a "challenge to the rational model of management" (p. 124).

Effective leaders must find constructive ways of reacting to the emotionality of organizational colleagues and understand the nature and process of conflict management styles and strategies, including identifying the emotional and cognitive antecedents of rational conflicts in the workplace (Gayle & Preiss, 1998). This is important because organizational conflict interactions have emotional consequences for supervisors, subordinates, and coworkers, which have the potential to damage organizational relationships and productivity. Based on these pioneering works, Jin (2010), based on a national survey of public relations leaders in the United States, pointed out that public relations leaders in general should have the ability to comprehend others' feelings, as well as to reexperience those feelings themselves, to communicate mutual understanding and compassion in the workplace.

Given the importance of integrating empathy, sensitivity, and self-awareness (the essential core of transformational leadership style) into future public relations practitioners' training and preparation, public relations educators can use several approaches in their classrooms to do so (Jin, 2010): First, empathy and self-awareness training and development should be integrated into leadership and management courses, with specific discussions, assignments and in-class activities on how to be more sensitive in detecting others' feelings and expressing one's feelings appropriately, to solve the problems in the most sensible and effective way.

Second, to apply the understanding and practice of at-work empathy to real-client settings, simulation team approaches should be taken in hands-on courses such as public relations campaigns. Student teams can be well structured internally, with a public relations manager and team members who are assigned specific roles. In addition, the team leaders would report to the client as well as to the instructor, who would facilitate practice of those teams' management skills and empathetic communication among employees and with the top management (the client and the instructor).

Third, empathy, sensitivity, and self-awareness skills and effectiveness should be incorporated and evaluated as an item on the team evaluation sheet so that each student team's demonstration of compassion and sensitivity can be observed and assessed from the management's perspective. In the mean time, the same empathy, sensitivity, and self-insight measures can be used in team member peer evaluations to assess the within-group employee communication quality and leadership effectiveness. As insightfully pointed out by one of the public relations leaders in Russia during the interview session, "The PR profession is not a profession of soldiers of fortune. It's a profession of intelligent and thoughtful people.

The Hardware or the Professional and Educational Structures

The hardware includes the following:

- Improve measurement skills and standards
- Bring ethical codes to life
- Increase knowledge of business, global environment

In addition to continuing to strengthen public relations research and measurement training for students and practitioners, more ethics training, business knowledge, and cultural orientation are critical pillars for constructing and supporting future public relations leaders, who must function and thrive at the global level.

Organizational structural support is one of the facilitators, according to recent research studying how public relations practitioners perceive and handle work–life conflicts in the United States. For instance, in examining public relations practitioners' work–life conflict experiences and coping mechanisms, Shen, Jiang, Jin, and Sha (2013) found a significant impact of the larger organizational environment and professional association on public relations practitioners' conflict experiences: A negative work environment could increase workers' self-reported levels of work–life conflict, whereas a strong identification with their profession and larger professional community could help mitigate such conflict. As the authors pointed out, the heightened level of work–life conflict could sharply discourage workers' proactive coping mechanism.

Global public relations education has been a priority item for public relations educators. The Commission on Public Relations Education (2012) recommended a wide range of strategic public relations management skills, including the following:

- Understanding reasons for varying definitions of public relations, strategic communication and communication management in different parts of the world.
- Understanding how social, economic, political and cultural dimensions influence how public relations is practiced.
- Understanding how public relations is practiced and studied in different parts of the world and the differences and similarities that exist.
- Having knowledge of major public relations theories, approaches and schools of thoughts developed in EU, Americas, Asia and Australia.
- Appreciating how cultural distinctions and socio-economic and political particularities influence public relations practice in different regions and countries throughout the world.
- Recognizing the social, political, economic and cultural factors that may alter public relations practices, even within one country.
- Appreciating how advanced global public relations theories can be used and applied in strategic decision-making.
- Appreciating cross-cultural and intercultural communication influences on public relations globally.
- Understanding relationship-building and relationship management across national and regional borders. (p. 15)

The preceding recommendations, many of which reflect the crucial need for cultural knowledge and a global vision for practice, need to be implemented more fully during public relations curriculum revision and innovation, especially for advanced professional education and training programs.

Conclusion: Crossing Over to the Future

How to build stronger public relations leadership is an essential agenda item for researchers and practitioners. Berger and Reber (2006) found that to "strengthen leadership skills in the profession" is one of the most important public relations issues, and "stronger PR leadership" emerged as the most needed public relations resource.

As summarized in Jin's (2010) study, it is crucial for public relations educators and professional associations to integrate transformational leadership elements, such as empathy, compassion, sensitivity, relationship building, and innovation, in classrooms and workshops to help prepare leaders for the future. Excellent public relations leaders should not only be good at motivating and sharing positive emotions, but also should be skillful in comforting employees under stress and channeling the negativity out of the workplace.

In the context of managing conflict with high emotional intelligence, Jin's (2010) study also shed light on the following indicators of public relations leadership competency, which imply that future public relations leaders should:

- demonstrate empathy as a core emotional trait, which drives public relations leaders' accurate assessment of employees' emotions and helps leaders to address those emotions with sensitivity and understanding;
- be flexible in decision-making power sharing, and be strategic in the power-sharing negotiation process at the same time;
- be experienced in motivating and maintaining optimism in the workplace by creating enthusiasm and excitement among employees;
- know how to take accommodative actions and express them when confronted by disagreeing employees, if resolving the disagreement will lead to task efficiency; and
- enhance negotiation and influence gaining knowledge and skills when communicating disagreements with top management in decision-making conflicts.

When the core quality of leaders is touched upon, Florence Mpaayei (2008) said,

> The moral authority of leaders is an essential ingredient to human security. Our attitudes determine whether we are able to resolve conflict. It requires real listening and a readiness to consider new ways. And if we are to be a bridge, we have to be willing to be walked on.

The essential ingredients here include the right attitude, conflict resolution skills, real listening, and readiness for new ideas and innovation. Yes, indeed, the future is uncertain. The findings of our global public relations leadership study shed light on what's needed for those who want to be ready and who are willing to cross over.

References

Aldoory, L., & Toth, E. (2004). Leadership and gender in public relations: Perceived effectiveness of transformational and transactional leadership styles. *Journal of Public Relations Research, 16*(2), 157–183.

Bass, B. M. (1985). *Leadership and performance.* New York, NY: Free Press.

Berger, B. K. (2012, Winter). The need for speed: public relations leadership study highlights global trends, future needs. *The Public Relations Strategist,* pp. 8–9.

Berger, B. K., & Reber, B. (2006). *Gaining influence in public relations.* Mahwah, NJ: Erlbaum.

Commission on Public Relations Education (2012, October). The curriculum in a master's degree program. In *Standards for a master's degree in public relations: Educating for complexity* (pp. 11–16). New York: Public Relations Society of America.

Dasborough, M. T., & Ashkanasy, N. M. (2002). Emotion and attribution of intentionality in leader-member relationships. *The Leadership Quarterly, 13*(5), 615–634.

DeSanto, B., Moss, D., & Newman, A. (2007). Building an understanding of the main elements of management in the communication/public relations context: A study of U.S. practitioners' practices. *Journalism & Mass Communication Quarterly, 84*(3), 439–454.

Fox, S., & Spector, P. E. (1999). A model of work-frustration aggression. *Journal of Organizational Behavior, 20,* 915–931.

Gayle, B. M., & Preiss, R. M. (1998). Assessing emotional organizational conflicts. *Management Communication Quarterly, 12*(2), 280–302.

Grossman, D. R. (2012, Winter). 13 ways to become a better leader: Focusing your energy in the new year. *The Public Relations Strategist*, pp. 12–13.

Grossman, D. R. (2013, Summer). How to think like a CEO: Become a better leader. *The Public Relations Strategist*, pp. 6–8.

Humphrey, R. H. (2002). The many faces of emotional leadership. *The Leadership Quarterly, 13*(5), 493–504.

Jin, Y. (2010). Emotional leadership as a key dimension of public relations leadership: A national survey of public relations leaders. *Journal of Public Relations Research, 22,* 159–181.

Jin, Y., Sha, B-L., Shen, H., & Jiang, H. (2012, October). *Tuning in to the rhythm: The role of coping in strategic management of work-life conflicts in the public relations profession.* Paper presented at the Annual International Conference of Public Relations Society of America, San Francisco, CA.

Luttrell, R., & McLean, D. (2013, April). A new generation of professionals: Working with millennials in 5 easy steps. *Public Relations Tactics*, p. 15.

Mpaayei, F. (2008, July). Addressing the Root Causes of Human Insecurity. Remarks given at Caux Forum for Human Security, Caux, Switzerland.

Meng, J. (2012). Public relations leadership: An integrated conceptual framework. *Public Relations Review, 38,* 336–338.

Meng, J., & Berger, B. (2013). An integrated model of excellent leadership in public relations: Dimensions, measurement, and validation. *Journal of Public Relations Research, 25*(2), 141–167.

Moss, D., & Green, R. (2001). Re-examining the manager's role in public relations: What management and public relations research teaches us. *Journal of Communication Management, 6*(2), 118–132.

Moss, D., Newman, A., & DeSanto, B. (2005). What do communication managers do? Defining and refining the core elements of management in a public relations/corporate communication context. *Journalism & Mass Communication Quarterly, 82*(4), 873–890.

Salovey, P., & Mayer, J. D. (1990). Emotional intelligence. *Imagination, Cognition and Personality, 9*(3), 185–211.

Shen, H., Jiang, H., Jin, Y., & Sha, B.-L. (2013, June). *Work-life conflict and coping: Challenging the individual-centric norm.* Paper presented at the Annual Conference of International Communication Association, London, England.

White, J., & Verčič, D. (2001). An examination of possible obstacles to management acceptance of public relations' contribution to decision making, planning and organization functioning. *Journal of Communication Management, 6*(2), 194–200.

Yeomans, L. (2007). Emotion in public relations: A neglected phenomenon. *Journal of Communication Management, 11*(3), 212–221.

9

PERCEPTIONS OF LEADERS, ORGANIZATIONS, AND THE PROFESSION

Elina Erzikova and Baiba Pētersone

The complex nature of contemporary public relations calls for a better understanding of professional leadership. The diversity of current public relations activities requires that public relations managers develop strong leadership skills including relationship building, strategic planning, decision making and problem solving, and so on.

A number of recent studies (Berger & Reber, 2006; Choi & Choi, 2009; Jin, 2010; Meng, Berger, Gower, & Heyman, 2012; Meng, Berger, & Heyman, 2011; Werder & Holtzhausen, 2009) have taken an in-depth look at a variety of aspects of public relations leadership. For example, Choi and Choi (2009) found that assertiveness, commitment, confidence, and responsibility are important public relations leadership traits. In addition, the researchers argued that such behaviors as providing a clear vision and acting as a change agent are most essential in demonstrating the importance of public relations contributions to organizational success.

The current study takes research on public relations leadership to a new—global—level. This chapter focuses on individual perceptions of public relations practitioners from 23 countries who participated in the global online survey. It explores their insights about leaders and leadership, the role of gender in leadership, organizational conditions for excellent leadership, and status of the profession worldwide.

Findings

In the following section, the findings are organized in five subsections. The first four sections discuss self-perceptions about (a) leaders and leadership, (b) gender, (c) organizations, and (d) the public relations profession (Table 9.1). The Summated Leadership Index—scores that describe the conditions for leadership in each country and two regions (Chinese-speaking and German-speaking countries) of the study—can be found in the fifth subsection (Table 9.2). We used the mean scores of participants in the 10 countries and two regions (Chinese-speaking and German-speaking countries) for comparisons in this chapter. Given the wide range in the number of survey participants in these countries and regions, the comparisons are largely descriptive. The survey instrument used a 7-point Likert-type scale ranging from 1 (*strongly disagree*) to 7 (*strongly agree*).

Perceptions About Leaders and Leadership

Three survey items examined respondents' self-perceptions about leaders and leadership development (Table 9.1, Items 1–3). In this regard, Meng et al. (2012) argued that the desire and passion to lead is one of nine characteristics of excellent leadership. In our study, many respondents considered themselves leaders in the field ($M = 5.66$), and most in this study desired to be leaders ($M = 6.15$). Further, men perceived themselves as leaders more strongly than did women.

Participants from the United States ($M = 6.17$), United Kingdom ($M = 5.91$), and Germany ($M = 5.85$) believed more strongly that they were leaders than did respondents from most other countries. Respondents from these three countries also expressed the strongest desire to become leaders. Russia ($M = 4.41$) was at the bottom of the list on the statement "I consider myself to be a leader in communication management," and Estonian and Latvian respondents ($M = 4.99$) showed the weakest aspirations to become leaders.

Apparently, Russian respondents hesitated to call themselves "leaders." There are at least two explanations for this. First, compared to the United States, those who head Russian organizations are not commonly called "organizational leaders." They are labeled a "director" or "manager." In Russian culture, a leader is an individual who has been *publicly recognized* for his or her leadership effort. In other words, people perceive a company's head to be a leader if his or her deeds transcend the organizational boundaries.

Second, Russian participants were younger than their global peers, and it is possible that their relatively short work experiences did not allow them to call themselves "individuals who lead the industry or organization." The same explanation may also apply to Estonia and Latvia, two other countries in which the respondents' inclination to describe themselves as leaders was weaker. Research on public relations in Central and East Europe shows that the application and growth of Western-style public relations is very recent (e.g., Ławniczak, 2001; Ławniczak, Rydzak, & Trębecki, 2003; Pētersone, 2006; Pūre, 2011; Tampere, 2004; Verčic, Grunig & Grunig, 1996). Here, the first public relations developments can be traced to the early 1990s. It is possible that in such a relatively short time, public relations practitioners have not been able to advance to senior leadership positions and, therefore, cannot describe themselves as leaders.

At the same time, respondents from the three countries—Estonia, Latvia, and Russia—appeared to be ambitious, because many of them did want to become leaders in the field. This desire perhaps contributed to respondents' optimism about the future of public relations in their countries.

TABLE 9.1 Mean Comparisons on Leadership Perceptions Across 12 Units ($N = 4,464$)

Statement #	German-speaking countries	Chile	Chinese speaking countries	Latvia & Estonia	Mexico	Russia	South Korea	Spain	U.K.	U.S.	Brazil	India	Total	F Value
	$n = 1,773$	$n = 156$	$n = 141$	$n = 142$	$n = 213$	$n = 215$	$n = 205$	$n = 210$	$n = 139$	$n = 827$	$n = 303$	$n = 140$	$N = 4,464$	$df = 11, 4,452$
1	5.85	5.37	5.23	5.17	5.54	4.41	5.20	4.78	5.91	6.17	5.50	5.68	5.66	40.15**
2[a]	6.45	5.65	5.42	4.99	5.81	5.61	5.35	5.54	6.29	6.40	6.21	6.39	6.15	36.90**
3	4.96	4.87	5.67	4.88	5.31	5.13	4.11	4.89	5.81	5.75	4.68	5.57	5.13	31.17**
4	6.58	6.77	6.23	5.78	6.74	6.21	4.80	6.73	6.73	6.73	6.75	6.41	6.50	74.45**
5[a]	5.63	5.01	4.27	4.64	5.20	4.12	3.87	5.70	5.68	5.24	5.16	5.11	5.25	31.67**
6[a]	4.09	4.12	3.76	4.51	4.43	4.23	4.05	4.54	4.99	4.66	4.20	3.96	4.27	9.39**
7	4.61	4.71	4.82	4.75	5.26	4.14	4.00	4.70	4.50	4.86	4.45	5.23	4.66	8.79**
8	4.63	4.57	4.96	4.70	5.05	4.48	4.55	4.44	4.58	4.82	4.25	5.50	4.67	7.51**
9[a]	5.39	4.72	5.10	5.15	5.00	4.94	4.82	5.25	5.34	5.09	4.39	5.71	5.16	9.59**
10	3.62	4.44	4.31	3.54	3.83	4.02	4.59	3.99	2.75	3.54	3.76	3.94	3.73	12.13**
11	3.32	3.34	4.04	3.30	3.55	3.19	4.11	3.31	3.47	3.62	3.17	3.61	3.44	8.01**
12	4.98	5.03	5.22	5.35	5.79	5.30	4.95	4.75	5.06	5.14	5.77	5.97	5.16	17.39**

Note: Statements of leadership perceptions: Statements of leadership perceptions: 1. I consider myself to be a leader in communication management. 2. I want to be a leader in communication management. 3. I learn more about excellent leadership from role models and/or mentors on the job than from university education or management development programs. 4. Males or females can be equally capable leaders in public relations. 5. I prefer to work for a male leader on the job. 6. Females have better interpersonal communication skills than males. 7. The highest ranking PR professional in my organization is an excellent leader. 8. My organization encourages and practices two-way communication. 9. The CEO or top executive in my organization understands the value of PR. 10. Leadership in public relations is different from leadership in other fields. 11. Leadership skills are more important than communication skills in leading a public relations unit or department. 12. I am optimistic about the future of the public relations profession in my country.

** $p < .01$.

[a] Reverse-coded item.

Participants indicated that they learned more about excellent leadership from role models and/or mentors on the job than from university education or management development programs ($M = 5.13$). More experienced professionals (>20 years) rated the power of role models significantly higher than did less experienced professionals. Countries with the highest mean scores for this statement included the United Kingdom ($M = 5.81$), United States ($M = 5.75$), China ($M = 5.67$), and India ($M = 5.57$). South Korea ($M = 4.11$) and Brazil ($M = 4.68$) had the lowest mean scores.

The preference for learning about excellent leadership from role models and mentors rather than university programs opens an interesting avenue for discussion about the quality of higher education curricula in public relations. Does it mean that universities do not provide their graduates with leadership training opportunities? This question becomes especially valid at a time when university programs around the world continue to increase.

For example, two studies in Latvia (Pētersone, 2006; Pūre, n.d.), more thoroughly discussed later in this book, showed that industry professionals believed that university graduates do not possess practical communication job-related skills and have to be retrained by their first employers. Of course, it's possible that the respondents in their evaluation of learning experiences focused only on their most recent and applied leadership skill acquisition opportunities on the job, such as team management and coordination, strategic planning, budgeting, and so forth. More academic leadership qualities that are encouraged in educational settings, including critical thinking, analytical reasoning, and reflectiveness may become taken for granted over time.

Perceptions About Gender

A set of survey items focused on perceptions of gender and leadership in public relations (Table 9.1, Items 4–6). Participants strongly agreed that women and men can be equally capable leaders in public relations ($M = 6.50$). Mean scores were highest in Chile ($M = 6.77$) and Brazil ($M = 6.75$) and lowest in South Korea ($M = 4.80$). Although respondents believed that women and men can succeed as leaders, both women ($M = 5.09$) and men ($M = 5.41$) indicated that they preferred to work for a male leader. This preference was expressed most strongly in Spain ($M = 5.70$), the United Kingdom ($M = 5.68$), and Germany ($M = 5.63$), but far less so in South Korea ($M = 3.87$), Russia ($M = 4.12$), and China ($M = 4.27$).

Across the countries and regions in the study, men ($M = 4.70$) felt more strongly than women ($M = 3.88$) that women have better interpersonal communication skills. Ratings were highest in the United Kingdom ($M = 4.99$) and the United States ($M = 4.66$) and lowest in China ($M = 3.76$) and India ($M = 3.96$).

It appeared the study brought contradictory results: Although strongly believing that women and men can perform as leaders equally well, our participants nevertheless said they preferred to work for a male leader. This finding possibly indicates socially desirable responses to the question about equal capability. Another explanation may be derived from the wording of the statements: The first statement sounded general and hypothetical—"Males or females can be equally capable leaders in public relations"—whereas the second was concrete and personal—"I prefer to work for a male leader on the job." Finally, participants might have been trying to be realistic in their preference because the majority of leaders worldwide are men (Zenger & Folkman, 2012). The preference for male leadership may simply reflect the existing hierarchies in organizations today.

This study seems to support research on sex stereotypes, which illustrated that despite the rise of women as leaders and managers during the last quarter of the 20th century, leadership and management are still perceived as masculine attributes (Bass & Bass, 2008). This implies that women face a double challenge in organizations: They need to prove their personal legitimacy as both professionals and leaders.

The study revealed a gender bias among public relations practitioners we surveyed, supporting Zenger and Folkman's (2012) statement that there is, if not actual then certainly, perceptual discrimination toward women in the workplace. In U.S. public relations, an empirically documented gendered pay gap has existed for 30 years (Dozier, Sha, & Shen, 2013). After controlling for such variables as years of professional experience, manager role enactment, participation in management decision-making, income-suppressing career interruptions and career specialization, these researchers concluded that "women are paid less than men because they are women" (Dozier et al., 2013, p. 13).

Meanwhile, an integrative biosocial approach in the psychology of gender has led to a proposition that "in many ways, men and women within any culture are more alike than they are different" (Kenrick, Trost, & Sundie, 2004, p. 75). Although, for example, women are less aggressive and more nurturing than are men (Hines, 2004), environmental factors (e.g., social, cultural, developmental) can alleviate or accentuate the sex differences induced by hormones (Hampson & Moffat, 2004).

Further, public relations scholars Aldoory and Toth (2002) argued that "there are differences between women and men, not based on biological gender, but rather based on gender role orientations that predict behavior" (p. 125). Accordingly, Bass, Avolio, and Atwater (1996) found that women's leadership styles appeared to be more transformational, whereas men's behaviors tended to be more transactional. This finding is another reason to support women on their road to leadership positions.

Perceptions About Organization

Three items explored the organizational conditions for excellent leadership in public relations (Table 9.1, Items 7–9). When asked to rate the performance of the highest ranking public relations practitioner in the organization, top leaders rated themselves significantly higher ($M = 5.32$) than did professionals who were one level below the top leader ($M = 4.28$) and those who were two levels or lower in the organizational hierarchy ($M = 4.14$). Ratings were lowest in South Korea ($M = 4.00$) and Russia ($M = 4.14$). There were statistically significant differences between leaders' self-perceptions of their performance and followers' assessments ($F = 204.41$) across all countries and regions.

The study revealed that the lower the positions participants occupied in the organizational hierarchy, the less favorable opinions they held about the top PR leader's performance. This finding suggests that "minding the gap" within a public relations unit is a vital process. Otherwise, this gap may affect not only internal but also external relationship dynamics. It is logical to assume that a public relations leader failing to create understanding and harmony in his or her unit might not be able to build effective relations with external publics.

Further, top leaders ($M = 5.05$) believed more strongly than did followers (at one level below, $M = 4.48$, and two or more levels lower, $M = 4.35$) that their organizations encourage and practice two-way communication. Scores across countries and regions were quite consistent.

Top-level leaders also rated their CEOs' understanding of the value of public relations significantly higher ($M = 5.41$) than practitioners who were one level removed ($M = 5.11$) and two levels or more removed ($M = 4.86$). Ratings were highest in India ($M = 5.71$), Germany ($M = 5.39$), and the United Kingdom ($M = 5.34$), and lowest was in Brazil ($M = 4.39$).

Importantly, the CEOs' understanding of the value of public relations ($M = 5.16$) was rated significantly higher than was the performance evaluation of top communication leaders ($M = 4.66$).

Perceptions About the Profession

The respondents were also asked to reveal their insights on the profession of public relations and its future (Table 9.1, Items 10–12). Participants appeared to believe that leadership in public relations is not very different from leadership in other fields ($M = 3.73$). The mean score was highest in South Korea ($M = 4.59$) and lowest in the United Kingdom ($M = 2.75$).

Participants thought communication skills may be a little more important than leadership skills ($M = 3.44$). Almost all countries scored low on this issue; the largest gap was between South Korea ($M = 4.11$) and Brazil ($M = 3.17$).

It appeared that participants believed in a universal nature of leadership. Indeed, at least 22 universal positive attributes of leadership (e.g., honesty, trustworthiness, informed, dynamic, just, dependable) have been identified (House, Hanges, Javidan, Dorfman, & Gupta, 2004). In other words, a complex and multidimensional concept of leadership transcends boundaries of organizations, occupations, and cultures. This gives the opportunity for public relations practitioners to collaborate with other communication disciplines (e.g., adverting, marketing) in leadership training. To reach the highest degree of effectiveness, this endeavor should be coupled with instruction in the communication skills that our participants regarded as being a little more important than leadership abilities.

Respondents seemed to be optimistic about the future of the public relations profession in their countries ($M = 5.16$), with India ($M = 5.97$), Mexico ($M = 5.79$), and Brazil ($M = 5.77$) expressing the highest degree of optimism. Spain ($M = 4.75$), South Korea ($M = 4.95$), and Germany ($M = 4.98$) appeared to be the least optimistic.

The Summated Leadership Index

In order to understand the conditions for leadership on a country and/or region basis, we summed the mean scores of three statements that dealt with the performance of the highest ranking public relations practitioner, the extent of two-way communication in the organization, and the CEO's understanding of the value of public relations (Table 9.1, Statements 7–9). We drew these items from Excellence Theory (J. E. Grunig, 1992), which suggests that the extent to which public relations functions and practice can be effective and excellent are affected by a number of factors. These include the quality and vision of the communication leader, the extent to which two-way communication and shared power are present in the organization, the level of support of top executives in the organization, involvement in strategic decision making, the separation of public relations from marketing functions, the extent to which communication units are integrated in organizations, and so forth.

The reliability test (Cronbach's alpha) on the three items was .66. After Statement 9 was dropped, the alpha reached the level of .70, which is a universal criterion (Nunnally, 1978). However, we left this variable in for descriptive comparisons (Table 9.2). The analysis of variance (ANOVA) test showed a significant F value ($F = 9.53$, $df = 11, 4452$, $p < .01$).

TABLE 9.2 Summated Leadership Index

Country/Region	n	Mean	Standard Deviation
India	140	16.44	4.26
Mexico	213	15.31	4.55
Chinese-speaking countries	143	14.87	4.29
United States	828	14.76	4.47
German-speaking countries	1773	14.62	4.07
Latvia/Estonia	142	14.60	3.96
United Kingdom	139	14.42	4.89
Spain	210	14.39	4.89
Chile	156	14.00	4.51
Russia	215	13.56	4.59
South Korea	205	13.37	2.14
Brazil	302	13.09	4.61
Total	4,464	14.49	4.26

Note: The Summated Leadership Index includes Statements 7, 8, and 9 (see note to Table 9.1 for list of statements).

In our index, the higher the mean, the better or richer is the organizational condition for leadership (the highest possible mean score for the leadership index would be 21.00). The mean of the leadership index for all participating countries was 14.49. India topped the list with a score of 16.44, which was significantly higher than most other countries. Mexico followed with a score of 15.33, which was significantly higher than the lowest three countries—Brazil (13.09), South Korea (13.37) and Russia (13.56).

As for India's score, based on literature (e.g., Cappelli, Singh, Singh, & Useem, 2010) and e-mail correspondence with Nilanjana Bardhan and Padmini Patwardhan, the authors of the chapter on India, we can imply that collectivist traditions of societal culture manifested themselves in participants' responses. Indian collectivist culture seems to define relationships within organizations, and this influence is much stronger than the rules of developing capitalism. Particularly, Indian organizations tend to prioritize people over profit (without diminishing the importance of profit) and CEOs feel personally responsible for nurturing this type of organizational culture. According to Bardhan and Patwardhan, India's long-standing tradition of corporate social responsibility also seems to add a favorable perception to a culture for communication. In addition, the field of public relations is on the rise in the country (the projected growth is 25%–30% in 2013), and respondents' optimism may have also led to a higher score on the Summated Leadership Index.

Discussion

The global survey results shed light on a variety of perceptions about leadership in public relations. Our findings also posed new questions for both public relations practice and research. As in previous studies supported by the Plank Center (e.g., Meng et al., 2012), many practitioners in this study considered themselves to be leaders or to aspire to leadership. At the same time, this study illustrated a striking gap between top public relations leaders and their followers regarding leadership performance. The fact that leaders rated their own performance significantly higher than did the followers may hint at a more traditional leadership style being adopted by public relations leaders.

According to Burns (1978), the transactional leadership style is based on exchanges of valued things between the leader and his or her followers (e.g., a reward for a good performance by subordinates). In contrast, transformational leaders strive to connect with followers, recognize their needs, and help the followers reach their full potential by inspiring and mobilizing them. Burns described the result of transformational leadership as "a relationship of mutual stimulations and elevation that converts followers into leaders and may convert leaders into moral agents" (1978, p. 4).

The transformational leadership style seems to be more appropriate when public relations is employed to develop effective trusting relationships with internal and external audiences by empowering them. This leadership style may not only "close the gap" within a communication unit but may also help public relations practitioners build strong "bridges" with external stakeholders.

As discussed earlier, respondents below the top leader evaluated their leaders' performance as average. At the same time, the participants clearly indicated that learning from mentors on the job about excellent leadership is more effective than university/workshop training. This may mean that (a) management/leadership development programs are weak or sparse or (b) at some point in their careers, participants did have excellent mentors, or (c) both. Overall, these findings may suggest the need to develop more on the job mentoring programs and possibly offer shadowing exercises with practitioners. Such approaches are highly likely to be supported by organizational CEOs because their understanding of the value of public relations was rated quite high by survey participants—higher than immediate public relations supervisors' performance.

The leadership study also revealed some thought-provoking findings about gender and leadership. Men perceived themselves to be leaders in public relations significantly more often than did women (Berger, 2012). This finding opens up a number of interpretations in the context of an earlier worldwide study by Zenger and Folkman (2012), who discovered that women are regarded as better leaders than are men. What does this imply for public relations? Does it mean that women in public relations still tend to keep their heads down because of a perceived glass ceiling (L. Grunig, Toth, & Hon, 2001)? Do they voluntarily choose to decline more demanding leadership roles to be caretakers? Do they have fewer opportunities to become leaders? Moreover, how does this finding relate to both female and male respondents' preferences to work for a male rather than female leader?

Another finding—participants did not see much difference between leadership in public relations and other occupations—deserves further investigation as well. Indeed, leadership competencies span different occupations. Yet, there is still the need to emphasize specifics of public relations leadership to maintain legitimacy of the occupation and strengthen leadership effort. The normative role of public relations specialists is quite broad. It includes but is not limited to being (a) a double advocate in representing the interests of both the client and the public, and promoting dialogue and debate (Fitzpatrick & Bronstein, 2006); (b) the eyes and ears of an organization's values and relationships (Allert, 1999); and (c) the "ethical conscience of the organization" (Bowen, 2007; Pratt, 1991).

When this complexity is taken into consideration, public relations leadership is seen as the process that differs somewhat from other occupations (who else is managing the sometimes opposite interests of the client and publics and is thinking about a societal interest at the same time?). The study results suggest that creating a public relations leadership discourse would benefit the industry by helping practitioners better articulate their roles and duties. Professional self-identification is crucial to the process of demonstrating the value of public relations to the success of the organization—a hot topic in the field today.

No less an important topic is gaining access to the dominant coalition, or decision-making authority, in the organization (Berger & Reber, 2006). Leadership is seen as one of the main routes to the dominant coalition by senior practitioners in the United States (Bowen, 2009). However, there is not unanimous enthusiasm in the U.S. academic community regarding a public relations specialist's membership in the dominant coalition (Erzikova & Berger, 2012). In addition, we do not know if a concern over a public relations person's strong association with top management—he or she is "one of them"—might weaken the public's trust in public relations activities in other countries.

Trust is an important indicator of public relations effectiveness (Rawlins, 2007), and effectiveness is affected by an organizational culture. In this regard, the Summated Leadership Index is an intriguing descriptive of the organizational condition for leadership worldwide (Table 9.2). The fact that the highest mean score was 16.44 (India) implies that there is room for leadership improvement in every country and region in the study. Although many forces contribute to the organizational condition for leadership (J. Grunig, 1992), public relations practitioners should nevertheless actively attempt to influence these forces, rather than allowing them to produce an undesirable effect.

Implications

This study supported the conceptualization of leadership as a simultaneously universal and culturally bound phenomenon (Bass & Bass, 2008). Although public relations leadership practices and strategies are certainly globalized in some respects, they are still culturally diverse, are oftentimes unique, and deserve more cultural specific attention from researchers.

A statistically significant difference between followers and top leaders' evaluations of the highest ranking public relations professional is an important finding—a wakeup call that encourages practitioners to self-reflect on routines and perhaps re-consider their internal practices. For researchers, the perceptual gap calls for a thorough examination of both the quality of leaders' performance and followers' expectations. Particularly, the leader–member exchange (LMX) theory of leadership (Graen & Uhl-Bien, 1995) might provide a useful framework to study the leader's relationships with each subordinate (not a group) since the leader might act differently toward different followers, especially in such a gendered occupation as public relations (Grunig et al., 2001).

The U.S. public relations field was 95% male populated when a female pioneer, Betsy Plank, entered the profession in the 1940s (Berger, 2012). Today, women compose at least 70% of the U.S. public relations field, and the number of women in leadership positions is ascending (Berger, 2012). The same dynamic is observed in many other countries. However, the majority of leaders worldwide are still men, and the higher the position level, the more men there are (Zenger & Folkman, 2012).

Further, Touhey (1974) argued that the perception of an occupation's prestige and desirability lowers when proportions of female practitioners increase. This is a serious concern for the field that strives to attract the best and brightest. At the same time, public relations experts are equipped with the knowledge of relationship building and persuasive strategies to elevate the status of women practitioners. Not only public relations but also other occupations will benefit from the effort. In addition, more research is warranted to examine why positive attitudes toward women leaders have not been reflected in a strong behavioral intention to work for them.

This section's results also bear implications for public relations education worldwide. Formal public relations education and training is young not only in the United States (Commission on Public Relations Education, 2006) but also in many other countries. Striving for legitimacy within academia, public relations programs request practitioners' help (Commission on Public Relations Education, 2006). Recent research (Shen & Toth, 2013) has shown that educators and practitioners agreed on the competencies (e.g., strategic management, business, globalization) that master's-degree students should develop during the course of study. This conversation needs to continue. Practitioners and educators worldwide should consistently engage in dialogue about the best way to prepare future public relations leaders who will reinforce the value of the public relations function within the organization, and contribute to the betterment of the profession and its contributions to the broader society.

References

Aldoory, L., & Toth, E. (2002). Gender discrepancies in a gendered profession: A developing theory for public relations. *Journal of Public Relations Research, 14*(2), 103–126.

Allert, J. R. (1999). Ethics in communication: The role of public relations. In S. K. Chakraborty & S. R. Chatterjee (Eds.), *Applied ethics in management: Towards new perspectives* (pp. 187–203). New York, NY: Springer-Verlag.

Bass, B. M., & Bass, R. (2008). *The Bass handbook of leadership: Theory, research, and managerial applications* (4th ed.). New York, NY: Free Press.

Bass, B. M., Avolio, B. J., & Atwater, L. (1996). The transformational and transactional leadership of men and women. *Applied Psychology: An International Review, 45*(1), 5–34.

Berger, B. K. (2012). *The cross-cultural study of leadership in public relations and communication management: Key themes and findings.* Tuscaloosa, GA: Plank Center for Leadership in Public Relations. Available online at http://plankcenter.ua.edu/wp-content/uploads/2012/10/Summary-of-Themes-and-Findings-Leader-Survey.pdf

Berger, B. K., & Reber, B. H. (2006). *Gaining influence in public relations: The role of resistance in practice.* Mahwah, NJ: Erlbaum.

Bowen, S. A. (2009). What communication professionals tell us regarding dominant coalition access and gaining membership. *Journal of Applied Communication Research, 37*(4), 418–443.

Burns, J. M. (1978). *Leadership.* New York, NY: Harper & Row.

Cappelli, P., Singh, H., Singh, J., & Useem, M. (2010, March). Leadership lessons from India. *Harvard Business Review*, pp. 1–9.

Choi, Y., & Choi, J. (2009). Behavioral dimensions of public relations leadership in organizations. *Journal of Communication Management*, *13*, 292–309.

Commission on Public Relations Education. (2006). *The professional bond—public relations education and practice.* New York, NY: Public Relations Society of America.

Dozier, D. M., Sha, B-L., & Shen, H. (2013). Why women earn less than men: The cost of gender discrimination in U.S. public relations. *Public Relations Journal*, *7*(1), 1–21.

Erzikova, E., & Berger, B. (2012). *Leadership education in the public relations curriculum: Reality, opportunities, and benefits. Public Relations Journal*, *6*(3), 1–30. Available online at www.prsa.org/Intelligence/PRJournal/Documents/2012ErzikovaBerger.pdf

Fitzpatrick, K., & Bronstein, C. (2006). *Ethics in public relations: Responsible advocacy.* Thousand Oaks, CA: Sage.

Graen, G. B., & Uhl-Bien, M. (1995). Relationship-based approach to leadership: Development of the leader-member exchange (LMX) theory of leadership over 25 years. *Leadership Quarterly*, *6, 219*–247.

Grunig, J. E. (Ed.). (1992). *Excellence in public relations and communication management: Contributions to effective organizations.* Hillsdale, NJ: Erlbaum.

Grunig, L.A., Toth, E. L., & Hon, L. C. (2001). *Women in public relations: How gender influences practice.* New York, NY: Guilford.

Hampson, E., & Moffat, S. D. (2004). The psychology of gender. Cognitive effects of reproductive hormones in the adult nervous system. In A.H. Eagly, A. E. Beall, & R. J. Sternberg (Eds.), *The psychology of gender* (pp. 38–64). New York, NY: Guilford.

Hines, M. (2004). Androgen, estrogen, and gender. Contributions of the early hormone environment to gender-related behavior. In A.H. Eagly, A. E. Beall, & R. J. Sternberg (Eds.), *The psychology of gender* (pp. 9–37). New York, NY: Guilford.

House, R., J., Hanges, P. J., Javidan, M., Dorfman, P. W., & Gupta, V. (2004). *Culture, leadership, and organizations: The GLOBE study of 62 societies.* Thousand Oaks, CA: Sage.

Jin, Y. (2010). Emotional leadership as a key dimension of public relations leadership: A national survey of public relations leaders. *Journal of Public Relations Research*, *22*(2), 159–181.

Kenrick, D.T., Trost, M.R., & Sundie, J. M. (2004). Sex roles as adaptations. An evolutionary perspective on gender differences and similarities. In A.H. Eagly, A. E. Beall, & R. J. Sternberg (Eds.), *The psychology of gender* (pp. 65–91). New York, NY: Guilford.

Ławniczak, R. (2001). Transition public relations: An instrument for systematic transformation in Central and Eastern Europe. In R. Ławniczak (Ed.), *Public relations contribution to transition in Central and Eastern Europe: Research and practice* (pp. 109–119). Poznan, Poland: Biuro Uslogowo-Handlowe.

Ławniczak, R., Rydzak, W., & Trębecki, J. (2003). Public relations in an economy and society in transition: The case of Poland. In K. Sriramesh & D. Verčič, D. (Eds.), *The global public relations handbook: Theory, research, and practice,* (pp. 257–280). Mahwah, NJ: Erlbaum.

Meng, J., Berger, B. K., Gower, K. K., & Heyman, W. C. (2012). A test of excellent leadership in public relations: Key qualities, valuable sources, and distinctive leadership perceptions. *Journal of Public Relations Research*, *24*, 18–36.

Meng, J., Berger, B. K., & Heyman, W. C. (2011). Measuring public relations leadership in the trait approach: A second-order factor model in the dimension of self-dynamics.

Journal of Public Relations, 5(1), 1–24. Available online at www.prsa.org/Intelligence/PRJournal/Documents/2011MengBergerHeyman.pdf

Pētersone, B. (2006, June). *The status of public relations in Latvia.* Paper presented at the meeting of the International Communication Association, Dresden, Germany.

Nunnally, J. (1978). *Psychometric theory* (2nd ed.) New York, NY: McGraw-Hill.

Pratt, C. B. (1991). Public relations: the empirical research on practitioner ethics. *Journal of Business Ethics, 10,* 229–236.

Pūre, I. (2011, July). *Development of public relations in Latvia: Pre-history and periods of development.* Paper presented at the History of Public Relations Conference, Bournemouth, England.

Pūre, I. (n.d.). *The development and conceptual diversity of public relations in Latvia: 1991–2010.* Ongoing doctoral research project, School of Business Administration, Turiba, Riga, Latvia.

Rawlins B. L. (2007, October 29). Trust and PR practice. Available online at www.instituteforpr.org/topics/trust-and-pr-practice/

Shen, H., & Toth, E. (2013). Public relations master's education deliverables: How practitioners and educators view strategic practice curriculum. *Public Relations Review 39*(5), 618–620. Tampere, K., 2001. Organizational communication in a post-communist society. In R. Ławniczak (Ed.), *Public relations contribution to transition in Central and Eastern Europe: Research and practice* (pp. 209–213). Poznan, Poland: Biuro Uslogowo-Handlowe.

Touhey, J. C. (1974). Effects of additional women professionals on ratings of occupational prestige and desirability, *Journal of Personality and Social Psychology, 29*(1), 86–89.

Verčič, D., Grunig, L. A., & Grunig, J. E. (1996). Global and specific principles of public relations; Evidence from Slovenia. In H. M. Culbertson & N. Chen (Eds.), *International public relations: A comparative analysis* (pp. 31–65). Mahwah, NJ: Erlbaum.

Werder, K. P., & Holtzhausen, D. (2009). An analysis of the influence of public relations department leadership style on public relations strategy use and effectiveness. *Journal of Public Relations Research, 21,* 404–427.

Zenger, J., & Folkman, J. (2012, March 15). Are women better leaders than men? [Blog entry]. Available online at http://blogs.hbr.org/cs/2012/03/a_study_in_leadership_women_do.html

SECTION III

Conversations With Leaders in Public Relations

This section provides a close-up look at public relations leadership in 10 countries and regions, each of which is examined in a chapter, as follows: the Chinese-speaking countries, India, South Korea, the German-speaking countries, Latvia, Russia, Spain, Brazil, Mexico, and the United States. Each chapter explores the key issues in the country or region, how these issues affect leadership roles and practices, and organizational cultural and structural factors that facilitate or impede excellent practice. The 10 chapters are heavily grounded in 137 depth interviews (68 women, 69 men) conducted with senior leaders in the countries. Overall, these chapters provide rich cultural perspectives on the leadership concept.

10

PUBLIC RELATIONS LEADERSHIP IN THE CHINESE-SPEAKING COUNTRIES

Talent Development in the Dynamic, Digital Age

Chun-ju Flora Hung-Baesecke, Yan Jin, and Juan Meng

This chapter discusses in-depth the important issues from public relations leaders' views and perceptions on leadership development. Public relations development in the Chinese-speaking countries (mainland China, Hong Kong, Singapore, and Taiwan) had unique beginnings because of historical, social, political, and economic factors.

In mainland China, due to the economic reform and opening-up policy in 1978 (He & Xie, 2009), public relations departments and Sino–foreign joint venture public relations firms first began in the coastal cities. To date, public relations and communication practice in mainland China has been moving in the direction of a strategic and managerial function, especially in multinational corporations and public relations agencies. Some local agencies also were launched and have tried to apply diverse strategies and actions, although the majority of communication services are still limited to event planning, press conference hosting, and basic media relations (Jin, 2010a).

In Hong Kong, public relations started in the 1950s when the British introduced the modern concept of public relations and established a public relations office for the purposes of providing information to the media (Cheng, 1999). After the handover of Hong Kong to the People's Republic of China in 1997, the developing public relations industry has been characterized by a growing body of professional public relations associations, practices, and functions that go beyond media relations and consumer marketing communication. There's been greater emphasis on relationship building, accompanied by accelerated development, following the ever-growing influence from mainland China (Martin, 2009).

The practice of public relations in Singapore has evolved from the models used by the British colonialists to a professional status, but it was also heavily influenced by Chinese culture (Chay-Nemeth, 2009). Although the development of the profession itself has advanced rapidly, there still are differences between multinational firms and local public relations agencies in understanding the importance and functions of public relations (Chay-Nemeth, 2009).

Public relations in Taiwan developed with changes in government regulations and policies (Sha & Huang, 2004). A more democratic society allowed different voices to rise, and the "election-driven" (Wu, Taylor, & Chen, 2001, p. 319) political environment provided opportunities for public relations to grow. However, despite decades of professional development in Taiwan, the majority of public relations functions still fulfill the technician role (e.g., media relations and event planning; Wu & Taylor, 2003).

Because of differences in historical, social, and economic developments, these four areas had different foci in the public relations practices. However, with more frequent interactions among these areas, corporations inevitably have to expand their business across the region, which creates more opportunities for public relations in the region. Thus, this chapter provides a closer look at some of the opportunities and presents the findings based on in-depth interviews with senior public relations executives in the region as part of the global project.

Method

In-Depth Interviews

In this region, 22 public relations leaders were interviewed about their views on the important issues in their daily practices, the strategies they adopt to deal with the issues, and their visions for developing future leaders for public relations (see Appendix B for the Interview Guide). We recruited the 22 industry leaders through convenience sampling strategy (i.e., snowball sampling). The interviews were conducted via telephone or face-to-face communications between January and May 2012. Two participants are presidents of local public relations associations, and the other interviewees serve as heads of corporate communication, directors of local public relations firms, and regional heads of multinational public relations firms in the region.

Participants in the interviews work for diverse organizations (e.g., public relations agencies, private corporations, publicly held corporations, state-owned enterprises, and educational institutions). The average years of working experience in the profession is 13.75, with a range of 2 to 25 years. The interviews ranged from 30 to 60 minutes in length. All the interviews were recorded, transcribed, and analyzed by the research team. The following section presents the major interview findings.

Findings

Top Issues for Leaders

Based on the interviews, the top three issues identified by the 22 leaders were (1) recruiting, training, and maintaining talent; (2) managing social media practices; and (3) improving client management.

Issue 1: Recruiting, Training, and Maintaining Talent

DeKrey, Messick, and Anderson (2007) contended that hiring and retaining talent has become a very important element in business operations in Asia, and it is one of the major responsibilities for top management. The issue of developing talent was mentioned a few times in the interviews. Participants indicated that public relations is a "people" business, which requires skills and knowledge in communicating and dealing with different groups of people and their demands. As a result, one senior executive from a multinational public relations firm expressed concerns over the lack of talent and the growing urgency to find "experienced, qualified, and capable talent to meet . . . the need for client servicing in terms of providing the all-round capabilities of fielding the various challenges for today's communication environment." The CEO of a public relations group in Taiwan shared her company's system and incentive plans for recruiting and keeping talent:

> Public relations is also a profession that requires creativity. In this creative profession, lacking professional management executives is a common problem. Senior executives need their successors. To prepare for a smooth succession and the company's continuity, we have an "Eagle Planning," a tailored training course to prepare professionals to become "eagles" in the future.

Although some participants mentioned the importance of providing training for developing future leaders, some also voiced concern in this aspect: The high turnover rate in this profession has discouraged some employers from offering more advanced training courses because of the fear of talent lost as commented by a senior public relations executive:

> There are a lot of young people in our profession. They also have many opportunities in the job market. So, offering high salary probably can keep them . . . Yet, the depth and levels of training courses cannot keep up with the demands in the market. Why? These companies are quite pragmatic: If the companies provide solid training courses, they are concerned that these talents will leave and work for other companies. So, many employers are reluctant to offer training courses.

Issue 2: Managing Social/Mobile Media Practices

The most recently published Mindshare's Digital Normalness Index 2013 (Mindshare, 2013) revealed that China scored highest in two motivations for going online: (a) self-expression and communication (e.g., visiting social network sites, posting comments, updating status, and communicating via instant messaging services) and (b) transaction (e.g., purchasing and online banking). Our interview data reflected such marketing research results. The prevalence of Weibo, WeChat, Line, QR codes, and other mobile apps have provided a handy communicating environment for young people. Such heavy usage in social/mobile media also presents a challenge in recruiting qualified professionals to manage related public relations functions. The Asia Pacific CEO of a public relations firm commented that "given the phenomenon of information overload nowadays due to the social media explosion, companies now have their digital departments, and public relations services ought to follow suit. Hence, hiring young talents who were digital savvy became important."

The participants highlighted several aspects of the social/mobile media practice that need a particular attention:

- **Using social media strategies in campaigns:** Most of the interviewees shared their experiences on using social media strategies in their campaigns; specifically, Weibo has become a widely used social media platform for many campaigns in the Chinese market. Consequently, the term *EPR* (electronic public relations) has become commonly known among public relations practices and has been a dominating method in practices. However, the effectiveness of such electronic public relations practice is still under debate due to lacking reliable measures.
- **Increasing stakeholder engagement:** Corporations and consultancies have been using social media to engage internal and external stakeholders. For example, Facebook, although the access is blocked in China, is still a pervasive social media channel that has been widely used in other Asian countries. Participants mentioned they use Facebook to create fan pages and provide content for key stakeholders to share. They acknowledged it is effective to increase stakeholder engagement and facilitate community building.
- **Reaching young audiences:** Participants also mentioned the salient information consumption habit of young audiences. The Internet has become the major or the only source of information for the younger generation. Young people go to Facebook, Twitter, Weibo, or Ren Ren to access information on companies, or to read and respond to comments. Hence, organizations have to react quickly in order to satisfy the expectations of the younger generation, both in speed of the response and in depth of the content.

Issue 3: Improving Client Management

Improving professional development of the public relations profession itself is still a long-term goal for practitioners in this region. As an important indicator of professionalism, improving client management is another issue participants addressed in the interviews.

Clients usually have high expectations, especially multinational ones. International brands usually are more mature because they have been developed over quite a long time. However, the markets in the region are still developing, and consumer behavior is sometimes not rational as commented by a leader from a local firm in China: "This kind of cultural conflict between the East and the West became the alert for consultancies in China in striving for providing satisfactory services in keeping clients."

Another reason for finding effective approaches to client management is a result of information overload. Interestingly, this point is relevant to one of the issues the interviewees identified: dealing with the speed and volume of information flow. Clients receive information online and off-line from various channels. Integrating information channels and providing useful and relevant information to clients has become a challenging task for consultancies.

On a pragmatic level, participants working in public relations firms acknowledged the interdependent relationship between the firms and their clients. The CEO of a public relations firm said, "After all, making profit is still very important. Managing clients well will allow my firm to secure stable profits."

Emerging Future Issues in the Region

When asked to identify new issues in the next 3 to 5 years, participants believed that some of the issues identified will remain as critical ones, for example, training and retaining talent and the integration of social media into communication strategies. Participants also named a few new issues that are highly relevant to the macro socioeconomic environments globally, such as organizations' social and environmental responsibilities, the impact of the 2008 financial tsunami on business behaviors, the engagement strategies with younger generations, and the city image management in China.

Although the Greater China region, compared with other countries in the Americas and Europe, was not heavily affected by the 2008 financial crisis, the domino effect from the global and euro economic crises will very likely affect this region more. Thus, it presents more challenges in communication practice as noted by one chief business officer, "The macroeconomic effects will bring impacts on business behaviors and budget allocation, which will eventually affect the communication strategies readjustments and the hiring of consultancies."

However, while corporations are struggling to recover from the damages of the global financial tsunami, publics still expect to see social and sustainable responsibility initiatives demonstrated by organizations. A general manager said, "Each corporation is related to each public in the society, and nowadays, people pay more attention to their well-being part; they will look for a better environment in the future, and they will pay attention on the earth." Thus, the issue of corporate social responsibility and sustainability will continue to get more attention.

Engaging with the new generations and city image management are two unique issues. The so-called post-80ers or post-90ers are considered the new generations in China, inasmuch as they grew up in a more affluent society and their behaviors, either purchasing products or commenting on issues, are a lot different from their seniors or their parents' generations. Their relatively more outspoken behaviors have influenced how organizations communicated with them. Therefore, practitioners considered it is important to "understand their knowledge structure, their values, their approach to life and work, and their communication consumption patterns."

With the booming market economy, city development in China has extended beyond the coastal or first-tier cities. Today, inner or second-tier cities are attracting both business investments and tourists. In order to succeed, these cities have launched new promotion and image campaigns in China or overseas. Such efforts present many opportunities in strategic planning in public relations and communication.

Cultural/Structural Factors Affecting Leadership Effectiveness

Factors Facilitating Leadership Effectiveness

When discussing cultural and organizational structural factors that might influence their leadership initiatives in organization, participants identified three leading factors.

Factor 1: Supportive senior leadership and organizational structure. Participants addressed the importance of having a supportive senior leadership at the organizational level in facilitating excellence in communication management. They expressed that there is a need for regular meetings between the top management team and the communication/public relations department to ensure communication transparency and information flow. Likewise, top management support and demonstrated appreciation were considered beneficial. Both should be connected to a flexible and supportive general culture within the organization. The chief business officer commented that "the culture of working together, combined with a very strong infrastructure with hardware and process support within the organization is crucial." Moreover, participants addressed the importance of having public relations executives be part of the top management team within the organization.

Factor 2: Effective inter-departmental communication. According to the participants, interdepartmental meetings were viewed as allowing communication managers and other departmental leaders to share ideas and discuss how to better serve the stakeholders. This beneficial relationship is enhanced if and when "a leadership team across different departments is composed in such a way and structure that people can speak a common language across various parts of the business and have common goals," according to a multinational public relations director in Singapore.

Factor 3: Efficient teamwork embracing individual creativity. To have an organization perform at its best, effective teamwork in all projects was seen as essential. A leader from a local public relations firm in Shanghai said, "When it comes to getting things done, there is no hierarchy or barriers based on titles or ranking." Likewise, a degree of flexibility was considered an asset. "Efficiency and flexibility" was referred to as a type of best practice because they foster the building of close relationships among employees and with clients. One leader in Shanghai said, "Such relationship among employees will be enhanced in an atmosphere that stimulates a positive form of competition while maintaining a spirit of collaboration at the same time."

Barriers to Leadership Effectiveness

The interviewees also identified the following cultural/structural factors in an organization that may impede or prevent excellence in the communication management.

Factor 1: Organizational temperament. Some interviewees raised the concern that a fearless and free culture unavoidably tended to be loose, especially in the creative industry. Hence, there is a strong need to balance this with more structure, policy, and stability. In addition, for some organizations, organizational culture does not always motivate the same level of work ethic among employees, which raises issues regarding employee accountability and expectations of equality.

Factor 2: Interdepartmental conflict and structural issues. Organizational size sometimes caused problems for leadership effectiveness. First, due to the large size and the marketing nature of some companies, many decisions tend to be skewed in the direction of marketing and financial concerns, rather than communications priorities. Second, sometimes there is lack of control of communication (in terms of where to get it and who gets it) because noncommunication departments either deliberately withhold information or share the information with media without consultation with the communication department. This creates communication work frustration and embarrassing situations that public relations leaders have to handle. Last, in the process of mergers and acquisitions that leads to the creation of large conglomerates, there tends to be communication problems among the constituent parts of the newly formed entity.

Factor 3: Resource and knowledge insufficiency. Most comments on this topic came from the agency perspective. In some client areas, the agencies might lack certain expertise, resources, or knowledge to obtain as well as to retain clients. Time management is another issue as the leader from Singapore said, "The agency bills by time and service delivered." A consequence of such issue is that there is a skewed focus toward implementation, far less on strategy, for some public relations agencies. One leader from Chengdu in China said, "A credible strategy plan is based on comprehensive and in-depth understanding of the market, based on research. We need to develop our research team."

Factor 4: Adopting appropriate leadership style. This concerns the impact of leaders' knowledge and their styles on communication effectiveness. In terms of leaders' knowledge, participants said they were still exploring how to build brand and add value to their work. In addition, given the development of new media and new market needs, a longer serving senior leader may be liked by clients but may not have the newest ideas or skills to meet the expectations of new technologies.

In terms of leadership styles, some leaders were expected to keep balance between being "too nice" and "too harsh." One leader in Shanghai said, "When the leadership style and organizational culture are both too loose, there can be a lack of direction or determination, and a lack of real support for employee initiatives." In addition, some leaders could not maintain emotional balance at work; they overtly exerted their emotions, including anger and venting to colleagues. Another detrimental aspect of leadership style was demonstrated by leaders and by their team when they showed complacency and arrogance, based on prior successes. Philosophically and practically, the Asia Pacific president and CEO said, "Leaders need to be aware of the business cycle and never get too complacent with their existing reputation."

Characteristics and Qualities of Excellent Leaders

In the interviews, we also asked participants to identify the most important characteristics or qualities of excellent leaders in public relations. These characteristics and qualities are included in the following checklist and are somewhat consistent with Meng and Berger's (2013) seven dimensions of excellent leadership in public relations:

- Having the ability to identify, develop, train, mentor, culture, and retain talent
- Having both passion and vision
- Communicating clearly with clients and leading employees

- Excelling in strategic planning and resource management
- Being ethical and socially responsible
- Possessing likable personality and charisma
- Having strong professional background and ever-learning spirit
- Maintaining authenticity in communication
- Having integrity, creativity, sustainability, and flexibility
- Being able to understand the trends and anticipate future development
- Being able to listen and to trust, demonstrating two-way communication

Summarizing the compiled list, we found that the most important characteristic of a leader for public relations is to be a capable communicator because, as the chief business officer of a multinational public relations firm commented, "The ability to communicate . . . [is] increasingly very critical to how leadership is being viewed as effective or not." However, being able to communicate is not enough. This interviewee further highlighted the need for authenticity of the communication, meaning the alignment of a leader's actions with the communication content.

Besides the consistency of our checklist with Meng and Berger's (2013) dimensions of excellent leadership, identifying and retaining talent was also mentioned by several participants. One leader in Shanghai went further by saying,

> No matter which profession the leader is in, he or she should know how to select talents and place them in the most suitable positions so that it allows them to fully show their potential in their duties. This is the capability a leader should have.

How Will Future Leaders Be Different?

Participants' visions for future leaders in public relations reflected the current phenomena of social media penetration and globalization. The excellence study (Grunig, Grunig, & Dozier, 2002) has advocated the role of public relations in the dominant coalition. As commented by the participants, the vision for future leaders in public relations in the region will hopefully include "having a seat at the table of the top management . . . to serve on and play much more key roles in communication management, as a company's top leader sitting at the top table of decision-making processes that drive business." In addition, one participant addressed the importance of having more visionary leaders for the profession in the future:

> We know for sure that PR firms will continue to get much bigger in the future because of social media, but what we do not have is a large number of executives who are PR people who have run large scale enterprises. There is a lack of commercial sensibility. In the future, we

are going to have far more PR leaders who really know the business and could run large scale businesses. That's the biggest difference I am looking forward to.

However, in reaching that status, participants raised the concern that many public relations leaders today still lack "professional confidence." Unfortunately, given the fact that executives from other departments in the organizations usually consider public relations to be "window dressing" or "spin doctoring," the confidence of public relations executives to lead communication initiatives is threatened. Therefore, participants highlighted the importance of improving the professional image and suggested that public relations should "feel big, not small, when it comes to placing ourselves in the world in our own competence."

As an important part of improving professionalism, future leaders should not only focus on profit making but also demonstrate moral values and ethics to the entire profession and young practitioners. For example, the CEO of a public relations group in Taiwan considered being loyal to vendors and clients very important in her work ethic and said she would not accept clients from the tobacco industry because smoking is harmful to health.

With the rise of the digital revolution, some participants suggested future leaders in communication should "to be able to communicate with people using all kinds of electronic social media and to know different skills when using different methods to interact with people." This point was echoed by some others in the interviews, who said future leaders should be digitally savvy and skillful in using various forms of social media, for example, Facebook, Line, Whatsapp, and so forth. They will use social media not only for personal communication but also for client or organization projects.

Digitalization also is accompanied by the following qualities that leaders should possess: globalization, transparency, and the fine line between personal and work lives. In terms of globalization, the general manager of corporate communication from the property group said,

> In the past, you can just do benchmarking within Hong Kong, but now we have to do something ahead, we have to invade, make improvement, have innovation, and we can't just benchmark locally. You have to reach Mainland China; you are talking about whole China. Going beyond China—you have to think about the world.

In terms of transparency, the influence of Weibo in mainland China will help enhance government transparency and business operations. In terms of the changes in personal lives, the director from Singapore commented that "communication will evolve to a point where it's essentially instantaneous, it's essentially happening all the time. They're going to be expected to be a lot more mobile than what we are expected to be at the moment."

Finally, there will be more future leaders with a major in communication. To date, many leaders lack the theoretical training in public relations that comes through higher education. Instead, they learned how to practice public relations directly from the field. The interviewee from a major soft drink company in Singapore considered that "the communication education will be more applied and more relevant to corporate communication needs, as well as corporate management experiences. They will also have more channels to obtain information." As a result, more future public relations leaders will be developed and equip themselves with more solid professional and theoretical knowledge before they enter the field.

Tipping Points for Leadership Success

Many of the "tipping points" mentioned by the interviewees are quite relevant to the attitudes the leaders held in their career—taking risks, work ethics and passion, persistence and perseverance, and getting out of one's comfort zone. Other tipping points included their diverse/overseas working experiences, their being culturally savvy, their professional training, and the influence of their role models and mentors at work.

One participant shared his own experiences of creating the first Canadian public relations firm in the United States market, and then creating a firm from scratch in Japan, as his risk-taking experiences. He said, "Diving into new markets in the hardest possible situations provided the most learning that allows you to progress." Similar to risk taking, the participant said that "getting out of his comfort zone" made him what he is today.

Several leaders mentioned work ethics, persistence, and perseverance. Because of their hardworking attitudes, observed over a long time by their supervisors or companies, they were promoted to more senior positions and took on more responsibilities. In addition, the general manager of a public relations firm in Taiwan highlighted the importance of persistence and perseverance:

> In our field, many outstanding practitioners gave up half way and many of them were my seniors. They either considered this field was too demanding, or the market in Taiwan was too small. I worked hard and learned quickly. After changing a few jobs, I found one career that I can fully devote all my capabilities to. I like taking challenges. Persistence is what has always supported me.

Current State of Leadership Development

Vicere (1997) identified new trends in leadership development: distance learning, the move toward experience-based methodologies, performance feedback, and flexibility and adaptability as most important competencies. There is no existing research specifically on public relations leadership development in Chinese-speaking countries. As for leadership development in general, Qiao's (2006) study revealed the approaches to develop leaders by successful companies in mainland China as being the linking of the leadership competence model with performance reviews, connecting succession planning with the company leadership development process, conducting training, and linking the company's strategic imperatives with talent development initiatives.

Our research showed some consistent findings in effective approaches to developing leaders. A few successful cases were (a) organizations provided internal or external training programs, (b) organizations developed tailor-made succession plans to prepare future leaders, (c) organizations used well-established mentor–leadership programs, and (d) leaders were provided different responsibilities to equip themselves with leadership qualities.

So far, in this region, the China International Public Relations Association (CIPRA) has taken a lead in offering diverse seminar and training programs for practitioners for their career advancement. This association also holds biannual nationwide university student campaign planning competitions. The winning students are provided cash rewards and are awarded internship opportunities in some major corporations. The same kind of association and university collaborations on student competitions and internship opportunities for winning students also can be seen in Hong Kong and Taiwan. In addition, local public relations associations collaborate with corporations and universities in developing training programs. The Council for Public Relations Firms Hong Kong annually organizes a university student and young professional talent competition to encourage talent development.

Some public relations firms in mainland China, Taiwan, and Hong Kong have developed systematic internship programs for university students, and mentors are assigned in assisting students' career orientation. Most of the time, students are no longer only assigned the duties of photocopying and media contacts. They are provided opportunities to participate in the proposal planning process and campaign executions. This approach has been win–win for both public relations firms and universities because the firms are able to identify talent for the company's operation continuation, and the students obtained practical experiences and career opportunities.

In terms of public relations curriculum development, different views on the values of public relations exist, and the emphases of the curricula vary in universities. Most of the universities still have marketing elements in their curriculum, due to the strong market orientation in this region. Moreover, the perception of whether public relations is the managerial role or the technician role in an organization is also reflected in the curricula designs.

Those universities considering public relations as a technical profession usually offer more skill courses. Others with the vision that public relations should be part of the dominant coalition and participate in the strategic decision-making process usually incorporate elements of management in their curricula. From a practitioner's viewpoint, Yen (2010) considered that the required core knowledge for public relations education should include the areas of management, social science, analytical ability, and communication skills. To keep up with developments in the field, external professional leaders have been invited to serve on the school advisory board at many universities to provide suggestions in the curriculum design.

Leadership Needs for the Future

Our research findings have demonstrated that the rapid development of public relations in this region has resulted in a great demand for public relations talent. Best-practice organizations (e.g., Johnson & Johnson and General Electric) view leadership development as a critical way to increase competitive advantage and support organizational strategies (Fulmer & Goldsmith, 2001). Similarly, one of the most important factors to facilitate the advancement of the public relations profession is to enable the development of highly qualified professionals who will become future leaders not only in the organization but also for the profession.

Leaders can be developed and improved, especially in such a dynamic profession that is experiencing rapid development under the influence of media, cultural, and social changes (Servaes, 2012). Best-practice organizations suggested viewing leadership development programs as a way to increase competitive advantage and support corporate strategy (e.g., Fulmer & Goldsmith, 2001). Thus, leadership development can be achieved in multiple approaches: an individual's experiences, formal or structured leadership development programs, educational programs or other types of interventions, formal training developed by organizations, and the influence of role models, mentors, and coaches (e.g., Conger & Fulmer, 2003).

In addition, research on leadership in general has revealed the characteristics (benevolence, morality, and authoritarianism) of the paternalistic leadership styles in this region (Redding, 1990; Sheer, 2012; Silin, 1976). The elements of morality and benevolence have been the indigenous characteristics for leaders in this region and can be incorporated into developing benevolent leaders for today.

Furthermore, Jin (2010b) posited that responding to the emotionality of employees is an important element for effective leadership. In the Chinese-speaking region, where human relationship is greatly emphasized, emotional skills facilitate building trusting relationships with employees. The relationship cultivation strategies Hung and Chen (2009) identified, such as being attentive, emphasizing education and engaging in personal relationships, keeping promises/ organizational credibility, and adhering to cultural and relations rules can be applied in developing effective leadership for this region.

Research also suggests the importance of the role of experience in developing leadership talent. Although an individual's naturally occurring life experiences, and what he or she learns from those experiences, have been confirmed as generating a significant impact on a leader's development (Bennis, 2009), organizations are also critical in helping talented employees get the right experiences at the right time to accelerate their development as leaders (e.g., McCall, 2010; McCauley et al., 1994).

To summarize, McCall (2010) identified five leveraging points organizations can use to create a supportive institutional context for leadership learning and development: (a) identifying developmental experiences, (b) identifying people with potential to be leaders, (c) developing processes for getting the right learning experience, (d) increasing the odds that learning will occur, and (e) taking a career-long perspective with a focus on critical career transitions. Such key leveraging points would greatly benefit the development of communication leaders in the rapidly changing Chinese society.

References

CIPRA. (2013). *The Annual Survey on Public Relations in China, 2012.* Beijing: China International Public Relations Association. Available online at www.chinanpr.com.cn/article-716349–1.html

Bennis, W. G. (2009). *On becoming leader* (4th ed.). Philadelphia, PA: Basic Books.

Chay-Nemeth, C. (2009). Becoming professionals: A portrait of public relations in Singapore. In K. Sriramesh & D. Vercic (Eds.), *The global public relations handbook, expanded and revised edition* (pp. 155–174). New York, NY: Routledge.

Cheng, K. (1999, September). The public relations in Hong Kong: Its past, present, and future. *Asian Studies,* pp. 123–144.

Conger, J. A., & Fulmer, R. M. (2003). Developing your leadership pipeline. *Harvard Business Review, 81*(12), 76–84.

DeKrey, S. J., Messick, D. M., & Anderson, C. (2007). *Leadership experiences in Asia: Insight and inspiration from 20 innovators.* Singapore: Wiley.

Fulmer, R. M., & Goldsmith, M. (2001). *The leadership investment: How the world's best organizations gain strategic advantage through leadership development.* New York, NY: AMA.

Grunig, L. A., Grunig, J. E., & Dozier, D. (2002). *Excellent public relations and effective organizations: A study of communication management in three countries.* Mahwah, NJ: Erlbaum.

He, C., & Xie, J. (2009). Thirty years' development of public relations in China Mainland. *China Media Research, 5*(3), 1–6.

Hung, C. J. F., & Chen, Y. R. (2009). Types and dimensions of organization-public relationships in Greater China. *Public Relations Review,* 35, 181–186.

Jin, Y. (2010a). At the fork of the road: A research review of public relations in China (2003–2008). *Media Asia, 36(2),* 63–71.

Jin, Y. (2010b). Emotional leadership as a key dimension of public relations leadership: A national survey of public relations leaders. *Journal of Public Relations Research, 22,* 159–181.

Martin, E. F. Jr. (2009). Hong Kong public relations: Resilient in the face of challenges. *Media Asia,* 36(2), 72–79.

McCall, M. W. Jr. (2010). The experience conundrum. In Nitin Nohria & Rakesh Khurana (Eds.), *Handbook of leadership theory and practice* (pp. 679–708). Boston, MA: Harvard Business Press.

McCauley, C., Ruderman, M., Ohlott, P., & Morrow, J. (1994). Assessing the developmental components of managerial jobs. *Journal of Applied Psychology, 79*, 544–560.

Meng, J., & Berger, B. (2013). An integrated model of excellent leadership in public relations: Dimensions, measurement, and validation. *Journal of Public Relations Research, 25*(2), 141–167.

Mindshare (2013). Are you digitally normal: Digital culture and the digital normal index. London, Mindshare. Available online at assets.mindshare.br.isotoma.com/xt-98f180b6-059f-11e3-ada9-0024e85b3c0c/1.AreYouDigitallyNormal-DigitalCultureandthe DigitalNormalIndex_FINAL.pdf

Qiao, X. J. (2006). *How the companies develop their leaders and what critical factors contribute to enhancing the effectiveness of leadership development practices.* Unpublished doctoral dissertation, Pennsylvania State University, University Park.

Redding, S. G. (1990). *The spirit of Chinese capitalism,* Berlin, Germany: Walter de Gruyter.

Servaes, J. (2012). Soft power and public diplomacy: The new frontier for public relations and international communication between the US and China. *Public Relations Review, 38*, 643–651.

Sha, B.-L., & Huang, Y.-H. (2004). Public relations on Taiwan; evolving with the infrastructure. In K. Sriramesh (Ed.), *Public relations in Asia: An anthology* (pp. 161–185). Singapore: Thomson Learning.

Sheer, V. C. (2012). In search of Chinese paternalistic leadership: Conflicting evidence from samples of mainland China and Hong Kong's small family business. *Management Communication Quarterly, 27*(1), 34–60.

Silin, R. F. (1976). *Leadership and values.* Cambridge, MA: Harvard University. Vicere, A. A. (1997). *Changes in practices, changes in perspectives: The 1997 international study of executive development trends.* University Park, PA: Institute for the Study of Organizational Effectiveness.

Yen, X. T. (2010). *A study on public relations professionals' views on public relations curriculums in universities* (Unpublished master's thesis). National Chengchi University, Taiwan.

Wu, M-Y., & Taylor, M. (2003). Public relations in Taiwan: Roles, professionalism, and relationship to marketing. *Public Relations Review, 29*, 473–483.

Wu, M.-Y., Taylor, M., & Chen, M.-J. (2001). Exploring societal and cultural influences on Taiwanese public relations. *Public Relations Review, 27*, 317–336.

11

LEADERSHIP IN A TRANSFORMING ENVIRONMENT

Perspectives from Public Relations Leaders in India

Nilanjana R. Bardhan and Padmini Patwardhan

The challenges facing public relations around the world are many and varied, particularly when rapid economic, technological, and cultural changes are transforming the professional landscape. According to Kruckeberg (2000), public relations practitioners must "first acknowledge their own professional ideology, values, and belief systems before they can address the same for their corporations" (p. 164). The role of leaders is central to this discussion because they set the tone, tenor, and pace of change in the profession. This chapter presents viewpoints of Indian public relations leaders on issues pertinent to the profession in India's transforming environment and offers a qualitative analysis of current leadership and practice in the region.

Addressing the complexity and dynamism of leadership in public relations, and drawing upon various streams of leadership literature, Meng and Berger (2013) define public relations leadership as

> a dynamic process that encompasses a complex mix of individual skills and personal attributes, values, and behaviors that consistently produce ethical and effective communication practice. Such practice fuels and guides successful communication teams, helps organizations achieve their goals, and legitimizes organizations in society. (p. 143)

Further, societal and organizational culture (as well as structure) play a central role and influence leadership performance.

Using this definition/model, and merging it with literature on leadership in an Indian context, we provide an in-depth look at leadership issues in the public relations industry in India. Keeping societal context in mind, we offer a qualitative analysis of the top communication issues that have an impact on public relations leaders in India, cultural and structural factors that assist and constrain their work, qualities of excellent leadership in Indian public relations, and current state of leadership development. We also chart some significant leadership needs for the future.

Brief History of Public Relations in India

Some have argued that public relations in India can be traced to ancient times (Reddi, cited in R. Singh, 2000). For example, Emperor Ashoka used rock tablets around BC 320 to propagate his vision to his publics (Kaul, 1988). Systematic and organized public relations developed in the colonial period (Ghosh, 1994). Some examples include (a) an external campaign by the Great Indian Peninsular Railway to promote tourism in India and (b) the establishment by the British of the Central Publicity Board in India for government relations—forerunner to today's Press Information Bureau. Freedom fighters like Mahatma Gandhi also used public relations effectively to oust the British from India (Desai, 1999). In the 1940s, domestic and multinational companies such as the Tata Group and Unilever began using modern forms of public relations. After independence in 1947, India adopted a mixed economy in which strategic industries were mainly government controlled. This gave rise to the public sector style of public relations (the norm until the 1980s): more bureaucratic than competitive with a high emphasis on national development. The private sector, strong but lean compared to the public sector, began to burgeon only after the late 1980s (Bardhan & Patwardhan, 2004; Bardhan & Sriramesh, 2004).

Since economic liberalization in the 1990s, and a corresponding surge in the private sector, there was an explosion of domestic public relations firms in India. Major multinational firms set up shop, often in affiliation with local outfits. Subsequently, the industry grew at a fast pace with a marked effort to improve professionalism and widen strategic scope of the public relations function (Bardhan, 2003; Gupta, 2007). Industry associations have also burgeoned. The Public Relations Society of India (PRSI), established in 1958, is large and comprised mainly of public sector professionals. More recently, other private sector oriented associations (e.g., the Public Relations Consultant Association of India—PRCAI) have been established (Bardhan, 2003). Indian practitioners, like in other transitioning economies, work in an environment that honors traditional practices and beliefs and is simultaneously future oriented. They also operate in a vastly diverse communication environment characterized by numerous languages, ethnicities, and religions (Bardhan & Sriramesh, 2004).

Scholarship on Public Relations in India

Sriramesh pioneered research on public relations in India in the early 1990s. Through an ethnographic study of public relations in southern Indian organizations, he developed the personal influence model (Sriramesh, 1996) that defines public relations practice in the high power distance Indian collectivist society. According to this model, building relations with strategically placed individuals through personal communication forms the bedrock of how practitioners function within India. In subsequent studies, Sriramesh (2000) and Bardhan (2003) found further support for this model. Other studies have focused on cultural similarities and differences from public relations in the West, standards of professionalism (Gupta, 2007; Newsom & Carrell, 1994), corporate social responsibility in India (e.g., Arora & Puranik, 2004; Chaudhri & Wang, 2007; Dhanesh, 2012; Sagar & Singla, 2004), multinational corporate public relations in India (Bardhan & Patwardhan, 2004; Berg & Holtbrügge, 2001) and crisis communication (Patwardhan & Bardhan, 2006). To our knowledge, no research solely focuses on public relations leaders and excellent leadership qualities in Indian industry.

The Study

As India project directors for a larger 23-country study of leadership in public relations and communication management by the Plank Center for Leadership in Public Relations at the University of Alabama, we conducted qualitative depth interviews with public relations leaders in India to gauge leadership issues, cultural contexts, and professional practice in the region. This chapter is primarily based on data from the interviews. Wherever possible, applicable findings from a larger survey of Indian practitioners--conducted during Phase 1 of the study, details of which are reported in a forthcoming article (Patwardhan & Bardhan, n.d.) are integrated, as is general literature on public relations and leadership in India.

Phone interviews were conducted with 13 public relations leaders in India. Interviewees were recruited through personal contacts, contacts made during the survey phase, and through LinkedIn solicitations. Interviews, lasting between 35 to 90 minutes, were conducted between August and November 2012. All were transcribed verbatim using a professional service. Seven interviewees were men, and six were women. All were located in one of the following metropolitan areas: Mumbai, Delhi, Kolkata, Chennai, and Bangalore. Seven were employed with agencies (two subsidiaries of multinational agencies and the rest Indian agencies) and six in corporations (two Indian corporations and the rest multinationals). None worked for the public or nonprofit sector. All served in leadership roles in their current organization, with industry experience ranging from 12 to (the majority) more than 25 years.

Top Issues for Public Relations Leaders in India

Overall, public relations leaders reported that the socioeconomic and media landscape in India is dynamic and that current and future public relations leaders need to skillfully navigate this landscape, balance human and technological communication, and educate clients/management about the full strategic potential

TABLE 11.1 Top Public Relations Issues in India

Issues	Frequency	Percentage
Finding, developing and retaining highly talented communication professionals	27	19.3
Improving the measurement of communication effectiveness to demonstrate value	22	15.7
Dealing with the speed and volume of information flow	17	12.1
Managing the digital revolution and rise of social media	15	10.7
Improving the image of the public relations/ communication management profession	15	10.7
Being prepared to deal effectively with crises that may arise	14	10.0
Improving employee engagement and commitment in the workplace	11	7.9
Meeting communication needs in diverse cultures and globalizing markets	10	7.1
Dealing with growing demands for transparency of communications and operations	7	5.0
Meeting increasing demands for corporate social responsibility	2	1.4

of public relations. Professional training, lack of sufficient talent along with a high turnover rate, issues with measurement of communication effectiveness, and education were weaknesses having an impact on the profession and the industry. These issues, as they relate to leadership, are elaborated in the rest of the chapter.

Survey participants in Phase 1 ($n = 140$) identified talent recruitment and retention, need to improve measurement of communication effectiveness, and need to deal with the speed and volume of information flow as the top three issues for India (Table 11.1). Interviewees corroborated these findings but also identified two additional top issues: (a) view of public relations in India mainly in terms of media relations and (b) insufficient recognition of its full scope as a strategic function and how social and digital media are changing the public relations landscape. Taken collectively (both survey results in Phase 1 and interviews in Phase 2), these views demonstrate remarkable similarity with observations from the aggregated global data for the overall leadership study. We next look at these issues from an Indian perspective along with strategies adopted and/or recommended by leaders.

Lack of Perception of PR's Strategic Role

In depth interviews conducted 10 years ago, Bardhan (2003) found a tendency of equating public relations with media relations a common problem in India. Our interviews suggest Indian practitioners still wrestle with the same issue, partly due to client misperceptions about the role of public relations. Many clients see public relations as getting press coverage, with low recognition of its other functions. A senior executive with more than 20 years of agency experience observed,

> I still feel there is huge lack of understanding about what PR does and what it delivers. Clients still tend to think that it's all media management. They don't understand that public relations is a complete package. . . . It involves a lot . . . many more elements than just having interviews placed in the media.

How do public relations leaders in India counter this? Educating clients, formally and informally, about the scope of public relations and the difference between public relations and marketing is one strategy. A senior professional with more than 25 years of agency experience also pointed to another strategy: a need to educate another stakeholder group—students. Therefore, he gives guest lectures at colleges and universities offering public relations degrees and certificates and conducts seminars and workshops for clients and colleagues.

Talent Recruitment and Retention

The second leading issue was lack of skilled professional talent and a high turnover rate, particularly in agencies. Public relations training in India is a hit-or-miss affair, with both educational institutions and industry contributing to the problem. One agency-based leader, active in the profession since early 1990s economic liberalization, observed that the industry has grown too fast and education has not kept pace. As a result, demand appears to have outstripped supply. He said, "We don't have great schools. We have very few schools that teach communication [or PR]. These are all cottage courses. There are very few structured communication courses [or degrees] that make true blue professionals."

In addition, public relations programs at academic institutions tend to be overly theory-based and driven mainly by non-Indian (mostly U.S.) textbooks and concepts that do not translate well in Indian contexts. An alternate solution offered by several agencies is some on-the-job training. The same agency leader described starting an internal training/education program to develop talent at agency cost. Several others mentioned similar efforts to nurture and retain employees and offer greater job satisfaction. However, beyond occasional workshops or guest lecturing, lack of collaborative academia–industry partnerships contributes to the problem from a long-term perspective. As a result, public relations education in India does not generate a sustainable entry-level talent pool or provide systematic training for leadership roles.

Digital Media, Speed of Information and the Public Relations Landscape

The third leading issue was the impact of social and digital media on the public relations landscape, a reality seen as a double-edged sword for leaders and practitioners. Associated with this is the speed of information flow and ways in which it needs to be harnessed and managed. An in-house practitioner for a large multinational auto company explained that the days of preplanning using traditional media are long gone. She said, "We've got to play it by the day and there is no set example, because it's an evolving field . . ." She provided the example of launching a new car model and said, "when someone "wants to buy a car, the first thing they do is to go on the internet and search for it. So, nobody is going to wait for you to get a review in a print publication, before they make the choice on the car." One of the first things she does is make sure the news is on Facebook and auto blogs. Thus, the consensus seemed to be that future leaders, as one interviewee put it, will have to be "comfortable with multiple platforms at multiple levels and almost work with them at the speed of light."

Although supportive of social and digital media in general, participants cautioned that practitioners need to better understand strategic use and effects. Broadly speaking, in an Indian setting where more collectivist social values prevail, social media are not seen as a substitute for human communication. Also, not all stakeholders in India are equally engaged with social and digital media. Therefore, although the importance of these media cannot be denied, they need to be part of a wider variety of communication platforms.

Effectiveness Measurement Challenge

Measuring communication effectiveness is a continuing challenge for public relations in India. A majority of interviewees considered the advertising equivalency measure (although still widely used) an inaccurate measure of public relations success. As one agency-based leader said,

> Measurement is still working in the old archaic way, advertising value equivalent. We have tools which have been brought in by some of the multinational PR firms that have come in, but have still not found acceptance. These things take a while. . . . Today the media world exponent has exploded. There are so many platforms you have to measure.

Leaders believed that the focus should be on measuring perceptions, awareness, and attitude change. Several reported developing quantitative and qualitative measures for their organizations/agencies and clients, although these have not been standardized across the industry.

Leadership in Indian Public Relations

In the leadership literature on India, much of the focus is on ancient culture and traditions and on how they mingle with current changing times (Sekhar, 2001; N. Singh & Krishnan, 2005). Earlier studies on leadership in India indicate two broad styles of leadership practice. One is the authoritarian and bureaucratic style (high power distance) mostly emphasizing task accomplishment. The other is the nurturing, participative (democratic) and empowering style in which the "personal touch" is very important. However, effective leadership in India depends not just on personality traits but also on the ability to navigate the larger environment, including organizational climate (Sinha, 1984).

According to a recent study published in the *Harvard Business Review* (Cappelli, Singh, Singh, & Useem, 2010), leaders of some of the top Indian corporations see themselves as being responsible for strategic input, developing a social mission, and as keepers of organizational culture. They also focus heavily on training and human capital development (Cappelli et al., 2010). Other leadership values, mostly in keeping with collectivism, include expertise, simple living, giving and receiving loyalty to and from employees, a self-sacrificing attitude, giving to others rather than focusing on self, a strong sense of duty which supersedes individual rights, and a very high focus on kinship and personal relationships. Internal rather than external relations seem to be a priority (N. Singh & Krishnan, 2005, 2007).

More recently, there is evidence of a shift away from high power distance and toward individualist values, transparency, and horizontal decision making (Cappelli et al., 2010; Chokkar, 2002; Kunnanatt, 2007). With India's transition to market capitalism and globalization, leaders able to mix traditional (authoritarian) leadership styles with more democratic styles appear to be much in demand. The mix depends on the nature of the industry or organization, with some being more traditional and others more change oriented.

Transformational leadership seems to be the need of the day. Transformational leadership, according to Burns (1978), is a style of leadership in which the leader and employees engage each other mutually so that both are able to rise to higher levels of performance and morality. Bass (1997) further noted that transformational leadership not only has universal traits but is also culture specific. The literature on India also emphasizes humane leadership, and the need for the leader to be able to motivate and be accountable to employees. Cappelli et al. (2010) observed that because Indian leadership is groomed in a highly uncertain environment, leaders are not as disturbed by change and are able to perform creatively in transforming environments.

Within the public relations context, leaders we interviewed demonstrate several traits and abide by many values highlighted in the general leadership literature on India. They seem to lean toward the democratic, nurturing, and empowering approach rather than the more traditional authoritarian/bureaucratic one. We note that none of our interviewees worked for public-sector companies, in which the bureaucratic approach is more prevalent. They represent the "new breed" of practitioners that emerged during the growth of market capitalism (Bardhan, 2003).

Interviews also revealed that public relations leaders are following leadership patterns that have evolved in the transforming climate of the last 20 years. The forces of economic privatization and globalization having an impact on cultural values as outside influences are merging with traditional and even ancient values. Although traditional modes of communication (i.e., high focus on interpersonal and human communication) and certain collectivist values are not being abandoned, leaders are generally supportive of leadership styles that involve less power distance and more individualism, transparency, horizontal structures and decision making, teamwork, and empowerment of employees. Within this more democratic approach to leadership, the public relations leaders interviewed did not emphasize traditional leadership values such as loyalty and self-sacrifice as much (N. Singh & Krishnan, 2005).

Cultural and Structural Influences on Public Relations Leadership in India

Overall, cultural and intra-organizational structural factors influencing the work of public relations leaders in India seem to mostly aid rather than hinder their performance, as interviewees report. The organizational culture in which they work places high value on ethics, integrity, innovation, and attention to people and knowledge. From a cultural perspective, human relations and the "personal touch" approach described earlier seem to largely guide their actions. Interviewees reported a strong sense of duty toward maintaining organizational culture and internal relations. Employee communication and attention to human capital development were described as top priorities. Focus on enriching organizational climate was best described by a leader who heads public relations for a 100-year-old Indian corporate group operating in 13 business areas: "[The company] is rooted in the core values of respect for people and belief in empowerment. We have been provided with the power of empowerment in the organization."

Another leader described her company as having an "open culture" that values its people and focuses on diversity. According to her, there is a sense that every employee gets a "fair share of voice in all forums."

External relations are viewed as somewhat more tricky, particularly for agencies. Observing that "a lot of practitioners in the PR business keep away from clients unless they have good news to give," an agency leader criticized this practice. He called for making human relations an equally important external relations focus for leaders, stating a need to stay in touch with clients in good and bad times and be honest with them so they know that they are in "good hands." This helps create a good image for the profession and allows the team to work with integrity.

From a structural perspective, nearly all interviewees working in-house had direct access to top management, enjoyed their confidence, and noted all units worked well with public relations. A head of public relations for a multinational auto company in India said that she has the full confidence of her top management with no pressure to engage in unethical practices. She commented, "Even on behalf of the executive I can make a decision on what can be said and what cannot be said." Interviewees saw themselves as playing a key role in strategic planning and input. At the same time, they stressed the importance of performing and delivering consistently and well to earn and keep the trust of top management.

A majority (agency as well as in-house) described their organizational structure as horizontal rather than vertical, a fact that aids their work as leaders. Within the agency environment, leaders preferred working democratically because it was essential to inspire and empower employees in their work. As the CEO of an Indian agency said, "We have teams that are independent to function on their own within the parameters of the strategy, etc., and also develop their own strategies, and develop their own ideas . . . It's a think-tank at all levels."

Another interviewee who manages offices of a multinational public relations firm in India described the culture of his agency as "flat" and "not very hier-archic." For example, he always has direct access to and communicates with the U.K.-based person who started the agency. He also described organizational culture as more "informal." This, he believes, facilitates information sharing within and across all offices in India, ensures that work doesn't slow down, and keeps clients satisfied. He said, "It's like we're one whole team and one fam-ily. . . . If a team needs support from another city and we have some time on our hands, we will jump in and do whatever they need."

On the corporate side, the head of public relations with the 100-year-old Indian company (with more than 29,000 employees) also reported a decentral-ized structure, well-defined responsibilities, and clear lines of communication helping him run corporate communications smoothly. The public relations head for a multinational electronics company observed a unique feature of her (global) company: no global headquarters. Instead, it has management hubs with meetings convened in different places (or virtually) as needed.

Finally, regarding societal culture, all interviewees acknowledged that the multicultural and multilingual nature of India, with several religions and ethnici-ties, makes communicating across cultures and languages a constant challenge. However, being rooted in the diverse Indian environment makes leaders value and pay close attention to diversity in all its forms, particularly in stakeholder communication and relationship building. One leader expressed preference for hiring multilingual practitioners. Another noted that Indian practitioners, in general, are highly skilled at working with diversity and can serve as role models for practitioners in other parts of the world.

Two major structural hurdles in the professional development of the public relations industry were also identified: limited platforms for sharing best practices and uneven quality of public relations education. Limited information and best practices sharing in industry hampers professional growth of Indian practitioners and leaders. Lack of good infrastructure for public relations education has an impact on quality and the availability of professionally trained talent.

Characteristics and Qualities of Excellent Leaders

Meng and Berger (2013) conceptualized and validated a concept of excellent public relations leadership with six dimensions: self-dynamics (self-insight, shared vision), team collaboration, ethical orientation, relationship building (internal and external), strategic decision-making capabilities, and communication knowledge management. Using aggregated survey data in the overall global study, this was also validated in a cross-cultural context. Our in-depth interviews offer support for all six dimensions of leadership as essential for effective public relations leadership in India.

There were, however, two exceptions. First, although external stakeholder relationships were important, leaders spoke at length about their role and responsibility in building internal relationships (including employee relations and human capital development). This may be explained by the collectivist leaning of cultures in India in general, despite a move towards more individualistic values today (Chokkar, 2002). Second, communication was discussed more in terms of cultivating human relations. The term *management*, which has a more instrumental connotation, was used in relation to knowledge and information; that is, the importance of skillfully "managing" knowledge and information was expressed by several of the leaders interviewed.

Based on the interviews, we conclude that excellent public relations leaders should do the following:

- Be good human beings and maintain high ethical standards for self and profession.
- Value transparency and be accountable to employees.
- Lead by example and serve as role models.
- Be self-motivated and not depend on external affirmation.
- Be responsible for mentoring future talent. For example, one agency-based leader said that good leaders should "be able to impart knowledge and groom a line of people who can take on the mantle, which is where we're really lacking. We're not investing in the future."
- Have a mature and holistic (i.e., political, social, etc.) view of the public relations landscape.
- Be well informed and knowledgeable in many areas, and manage and apply their knowledge appropriately and persuasively. They should constantly learn and should not become stuck in boxes. They should also develop better information-sharing skills.

- Possess outstanding communication skills in general, be good communicators (articulators of viewpoints and negotiators of conflict) and listeners, and connect with diverse stakeholders in their own language.
- Be good counselors to management and not succumb to becoming "yes" people. According to one in-house leader, it is necessary to take a "courageous approach towards PR in one's company. They [leaders] should be good listeners, but also be good counselors to the executive." Good counseling, according to her, involves saying no when necessary, and this requires courage. Similarly, leaders should be responsible for strategic input and planning.
- Foster teamwork rather than competition among employees, and be team players and vision builders.
- Balance human and technical communication and be skilled at providing the "personal touch" for building relationships. Too little emphasis on human communication is detrimental to relationship building.
- Be able to juggle many communication platforms, "cross pollinate" between platforms, and navigate the speed of information flow. They should also be skillfully navigate the fast changing sociocultural, economic, and political landscape in India as well as maintain high standards in their work.

Some leadership qualities specific to Indian public relations expressed in the interviews were the role of the leader as a mentor/trainer of talent for the future (due to the lack of quality education) and the need to skillfully manage uncertainty and to create vision in a transforming society. In other words, transformational public relations leadership is important as well as necessary in the highly fluid Indian landscape.

Current State of Leadership Development and Future Leadership Needs

Combined survey and depth interview data suggest that, at present, there is no formal structure for public relations leadership development in India. The overly fluid/transitional nature of the industry may be a compelling explanation. The more established public sector style of public relations (assisted through the activities of the PRSI) is being challenged by an emerging private-sector style that, although growing in dominance, has not yet developed a solid leadership structure. A cohesive industry approach combining the two styles does not exist either. Although several outstanding leaders are informally guiding the industry in times of change, training and professional development in public relations is not where it could be. More focus, more direction, and a stable industry-level support structure are necessary for future development.

An important factor having an impact on leadership development in India is lack of emphasis on communication education in general, and public relations training in particular. New hires may or may not have an educational background in communication/public relations and may mostly learn on the job or through in-house training. Despite increased focus on communication and public relations education in the last decade at an undergraduate level (as several interviewees explained), theory-based pedagogy offers less practical value and is dependent on content developed outside India (mostly the United States).

In all likelihood, nonavailability of Indian material and limited public relations research on India are factors responsible for this situation. About 10 years ago, Bardhan (2003) found a handful of postgraduate degree/diploma opportunities in public relations education, some offered through established and reputed universities and institutes. Since then, given rapid growth of private-sector public relations, numerous education "shops" have mushroomed with courses taught by professionally inexperienced educators. In sum, leadership development is hampered by the lack of strong basic, culturally relevant communication education at the beginning of a public relations career.

Second, the industry still lacks an overall strong, cohesive structure despite existence of national level associations such as the PRSI and private-sector bodies such as the PRCAI. Thus, venues for information sharing among leaders about how to navigate the changing landscape and other issues of professional importance (such as strategic use of social media and communication effectiveness measurement) are somewhat limited. Although conferences, seminars and workshops are held frequently (especially by PRSI), some interviewees reported that they do not center on more pressing issues facing practitioners. The lack of a cohesive professional industry structure also limits formal apparatus for training and professional development at industry level. Most leaders interviewed were trained by good mentors and are successful because of their personal efforts and hard work. The lack of strong role models also adds to the difficulty of cultivating and setting leadership standards at an overall level.

Literature on leadership in India and the interviews reveal a collectivist tendency among public relations leaders in India to focus more on internal rather than external relationship building. At one level, this is a strength contributing to a strong organizational culture. At another, it is a weakness if it occurs at the expense of building relations and networking with colleagues across industry in various settings and organizations (agency, in-house, private sector, public sector, and nonprofit). Furthermore, the industry has grown rapidly but in an ad hoc manner. This growth now needs to be channeled in a more focused manner. Finally, the schism between the public- and private-sector subcultures of public relations needs to be bridged through dialogue and cooperation for the industry to progress with confidence and to produce more outstanding leaders.

Based on the preceding, we offer three prescriptive recommendations to address leadership development needs for public relations in India:

1. First, academia and industry should find ways to work together to develop context-specific curricula and devise an appropriate balance between theory

and practice. Educators should engage in more research to develop content. Industry should help by providing structured internship and shadowing opportunities. Professionals and leaders should also invest more time giving guest lectures at educational institutions.

2. Second, practitioners and leaders from within various public relations subcultures in India should find ways to dialogue and jointly build a more cohesive professional industry structure. This would provide future focus and serve as a platform for systematic training and professional development for practitioners at all levels, including leaders. It would also lead to better information sharing across industry and provide a united front for diverse forms of the public relations practice within India.

3. Third, those already in leadership positions, whatever style of public relations they may practice, should make it their priority to think at a level larger than the organization and to work together to create networking and relationship building opportunities at an industry level.

Collectively, these efforts can contribute synergistically toward strengthening the structure and culture of leadership within the public relations industry in India.

Conclusion

The public relations industry in India is old as well as new. It is old because if one goes back thousands of years, one can see how rulers and leaders in India, over time, have made excellent use of communication for galvanizing social and political movements. It is new because it has been only slightly more than 60 years since Indian independence, when the nation began developing its own infrastructure for industry and the service sector, including public relations. It is now a matter of working diligently to bring old and new together to chart a cohesive path for the growth of industry and leadership culture.

Our analysis of the state of leadership in public relations in India is not intentionally negative. We simply bring to light some issues that stand in the way of developing a stronger leadership culture for the future. As noted previously, Cappelli et al. (2010) observed that leaders of thriving companies in India could be role models for the rest of the world. The public relations industry in the region is well positioned to learn from these leaders and to systematically strengthen local practice. Operating in a climate of uncertainty, they are actually at an advantage when it comes to navigating change. They are also experienced at working with multicultural publics given the vast cultural diversity. Finally, with the largest population in the world, with a median age of 28, there is no dearth of young talent that can be cultivated to promote emergence of prospective public relations leaders in India by making a collective investment in the future.

References

Arora, B., & Puranik, R. (2004). A review of corporate social responsibility in India. *Development, 47*(3), 93–100.

Bardhan, N. (2003). Rupturing public relations metanarratives: The example of India. *Journal of Public Relations Research, 15*(3), 225–248.

Bardhan, N., & Patwardhan, P. (2004). Multinational corporations and public relations in a traditionally resistant host culture. *Journal of Communication Management, 8*(3), 246–263.

Bardhan, N., & Sriramesh, K. (2004). Public relations in India: A profession in transition. In K. Sriramesh (Ed.), *Public relations in Asia: An anthology* (pp. 63–96). Singapore: Thomson Learning.

Bass, B. M. (1997). Does the transactional–transformational leadership paradigm transcend organizational and national boundaries? *American Psychologist, 52*(2), 130–139.

Berg, N., & Holtbrügge, D. (2001). Public affairs management activities of German multinational corporations in India. *Journal of Business Ethics, 30*(1), 105–119.

Burns, J. M. (1978) *Leadership.* New York, NY: Harper & Row.

Cappelli, P., Singh, H., Singh, J., & Useem, M. (2010, March). Leadership lessons from India. *Harvard Business Review*, pp. 1–9.

Chaudhri, V., & Wang, J. (2007). Communicating corporate social responsibility on the Internet: A case study of the top 100 information technology companies in India. *Management Communication Quarterly, 21*(2), 232–247.

Chokkar, J. (2002). Leadership and culture in India: The GLOBE research project. Available online at www.hs-fulda.de/fileadmin/Fachbereich_SW/Downloads/Profs/Wolf/Studies/india/india.pdf

Desai, R. (1999). *Indian business culture: An insider's guide.* New Delhi, India: Viva Books.

Dhanesh, G. (2012). Better stay single? Public relations and CSR leadership in India. *Public Relations Review, 38*, 141–143.

Ghosh, S. (1994). *Public relations today (in the Indian context).* Delhi, India: Profile Publishers.

Gupta, S. (2007). Professionalism in Indian public relations and corporate communications: An empirical analysis. *Public Relations Review, 33*, 306–312.

Kaul, J. (1988). *Public relations in India* (2nd ed.). Calcutta, India: Naya Prokash.

Kruckeberg, D. (2000). Public relations: Toward a global professionalism. In J. A. Ledingham & S. D. Bruning (Eds.), *Public relations as relationship management: A relational approach to the study and practice of public relations* (pp. 153–166). Mahwah, NJ: Erlbaum.

Kunnanatt, J. T. (2007). Leadership orientation of service sector managers in India: An empirical study. *Business and Society Review, 112*(1), 99–119.

Meng, J., & Berger, B. (2013). An integrated model of excellent leadership in public relations: Dimensions, measurement, and validation. *Journal of Public Relations Research, 25*(2), 141–167.

Newsom, D., & Carrell, B. (1994). Professional public relations in India: Need outstrips supply. *Public Relations Review, 20*(2), 183–188.

Patwardhan, P., & Bardhan, N. (n.d.). Worlds apart or a part of the world? Public relations issues and challenges in India. *Public Relations Review.*

Patwardhan, P., & Bardhan, N. (2006). The Bhopal Carbide disaster: A lesson in crisis communication. In M. G. Parkinson & D. Ekachai (Eds.), *International and intercultural public relations: A campaign case approach* (pp. 220–238). Boston, MA: Allyn and Bacon.

Sagar, P., & Singla, A. (2004). Trust and corporate social responsibility: Lessons from India. *Journal of Communication Management, 8*(3), 282–290.

Sekhar, R. C. (2001). Trends in ethics and styles of leadership in India. *Business Ethics: A European Review, 10*(4), 360–363.

Singh, N., & Krishnan, V. R. (2005). Towards understanding transformational leadership in India: A grounded theory approach. *Vision – The Journal of Business Perspective, 9*(2), 5–17.

Singh, N., & Krishnan, V. R. (2007). Transformational leadership in India: Developing and validating a new scale using grounded theory approach. *International Journal of Cross Cultural Management, 7*(2), 219–236.

Singh, R. (2000). Public relations in contemporary India: Current demands and strategy. *Public Relations Review, 26*(3), 295–313.

Sinha, J. B. P. (1984). A model of effective leadership styles in India. *International Journal of Management & Organization, 14*(2/3), 86–98.

Sriramesh, K. (1996). Power distance and public relations: An ethnographic study of southern Indian organizations. In H. Culbertson & N. Chen (Eds.), *International public relations: A comparative analysis* (pp. 171–190). Mahwah, NJ: Erlbaum.

Sriramesh, K. (2000). The models of public relations in India. *Journal of Communication Management, 4*(3), 225–239.

12

PAST, PRESENT AND FUTURE PUBLIC RELATIONS IN SOUTH KOREA

Issues, Work Environments, and Leadership

Jae-Hwa Shin, Jaesub Lee, Jongmin Park, and Kwang Hee Kim

Managerial leadership has been a central interest in organizations. Numerous scientific studies over the past century have addressed a variety of issues and concerns, including traits, personalities, skills, influence, power, effectiveness, functions, roles, styles, and contingencies (Yukl, 2006). Because public relations emphasizes a managerial function for practitioners in organizations, managerial leadership has become "an important and promising" area of inquiry in public relations (Meng, Berger, Gower, & Heyman, 2012). Meng and her colleagues (2012), however, also noted that "leadership in public relations has received little direct research attention," and accordingly, there is "a strong need for exploring the qualities and value of leadership in the practice of public relations" (p. 19). Research aimed at better understanding of leadership qualities and dimensions, they further claimed, will help develop practitioners' leadership competencies and augment the profession's value to the organization.

Given globalization, the diversity of the workforce, and worldwide strategic importance of the communication profession in a variety of organizations, cross-cultural leadership research in public relations is of crucial importance (Hofstede, 2001; Scandura & Dorfman, 2004; Shin, Heath, & Lee, 2011). This chapter reports on the issues and concerns of public relations leadership in South Korean contexts. More specifically, this chapter describes the developmental history of Korean public relations and presents an interview study that explores important current and future leadership issues and values, work environments, and practices in Korean public relations.

Contemporary Public Relations in Korea

In Korea public relations is called *Hong Bo*. It literally means "broadly informing." Its contemporary development in Korea coincides with the Japanese defeat during World War II (e.g., Kim, 2003; Rhee, 2002). As Japan retreated from

Korea, the U.S. Army assumed temporary governance over the southern half of Korea (South Korea) under the United Nations trusteeship in 1945. During this administrative transition, the term *public relations* was first used and professionally practiced in Korea. Early practice concentrated on controlling the press (e.g., censorship) to enhance the administration's positions on policies and regulations. Thus, Korean public relations practices began with U.S. style of media relations, but in an authoritarian context.

During the 1960s, public relations came to be widely practiced in Korean businesses, and increased significantly in the 1970s as the economy expanded rapidly. In particular, chaebols (large and often family-owned business conglomerates) needed to interact with various publics and required public relations. Chaebols were connected closely with the government and enjoyed special privileges such as preferential financial arrangements and contracts in exchange for political funds and other forms of support that were often perceived as illegal by the public at that point. Hence, chaebols established in-house public relations units to manage such perceptions. The primary task of public relations was to evade public criticism about chaebols' wrongdoings. Toward this end, public relations departments in chaebols focused largely on publicity to counter negative news reports on their collusive transactions with the government and monopolies in certain markets (Kim & Hon, 1998). Media relations is still the most frequent assignment, requiring about 95% of the public relations personnel (Korea Public Relations Association, 2003).

During the 1980s, Korean society was characterized by democratization movements and business internationalization. Many multinational corporations and large local companies needed more advanced public relations practices to keep up with changing political, cultural, and business environments. In particular, the 1988 Seoul Summer Olympic Games served as a significant catalyst in the development and transformation of the public relations industry. For the first time in Korea, "full-service" public relations firms were established, including Communications Korea (a Hill & Knowlton affiliate), Merit Communications (a Burson-Masteller affiliate), and KPR & Associates. As suggested earlier, before the 1980s, there were no independent public relations firms, only in-house departments in chaebol companies. In 1989, Korean public relations practitioners established their first professional association, the Korea Public Relations Association (KPRA).

In the early 1990s, the Korean public relations industry expanded steadily, growing at a rate of 30% to 40% annually (Park, 2001). However, in the late 1990s, the economic crisis in Korea slowed the growth of the public relations industry. During the International Monetary Fund (IMF) crisis (harsh austerity measures imposed by the IMF in exchange for a financial bailout during 1997–1998), corporate activities including public relations became somewhat stagnant (Rhee, 2002). Nonetheless, a strong economic recovery suggested the growing need and opportunity for public relations in Korea. As of 2009, the

Korean Public Relations Yearbook (2010) listed 30 major public relations firms, 58 public relations agencies, and 31 large in-house public relations departments in major Korean chaebols.

Practice Models

In line with an inordinate emphasis on media relations, public relations practitioners in Korea have tended to enact technical public relations (press agentry and public information) more frequently than managerial models (Kim & Hon, 1998). On the other hand, these same practitioners have expressed desire to practice managerial models. Although Korean public relations has enhanced its sophistication in its practices over time, on the whole, it is still very much in the formative stage relative to U.S. public relations (Kim & Hon, 1998; Park 2003).

Further, the Korean practice of press agentry (and for that matter most of public relations activities) is primarily enacted through the "personal influence model" in which public relations practitioners have mobilized various interpersonal relationships with key individuals in government, media, political entities, and activist groups in order to affect their organizational interests (e.g., Kim & Hon, 1998; Park, 2003). More specifically, Shin and Cameron (2003) found that informal relations enacted through unofficial calls, private meetings, regional/alumni/blood ties, press tours, bargaining advertising, and perks such as golf and hiking affected news coverage (what is news and how it is presented) at least moderately.

Jo and Kim (2004) examined the personal influence model by identifying three specific sub-dimensions: seeking informal relationships (easy access to or personal connection with journalists), providing monetary gifts (tactics such as gift offering, social gathering, and offering direct payments to maintain favorable relationships with journalists), and formal responsibility for public relations (e.g., developing and disseminating valuable news items and doing follow-up services for further inquiries). Such tactics are in some ways consistent with Korean cultural norms and values. Confucianism, in particular, encourages close, personal social ties and harmony among concerned parties (e.g., public relations practitioners and journalists; Kim & Bae, 2006). When faced with nonroutine crisis or conflict situations, Korean public relations practitioners place high value on "enactment competency," that is, balancing multiple interests, protecting valuable resources, balancing pragmatism and idealism, and maintaining flexibility (Shin et al., 2011).

Rhee (2002) suggested that the "excellence" models are being widely practiced by Korean public relations practitioners and are highly amenable to Korean culture. According to Rhee, Korean cultural characteristics such as collectivism, uncertainty avoidance, and Confucian dynamism correlated with characteristics advocated in the excellence models.

Looking to the future, Berkowitz and Lee (2004) predicted that a recent governmental declaration of the policy of the "tense regard," or more socially distanced relations with the press during the Roh Moo-Hyeon's government (2003–2008), may help Korean public relations grow beyond traditional media relations and move closer to the ideals of Western media relations practices. Consistent with personal, relational orientation of the society, Korean public relations practitioners may also take advantage of social networking websites, including Twitter, Facebook, and Flickr, and corporate blogging (Hwang, 2012).

Public Relations Education

The first independent academic department of public relations in Korea was established at Chung Ang University in 1974. Since then, educational endeavors have expanded substantially. As of 2010, 82 universities offer an undergraduate curriculum that includes public relations courses. Thirty-six universities offer undergraduate and graduate curriculums in which public relations is a subdiscipline (*Korea Public Relations Year Book*, 2010). Twenty-eight universities have an undergraduate program that includes "public relations" as part of the department name (e.g., department of advertising and public relations), and five graduate schools bear public relations program names (Korea Press Foundation, 2012).

Many professional and academic associations have focused on public relations. The major public relations affiliates include the Korea Public Relations Association, Korean Academic Society for Public Relations, Korean Association for Advertising and Public Relations, Korea Public Relations Consultancy Association, Korea Universities PR Association, Korea Business Communicators Association, and Korean Hospital Public Relations Association.

The Study

As noted earlier, Meng and her colleagues (2012) argued that "there is much to do and to learn on the leadership front in public relations" (p. 34). In their judgment, devoting attention to leadership is paramount to "the value, image, success, and future of public relations" (Meng et al., 2012, p. 34). Thus, as part of ongoing efforts to build a foundation upon which new leadership theories unique to public relations can be built, this interview study explored critical leadership issues, values of public relations to the organization/management, work environments in which public relations practitioners enact their roles, and future expectations of public relations leaders in South Korea. This interview study and the associated survey were conducted as part of a 23-country global-scale investigation of leadership in public relations and communication management sponsored by the Plank Center for Leadership in Public Relations at the University of Alabama.

This study focuses largely on findings from the interview data. When relevant, findings from the survey of 205 Korean practitioners are integrated.

Interviews

Ten interviews were conducted with experienced Korean communication and public relations practitioners. Interviewees consisted of seven men and three women, typically with more than 11 years of work experience in their practices. These veteran practitioners held leadership positions of team leader, manager, and director of public relations in diverse industries of public and private, domestic and international, and profit and nonprofit organizations. The smaller number of female interviewees reflects the relatively low number of female communication and public relations professionals at the managerial level in South Korea.

To identify prospective Korean interviewees in public relations and communication management, the list of names and their email addresses were withdrawn *Korea Public Relations Yearbook* (2010), which includes members and their contact information of Korea Public Relations Association (KPRA) and affiliate organizations such as Korea Society of the International Public Relations Association IPRA, Korean Academic Society for Public Relations, Korean Association for Advertising and Public Relations, and Korea Public Relations Consultancy Association. In addition, personal and informal inquiries were made about the potential interviewees through email and phone calls.

Interviews were arranged via personal contacts and conducted mostly in face-to-face meetings. In general, a prospective interviewee was first contacted by a researcher and, when they agreed to participate, met in their offices or public places. One interview was done through e-mail. In-person interviews lasted from 30 to 90 minutes. These interviews were audio recorded with the interviewee's agreement. Field notes were taken at the same time. All interviewees received token remuneration for their participation.

Interview questions were first developed in English following the guidelines in the 23-country cross-cultural investigation of leadership in public relations and communication management. Questions were primarily concerned with two broad areas: (a) current and future issues in public relations and communication management in Korea and (b) cultural, structural, and leadership environments (see Appendix A). Once finalized in English, the questions were then translated to a Korean version by two bilingual researchers. One researcher translated all the questions to a Korean version and the other reexamined the Korean version independently. Any differences in translation (e.g., word choices, sentence structures, and grammatical matters) were resolved through discussion. All interviews were conducted in Korean, and the transcripts in Korean were translated to English versions. Again, one researcher translated all the Korean transcripts to English versions, and, after independent inspections, any issues in translations were resolved by discussion and mutual agreements between the bilingual researchers.

Findings

Two Most Important Current Issues

The first area of inquiry in the interviews concerned the two most important issues in current communication and public relations practices in South Korea. Analysis of the findings suggested that the most important issue is social media. Social media involve use of electronic forms of communication via various channels, including Twitter, Facebook, YouTube, Flickr, blogs, photo- and file-sharing sites, wikis, and the like. They are often used to create, share, and exchange personal and/or business information, ideas, messages or other content. The practitioners were primarily concerned about understanding and utilizing social media and about tailoring messages or issues to the target audiences.

Practitioners recognize, and are expected to take advantage of, many capabilities of social media through which communication often becomes two-way or multi-way, fast, widely dispersed, and participative; social media help share and exchange information and interests rapidly and widely. Thus, social media have come to represent potentially useful and effective tools for the practitioners and organizations to influence the public's opinions, views, attitudes, behaviors, and participation. A related point is that social media represent changing media environments. Practitioners indicated they must be adaptive to new media environments, and in fact, today's clients demand social media service highly.

The impacts of social media were perceived in many ways and at many levels—the practitioner, department or unit, organization, and field. Social media present new opportunities and challenges to the practitioner and to the entire profession of communication and public relations. Practitioners are expected to acquire new skills to work with social media (e.g., social media research, content, and accessibility), often through training and development efforts (e.g., lectures and consultations from external experts). Social media are considered as means to a complete reorganization of the unit with more resources, forming a new taskforce/special project/action plans and to a greater sharing of ideas and fine-tuning of opinions among team members. The use of social media has become a measure of success/performance evaluation of the unit as well (and subsequent external businesses from such successes and greater direct and indirect revenue generation).

Accordingly, social media has elevated the unit's and the practitioner's status with greater recognition and more interest in the public relations role in the organization, especially by top management. In addition, social media have made it easier to send information to audiences in different countries, further leading to additional conversations via offline channels. One practitioner noted a dramatic impact that social media brought upon the unit:

> The possibilities of new [communication] technology led to a reorganization of the unit, which resulted in a new team in charge of public relations. We moved from the traditional media relations. We established a new team after addressing many concerns, including one person vs. a team for the task, hiring, new equipment, internal expertise vs. outsourcing, expenses, etc. Social media are currently taking a greater place in our practice.

The second most important issue was employee communication. Employee communication broadly refers to communicative interactions among employees or members of an organization (Berger, 2008). Specific concerns that were identified included enhancing internal communication competencies so that communication with various internal publics (sometimes across countries, gender, and generations) became open, smooth, and effective. The leaders interviewed cited the importance of employee communication in working well together with people with different backgrounds, generating effective work outcomes, meeting the demands of top management and critically contributing to the survival of the organization.

Employee communication affected communication and public relations in several important ways. First, improved internal communication ability helps to deal with conflicts; smooth and harmonious communication enhances mutual understanding of involved parties and resolves conflict in a positive way. Second, improved employee communication helps create or establish new communication channels with both internal and external publics (e.g., intranet, newsletters, opinion leaders). Third, it also increases employee attention to communication issues and organizational affairs. One firm that an interviewee works for established "spaces" for communication to help develop harmonious relationships among employees with sociocultural differences. Fourth, employee communication may enhance the value and development of the organization. Good employee communication helps form a taskforce, engage in special projects, and draw up future plans. One practitioner interviewed noted how employee communication reflects the essence of leadership qualities:

> At present, seven members work together in our team. I work as the team leader. One critically important thing to my role is open–mindedness— attitudes to share what I have with team members, not being secretive but open about what I do and what the team members do, which will then enhance the breadth of mutual understanding and counter conflicts. This sort of communication has a lot to do with internal smoothness in communication. In fact, I believe this [open–mindedness] is the core of leadership.

TABLE 12.1 Top Issues for Korean Public Relations and Communication Practitioners

Issues	Frequency	Percentage
Being prepared to deal effectively with crises that may arise	40	19.5
Improving the measurement of communication effectiveness to demonstrate value	29	14.1
Dealing with growing demands for transparency of communications and operations	29	14.1
Managing the digital revolution and rise of social media	27	13.2
Meeting increasing demands for corporate social responsibility	19	9.3
Dealing with the speed and volume of information flow	18	8.8
Finding, developing, and retaining highly talented communication professionals	17	8.3
Meeting communication needs in diverse cultures and globalizing markets	16	7.8
Improving the image of the public relations/communication management profession	8	3.9
Improving employee engagement and commitment in the workplace	2	1.0

Findings from the larger survey data generally corroborated the interview findings. The issue of managing digital revolution and rise of social media was cited often. Likewise, dealing with growing demands for transparency of communication and operations, largely a communication issue with employees (and perhaps with nonemployees as well) was a top concern, too. Survey participants also identified two additional top issues: effective crisis management and improvement in the measure of communication effectiveness (see Table 12.1).

Three Most Important Future Issues

The interviewees named three big issues in the coming 3 to 5 years: (a) managing complex aspects of social media, (b) the need for more face-to-face communication, and (c) a likely expansion of the practice. Social media and network-related issues loomed large in the minds of Korean communication and public relations leaders and practitioners for their future practice as well as their current activities. One practitioner commented that "the importance of SNS [social network sites] in public relations grows as time goes by, and social media will be the primary vehicle through which we practice public relations in a few years." Many practitioners felt that they would work on issues relating to social media content value and policy, strategic/tactical use, appropriateness in a crisis, right mix of message, and the generation gap in terms of the usage. However, practitioners indicated a counter issue to the greater reliance on social media—the need for face-to-face communication, as suggested in the following comment:

I would like more face-to-face or interpersonal relationship development with various publics. As the SNS becomes part of everyday interaction, it becomes invisible background. As communication channels become diverse, it's actually getting more difficult to communicate with targeted publics about public problems. It is like being poor in rich choices.

Expansion of the practice was the third issue. The following comment highlights this issue:

Currently public relations is focused on issues defined by the organization in Korea; in the future, public relations may need to get involved in various political, cultural and economic issues, and public relations should be ready for such broader tasks and responsibilities.

Influence of Culture or Structure of the Organization

Another area of inquiry in the interviews was to identify cultural or structural factors that contribute to successes and failures in the practice of communication and public relations. Public relations practitioners suggested that "togetherness" and "task competencies" are the two most important values in Korean organizations and relevant to their practice. One prevailing value or characteristic was "doing things together and for each other," as illustrated in expressions such as "working together," "finding value together," "serving the customers well together," "sharing the benefits with the community," "enjoying together," and "developing harmonious work relationships" among employees with different backgrounds. The other value was enhancing task competencies in the practice, including areas of task efficiency, client-focused approach, development of unique and creative talents, and effective communication.

Two success factors also were identified: interaction patterns and top management support. One critical factor was interactions with external publics that were visible, frequent, regular, and two way. Such interactions were perceived to be attainable when practitioners have access to inside information, are party to high-level management and committees, and are able to influence decision making. The other factor was top management involvement in terms of support, engagement, interest, value, and knowledge and understanding of communication and public relations.

Two additional factors were tied critically to failures in communication and public relations practices: misconceptions of the profession and unsuccessful role enactment. First, misunderstanding, and/or indifference toward communication and public relations from the top management and employees were seen as dooming the practice. For instance, some senior employees cited the misperception of public relations as a vanity or luxury with management failing to recognize its importance relative to sales and marketing on public views of the organization (e.g., brand and image). Another factor was unsuccessful role enactment by the professionals themselves. In such failure situations, the practitioners played "supportive" (technician) rather than "leading" (managerial) roles, lacked excellent functional leadership, or were ineffective in harmonizing different interests in policy formation and implementation.

Values of Public Relations and Communication Management

Korean communication and public relations units or leaders generally were viewed favorably by their top management or dominant coalitions, according to the public relations leaders interviewed. They received strong, full, and sufficient support from their CEOs and top managers; had direct reporting relationships with the management; and closely consulted with them. They also participated in high-level meetings and dealt with weighty assignments.

The interviewees reported attempts to showcase values of communication and public relations to the firm in many different ways, including improvement in the company's image, awareness, and recognition; value of media coverage and effective handling of negative media coverage; a favorable ratio of the expense and effectiveness relative to advertising impact and the number of articles or broadcasts per financial unit; and an increase of revenue size from winning business or projects from other companies. However, a few practitioners expressed concerns that they did not have good systematic measures to show the relative value of public relations to the organization yet. Most noted that existing measures are ambiguous, and they are uncertain about the values of such measures.

Leadership Qualities and Characteristics

Korean communication and public relations leaders perceived that the two most important characteristics or qualities of excellent leadership were communication competencies at multiple levels and managerial competencies for task and conflict. Practitioners noted that public relations professionals should enact communication competencies (abilities, skills, and effectiveness) at the personal (e.g., be open-minded, create an issue or a vision, generate and distribute content), relational (e.g., enhance relational ability, build social networks), and mediated levels (e.g., increase external interaction, work with media networks). The following comment illustrates the importance of communication and relationship competencies in current public relations leaders in Korea:

> The first characteristic is communication competence. Especially because we need to work on both internal and external communication simultaneously, the practitioner must be a communication expert. The other is relationship competence. This characteristic is closely related to

communication competence. Without building relationships or networks, internal and external communication may not work well.

The other leadership qualities are managerial competencies for task (task-centered, analytical and adaptable, objective, fair and square approaches) and conflict (harmony, careful consideration, deep positive emotional touch, love, and understanding of the organization and environment).

Future Korean communication and public relations leaders are expected to face familiar and new demands or problems. Some of the participants' comments indicated that future communication leaders will need greater learning, adaptability, and creative problem solving (e.g., technological potentials, lessons from experiences, changing work/communication environments such as media use, audiences/publics, public opinion setting, and SNS and other digital forms). Future leaders also must elevate their status, role, and importance and expand applications of public relations in many areas. Finally, there is growing recognition of different kinds of publics and corresponding expectations in the practice, as illustrated in the following comment:

> These days, consumers don't simply receive information from daily newspapers. They seek out information themselves; they are active consumers. Accordingly, public relations practitioners themselves must change in order to generate any positive outcomes in the practice. I believe this sort of change will accelerate. Thus, public relations practitioners themselves double their efforts to find out new methods that fit such changing work environments.

Discussion

Meng and her colleagues (Meng & Berger, 2013; Meng et al., 2012) indicated that little is known about leadership theories unique to communication and public relations, though it is critical to "the value, image, success, and future of public relations" (Meng et al., 2012, p. 34). This chapter represents an attempt to offer insight into research endeavors exploring many useful venues of leadership, including critical leadership issues, values of public relations to the organization/management, work environments in which public relations practitioners enact their roles, and future expectations of public relations leaders, in a South Korean context. Interview and survey data indicated that Korean professionals in communication and public relations perceived social media and employee communication as highly important issues in their current practice. They further saw that social media, face-to-face relationships, and an expansion of the practice are looming large in the next several years. They believed that togetherness (e.g., working and sharing together) and task competencies are valued most in their organizations. Critical success factors are interaction patterns and management support.

Korea has developed one of the most advanced and ubiquitous information technology infrastructures in the world. The country has led the International Telecommunication Union's so-called Digital Opportunity Index, which measures a country's information technology advancement in four categories, including coverage and affordability, access path and device, infrastructure, and quality. Korea also boasts the highest rate of high-speed Internet or broadband household penetration in the world, 95% as of 2008 (Strategy Analytics, 2009) and 97.2% in 2011 (OECD iLibrary, 2013). Flurry market research blog ranks Korea as the country with the fourth greatest number of active smart phones and similar devices (28 million active users) with 78% penetration rate among 15 to 64 years old (Farago, 2012).

Korean communication practitioners seem to be trying to take advantage of such cutting-edge national infrastructure or social media resources to reach out, or build relationships with, internal employees and external publics. In fact, their skillful use of social media may have elevated their status within the organization. Consistent with resource dependency theory (e.g., Pfeffer & Salancik, 1978), as the practitioners are able to utilize vital resources of social media environments to cope with organizational uncertainties such as crisis, relationship building, branding, image, and the like, they facilitate the redistribution of power inside the organization; the public relations function becomes more powerful and affects strategic decision making, which in turn influences organizational actions and structure.

This is clearly illustrated in the leaders' optimistic view of Korean communication and public relations professionals. They stated that top management recognizes the importance and value of the profession to the organization. They reported receiving strong, full, and sufficient support from their CEOs and top managers with changing media environments, enjoying direct reporting relationships with them, and closely consulting with the management. They also reported participating in high-level meetings and work on strategic organizational assignments. This changing work environment in Korean communication and public relations practice leads the practitioners to serve in more managerial than technical roles (e.g., Dozier, 1992).

On the other hand, misconceptions of the profession and unsuccessful role enactment have led to failures in practice. Korean practitioners felt that their firms value public relations highly and utilize many different ways to showcase the values to the firms. Yet, some were unsure of the effectiveness or the measures used. Korean leaders suggested that successful public relations leaders tend to enact communication competencies at different levels as well as managerial competencies for task and conflict.

It is quite obvious that important current and future leadership issues, critical success and failure factors, and leadership characteristics as a whole address underlying concerns of "harmonious relationship" in Koran practice of communication and public relations. Social media are tools of relationships in changing media environments. Effective employee communication is essentially designed to develop and maintain harmonious relationships with internal and furthermore external publics. Working together well, interacting well, developing supportive relationships with top management and resolving conflicts well—all such issues, concerns, and demands—are quite consistent with the traditional Korean focus on a relationship-based approach to public relations and communication management. In particular, they embody the Confucian focus on relationships in all daily (personal and business) matters (e.g., Kim & Bae, 2006; Lee & Jablin, 1992; Rhee, 2002).

Korean communication and public relations practitioners are expected to enact communication competencies or abilities, often serving as effective linkages, bridges and ties with internal and external publics. Such leadership qualities are culturally embedded in Korea. Appreciating relationships is in synch with sociocultural values of Confucianism—harmonious relationships as the code of conduct (Yum, 1988). In a way, this relational emphasis has been in the realm of media relations, the traditional practice of Korean communication and public relations. Korean practitioners with social media skills and managerial competencies may be well suited to advance their communication and public relations to the next level.

Meng and Berger (2013) advanced an integrated and measurement-based leadership theory in public relations and empirically identified six dimensions that contribute to effective communication and public relations practice: self-dynamics (e.g., personality, skills, values, envisioning ability), team collaboration, ethical orientation, relationship building, strategic decision making, and communication knowledge management (e.g., possessing, applying, and converting public relations knowledge and communication expertise into effective strategies and tactics). Korean communication and public relations leaders appeared to link their perceptions of leadership primarily to the dimension of relationship building and, to a lesser extent, communication knowledge management.

Korean leaders are implicitly aware of the importance of self-dynamics and ethical orientation in their practices. As they look at the current and future practice, Korean leaders have emphasized learning and acquiring new skills, creating vision, being open-minded, being adaptable, and reflecting on their roles and expectations. From the larger survey findings, dealing with growing demands for transparency of communications and operations were identified as top issues. As Korean public relations aspires to thrive on the global stage, Korean practitioners are likely to move in a direction that is consistent with the leadership theory in public relations.

In summary, effectively managing social media, having quality employee communication, developing face-to-face relationships, and expanding the practice are defining leadership issues. Further, such issues as working and sharing together, communication competencies, task/role competencies, management support, and dealing with misconceptions of the profession were identified as critical factors that affect daily success and failure at work. Korean practitioners perceived that their firms value public relations highly and utilize many different ways to showcase their values to the firms, though the measurement remains an issue.

Korean public relations leaders are perceived to enact communication competencies at the individual, relational, unit, organizational, and interorganizational levels as well as managerial competencies for task and conflict. Future Korean leaders are likely to ensure their success by focusing on learning, adaptability, creative problem solving, highlighting values to the firm, and self-reflecting on their roles and expectations. Korean communication and public relations professionals recognize that their professional work meaningfully contributes to their firms' strategic goals.

References

Berger, B. (2008, November 17). *Employee/organizational communications*. Gainesville, FL: Institute for Public Relations. Available online at www.instituteforpr.org/topics/employee-organizational-communications/

Berkowitz, D., & Lee, J. (2004). Media relations in Korea: Cheong between journalist and public relations practitioner. *Public Relations Review, 30*, 431–437.

Dozier, D. M. (1992).The organizational roles of communications and public relations practitioners. In J. E. Grunig (Ed.), *Excellence in public relations and communication management* (pp. 327–355). Hillsdale, NJ: Erlbaum.

Farago, P. (2012, August 27). iOS and Android adoption explodes internationally [Blog entry]. Available online at http://blog.flurry.com/bid/88867/iOS-and-Android-Adoption-Explodes-Internationally

Hofstede, G. (2001). *Culture's consequences: Comparing values, behaviors, institutions, and organizations across nations* (2nd ed.). Thousand Oaks, CA: Sage.

Hwang, S. (2012).The strategic use of twitter to manage personal public relations. *Public Relations Review, 38*, 159–161.

Jo, S., & Kim, Y. (2004). Media or personal relations? Exploring media relations dimensions in South Korea. *Journalism & Mass Communication Quarterly, 81*, 292–306.

Kim, Y. (2003). Professionalism and diversification: The evolution of public relations in South Korea. In K. Sriramesh & D. Verčič (Eds.), *The global public relations handbook: Theory, research, and practice* (pp. 106–120). Mahwah, NJ: Erlbaum.

Kim, Y., & Bae, J. (2006). Korean practitioners and journalists: Relational influences in news selection. *Public Relations Review, 32*, 241–245.

Kim, Y., & Hon, C. L. (1998). Craft and professional models of public relations and their relation to job satisfaction among Korean public relations practitioners. *Journal of Public Relations Research, 10*, 155–175

Korea Press Foundation. (2012). Media statistics information. Retrieved from www.kpf.or.kr

Korea Public Relations Association (2003). *KPRA research report 2003: An investigation on the current state of Korean public relations industry and perceptions*. Seoul, Korea: Author.

Korean Public Relations Year Book. (2010). Seoul, Korea: Korean Public Relations Association.

Lee, J., & Jablin, F. M. (1992). A cross-cultural investigation of exit, voice, loyalty and neglect as responses to dissatisfying job conditions. *Journal of Business Communication, 29*, 203–228.

Meng, J., & Berger, B. (2013). An integrated model of excellent leadership in public relations: dimensions, measurement, and validation. *Journal of Public Relations Research*, 25, 141–167.

Meng, J., Berger, B. K., Gower, K. K., & Heyman, W. C. (2012). A test of excellent leadership in public relations: Key qualities, valuable sources, and distinctive leadership perceptions. *Journal of Public Relations Research*, 24, 18–38.

OECD iLibrary. (2013). Country statistical profile: Korea. Available online at www.oecd-ilibrary.org/economics/country-statistical-profile-korea_20752288-table-kor

Park, J. (2001). Images of "Hong Bo (Public Relations)" and PR in Korean newspapers. *Public Relations Review*, 27, 403–420.

Park, J. (2003). Discrepancy between Korean government and corporate practitioners regarding professional standards in public relations: A co-orientation approach. *Journal of Public Relations Research*, 15, 249–275.

Pfeffer, J., & Salancik, G. R. (1978). *The external control of organizations: A resource dependence perspective*. New York, NY: Harper & Row.

Rhee, Y. (2002). Global public relations: A cross-cultural study of the excellence theory in South Korea. *Journal of Public Relations Research*, 14, 159–184.

Scandura, T., & Dorfman, P. (2004). Theoretical letters: Leadership research in an international and cross cultural context. *Leadership Quarterly*, 15, 277–307.

Shin, J., & Cameron, G. (2003). Informal relations: A look at personal influence in media relations. *Journal of Communication Management*, 7, 239–253.

Shin, J., Heath, R. L., & Lee, J. (2011). A contingency explanation of public relations practitioner leadership styles: Situation and culture. *Journal of Public Relations Research*, 23, 167–190.

Strategy Analytics. (2009). Strategy Analytics: U.S. Ranks 20th in Global Broadband Household Penetration. Press Release. Available online at www.strategyanalytics.com/default.aspx?mod=PressReleaseViewer&a0=4748

Yukl, G. (2006). *Leadership in organizations* (6th ed.). Upper Saddle River, NJ: Pearson Prentice Hall.

Yum, J. O. (1988). The impact of Confucianism on interpersonal relationships and communication patterns in East Asia. *Communication Monographs*, 55, 374–388.

13

LEADERSHIP IN COMMUNICATION MANAGEMENT

Enduring and Emerging Challenges in Germany, Austria, and Switzerland

Ulrike Röttger, Janne Stahl, and Ansgar Zerfass

As an organizational interface, public relations is largely affected by environmental dynamics and changes in the organizational environment. At the same time, the ability of public relations departments to act is strongly influenced by structural and organizational prerequisites in their respective organizations (Röttger, 2010). Both aspects have a major bearing on the performance of public relations leaders—a fact that is also illustrated by the results of the global study of leadership in public relations and communication management concerned with the German-speaking countries (Germany, Austria, and Switzerland) presented in this chapter.

As a general rule, the importance of public relations within differentiated media societies located at the heart of Europe is greater than ever before. This is the case because organizations are—whether they like it or not—faced with a multitude of different and rapidly changing observations and descriptions by other parties. Consequently, they are also confronted with different and sometimes divergent expectations (Preusse, Röttger, & Schmitt, 2013). A powerful dynamic prevails in this area because of factors such as the constant presence of companies in the media and the extensive opportunities for social participation and involvement on the Internet. This situation bears major challenges for public relations leaders. Their very task, after all, is to anticipate future sociopolitical developments and to prepare their departments in a way that enables them to master the communication tasks of tomorrow.

Within this context, *leadership* is defined as "a process whereby an individual influences a group of individuals to achieve a common goal" (Northouse, 2013, p. 5). With regard to public relations, Berger and Meng (2010) define leadership as

> A dynamic process that encompasses a complex mix of individual skills and personal attributes, values, and behaviors that consistently produce ethical and effective communication practice. Such practice fuels and guides

successful communication teams, helps organizations achieve their goals, and legitimizes organizations in society. (p. 427)

When defining leadership in communication management, the interaction of the public relations leader within the leadership structures of the organization should be taken into account. This chapter draws on a structuration theory perspective to describe how communication professionals in Germany, Austria, and Switzerland address the challenges within the framework of the structural and cultural conditions of their respective organizations.

To this end, the following section outlines the salient characteristics of the three countries, namely, Germany, Austria, and Switzerland, as well as the specific features of the occupational field of public relations in these countries. In a next step, the study design is described and empirical results are presented. In so doing, the chapter focuses on three thematic areas: top issues for leaders, cultural and structural influences on leaders, and characteristics and qualities of excellent leaders. The last section places the results in context and offers a perspective on the future.

Characteristics of the Countries: Germany, Austria, and Switzerland

The countries of Germany, Austria, and Switzerland share borders with one another in the heart of Europe. Germany is a federal state with 16 constituent states. It has an area of 357,121 square kilometers, has approximately 80.5 million inhabitants, and has a gross domestic product of 2.6 trillion euros (Federal Statistical Office of Germany, 2013). Switzerland, which has approximately 8 million inhabitants and an area of 41,284 square kilometers, and Austria, which has approximately 8.4 million inhabitants and an area of 82,409 square kilometers, border Germany to the south (Statistics Austria, 2013; Swiss Federal Statistical Office, 2013). German, among other languages, is spoken in all three countries. In Germany and Austria, German is the official language; in Switzerland, there are three other official languages alongside German.

All three countries are democratic states based on the rule of law and apply the principle of the separation of powers into legislative, executive, and judicial branches. Germany and Austria have 16 and 9 constituent states (*Bundesländer*), respectively, and Switzerland has 26 cantons (*Kantone*). All the countries are structured according to the principle of the *Sozialstaat*, a concept of a social state similar to that of the welfare state. The societies can be described as pluralistic societies with religious freedom and the separation of church and state. All the countries have a pluralistic and diverse media system with a distinction between private and public service offerings for radio and television. The public service offerings in this respect entail a remit to provide basic services financed by fees and based on a principle of independence from the State. The print and online offerings are extremely diverse and many of them can be classed as high-quality journalism.

Freedom of the press is regarded as a given. The differentiated media system serves an important critical function within the pluralistic democracies because it offers the citizens a diverse picture of the social, political, and economic situations within the countries and exerts an influence on political processes. Consequently, it is also colloquially referred to as the "fourth power in the state." Because these three countries share a common language, a common cultural environment, and numerous similarities associated with the occupational field of public relations, they are considered together in this chapter.

Overview of the Occupational Field of Public Relations

The growing importance of public communication for organizations from all sectors of society has caused the occupational field of public relations in Germany, Austria, and Switzerland to expand and become more differentiated as part of a process that began in the mid-1980s and continues to this day (Bentele & Seiffert, 2012). In parallel to this development, the professionalization of public relations—measured by factors such as the education level of PR practitioners and the number of academic educational institutions—has steadily progressed (Röttger, 2010). As part of this trend, the term *public relations* is used increasingly less frequently because everyday usage tends to equate this term with operational press and media relations work. Within the profession, the designations "communication management," "corporate communication," or simply "communications" have become established.

Access to the occupational field in the three countries is fundamentally open; in other words, access is not subject to standardization, and it is not tied to specific qualifications or educational prerequisites. From a scholarly viewpoint, this makes the approach and the task of fully documenting the occupational field considerably more difficult. It is probably also for this reason that there are currently no up-to-date, representative studies on the occupational field of public relations in its entirety in Germany, Austria, and Switzerland. There are some comprehensive older studies (Röttger, 2000/2010; Röttger, Hoffmann, & Jarren, 2003; Szyszka, Schütte, & Urbahn, 2009; Wienand, 2003) as well as surveys on specific aspects of the occupational field, such as gender research (Fröhlich, Peters, & Simmelbauer 2006), and surveys concerned with public relations practitioners in communication departments of companies and other organizations (Bentele, Dolderer, Fechner, & Seidenglanz, 2012).

Moreover, empirical data on all three countries are available from the annual *European Communication Monitor*, a research initiative that has been conducted since 2007 and surveys professionals in communication departments and agencies (Zerfass, Moreno, Tench, Vercic, & Verhoeven, 2013). Up to now, studies that explicitly address communication professionals in leadership positions with regard to the three countries of Germany, Austria, and Switzerland either did not exist or were concerned with specific aspects (Nothhaft, 2011).

Although no formally established educational prerequisites exist, it is apparent that the occupational field is highly dominated by those with an academic education. A university degree is nowadays more or less a mandatory prerequisite for a job in public relations: Approximately 90% of communication managers have studied at university (Bentele et al., 2012, p. 35). The majority of them studied a subject in the arts, humanities, or social sciences (66%), such as a degree in communication studies, sociology, or political science. Most public relations practitioners have completed a program of academic study at graduate level, and a significant proportion of top-level communicators in major companies have a doctorate.

Universities and colleges in Germany, Austria, and Switzerland today offer a large number of bachelor's and master's degree programs of various kinds, some of which are geared more strongly toward research and others place greater emphasis on practice. Moreover, many different areas of study offer the opportunity to cover public relations–specific topics by taking elective courses. In parallel, a wide range of programs is available to those wishing to pursue further training in public relations alongside their work commitments. The majority of these programs is offered by private providers, and a smaller proportion of them is available from universities and colleges.

At the time of writing, approximately every third communication professional has completed an educational or further training program specific to public relations (Bentele et al., 2012, p. 39). The Academic Society for Corporate Management and Communication (www.akademische-gesellschaft.com) has been promoting the exchange of ideas between public relations leaders in major companies and the public relations research community for some time. This network comprises nearly 30 chief communication officers of blue-chip companies and international market leaders based in German-speaking countries, as well as the top research universities in the field.

On the whole, hardly any specific leadership development programs exist to date in the communication industry in Germany, Austria, and Switzerland. Questions such as those concerned with the personal prerequisites for leadership in communication management, specific leadership qualities, and the associated training have so far received little attention both in the industry and within the German-speaking public relations research community.

The Study

Within the framework of the global leadership study supported by the Plank Center, the universities of Leipzig and Münster carried out a quantitative survey and a qualitative survey of leaders in communication management in the German-speaking countries. Both parts of the study—quantitative and qualitative—are briefly presented here. The subsequent analysis focuses on the findings of the qualitative interviews.

The quantitative study documents a sample of 1,766 participants taken from all three countries (1,402 from Germany, 222 from Austria, and 142 from Switzerland). The balance between the proportions of female and male survey participants is virtually even. Of the communication managers who participated in the survey, 855 see themselves as occupying a leadership position at the highest level, and 691 see themselves as occupying a leadership position at the second-highest level. The survey period lasted for 5 weeks from the end of November 2011 to the beginning of January 2012 (Röttger, Zerfass, Kiesenbauer, & Stahl, 2013).

For the qualitative study, 12 guided interviews were conducted by phone with senior communication executives in the German-speaking countries between July 9 and August 23, 2012. The interview language was German, and the interview guide used was a translated version of the original English guide. The average interview had a length of 57 minutes (range: 46–80). The sample consisted of five female and seven male interviewees, all of whom worked in large companies with more than 1,000 employees (range: 1,000–145,000) and had an average of 17 years of experience in communication management (range: 11–25).

The majority of companies were located in Germany, three were located in Austria, and one was located in Switzerland. Two of the organizations were (partly) state-owned companies; the rest were either joint stock or private companies. Each of the 12 interviewees was the most senior communication manager in his or her company and had a job title such as "head of corporate communications," "director corporate communications," or "head of corporate and market communications." As the last title indicates, marketing communications and general marketing decisions were also part of the job descriptions for some of the interviewees. Furthermore, some of the interviewees were part of the top-level corporate management team.

Top Issues for Public Relations Leaders in the German-Speaking Countries

The communication managers who participated in the interviews very frequently named the most important issues in communication management as being aspects concerned with strategically aligning communication. Another area of focus was handling and making use of social media as part of communications.

With regard to the issue of strategically aligning communication, the interviewees referred especially frequently and emphatically to the need for integrated communication:

> Of course, it's important in this respect that the various communication channels work in good times as well as in bad times. In other words, not just in crisis situations—I mean, it's of paramount importance in such cases—but, fundamentally, it's important that we communicate, hand-in-hand, in a coordinated way during normal operations too.

Other issues including formulating and implementing the communication strategy, stakeholder management, and interweaving communication strategy and corporate strategy also were mentioned:

If we take a strategic view, the issue is one of "stakeholder management." I'm reluctant to draw a distinction between this issue and what strategic communication is generally taken to mean. In principle, stakeholder management is, of course, part of strategic communication, and it is indeed the case here that not only do you have to concern yourself with content, but you also have to concern yourself with the question of what you are communicating to which target group and with what kind of tonality, with what kinds of interactions. In other words, anticipating interactions is becoming increasingly important in communication. It's no longer just about simply conveying a company message.

Another communication leader said,

Well, we have really close links with the board too, of course; we also have our own strategy office and the communication department links up with this too. So, all our planning is aligned with this strategy. This means that even the budget planning is always aligned with our strategic goals in a totally clear way, and that, in fact, is the big change. We were—this may sound a little old-fashioned—but, a few years ago, we were still not in a position where we were able to say that we now have a completely clear strategy and that we're even guided by it when preparing the budget, when drawing up the communication plan.

Of the 12 communication managers who participated in the interviews, only 1 named social media as the most important issue at the present time. At the same time, it was established that even companies operating in business-to-business (B2B) markets can have a major interest in social media: By presenting industry-specific information in an entertaining way on a Facebook page, a company can reach a very large number of stakeholders and secure their loyalty to the company. Moreover, organizations are increasingly using their Facebook to recruit staff. Four other communication professionals named social media as the second most important issue in communication management, for example:

From my point of view, it [the rise of social media] is important because it entails, or serves, completely different forms of communication. . . . Every sender is a recipient and every recipient is a sender. In other words, we see everyone having a say, everyone joining in the conversation. With the issue of Web 2.0, of course, we're dealing with an entirely different speed when it comes to responding and communicating. You have other demands to meet. And you have—and this is the interesting thing—several colleagues who are worried about losing their communicative supremacy and their overview of the situation, their power to shape things.

For the most part, the other public relations leaders also attributed a high level of importance to social media when asked. A few of them emphasized that the relevance of social media depends on the industry in which they operate. One leader said,

> Fundamentally, I would first of all invite people to consider that it always depends on the industry in which you're operating. I don't share the general hype, which is, no doubt, triggered to a certain extent by agencies and other service providers that are looking to sell the relevant services, but I also currently have no desire to critique the system.

Another communication leader said,

> The issue of "social media" naturally has a high degree of relevance simply because—for a start—it expands the stakeholder front for a company; because we stopped talking about the communicative supremacy of a company a long time ago; because the depth of impact, because the reach is significantly increased through social media; and, in this respect, it's an issue that—at least in theory—has to be faced up to. Whether or not every company has to do so in practice is something that must be determined on the basis of the industry.

Overall, the qualitative study shows that social media are very important for communication management—although it will still take some time before some companies use social media on a professional basis. This point is also borne out by a Delphi study of social media communication in Germany (Linke & Zerfass, 2012). It is to be assumed that industry-specific differences in the ways in which social media are used will also continue to exist in the future.

Aside from the aforementioned issues of social media and the process of strategically aligning communication, the issues of employee management/the qualification of employees, communication controlling, and corporate social responsibility (CSR) communication were also occasionally named as top issues in communication management in the qualitative interviews.

The results of the quantitative study also confirm the high level of importance assigned to the issue of social media. These results rank handling social media and the digital revolution as the second most important challenge for leaders in communication management (see Figure 13.1).

If consideration is given not only to the matter of which issue was named as the most important in the quantitative study but also to the assessment of the issues taken altogether, it is apparent that the German-speaking participants actually assigned the highest level of importance to social media (see Figure 13.2).

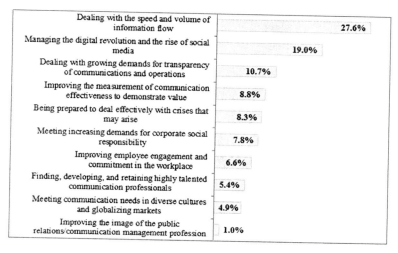

FIGURE 13.1 Most Important Issue for Leaders in Communication Management in Germany, Austria, and Switzerland

Note: Leadership Survey (2012); *n* = 1,766 public relations professionals from Austria, Germany, and Switzerland: Question: Please indicate which one of these 10 issues, in your opinion, is the most important issue for your communication leader (or you, if you are the leader).

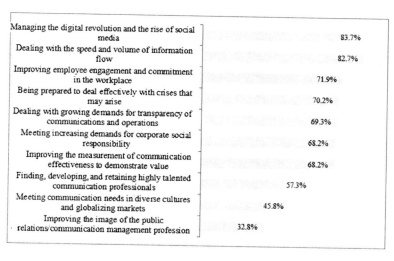

FIGURE 13.2 Overall Importance of Issues for Leaders in Communication Management in Germany, Austria, and Switzerland

Note: Leadership Survey (2012); *n* = 1,766 public relations professionals. Question: Please indicate to what extent you agree that each of the following issues is important to your communication leader (or you, if you are the leader) in your organization today. Scale: 1 (*A little bit*) to 7 (*A great deal*). Bars indicate the percentage of respondents who marked scale points 5 through 7, that is, who clearly stated that the issue is important.

Cultural and Structural Influences on Leaders

The communication professionals who participated in the interviews opened up a very broad area with their answers regarding the influence of cultural and structural factors that support the communication function or make communication more difficult.

The public relations leaders placed particular emphasis on the structural factor of the link established between communication management and the CEO or chairperson of the board. This factor provides a very high level of support to the communication function. Proximity to the CEO was regarded as highly important in practically all the interviews, and the participants indicated that very good connections existed in almost all the companies to which the interviewees belonged. In almost every case, the chairperson of the board valued the work of the communication function and collaborated closely with this function. Only in one case did the interviewee indicate that the CEO did not assign a high status to public relations. Moreover, it was in this very case that the interviewee also emphasized that proximity to the CEO was not a crucial factor for effective communication work. In all other interviews, however, the public relations leaders named the structural link to the board as one of the most important factors for effective public relations, as indicated in these two comments:

> I report directly to the CEO. I also believe that this is really important. Otherwise, you wouldn't be able to do it [communication work] because then you wouldn't become aware of anything at all—that's my opinion. I'm informed at an early stage—and usually by him in person—when anything needs to be dealt with, but I'm also informed by the other members of corporate management . . .
>
> Also spatial proximity [to the CEO] . . . so that the board is accessible. There simply needs to be a good exchange of ideas.

Aside from this special link to the CEO, it is important from a structural standpoint that the communication managers are represented on all the major bodies, as reflected in these three comments:

> In structural terms, by means of a process of becoming appropriately anchored within the company from a hierarchical point of view and by means of appropriate powers to lay down guidelines. . . . establishment of a link between corporate communication and the CEO and a presence at all board meetings. We have access to all documents, including those of the supervisory board.
>
> I'm automatically represented everywhere alongside whoever else. In other words—I also said right away at the beginning that this was very important—I'm represented on all the relevant bodies and committees—including those at board level—and I become aware of the information.

I attend the important meetings, which means that I pick up on things that, in turn, provide me with a context . . .

Besides the process of structural anchoring that takes place in the company, the conception of public relations that exists within the company also plays an important role:

> The understanding of management is also extremely important in communication. It's about it [communication] being seen as a task of management rather than there somehow being a perception that we're a service department—and somehow this does happen—but, instead, it's about recognizing that communication is part of management. I believe that this is also an important factor in the culture.

These statements reveal that the structures and the perception of communication in a particular organization strongly influence the actions of the leading communication manager. This insight is also supported by the results of the quantitative study, in which involvement in the strategic decision-making processes of the organization was identified as the most important prerequisite for leadership in communication management. Many opportunities are open to communication management if the prerequisites, such as a close link to company management, are in place.

Except in one instance, important structural factors that support the communication function are present in all the companies whose communication managers participated in the interviews. The findings of the quantitative survey also paint a comparable picture. The statement "The CEO or top executive in my organization understands the value of public relations" scored a mean value of 5.4 on a scale of 1 (*strongly disagree*) through 7 (*strongly agree*) in the German-speaking countries, a result that is outstanding by international comparison. These results indicate good structural foundations for communication management in Germany, Austria, and Switzerland.

The public relations leaders identified other structural factors that support the communication function as follows: a decentralized approach toward organizing communication (each business unit has its own communication department), clear staffing and resourcing, the qualification of employees, a good flow of information that starts with top management and progresses down the hierarchy in individual stages, interconnections linking individual company departments to communication management, and good international arrangements for localizing themes in the relevant countries.

According to the interviewed public relations leaders, the following cultural factors have a positive effect on the communication function: the regular exchange of ideas and meetings in person with communication professionals from subsidiaries, a high regard for the communication function throughout the entire company, communicative openness and trust in the communication function (a willingness to "convey information and issues"), and a communication department whose members are drawn from a variety of cultural backgrounds.

The communication managers also answered questions about culturally and structurally relevant factors that make communication management work more difficult. The problem posed by internal communication, and by an absence or restriction of openness toward the communication function within the company, was the most frequently discussed issue in this context. For example, a recurring complaint was that relevant information did not reach employees because department or team leaders either did not pass it on or did not pass it on quickly enough. Moreover, individual interviewees also mentioned the following aspects: cost pressure/savings, the conception of communication as part of marketing, poor integration of the communication department within bodies, and CEOs who did not adequately embrace their communication duties.

It is clear that the structural and cultural factors strongly influence communication management work. The cultural and structural conditions define the framework in which leaders in communication management are able to push ahead with professional communication activities. However, the interviews also reveal that the leading communication managers are able to influence structures within the company if they commit themselves to doing so.

Characteristics and Qualities of Excellent Leaders

The communication managers particularly regarded personal leadership characteristics, general leadership competencies, and communication competencies as important characteristics and qualities of excellent leaders.

The participants very frequently mentioned personal leadership characteristics, such as *the ability to listen*, *the ability to delegate*, or *the ability to assert oneself*. The naming of these characteristics confirms the important role played by the leadership personality in the observation of leadership, which is also emphasized in the literature (for an overview, see, among others, Bass, 1990; Northouse, 2013).

The survey participants also considered general leadership competencies to be exceptionally important. Within this context, they mentioned factors such as loyalty toward employees, prudence in putting together and managing teams, and the ability to empower and to give challenges to employees. The interviewees did not mention any typical management competencies, which can be considered as a subgroup of general leadership competencies and include, for example, the ability to develop coalitions within and outside the organization.

The public relations leaders saw communication competencies as important qualities for a leader. Communication competencies include, on the one hand, specialist communication knowledge:

> In a sense, having specialist knowledge so that you can make a good assessment of things and be ready with the right arguments; that the

communication leader has really learned how to do the job . . . I really don't think all that much of out-and-out career changers, but what I value instead are really good communication skills.

On the other hand, communication competencies encompass analytical and visionary skills that depend on the specialist field. In this context, participants mentioned factors such as *conciseness in analysis, consistency in implementation, and a huge amount of composure.* Another statement reads "The public relations leader must be a visionary." When compared with the United States (see Chapter 19), it is apparent that the communication professionals from Germany, Austria, and Switzerland do not see business knowledge as an important quality for leaders; instead, they emphasize classical leadership qualities (personal characteristics and general leadership competencies). In India (see Chapter 11), the ability to develop external and internal relationships plays a prominent role by comparison with the German-speaking countries.

The results of the quantitative study also indicate the high level of importance of communication and team leadership competencies for communication managers in the German-speaking countries. With mean values ranging from 5.9 through 6.1 on a scale of 1 (*minor importance*) through 7 (*very high importance*), these competencies were considered to be very important prerequisites for leadership in communication management. However, the interviews illustrate that good leadership of employees—including where such leadership takes place independently of the team—and personal leadership characteristics are also seen as important qualities for a leader.

Other quantitative results reveal the high level of importance assigned to measures aimed at developing the personal competencies of future leaders. This finding is congruent with the responses from the interviews, which identified personal characteristics and general leadership competencies as important qualities for communication managers.

Meng and Berger (2013) identified six dimensions of excellent leadership as follows: self-dynamics, team collaboration, ethical orientation, relationship building, strategic decision-making capability, and communication knowledge management. If these dimensions are compared to the characteristics and qualities that the survey participants named as being associated with excellent leaders, it becomes apparent that the interview participants did not mention some dimensions at all. This applies to the ethical orientation and relationship building dimensions in particular.

Leadership Needs for the Future

Social media are—as already mentioned—a special challenge for communication management. New opportunities are arising in this area, and the prospect of making successful use of them presents public relations leaders with demanding tasks. For example, communication professionals must decide how social media are used in their companies for the purpose of communication and how they are to be integrated into the overall communication concept. At the same time, social media represent a new form of communicative networking that tends to be at odds with the traditional aspiration to exert control that is associated with public relations. Companies actively involved in Web 2.0 must learn that they can only have very limited control over the content of their offerings.

It is possible to view this situation as a paradigm shift in communication management that is closely related to a perennial communication management issue: the adequate prerequisites for strategically understanding and strategically aligning communication. In this respect, once again, the empirical studies indicate the outstanding importance of a close structural link between communication management and the CEO as well as a general openness within the organization toward communication management. This notion encompasses an understanding of the need for communication management as well as the tasks and opportunities that it entails.

The issue of "strategically aligning communication" has occupied the attention of the industry in Germany, Austria, and Switzerland from the outset, and it does not seem to have lost any of its topicality to date. Strategically aligning communication represents a long-term challenge that requires constant attention. Yet this is not to say that extensive shortcomings are to be noted in this area: The findings of both studies indicate that the conditions for leadership in communication management are good in the countries examined in these studies. An appropriate framework for carrying out public relations activities, therefore, is in place in many cases.

In order for communication professionals not only to make the right strategic decisions but also to lead employees effectively, it is important, on one hand, that they possess the necessary leadership characteristics. On the other hand, it is important that they receive an education and further training in specific leadership competencies. Except for a few master's degree programs, this latter point has so far received little attention in terms of public relations practice and public relations training in Germany, Austria, and Switzerland. The ongoing professionalization and differentiation of the occupation entail a need to design and offer specialized educational and further training programs for public relations leaders, too. A greater awareness of the demands and prerequisites of leadership in the public relations industry is necessary to meet this need.

The issue of "leadership in communication management" has so far been almost completely overlooked in the German-speaking public relations research community. The study of Germany, Austria, and Switzerland presented in this chapter offers initial findings and indicates that a more intensive examination of the relevant questions holds much potential. In this respect, an interdisciplinary and international perspective is indispensable. Such a perspective is entirely in keeping with the prevailing transition in Europe from traditional public relations research to a more extensive engagement with questions of communication management and strategic communication.

Acknowledgments

The global leadership study has been supported in the German-speaking countries by the Academic Society for Corporate Management and Communication, and Convento, Neuss, which provided a database of communication professionals in the region for the quantitative survey. Katharina Simon at the University of Leipzig was responsible for project management and online survey administration. Johannes Schulte at the University of Münster did a great job of conducting and transcribing qualitative interviews with communication leaders.

References

Bass, B. M. (1990). *Bass & Stogdill's handbook of leadership: Theory, research, and managerial applications.* New York, NY: Free Press.

Bentele, G., Dolderer, U., Fechner, R., & Seidenglanz, R. (2012). *Profession Pressesprecher 2012.Vermessung eines Berufsstandes* [The profession of the spokesperson 2012. Measuring the occupational field]. Berlin, Germany: Helios Media.

Bentele, G., & Seiffert, J. (2012). Public relations and culture in Germany: Between the iron cage and deliberative democracy. In K. Sriramesh & D. Vercic (Eds.), *Culture and public relations* (pp. 124–141). New York, NY: Routledge.

Berger, B. K., & Meng, J. (2010). Public relations practitioners and the leadership challenge. In R.L. Heath (Ed.), *The SAGE handbook of public relations* (pp. 421–434). Thousand Oaks, CA: Sage.

Federal Statistical Office of Germany (2013). Retrieved from https://www.destatis.de

Fröhlich, R., Peters, S. B., & Simmelbauer, E.-M. (2006). *Public Relations. Daten und Fakten der geschlechtsspezifischen Berufsfeldforschung* [Public relations. Data and facts from gender-specific research of the occupational field]. Munich, Germany, and Vienna, Austria: Oldenbourg.

Linke, A., & Zerfass, A. (2012). Future trends of social media use in strategic communication: Results of a Delphi study. *Public Communication Review, 2*(2), 17–29.

Meng, J., & Berger B. (2013). An integrated model of excellent leadership in public relations: Dimensions, measurement, and validation. *Journal of Public Relations Research, 25*(2), 141–167.

Northouse, P. G. (2013). *Leadership: Theory and practice.* Los Angeles, CA: Sage.

Nothhaft, H. (2011). *Kommunikationsmanagement als professionelle Organisationspraxis. Theoretische Annäherung auf Grundlage einer teilnehmenden Beobachtungsstudie* [Communication management as professional organizational practice. A theoretical approach based on a participatory observation study]. Wiesbaden, Germany: VS Verlag für Sozialwissenschaften.

Preusse, J., Röttger, U., & Schmitt, J. (2013). Begriffliche Grundlagen und Begründung einer unpraktischen PR-Theorie [Conceptual basis and justification of a nonpractical PR theory]. In A. Zerfass, L. Rademacher, & S. Wehmeier (Eds.), *Organisationskommunikation und Public Relations. Forschungsparadigmen und neue Perspektiven* [Organizational communication and public relations. Research paradigms and new perspectives] (pp. 117–142). Wiesbaden, Germany: Springer VS.

Röttger, U. (2010). *Public Relations? Organisation und Profession. Öffentlichkeitsarbeit als Organisationsfunktion. Eine Berufsfeldstudie* [Public relations? Organization and profession. Public relations as an organizational function. A field study]. Wiesbaden, Germany: VS Verlag für Sozialwissenschaften.

Röttger, U., Hoffmann, J., & Jarren, O. (2003). *Public Relations in der Schweiz* [Public relations in Switzerland]. Constance, Germany: UVK.

Röttger, U., Zerfass, A., Kiesenbauer, J., & Stahl, J. (2013). *Führung im Kommunikationsmanagement – Herausforderungen im internationalen Vergleich* (Forschungsberichte zur Unternehmenskommunikation Nr. 1) [Leadership in communication management – An international comparison of challenges [Research Reports on Corporate Communication (No.1)]. Leipzig, Germany: Akademische Gesellschaft für Unternehmensführung und Kommunikation [Academic Society for Corporate Management & Communication].

Statistics Austria. (2013). Available online at www.statistik.at

Swiss Federal Statistical Office. (2013). Available online at www.bfs.admin.ch

Szyszka, P., Schütte, D., & Urbahn, K. (2009). *Public Relations in Deutschland. Eine empirische Studie zum Berufsfeld Öffentlichkeitsarbeit* [Public relations in Germany. An empirical study of the occupational field of public relations]. Constance, Germany: UVK.

Wienand, E. (2003). *PR als Beruf. Kritische Analyse eines aufstrebenden Kommunikationsberufes* [PR as a profession. Critical analysis of a communication profession on the rise]. Wiesbaden, Germany: Westdeutscher Verlag.

Zerfass, A., Moreno, A., & Tench, R., Vercic, D., & Verhoeven, P. (2013). *European communication monitor 2013. A changing landscape? Managing crises, digital communication and CEO positioning in Europe. Results of a survey in 43 countries.* Brussels, Belgium: EACD/EUPRERA, Helios Media.

14

ADDRESSING ORGANIZATIONAL AND SOCIOPOLITICAL CHANGES THROUGH LEADERSHIP IN PUBLIC RELATIONS IN LATVIA

Baiba Pētersone and Bryan H. Reber

The development of contemporary public relations in Latvia can be traced to the early 1990s when the country regained its independence after more than 50 years of Soviet occupation. Although it is possible that public relations was practiced in the independent Latvia between 1918 and 1939, public relations researchers generally agree that Soviet-style propaganda, common also in Latvia during the years of the Soviet dominance, was not public relations (e.g., Bentele & Peter, 1996; Guth, 2000; Karadjov, Kim, & Karavasilev, 2000; Scholz, 1998; Verčič, Grunig, & Grunig, 1996). As observed by Verčič et al. (1996), propaganda is not about communication but "discommunication" (p. 42). It "dissolves communication between people in order to disable their ability to form publics" (Verčič et al., 1996, p. 42). The sole purpose of propaganda is to spread "information about the constraints that a system places on lateral communication" (p. 44). In these circumstances, public relations that aims to build reciprocal relationships between organizations and their publics cannot exist.

Like other countries under the Soviet sphere of influence, Western-style public relations in Latvia emerged in response to political and economic changes (Pētersone, 2006; Pūre, 2011). Ławniczak (2001), who researched public relations developments in Poland, coined the term "transition public relations" to describe this particular kind of communication management. He observed that public relations was a crucial instrument in "introduce[ing] and adopt[ing] the mechanisms and institutions of the market economy and democracy" (Ławniczak, 2001, p. 14).

Following is a brief overview of public relations developments in Latvia, a country with a population of approximately two million people located in northeast Europe on the Baltic Sea between Estonia and Lithuania. A qualitative study based on in-depth interviews with the first Latvian public relations practitioners (Pētersone, 2004, 2006) showed that the initial public relations–like activities were practiced by anti-Soviet dissident groups in the late 1980s. This citizen movement used the instruments of Western style communication to organize large-scale demonstrations to oppose the Soviet occupation of Latvia and lobby their cause in the Western media. One such example was "Baltic Way," an event held in summer 1989 to commemorate the secret Molotov–Ribbentrop Pact of 1939 that divided Europe in the Soviet and Nazi spheres of influence. Almost 2 million people formed a human chain, linking hands from Estonia through Latvia to Lithuania.

In addition to the facilitation of political changes, Pētersone's (2004, 2006) research showed that after formal independence was ensured in 1991, public relations was employed to support the country's free-market orientation. For instance, public relations facilitated the privatization of formerly state-owned enterprises, introduced free-market products and services, helped the government attract foreign investments and create local support for foreign enterprises, and promoted Latvian products abroad.

Pūre (2011) divided the Latvian public relations history in three periods: warm-up, the beginnings, and ongoing professionalization. During the *warm-up* years (1991–1994) government ministries hired the first press secretaries, and public relations was used by political parties and individual politicians for image-making purposes. The first public relations practitioners were former journalists whose jobs exclusively focused on creating publicity for their clients. Despite democratization, Pūre found that in the early 1990s there was very little concern for public opinion. She concluded that "propaganda was [still] openly used" (Pure, 2011, p. 248).

During the next period, labeled *beginnings* (1995–2000), the public relations industry experienced speedy growth. The Western companies that had recently entered the Latvian market created a need for public relations agencies that could promote their products and lobby the national government to adopt legislation consistent with their business interests. In response to these market demands, Consensus PR, the first Latvian public relations agency, was established in 1995. It was followed by many other local and a few international agencies. In 1996 the first public relations units were formed at a number of finance institutions such as the Bank of Latvia and state-owned enterprises. The same year Vidzeme University College opened the country's first full-degree university program in public relations. During this period, public relations was still practiced on a tactical rather than a strategic basis.

The period of *professionalization* began in 2001 and is still in progress. The Latvian Association for Public Relations Consultancies and the Latvian Association for Public Relations Professionals were both established in 2004. Since then these associations together have organized Baltic PR Awards, the best practice competition that in later years has been expanded to include campaigns implemented in Estonia and Lithuania. During this period most public and private sector organizations have formed in-house public relations units. The agency sector also has continued to expand. A recent Klynveld, Peat, Marwick, and

Goerdeler KPMG (2001) audit showed that 65 firms in Latvia offered public relations services between 2009 and 2011. Currently most universities provide programs and courses in public relations at all levels of study.

Despite these developments, Pūre (2011) found that advanced and ethical forms of public relations practice are still frequently replaced by manipulation and propagandistic communication. Similar conclusions were drawn by Pētersone (2004, 2006), who learned that a lack of understanding about lateral exchanges still prevailed in Latvia, and withholding information was used as a tool of power. Nevertheless, both researchers observed there is also cause for optimism. An understanding of public relations as a strategic management function that is based on reciprocity between organizations and their publics has strengthened, as suggested by Pūre (2011), especially in the aftermath of the severe economic crisis that Latvia experienced between 2008 and 2010.

To further explore the status of public relations in Latvia, the global leadership study aimed to investigate issues that are important to public relations leaders and their followers, and to learn how they manage those issues. In the remaining part of this chapter, the quantitative and qualitative findings of the Leadership Study in Latvia are discussed.

The Global Study of Leadership in Public Relations

The global 58-item online leadership survey was translated into Latvian and was posted on the international survey site. At first the members of the Latvian Association for Public Relations Professionals and the Latvian Associations for Public Relations Consultancies were invited to participate in this study. The small size of these associations and a low response rate from their members required employing other means of participant solicitation. A research assistant was hired to compile a contact list of public relations managers at Latvian public-, private-, and nonprofit-sector organizations. Everyone on this list was invited to respond to the online survey.

Of 462 recipients, 111 public relations practitioners fully completed the survey. Most respondents were employed by the private sector (40.5%), followed by those working for the nonprofit and government organizations (29.7%), agencies (8.1%), and publicly traded companies (7.2%). Only 2.7% of respondents were self-employed. Public relations units in respondents' organizations were small: fewer than five employees (67.6%), five to 15 employees (30.6%), 16 to 25 employees (0.9%) and more than 25 employees (0.9%). Of the respondents, 48% described themselves as top leaders, 32.4% as one level below the top leaders, and 18.9% as two or more levels removed from the top leader.

Public relations is a new profession in Latvia. It was also reflected in the respondents' years of experience in the field: 67.6% had fewer than 11 years of experience, 27.9% had between 11 and 20 years of experience, and the remaining 4.5% had more than 20 years of experience. The majority of respondents had earned a university degree: master's (54.1%), bachelor's (36.0%), and doctoral (5.4%). The rest had a high school diploma (2.7%) or other forms of training (1.8%). Among those with university degrees, the primary areas of study included public relations (23.4%), social sciences (18%), communication and media (13.5%), business and management (12.6%), humanities (9.0%), journalism (5.4%), advertising and marketing (3.6%), math and natural sciences (1.8%), computer science (0.9%), and other majors (9.9%).

Most respondents were women (85.6%), with men constituting only 14.4% of the study's respondents. The largest age group was 25 to 35 (55.0%); the next two largest age groups were between 36 and 45 (25.2%) and 46 to 55 (16.2%). A small number of respondents were older than 55 (3.6%), and none were younger than 25.

Descriptive and inferential analyses were used to study the survey data. These analyses included simple frequency review and means comparison as well as one-way analysis of variance (ANOVA) using the Statistical Package for the Social Sciences (SPSS) computer software.

Researchers also conducted interviews with eight senior public relations executives to gain in-depth understanding of issues pertaining to public relations leadership in Latvia. McCracken (1988), who also suggested the same size of eight, believed that for qualitative studies it is essential to work in-depth with a few participants rather than superficially with many. The interviewees were selected based on the purposive and maximum variation sampling strategies. All participants held the highest public relations position in their organizations or headed a public relations consultancy. They represented the following sectors: national government (1), local municipality (1), banking (1), service providing business enterprise (1), health care organization (1), university (1), and public relations consultancy (2). Six participants were women and two were men. Their work experience in public relations ranged from 7 to15 years.

Semistructured, approximately hour-long interviews, based on the global interview protocol, were conducted in Latvian with each participant. The first part of the interview involved an in-depth discussion about issues that were important to the participants in their public relations leadership roles; the second part of the interview centered on the culture and structure of the participants' organizations. The data analysis involved searching for common themes among the interviews.

Top Issues for Leaders

Both the survey and in-depth interviews inquired about the issues that were the most important to public relations leaders in Latvia. The four leading issues, discussed in this section, included dealing with information flow and social media, addressing crises and changing policy environments, cultivating human capital, and establishing the strategic and monetary value of public relations to the organization (see Table 14.1).

TABLE 14.1 Frequencies and Means of Top 10 Issues in Latvia

Issues	Mean
Dealing with the speed and volume of information flow ($n = 36$)	6.24
Being prepared to deal effectively with crises that may arise ($n = 17$)	6.18
Increasing employee engagement and commitment in the workplace ($n = 14$)	5.72
Managing the digital revolution and the rise of social media ($n = 9$)	5.32
Meeting demands for transparency of communications operations ($n = 9$)	5.40
Finding, developing and retaining highly talented professionals ($n = 8$)	5.20
Meeting communication needs in diverse cultures ($n = 7$)	4.92
Improving measurement of communication to demonstrate value ($n = 5$)	5.59
Improving the image of the profession ($n = 4$)	4.86
Meeting increasing demands for corporate social responsibility ($n = 2$)	5.05

Dealing With Information Flow and Social Media

The issue of "dealing with the speed and volume of information flow" ($M = 6.25$) was rated as the most important by the survey respondents. To address this issue public relations practitioners in Latvia used new technologies to collect, analyze and distribute news and information faster ($M = 5.58$), and developed new skills and/or improved work processes in their units ($M = 5.44$).

The changing communication environment was also a common theme among the interviewed executives. They especially emphasized the significance of social media and ways that it has shaped the overall communication environment. A public relations director, who headed a public relations unit at a service provider, said social media required his team to "keep up with the times." His colleague from a local municipality discussed "the need to understand the development of communication technologies and opportunities provided by them." Knowledge of how to reach publics through social media was described as "an absolute must" by a research participant employed by a public relations consultancy.

The interviews also shed light on ways that social media has shaped the work of public relations units. It has required reallocation of human resources, rene-gotiation of work schedules, continuous monitoring of trends in communication technologies, and changes in communication content and delivery.

Addressing Crises and Changing Policy Environments

According to the survey participants, being prepared to deal effectively with crises that may arise ($M = 6.11$) was the second most important issue for com-munication management leaders in Latvia. The two most frequently applied strategies to deal with this issue involved: developing effective crisis communica-tion plans for action ($M = 5.78$), and implementing effective issues management programs to reduce the risk of crises ($M = 5.50$).

The need to react to crises and issues was also voiced by the interviewees, especially from public- and nonprofit-sector organizations with turbulent policy environments. For example, the head of a public relations unit at a national government institution explained the context in which her unit operated:

> Sometimes our environment is predictable, but most frequently it's not. Under these circumstances we must function almost like forecasters. We must know how to predict what's next. We have to have good intuition . . . to know ahead of time how best to organize our work.

Her colleague from a health care organization had similar experiences:

> What surrounds us is always changing. We have to react to all these sudden excesses in healthcare. They make your plans and routines shudder in an instant. We have to know how to react. We often have to work in a crisis communication mode.

Cultivating Human Capital

"Improving employee engagement and commitment in the workplace" ($M = 5.74$) was selected as the third most important issue by the survey respondents. To accomplish this task, public relations leaders had to create a positive communication climate in the organization ($M = 5.95$), honor employees through reward and recognition programs ($M = 5.63$), and increase accessibility to and visibility of senior leaders" ($M = 5.63$).

Like the other two most important issues, human capital cultivation was also acknowledged by most of the interviewees. Public relations executives "built teams within the public relations unit and with colleagues in other organizational structures," "encouraged [employee] initiative," "facilitated communication between public relations professionals and other employees about matters that are important to the business," and "tried to involve all employees in external communication about the organization." A head of a public relations unit at a city council illustrated the value of strong teams: "If I don't connect with people, I cannot implement various ideas and activities. If I fail to materialize these ideas and activities, I cannot reach my unit's goals and the goals of our council."

Establishing the Strategic and Monetary Value of Public Relations to the Organization

Another issue that was important to the interviewees, especially from the business sector and the agencies with many corporate clients, was establishing public relations as a function that provides significant contributions to the overall management of the organization. A consultancy head said that for several of his clients it was a great challenge to persuade the top management of the need to integrate public relations into the overall organizational strategy. He said, "For us, it is important to place communication in the big picture . . . to make the management understand that communication management is part of the business' final success."

A public relations head at a leading bank believed that public relations leaders should ensure that the public relations function is included in the organization's team of decision makers because "if we look at the very core of the issue, there is a direct link between successful organizational decisions and good communication."

Both consultancy heads and the previously mentioned public relations director at the bank discussed the importance of the public relations leader's ability to demonstrate to senior management the monetary returns of communication initiatives. The latter explained the challenge: "How do we measure the impact of communication? It's not enough to limit ourselves to broad reputational measurements. How do we show the value of our work? How do we demonstrate that communication matters?"

The need to establish the strategic and monetary value of public relations to the organization, however, did not prevail among the survey respondents. Among the 10 most important issues included in the survey, "improving the measurement of communication effectiveness to demonstrate the value [of public relations]" ($M = 5.59$) was rated eighth. Only 5 of the 111 respondents named it as the most important issue. Strategies that these five respondents selected to deal with this issue were attending workshops on measurement to learn and adopt best practices ($M = 6.40$) and focusing more on nonfinancial performance indicators than financial measures ($M = 6.40$).

Cultural and Structural Influences on Leaders

Conversations with public relations executives provided insights on factors that shaped the leadership in and practice of public relations in Latvia. The first part of this section addresses those influences that came from the external environment, whereas the second part deals with factors that are determined by internal organizational patterns.

Environmental Influences

Many of these influences were closely related to the above described most important issues. Several research participants acknowledged that the *growth of social media* has changed and that it continues to modify the practice of public relations in Latvia. A public relations manager working for a university labeled this factor as "continuous development of the communication space." The growth of social media has required public relations units to acquire new resources such as additional staff, time, and knowledge. Furthermore, the expansion of social media has also influenced the content of communication by shifting the focus from written to visual messages.

Another environmental influence directly tied to one of the most important issues was unpredictable policy environments. This factor was especially singled out by participants working for the public and nonprofit sectors. A senior public relations manager from a local municipality said, "[You have to] be able to see five steps ahead and predict what will happen." Several research participants linked these changes to ongoing political and economic transformations in the country.

The interviewees who work for the private sector believed that the Latvian *economic crisis* between 2008 and 2010 contributed to a better appreciation of public relations in Latvian organizations. A public relations executive from a bank called this crisis a "turning point that demonstrated the value of public relations." She concluded,

> Communication was absolutely necessary. It created trust. It provided people with encouragement. We were assigned a larger budget and more people. If others said that everything was taken from them during the crisis, for us [the public relations unit] it was the opposite. We received more.

The link between crises and perceived increased value of the public relations function is reinforced in the literature. Grunig, Grunig, and Dozier (2002) noted that crises "have the potential to enhance career opportunities of public relations practitioners" (p. 477). Another study (Berger & Reber, 2006) found that most public relations practitioners said they have the most influence in an organization when the organization is in crisis (p. 100).

The interviewees identified the changing body of public relations practitioners as another environmental influence shaping the field in Latvia. These interviewees suggested that in the early years of the field's development former journalists were employed as public relations practitioners. Their primary focus was on publicity and media relations. Since then, the field has grown. The research participants believed that currently many professionals with formal education and knowledge in public relations have entered the field. This next generation of public relations professionals understands the more complex nature of public relations, especially its role in organizational decision making and facilitation of internal communication.

The development of public relations from serving primarily a media relations function to its evolution into a key strategic function may be a typical trajectory around the world. For example, Ivy Lee and Basil Clarke, early-20th-century public relations figures in the United States and the United Kingdom, respectively, began their careers as journalists (Hallahan, 2002; L'Etang, 2004). Although anecdotal, public relations development in Latvia today may be similar to those in other countries.

Organizational Influences

Public relations in Latvia has also been shaped by organizational factors. One such factor was the *authoritative style of management* that, the research participants believed, senior executives had inherited from the Soviet era. Although not descriptive of her organization, a research participant from a public institution described a common management practice in Latvia: "I think we have a lot of authoritarian managers. They do not trust their own people. They always want to make subjective decisions. They never listen to their employees. They never analyze situations. They don't weigh pros and cons." She continued by attributing this authoritarian style of management to the transitional context: "Maybe this is not isolated. Maybe this needs to be measured against the overall level of democracy in our country. It is possible that our business and management cultures are still continuing to develop."

However, this trend was not common in the Latvian branch of international companies. For example, a public relations director employed by a Scandinavian company said,

> A crucial part of Nordic cultures . . . and also our [organizational] value is people. It's all about people. In Nordic countries there is a high regard for consensus. We practice the same [in Latvia]. We always reach a consensus before we proceed with a project.

Another common organizational influence that put strains on the public relations work was the lack of management's understanding of the role of public relations. Organizational management was not aware of what public relations can do for its organizations. According to a public relations head employed by a government institution, "Public relations practitioners must always be capable of providing a rationale for their actions." Research participants also acknowledged that it was their responsibility to help management and other employees understand public relations. One research participant said she had "to do PR for PR." To help management understand public relations, communication executives had to continuously introduce management and others to public relations outcomes, maintain continuous communication with the management and react to the management's feedback, as well as take the initiative in helping the management reach organizational goals.

Characteristics and Qualities of Excellent Leaders

This section focuses on leadership traits that were valued among public relations professionals in Latvia. It begins with a discussion of general leadership characteristics and qualities identified across the issues, and concludes with leadership traits that are related to a specific issue.

General Leadership Characteristics and Qualities

The survey revealed that the three highest rated traits across the survey's 10 important issues included, first, an ability to participate in the organization's strategic decision-making regarding the issue ($M = 6.26$). During the in-depth interviews, several public relations executives, especially from the corporate and agency sectors, discussed a similar trait. They emphasized the significance of the public relations leader's ability to provide public relations contributions to the overall business goals. A public relations head from the bank illustrated, "[the public relations unit] must provide maximum added value to everything that the company does."

The second highest rated trait was the ability to build and manage professional work teams to address the issue ($M = 6.16$). Team management skills were also one of the most frequently discussed qualities by the interviewees. The research participants believed that this quality involved motivating and supporting public relations teams, facilitating the team's and its individual members' professional growth and development, coordinating and leading teamwork, taking responsibility for the final outcome of the teamwork, and reducing the turnover of team members. Several female participants emphasized the importance of empathy. One of them said,

> It is important that we do not think only about work. We also need to talk about other things that are important in life . . . that we do to make everyday more pleasant. We are all human. We are one team. We spend more time with our colleagues than with our families. It is essential to create a good working environment. We need to ensure that we invest in the time that we spend together.

The third leadership skill named by the survey respondents was the ability to provide a compelling vision for how communication can help the organization ($M = 6.06$). This trait also resonated among the interviewees who suggested that a good leader in Latvia must possess an ability to demonstrate the value of public relations to management and other colleagues. This ability involved explaining decisions, actions and directions, and outcomes related to public relations. Several participants believed that to demonstrate the contribution of public relations to the organization, the leading public relations practitioners must maintain good ongoing relationships with the management.

Another general leadership quality revealed through the interviews was labeled by one participant as *professionalism*. She described it as "being systematic, professionally loyal and concise in communication with colleagues. It also means that one must be able to clearly define goals and have the expertise to meet them." Some other elements mentioned during the interviews and could possibly be added to this trait were impartiality in decision making, critical analytical skills, and knowledge about public relations.

Issue Specific Leadership Traits

The following paragraphs link the three most important issues with specific leadership traits. "Dealing with the speed and volume of information flow" was selected as the most important issue by the survey respondents. Public relations practitioners believed that the four leadership traits that help leaders best address this issue are possessing communication knowledge to develop appropriate strategies, plans, and messages ($M = 6.31$); participating in the organization's strategic decision making regarding the issue ($M = 6.27$); having the ability to build and manage professional work teams to address the issue ($M = 6.09$); and providing a compelling vision for how communication can help the organization ($M = 6.02$).

For the second most important issue, that is, *being prepared to deal effectively with crises that may arise*, two leadership traits received the high rankings of 6 or above on the 7-point scale. These traits were participating in the organization's strategic decision making regarding the issue ($M = 6.11$) and having the ability to build and manage professional work teams to address the issue ($M = 6.11$).

Finally, the third most import issue was *improving employee engagement and commitment in the workplace*. Five leadership traits were selected as very important for this issue: participating in the organization's strategic decision making regarding the issue ($M = 6.37$), possessing a strong ethical orientation and set of values to guide actions ($M = 6.21$), having the ability to build and manage professional work teams to address the issue ($M = 6.42$), providing a compelling vision for how communication can help the organization ($M = 6.05$), and having the ability to develop coalitions in and outside the organization to deal with the issue ($M = 6.05$).

Current State of Leadership Development

This section focuses on the role of universities and professional associations in leadership development and training in Latvia. During the past 17 years, a great number of Latvian universities have opened programs in public relations at four different levels. Pūre's (n.d.) doctoral research shows that there are five associate level programs, nine bachelor's programs, four master's programs, and two doctoral programs. Five bachelor's and three master's programs have a more professional orientation as opposed to those with more academic studies. Graduates of professionally oriented programs receive either the qualification of "public relations manager" or "manager of the public relations structural unit." These programs are very popular among Latvian students.

The curriculum for the professional programs is based on either the professional qualification standards for public relations managers or the managers of public relations structural units. Both standards have been developed by national committees consisting of educators and practitioners. The existing standard for public relations managers is currently being revised. Andris Pētersons (personal communication, September 6, 2013), the head of the working committee on the professional standard for public relations managers, acknowledged that leadership skills are an important aspect of public relations education. He said,

> Public relations managers should be leaders. Leadership skills are required by both the job market and the professional qualification standard that is based on the demands of the job market. . . . Public relations programs most certainly should encourage and develop students' leadership abilities.

Although the programs of study are aimed towards developing managerial skills, the Leadership Study and other investigations (e.g., Pētersone, 2006; Pūre, n.d.) reveal that Latvian public relations practitioners are critical of public relations education. For example, a head of a leading public relations consultancy encountered difficulties in finding highly skilled public relations consultants who could advise senior-level executives at client companies. He believed that many institutions of higher education fail to prepare well-rounded professionals. He preferred to hire political science or business majors rather than their public relations and communication counterparts. He said he found that the latter lacked an overall understanding about current affairs and business practices.

Other studies yielded similar findings. One of this chapter's authors (Pētersone, 2006) found that some industry leaders did not trust educational programs because they were delivered by educators who formerly were employed by the Communist Party as propaganda disseminators. Pūre's (n.d.) doctoral research revealed that public relations managers found that the graduates of Latvian higher education programs in public relations were unprepared for the current demands of the job market. These managers felt the graduates were well versed in communication theories, but lacked practical skills and training. Some of Pūre's interviewees aimed harsh criticism at Latvian universities. They said, "public relations is taught at every university that is not too lazy to teach it," and "[public relations programs] are an opportunity for an easy money [for universities]."

Of course, this complex issue cannot be viewed one-sidedly. The same study (Pūre, n.d.) showed that the industry practitioners, many of whom were not formally educated in public relations, may not have understood the more complex aspects of public relations. For these individuals, public relations was a synonym for publicity and media relations. It is true that most recent graduates lack strong ties with reporters. Therefore, their older colleagues, who only value publicity, may find them unprepared for the job. However, the authors of this chapter agree with Pūre's observations. The publicity perspective on public relations overlooks a range of contributions that public relations can offer to the organization. This publicity perspective limits public relations to a craft that requires a set of vocational skills rather than an independent professional field that values advanced capabilities such as critical thinking, strategic planning, management, visionary leadership, and so forth.

In addition to the vast educational opportunities at universities, there are two professional associations in Latvia, one for individual public relations practitioners and one for public relations consultancies. Both associations aim to facilitate the education of public relations professionals. The website of the Latvian Association for Public Relations Practitioners (n.d.) describes this organization as an independent professional body that "shapes the reputation of the public relations industry, ensures knowledge transfer among public relations professionals, promotes collegiality, as well as sets standards for professional quality and ethics" (para. 1).

> The mission of the Latvian Association for Public Relations Consultancies (n.d.) is to maintain and create a successful business environment for public relations consultancies in the Republic of Latvia, protect the professional and business interests of the Association's members, educate public relations service providers and their clients, follow the [public relations] industry's current trends and developments in Latvia and the world, [and] establish and manage collaborations with public relations and related industry partners at home and internationally. (para. 3)

A review of the two associations' websites show that they both hold best-practice seminars and educational events for their members and jointly organize the Baltic PR Awards, an annual multi-category competition that recognizes the best public relations campaigns in the three Baltic countries.

Nevertheless, research on public relations in Latvia (Pūre, n.d.) suggests that practitioners' skepticism also extends to these two professional associations, both of which are relatively small. According to the above mentioned websites, the association for public relations practitioners has more than 100 members (Latvian Association for Public Relations Professionals, n.d., para. 1) and the consultancies association's membership consists of only eleven firms (Latvian Association for Public Relations Consultancies, n.d., para. 2). A theme that emerged during Pūre's doctoral research suggests that some non-members perceive these associations as small cliques of elite public relations practitioners and agency heads whose sole purpose is to maintain their dominance in the market. Because of this situation, others do not see any value in joining them.

We believe five factors could contribute to leadership development in Latvia. First, educational institutions and the industry should engage each other in a discussion about the best ways to prepare future industry leaders. It seems that public relations students could strongly benefit from both strong academic backgrounds and solid internship experiences.

Second, the Leadership Study and other previously mentioned studies (Pētersone, 2004, 2006; Pūre, n.d.) showed that public relations practitioners believed that public relations graduates lacked knowledge about broader social, cultural, and political issues. This finding may suggest that the public relations education programs should encourage students to expand their horizons by integrating interdisciplinary knowledge in the curriculum.

Third, as better educated practitioners enter the field and some public relations graduates continue with higher level studies, the body of public relations educators may also change. The less qualified faculty may be replaced by academics and professionals with comprehensive understanding of the complex nature of public relations.

The fourth factor for strengthening leadership development in Latvia may include more inclusive public relations associations that work toward educating both their members and nonmembers. Many public relations practitioners lack formal education in public relations. It is possible that appropriate training programs offered by the two associations could help these individuals learn about the various functions of public relations that exceed media relations and publicity. These training programs could also benefit the development and strengthening of practitioners' leadership capabilities.

Finally, larger sociocultural changes can also contribute to the leadership development. The interview findings suggested that an authoritarian style of management inherited from the Soviet era is still common in Latvian organizations. It is likely that as the society continues moving toward openness and transparency, the authoritarian style of management will become less acceptable.

Leadership Needs for the Future

The leadership study also revealed practitioners' insights about the future of the profession and its leadership. Conversations with public relations executives singled out several aspects of public relations work that will require their attention in the coming years. Almost all interviewed public relations leaders believed that in the future the importance of *internal communication* will increase. For example, a public relations manager employed by a public university believed that as the management becomes more aware of various aspects of public relations, the better it will understand the role of this function within the organization. She said,

> The management knows that it can request more from public relations professionals. It's not just publicity. . . . We can see from recent job announcements that more and more companies understand the value of internal communication and seek internal communication specialists.

She also attributed this change to better educated and experienced public relations practitioners who have advanced expertise in public relations and can replace the publicity-focused former journalists.

The research participants also said that social media and communication technologies will continue to play a major role in public relations. The industry will need to catch up with the development of social media and communication technologies, as well as diversify the ways that organizations reach their publics. An interviewee explained, "If two years ago it was a question of whether we need social media, then today it's a question of how we use the social media."

Another issue that dominated the conversation about future needs in public relations involved the improvement of change management skills, especially in the aftermath of the economic crisis. Strengthening change management skills and capabilities was also identified by survey respondents as a way to develop future leaders ($M = 5.95$). The respondents also agreed with the growing importance of enhancing conflict management skills ($M = 5.82$).

Some other future leadership needs cited included learning to better measure public relations returns and contributions to business goals, integrating the public relations function into the organizational decision-making process, and managing public relations programs strategically. Overall, Latvian public relations practitioners were positively inclined toward the future of the profession in Latvia. The interviews allowed a conclusion that management's respect for public relations is increasing and public relations practitioners themselves are acquiring an advanced understanding about their profession. As observed by a public relations director at a city council, "Finally, public relations specialists are valued."

References

Bentele, G., & Peter, G. M. (1996). Public relations in the German Democratic Republic and the new federal German states. In H. M. Culbertson & N. Chen (Eds.), *International public relations: A comparative analysis* (pp. 349–365). Mahwah, NJ: Erlbaum.

Berger, B. & Reber, B. (2006). *Gaining influence in public relations: The role of resistance in practice.* Mahwah, NJ: Erlbaum.

Grunig, L., Grunig, J. & Dozier, D. (2002). *Excellent public relations and effective organizations: A study of communication management in three countries.* Mahwah, NJ: Erlbaum.

Guth, D. W. (2000). The emergence of public relations in the Russian Federation. *Public Relations Review, 26*(2), 191–207.

Hallahan, K. (2002). Ivy Lee and the Rockefellers' response to the 1913–1914 Colorado coal strike, *Journal of Public Relations Research, 14*(4), 265–315.

Karadjov, C., Kim, Y., & Karavasilev, L. (2000). Models of public relations in Bulgaria and job satisfaction among practitioners. *Public Relations Review, 26*(2), 209–218.

KPMG. (2011). *Study on the public relations industry in Latvia.* Rīga, Latvia: Author.

The Latvian Association for Public Relations Consultancies. (n.d.). About us. Available online at http://lasak.lv

The Latvian Association for Public Relations Practitioners. (n.d.). About us. Available online at http://lasap.lv/parmums

Ławniczak, R. (2001). Transition public relations: An instrument for systematic transformation in Central and Eastern Europe. In R. Ławniczak (Ed.), *Public relations contribution to transition in Central and Eastern Europe: Research and practice* (pp. 109–119). Poznan, Poland: Biuro Uslogowo-Handlowe.

L'Etang, J. (2004). *Public relations in Britain: A history of professional practice in the twentieth century.* Mahwah, NJ: Erlbaum.

McCracken, G. (1988). *The long interview*. Newbury Park, CA: Sage.

Pētersone, B. (2004). *The status of public relations in Latvia* (Unpublished master's thesis). University of Maryland, College Park.

Pētersone, B. (2006, June). *The status of public relations in Latvia*. Paper presented at the meeting of the International Communication Association, Dresden, Germany.

Pūre, I. (n.d). *The development and conceptual diversity of public relations in Latvia: 1991–2010* (Ongoing doctoral research project). School of Business Administration Turība University, Rīga, Latvia.

Pūre, I. (2011, July). *Development of public relations in Latvia: Pre-history and periods of development*. Paper presented at the History of Public Relations Conference, Bournemouth, England.

Scholz, J., 1998. *A normative approach to the practice of public relations in the eastern part of Germany* (Unpublished master's thesis). University of Maryland, College Park.

Verčič, D., Grunig, L. A., & Grunig, J. E., 1996. Global and specific principles of public relations; Evidence from Slovenia. In H. M. Culbertson & N. Chen (Eds.), *International public relations: A comparative analysis* (pp. 31–65). Mahwah, NJ: Erlbaum.

15

TAKING ON THE BEAR

Public Relations Leaders Confronting Russian Challenges

Elina Erzikova

Russia, one of the world's top economies, has a relatively young public relations field. In the past 20 years, the field has moved from being perceived as inferior (Tsetsura, 2011) to being recognized as quite mature and ambitious (Epley, 2012). The Russian public relations market is one of the fastest growing in Eastern Europe, with agencies opening offices around the world (Tsetsura, 2011). The burgeoning occupation is attractive for young Russians who perceive it as creative and prestigious (Erzikova & Berger, 2011).

Still, a number of issues impede the industry's growth. Particularly, the Russian field lacks professional standards and legislation and suffers from a low level of business transparency (Epley, 2012). In addition, the field does not seem to be developing equally across the country, supporting a geopolitical approach (Tsetsura, 2009) to study distinct public relations practices within a single country. Epley (2012) quoted a leading public relations practitioner who believed that in Russia, public relations practices outside of Moscow are somewhat "naïve," whereas PR in the capital is "more sophisticated, aggressive, and cynical."

However, regardless of a geographical location, Russian public relations practitioners intend to take a leadership role in tackling major social issues and building societal harmony (Epley, 2012). Systematic research on Russian public relations will help the field analyze best practices and develop a leadership style that effectively addresses the global—local continuum (de Vries, 2001). This task is not an easy one in any country, and Russia with its Soviet heritage—a deficient and bureaucratic managerial system—seems to be the most challenging place to implement leadership reforms.

Recent research has shown that a "tough love" approach (McCarthy, Puffer, May, Ledgerwood, & Stewart, 2008), or a leader's encompassing control, still dominates in Russian organizations. The culture of fear also inhibits organizational changes. Workers avoid showing initiative or sharing ideas for fear of mistakes or the appearance of superiority over a supervisor (McCarthy et al., 2008). Meanwhile, the strongest constraint affecting leadership in Russian organizations is the State, a hostile intruder of business operations (McCarthy et al., 2008).

Public relations leadership at the organizational level might be a factor in overcoming the Soviet administrative heritage and adapting to market needs (Dixon, Meyer, & Day, 2007; McCarthy et al., 2008). Indeed, Bass and Bass (2008) argued that leadership has a potential to become the single most important factor in organizational success or failure. In Russia's noncompetitive economy, the role of leaders becomes critical in orchestrating the process of adapting to new technology and the environment (Bass & Bass, 2008).

Elenkov (2002) found that excellent leaders in Russia demonstrate charisma, individualized consideration, and intellectual stimulation. Considering the Russian collectivist culture, a weak market, and the environment of uncertainty, charismatic leadership seems the most effective for achieving organizational goals (Elenkov, 2002). The proposition supports Bass's (1985) hypothesis that charismatic leadership suits best those organizations operating in a turbulent external environment.

The post-Soviet Russia is characterized by two new dynamics: the struggle of ordinary people to make ends meet and a widespread fascination with celebrities (Goscilo & Strukov, 2011). The current political leadership has contributed to the formation of celebrity culture in Russia (Goscilo & Strukov, 2011). Glamour, a by-product of celebrity culture, serves as a new Russian utopia promoted by Putin's regime. The political agenda is constructing a new identity, "*homo glamuricus*, to replace *homo sovieticus*," to build a new middle class "comprising owners of economic and social wealth" (Goscilo & Strukov, 2011, p. 4).

Not surprisingly, the nouveau riche actively seeks publicity opportunities. Lacking knowledge of normative public relations, they think of media exposure not as a part of public relations but as public relations, itself. One of the new-era businesspersons, Potapenko (2012) openly called organizational heads to fire public relations practitioners and become spokespersons for their own enterprises. Thousands of social media users, including some public relations leaders interviewed in this study "liked" Potapneko's (2012) proposition. A critical attitude toward the public relations field is not a new finding. Both publics and public relations practitioners themselves have been criticizing the public relations practice in Russia for a number of years (Erzikova & Berger, 2006).

The Global Leadership Study

Against this backdrop, Russian public relations practitioners participated in the global study of leadership in communication management carried out by The Plank Center for Leadership in Public Relations at the University of Alabama. Results of this survey in 23 countries (Berger, 2012) showed that Russian public relations practitioners' ($n = 215$) perceptions of public relations and its importance and challenges are in tune with their global peers; Russian public relations practitioners share many beliefs about professional leadership with their colleagues in other countries. Russian participants also indicated that (a) dealing with the speed and volume of information flow, (b) finding and retaining talented communication professionals, and (c) dealing with crises were the three most significant issues affecting the respondents' routine operations.

Like their global peers, Russian practitioners believed that the most important personal abilities for coping with on-the-job issues were participating in organizational strategic decision making, possessing communication knowledge to develop appropriate strategies, and having the ability to build and manage professional work teams to address the issue. Russian participants thought that strengthening change management skills and capabilities is the most important development need for future leaders, and they place high importance on moral education and business training.

Interviews with Russian Public Relations Leaders

The global leadership survey provided a baseline of data regarding practitioners' perceptions of key issues in the field, how they manage those issues, what the issues mean for leaders, and what future development needs and opportunities are important for the profession. Interviews with leaders in the field were then conducted with public relations leaders in each country and region in the study. The remainder of this chapter focuses on interviews that were conducted with professionals and leaders in Russia.

Participants and Data Collection

Thirteen Russian public relations practitioners (six women and seven men) participated in the study. A snowball sampling technique was used to recruit respondents. An effort was made to assure geographical representation and diversity based on gender, age, length of experience, education, and type of organization. Participants represented six different Russian regions. Respondents' ages ranged from 27 to 52. Their professional experience ranged from 5 to 20 years as public relations practitioners. Eleven participants had bachelor's degrees in public relations, humanities, or journalism; two respondents held PhD degrees in Russian language and literature.

Participants worked for different types of organizations, including public relations agencies, businesses, political organizations, and nonprofits. They held the first or second positions in their companies or communication units. Of 13 participants, 2 were heads of organizations. They were included in the study to reflect a growing number of organizational leaders who act as public relations representatives for their companies in Russia.

The interview process was guided by Kvale's (1988) suggestion that "the interview statements are not collected—they are coauthored by the interviewer" (p. 101). This approach implies that the interviewer was actively listening and following up after the answers were spoken (Kvale, 1988). A relatively small sample helped develop strong relationships with research participants and obtain rich data (L. Grunig, 2008).

Interviews were conducted in Russian and lasted 2 hours on average. Nine respondents were interviewed in their offices in Russia, and four participants were interviewed via Skype. Interviews were audio recorded and transcribed for analysis. Participants signed informed consent forms prior to interviews. Those who were interviewed via Skype received the informed consent form via e-mail.

Data Analysis

Strengths of qualitative data include but are not limited to providing vivid descriptions situated in a real context, focusing on "lived experiences" of people, locating the meanings people place on different phenomena, revealing complexity, and providing researchers with a possibility to understand a latent issue (Miles & Huberman, p. 10, 1994).

The Miles and Huberman's (1994) three-step approach to the qualitative data analysis was utilized to analyze transcribed interviews with Russian public relations leaders. The first stage—data reduction—included sorting, clustering, and summarizing data. The second step—data display—resulted in 18 short blocks of texts or "simplified gestalts" (Miles & Huberman, 1994, p. 11). The blocks (boxes) were further arranged to study patterns, trends, and a possible interaction between variables (e.g., between a low quality of public relations professionals and encroachment of the field). The final stage of data analysis included the process of preliminary conclusion drawing and verification that should be further tested using different methods and samples.

Top Issues for Leaders

Respondents indicated a number of important issues that have an impact on them and the practice of public relations. Two issues—misinterpretation of public relations and a low professional quality of practitioners—were addressed explicitly and implicitly in all interviews.

Misconception of Public Relations and its Consequences

The misconception of public relations appeared to be the number one concern. More important, misinterpretation of public relations encompasses different social strata in Russia, according to study participants. Whereas ordinary people consider public relations to be spinning (a lie), businesspeople and politicians see it as a quick fix, or media relations at best. Moreover, top executives encroach into public relations, seeing it as a publicity opportunity. Sadly, many public relations specialists themselves perceive public relations as hidden manipulation.

Ordinary-people level. Participants believed that although contemporary public relations practitioners distance themselves from the "prehistoric dirty political PR of the 1990s," the masses are still suspicious about public relations communications. As a participant said, "People are still trying to figure out at what point they would be duped." Another participant echoed that sentiment by expressing a strong belief that the state protects interests of the elites, not ordinary people, which make public institutions' efforts to reach out an "almost impossible mission."

Indeed, trust in public institutions in Russia is the lowest in the world (Shlapentokh, 2006). As a consequence, communications initiated by various organizations often times do not produce an intended effect among ordinary people. Coupled with a low professionalism of public relations practitioners, public relations actions might be even counterproductive, study participants believed. One respondent said, "I observe many PR managers, and I realize that without their 'work,' the situation would be better. For example, they decrease the leading political party's rating among the electorate, not increase it." Overall, the country's political, economic, and social environment appeared to turn ordinary Russians into a "PR resistant audience."

Organizational-heads level. Participants believed that organizational leadership does not have an adequate understanding of public relations, resulting in a tendency to either underestimate or overestimate a public relations function. A head of a public relations agency said, "Oftentimes, a PR specialist is not part of a strategic decision-making team. The PR specialist is simply given a task, for example, to organize the media coverage of an event."

The CEOs' misunderstanding of public relations leads to a belief that public relations is incapable of contributing to the bottom line. A head of a public relations agency said that return on investment (ROI) was a "difficult topic to discuss" with organizational heads because they still measure the public relations contribution by the number of published stories. The participant said even if public relations practitioners realize this is an outdated approach, they would not argue with the CEO.

Staying out of trouble, or practitioners' passivity in explaining public relations functions to their supervisors, appeared to be common across organizations in Russia. There is a clear discrepancy between practitioners' complaints about misunderstanding public relations functions and a shortage of practitioners who are willing to actively educate their bosses on professional issues. A public relations agency head said that for many years, he tried unsuccessfully to encourage PR practitioners to use advanced techniques and/or collaborate with his agency.

These days, he bypasses public relations departments and sells his agency's services directly to top management. In addition, he launches seminars and workshops for organizational heads on a variety of public relations professional issues. The participant thought his effort contributed to economic improvement in his region.

It appears that the process of acquiring public relations knowledge is a two-way street in Russia. Participants in this study said that increasingly more business owners and top managers seek an opportunity to educate themselves about public relations every year.

Whereas one category of organizational leaders undervalues the public relations potential, another category thinks about the practice as magic. A respondent said her boss believes a public relations effort produces an immediate result: "He doesn't understand that the effect doesn't happen overnight, especially in the bank industry." Another participant said that she is perceived as an emergency service: "Metaphorically speaking, the client appeals to PR experts when he is almost dead." Proactive public relations does not seem to be in great demand by the C-suite in Russia, study participants concluded. The C-suite refers to those highest level executives in the senior decision-making circle, such as the chief executive officer, chief financial officer, chief technology officer, and so forth.

Overall, there has been a change in Russian public relations leaders' perceptions during the last 7 years. Interviewed in 2005, leading public relations practitioners said Russians were not familiar with the concept of public relations (Erzikova & Berger, 2006). In 2012, they said that public relations is being misinterpreted by various publics. To some extent, the misinterpretation of the public relations function can be explained by the complexity of contemporary public relations practice. Today's public relations is "much more than just a corporate communication practice" (Botan & Taylor, 2004, p. 659) worldwide. Public relations is a multidimensional activity involving different expertise even in countries with developing professional practices. With complexity comes varying definitions of what it means to be a public relations practitioner—from a message creator to a crisis manager to an event planner. Therefore, it's no surprise that public relations is construed in many ways in Russia.

It appeared that the Russian top management has gone much further in its interpretation of public relations than practitioners expected. There is a tendency of organizational heads to perform public relations functions. A head of a publishing house said, "I'm involved in GR [government relations] every day. I can't imagine outsourcing this task to a PR person." She added that besides the intensity of government relations activities, she believes public officials would not deal with a staffer—only with the organizational head. For many reasons (e.g., distrust, a culture of secrecy), the top manager is usually the final and often the only decision maker. This is why, for example, strategic partnership projects are discussed at the executive level, not public relations practitioners' level, the publishing house head concluded.

The fact that organizational leaders perform tasks of public relations practitioners signals encroachment of the field. Traditionally in the United States, encroachment has been defined as "the assignment of non-public relations professionals to manage the public relations function" (Lauzen, 1993, p. 248). However, this practice does not seem to be a central concern of American public relations practitioners these days. Bruce K. Berger, first director of the Plank Center for Leadership in Public Relations at University of Alabama, said,

> I used to hear a lot about encroachment into the profession in the US a decade ago. But I hear about it far less today. Perhaps one reason is that social media have given practitioners some license to spread their reach inside organizations. (personal communication, March 18, 2013)

"Traditional" Western encroachment into the public relations function happens when one supposedly equal unit within an organization (marketing, human resources, or legal) subordinates public relations (Lauzen, 1993, Lauzen & Dozier,1992; Lee, Jares, & Heath, 1999). It appears that in Russia, encroachment crosses two organizational levels—top executives and public relations managers. There are several explanations for why executives desire to perform on the public relations stage.

First, the politics of glamour (Goscilo & Strukov, 2011) defines the need for becoming a media personality. Second, close ties with reporters are perceived as a means of protection from the State (Potapenko, 2012). Third, business owners and top managers' disappointment in the quality of public relations practitioners make them take on the public relations duty. Finally, the culture of secrecy and distrust seems to exclude public relations practitioners from the decision-making process, relegating them to a technician role.

Public relations–specialists' level. Study participants believed some practitioners carry old interpretations of public relations. Those who "are stuck in the past" might think about public relations as a solely creative and artistic activity. A head of a public relations agency thought a strong focus on creativity prevents PR practitioners from considering and mastering measurements of effectiveness. A political consultant with extensive experience said,

> PR people have to be energetic and resourceful; PR should be a drive for them, not just a job. I didn't mention "creativity" since too much emphasis has been given to this quality in the last 20 years. It's time to discuss professionalism based on knowledge of theory and research, not just creativity.

Another misperception of public relations—public relations is manipulation— also seems to originate in the past (e.g., information wars in the 1990s). The political consultant believed that many practitioners still think "PR is manipulation of public opinion." However, as the respondent explained, the growth of social media in Russia makes the "task of hiding manipulation tougher."

A political manager with 10 years of experience believed some of his colleagues still interpret public relations as a semisecret adventure. He said, "The PR profession is not a profession of soldiers of fortune. It's a profession of intelligent and thoughtful people." The manager believed that an oversimplified interpretation of public relations helps some practitioners justify "inertia and a comfy living." Overall, study participants believed a misinterpretation of public relations by practitioners can be also explained by a low quality of education and lack of desire for self-improvement.

Low Level of Professionalism

The second greatest concern was a low level of professionalism among public relations practitioners. One respondent said, "The situation is desperate because young practitioners do not have an adequate PR education and tend to avoid professional challenges." As for older practitioners, they "insist on doing PR in an ancient way." The head of a publishing house said,

> There are no fresh approaches in PR. Clients are more educated and sophisticated than PR practitioners. PR people offer strategies and tactics that disappoint the client: "Too old." This is an alarming trend—our client has outgrown our approaches. One of the explanations is a weak educational system. Not surprisingly, the client doesn't want to rely on PR people; he studies PR and comes up with his own methods.

A female head of a public relations agency that trains five or six interns every summer said that public relations curricula do not reflect the current needs of the industry; for example, universities do not teach digital public relations. Although public relations programs describe relations with traditional media as the most valuable form of public relations, graduating seniors cannot write a news release. In other words, public relations students "are indoctrinated to obey an outdated approach, and they are not trained in basic writing," the practitioner said.

According to study participants, public relations graduates do not understand fundamental concepts. For example, they do not know how to approach target audiences. As a result, in-house public relations practitioners "write for their boss—not for the readers," and mass audiences do not understand bureaucratic language or professional jargon, the head of a publishing house said.

Study participants thought that "PR students are left to survive" for several reasons. First, Russian universities are lagging behind Western universities in creating an effective learning environment. Second, organizations "do not educate staffers," meaning there is no continuum of education and training in practice.

Thus, "a student has to educate himself/herself to be prepared for PR work," according to the female head of a public relations agency.

Both survey and interview data showed respondents believed that the task of cultivating moral character should be not less important than developing professional skills of future public relations practitioners. Respondents saw a new generation of public relations specialists as being more technologically advanced and less ethical. In addition, participants did not think that industry practices are an example of ethical conduct. A public relations consultant to the head of a multibillion corporation said, "Looking at what is happening in PR now, I realize that the future generation will be less concerned with ethical issues."

Concerns expressed by participants—misconception of public relations and a low quality of professionals—might not be unique to Russia (Berger & Reber, 2006). However, two factors distinguish Russia among other countries: (a) the degree to which these interrelated problems are perceived as critical challenges and (b) strong external factors (e.g., a noncompetitive economy, politics of glamour) that hinder the industry from overcoming the challenges.

Cultural and Structural Influences on Leaders

Study participants indicated a number of cultural and structural dynamics that have an impact on their practice. Almost all respondents described organizational culture in positive terms: "a team spirit," "creative," "friendly," and "open." They also saw senior executives as being understanding of the public relations value and supportive of practitioners' initiatives. This finding somewhat contradicts the Russian survey results that revealed a modest evaluation ($M = 4.94; SD = 1.90$) of CEOs' understanding of the importance of public relations.

A head of a public relations agency said he promotes competition among his staffers: A manager who comes up with best ideas for a project becomes a team leader. Two participants said their organizations are akin to the army. Yet, as a respondent said, "The authoritarian style doesn't mean that needs of employees are disregarded for the sake of achieving goals. The tasks are indeed complex, but there is always a consideration of the comfort level of our employees."

Tension within a communication department was brought up by a participant who worked for a national resort: "If there is a winning situation, the victory is ascribed to advertising and/or marketing experts. If there is a failure, PR specialists will be blamed."

A relatively new phenomenon—chain enterprises—brought a challenge to regional communication professionals. They are subordinate to their organizations' headquarters located in the Russian capital. As the head of a publishing house said, "For Moscow, only profit is important." The Moscow headquarters office imposes identical communication plans for all regions, without recognizing local specifics. When such plans fail, regional communication professionals are blamed. At the same time, a chain enterprise provides some advantages.

According to the publisher, "If I have a problem, I will talk with other heads of regional branches. I can't ask my colleagues here, in the city, to help me—they are friends and competitors at the same time."

Other respondents also mentioned a conflict between their regional branches and a Moscow headquarters. As a practitioner said, "Sometimes we cannot meet the needs of VIP clients because of regulations imposed by Moscow."

Participants believed the industry has moved from basic measurement (e.g., the number of published stories) to a more complex form (e.g., before- and after-event surveys). However, they were concerned with the fact that the development of more thorough measurement techniques might be hindered by the lack of human and financial resources in public relations departments.

Further, the politics of glamour (Goscilo & Strukov, 2011) manifested in the business owners' and top managers quest for publicity slows the process of mastering public relations research and measurement. A female head of a PR agency said, "In some companies, if 'TVs' don't come, the news conference is considered a failure. Clients love to see themselves on TV, especially on national channels." Participants emphasized that while an average client sees public relations as an opportunity to appear on television, the emerging agenda (e.g., ROI) would not be a priority for public relations practitioners.

Interestingly, some respondents did not think their organizations had internal factors that impede successful communication. They focused on external factors, such as political authoritarianism, bureaucracy, and a low quality of reporters.

Traditional media, especially television stations, are not necessarily interested in covering events initiated by public relations practitioners. A respondent said, "Government-controlled TV channels conveniently consider any information that comes from sources other than government an advertisement, and they charge organizations for broadcasting it." This commercial approach is one of the reasons public relations practitioners have delved into Internet communication.

The rise of authoritarianism as a leadership style in Russia also was seen as a reason to "immigrate into a digital world." One of the participants said, "[O]ne of the obvious methods of resistance to the Kremlin is using the Internet as a means of communication." However, as a political public relations manager said, "It's not clear how information distributed via social media is processed. Everyone is saying the Internet has an impact, but we don't know *how* the Internet is affecting human communication." Overall, respondents thought that developing social media skills needs to be an integral part of public relations education.

Cultural Underpinning of Measurement and Evaluation

Although Russian public relations has emerged in the era of globalization and has been influenced by Western PR, the domestic practice nevertheless reflects its unique national culture (Guth, 2000). Unlike the Western brain culture, Russia is rather a heart culture, or a culture that does not necessarily believe that every-thing can be quantified (L. Grunig, 2008).

Public relations measurement and evaluation seemed to be an issue that especially clearly demonstrated differences between the West and Russia in interviews with participants. Whereas the West seems to consider quantitative approaches to be more valid and reliable than a qualitative analysis, Russia leans toward culturally based methods of evaluation, including reflexivity. A political consultant said he evaluates a "narrative factor by analyzing whether narratives that appeared during a campaign [in the media] correspond in spirit with a conceptualization of the campaign."

A public relations manager for a large corporation said peaceful relationships between a quite confrontational professional union and top management were achieved because of an ongoing internal communications program. Her measure-ment of success was the fact that "instead of attacking the CEO, union leaders ask, 'What should we do together to change the situation for the better?'"

Another public relations manager said her evaluation of a PR campaign is based on whether the campaign "produced cognitive dissonance in people's heads." She was proud to astonish 100 foreigners during a Night at the Museum event: "They saw ballerinas standing among dinosaurs and heard Tchaikovsky's music while passing by the history museum. The foreigners were stunned." Native Russians were interested in the event as well: The client required the public relations manager to secure attendance of 20,000 visitors during 2 months. She brought in 50,000 people.

Overall, these methods—measuring a narrative factor, the degree of union's friendliness, and cognitive dissonance—signal not only specifics of high-context culture (Hall, 1976) but also a weak business culture (McCarthy et al., 2008). In its turn, the fragile business culture reflects an outdated economic structure (de Vries & Shekshnia, 2008).

Characteristics and Qualities of Excellent Leaders

Discussing leadership characteristics, respondents linked a well-rounded educa-tion, professionalism, and trust. A PR manager for one of the best Russian universities said, "Professionalism is not only about the ability to create a good media kit but also about the ability to perform a reformist role in society." In his opinion, a change agent role presumes actions that increase trust at personal, organizational, and societal levels. The practitioner defined public relations leadership as a "drive to create a better future for an organization and society." Another practitioner emphasized that leader's actions speak loader than his or her words:

> The leader is a trusted person, who will be followed even if it is not easy for followers—to walk a tough road. A leader is a person, who is not only

constantly generates ideas, but also implements them. Overall, the leader is a person with concrete actions that followers understand and accept.

Other respondents contributed to this discourse by describing leadership as a "combination of vision and risk-taking" and seeing a "solid education and extensive experience" as most important leadership prerequisites. A head of a public relations agency believed reputation is the most important quality of a PR leader: "When I talk to a client, I don't talk about what I do. I simply tell them my name."

In accordance with the Russian collectivist culture, participants emphasized the ability to establish close relationships and "discuss with followers problems that are outside of work." They also underlined the necessity of a constant professional growth. In this regard, a political manager said many of his colleagues extensively use such a method of propaganda as a fear appeal: "If you don't vote for this particular candidate, tomorrow you will live even worse than today." The manager admitted he also capitalizes on this method, but at the same time, he is searching and developing new tactics that will help his candidate win elections tomorrow.

Study participants believed public relations leadership has not been manifested at the national level in Russia. Importantly, a perceived shortage of nationally recognized charismatic public relations leaders appeared to be a universal phenomenon (Berger & Reber, 2006). One Russian participant commented, "Sporadic attempts to lead the industry don't count." As in the previous study (Erzikova & Berger, 2006), leading public relations practitioners in the current research saw leadership as a way to elevate the status of public relations in the country. A PR manager for a national bank said, "Outstanding role models inspire people to become better professionals. 'Better' means 'educated, motivated and moral.'"

The theme of authoritarianism as a leadership style was brought into conversation by a number of participants. They thought the rise of authoritarianism in national politics has a negative impact on the country's present and future. However, respondents reserved their own right to be authoritarian to get the job done.

Current State of Leadership Development

There are 163 institutions of higher education that prepare public relations specialists in Russia. To the author's knowledge, there is not a specific public relations leadership course or discussion of leadership across the university curricula. As for indirect (but still important) efforts to develop future leaders, the Russian Public Relations Association's (RASO's) has conducted a national student competition, "Crystal Orange," since 2001. In addition, RASO has started rating institutions of higher education across all four categories—federal, national research, state, and commercial—to showcase the best programs and support initiatives aiming to improving the quality of public relations education in Russia. RASO also encourages different student activities—competitions, forums, and festivals—at the university level.

In 1998, the Moscow-based RASO launched a national public relations competition for practitioners, "Silver Archer." Since then, more than 1,800 projects have participated in the contest. "Silver Archer" also recognizes most successful and influential practitioners in the category, "Master."

Importantly, Russian provinces also have initiated professional contests. For example, "RuPoR" has been conducted in Central Russia since 2005. Public relations students and practitioners have an opportunity to learn from foreign practitioners during master classes at annual professional conventions (e.g., "PR Days in Moscow," "Baltic PR").

Because a new profession attracts risk takers (Bourdieu, 1984), there is hope that those individuals who choose a relatively new occupation in Russia—public relations—are able to move the industry forward by building trust and resisting encroachment from top management. Developing and supporting a profession's leaders seem crucial to achieving the goals. Research is warranted to investigate culturally relevant approaches to leadership development in Russia.

Conclusion

Interviews with leading public relations practitioners from different Russian regions revealed their perception of public relations as a "social practice" (White & Mazur, 1995, p. 266). Participants believed public relations should be used more actively to address Russia's economic, political, and social challenges.

Russia has demonstrated strong economic growth since 1999, but the "benefits of economic recovery are being distributed unequally—the rich are getting richer while the poor remain poor" (de Vries & Shekshnia, 2008, p. 238). As they have for the past century, average Russians still distrust the government and are skeptical about reforms (de Vries & Shekshnia, 2008). Meanwhile, Russia's new elite, wealthy individuals for whom Putin's regime provided an economic and political lift, fixates on glamour and celebrity. The elites perceive constant presence in media—a necessity to maintain a celebrity status—as public relations. *Piarit'sya*—a derivative from an abbreviation, PR—has become a common concept in Russia.

The pejorative term, *piarit'sya* or "seeking cheap publicity," hurts the public relations industry. First, the term reduces a multidimensional PR function to questionable promotional efforts and sends a misleading message to a variety of audiences. Second, a "do-it-yourself" approach leads to a call to fire "worthless" public relations staffers. Mass tabloidization of the media (as a perceived means to increase readership) intensifies misinterpretation of public relations by ordinary people.

Such a mix of dynamics creates a Russian environment that is quite challenging for the public relations profession. On the other hand, there is not an ideal setting anywhere in the world, and the art and science of public relations are the ability to minimize challenges and capitalize on strengths.

Mastering the public relations leadership concept might help different organizations to meet challenges of the globalized economy and thus, improve an overall situation in the country. Public relations leadership is not an effort to maintain control over others, but a systematic approach to cultivate trust and mutually beneficial relationships between organizations and their stakeholders. This philosophy seems a crucial pledge in a country still suffering from the consequences of a Soviet-like command system.

References

Bass, B. M. (1985). *Leadership and performance beyond expectations.* New York: Free Press.

Berger, B. (2012). *Key themes and findings: The cross-cultural study of leadership in public relations and communication management.* Tuscaloosa, AL: Plank Center for Leadership in Public Relations. Available online at http://plankcenter.ua.edu/wp-contentuploads/2012/10/Summary-of-themes-and-Findings-Leader-Survey.pdf

Berger, B. K., & Reber, B. H. (2006). *Gaining influence in public relations: The role of resistance in practice.* Mahwah, NJ: Erlbaum.

Botan, C., & Taylor, M. (2004). Public relations: State of the field. *Journal of Communication, 54*(4), 645–661.

Bourdieu, P. (1984). *Distinction. A social critique of the judgment of taste.* Cambridge, MA: Harvard University Press.

de Vries, M. K. (2001). The anarchist within: Clinical reflections on Russian character and leadership style. *Human Relations, 54*(5), 585–627.

de Vries, M. K., & Shekshnia, S. (2008). Vladimir Putin, CEO of Russia Inc. The legacy and the future. *Organizational Dynamics, 37*(3), 236–253.

Dixon, S. E. A., Meyer, K. E., & Day, M. (2007). Exploitation and exploration learning and the development of organizational capabilities: A cross-case analysis of the Russian oil industry. *Human Relations, 60,* 1493–1522.

Elenkov, D. S. (2002). Effects of leadership on organizational performance in Russian companies. *Journal of Business Research, 55,* 467–480.

Epley, J. S. (2012, April 4). Public relations in Russia: Keeping open a once closed society. *PR Tactics.* Available online at www.prsa.org/Intelligence/Tactics/Articles/view/9700/1046/Public_relations_in_Russia_Keeping_open_a_once_clo

Erzikova, E., & Berger, B. (2006, November). *Exploration of Russian flavor: Ethical aspects of PR practice in Russia.* Presented at the National Communication Association convention, in San Antonio, TX.

Erzikova, E., & Berger, B. (2011). Creativity vs. ethics: Russian and U.S. public relations students' perceptions of professional leadership and leaders. *Public Relations Journal, 5*(3), 1–24. Available online at www.prsa.org/Intelligence/PRJournal/Documents/2011ErzikovaBerger.pdf

Goscilo, H., & Strukov, V. (2011). Introduction. In H. Goscilo & V. Strukov (Eds.), *Celebrity and glamour in contemporary Russia: Shocking chic* (pp. 1–26). London, England: Routledge.

Grunig, L. A. (2008). Using qualitative research to become the "thinking heart" of organizations. In B. van Ruler, A. Tkalac Vercic, & D. Vercic (Eds.), *Public relations metrics: Research and evaluation* (pp. 120–136). New York, NY: Routledge.

Guth, D. W. (2000). The emergence of public relations in the Russian Federation. *Public Relations Review, 26*, 191–207.

Hall, E. T. (1976). *Beyond culture*. Garden City, NY: Anchor Press.

Kvale, S. (1988). The 1000-page question. *Phenomenology and Pedagogy, 6*(2), 90–106.

Lauzen, M. M. (1993). When marketing involvement matters at the managerial level. *Public Relations Review, 19*(3), 247–259.

Lauzen, M. M., & Dozier, D. M. (1992). The missing link: The public relations manager role as mediator of organizational environments and power consequences for the function. *Journal of Public Relations Research, 4*(4), 205–220.

Lee, J., Jares, S. M., & Heath, R. L. (1999). Decision-making encroachment and cooperative relationships between public relations and legal counselors in the management of organizational crisis. *Journal of Public Relations Research, 11*(3), 243–270.

McCarthy, D. J., Puffer, S. M., May, R. C., Ledgerwood, D. E., & Stewart, W. H. (2008). Overcoming resistance to change in Russian organizations: The legacy of transactional leadership. *Organizational Dynamics, 37*(3), 221–235.

Miles, M. B., & Huberman, A. M. (1994). *Qualitative data analysis: An expanded sourcebook* (2nd ed.). Thousand Oaks, CA: Sage.

Potapenko, D. (2012, January). "Uvolte svoikh piarshikov, osnovnoi rupor kompanii—vladelets and gendirektor." [Fire your PR people, the main mouthpieces of the company are the owner and CEO]. *Kommersant Sekret Firmy, 5*(319). Available online at www.kommersant.ru/doc/1913266

Shlapentokh, V. (2006). Trust in public institutions in Russia: The lowest in the world. *Communist and Post-Communist Studies, 39*(2), 153–174.

Tsetsura, K. (2009). The development of public relations in Russia: A geopolitical approach. In K. Sriramesh & D. Verčič (Eds.), *The global public relations handbook: Theory, research, and practice* (rev. and expanded ed., pp. 600–618). New York, NY: Routledge.

Tsetsura, K. (2011). Is public relations real job? How female practitioners construct the profession. *Journal of Public Relations Research, 23*(1), 1–23.

White, J., & Mazur, L. (1995). *Strategic communication management: Making public relations work*. Wokingham, England: Addison-Wesley.

16

SPAIN

Public Relations Leadership in an Age of Turbulence

Cristina Navarro Ruiz and Ángeles Moreno

Public relations in Spain represents a relatively young sector that, despite suffering the ravages of the current financial collapse, is keeping afloat and has even experienced a slight improvement in its results after the sharp decline in 2009. In fact, the turnover of the main communication companies rose by 11.2% in 2011 as compared with 2009, while trade benefits decreased by 20% over that time, due mainly to procedural expenses. These figures reflect the resilience of the sector despite the persistent crisis in the eurozone that has increasingly become a deep political crisis as well, particularly in Spain, where the outbreak of corruption, combined with ineffective institutional responses, has produced widespread dissatisfaction and distrust on the part of citizens (Villoria, Van Ryzin, & Lavena, 2013).

Currently, Spain has about 1,000 communication and public relations agencies (Puesto Base, 2011) and a business volume of 393 million euros ($525.33 million[1]). Although no official data are available, the number of people performing public relations is greater than ever, as many of the 10,000 journalists who lost their jobs between 2008 and early 2013 are trying to make a living out of freelance PR activities (Melida, 2013). However, the economic downturn in the region has resulted in a majority of consultancies operating on smaller budgets and thus unable to take advantage of the flood of potential employees now available for hire (International Communications Consultancy Organization [ICCO], 2012).

As in the rest of Southern European countries, public relations in Spain has been shaped by the late arrival of democracy and industrialization (C. García, 2013). In fact, PR began to develop further following the death of the dictator Francisco Franco in 1975, the gradual introduction of democracy, the liberalization of the communications media,[2] and greater openness to other countries and cultures. However, the real expansion of public relations began at the end of the 1970s with the new socioeconomic situation, and in the 1980s, the sector expanded in private and public enterprises. This development progressed rapidly through two major international events: the World Expo in Seville and the Olympic Games in Barcelona, both held in 1992 (Moreno, 2004; Rodríguez Salcedo, 2012).

The professional improvement of the 1990s and the first years of this century was due to the "economic miracle" that turned Spain into the world's 10th-largest economy (Organisation for Economic Co-operation and Development [OECD], 2010) and led the international expansion of many major companies. In addition, the birth of the Association of Public Relations and Communication Agencies (ADECEC) in1991, and the Association of Communication Directors (Dircom) in 1993 represented a step forward in the recognition of public relations as a consolidated discipline.

However, after 7 years of strong growth (2000–2007), the economic boom was reversed, and by the end of 2008 the country entered a deep recession, leaving over a quarter of Spain's workforce unemployed (Instituto Nacional de Estadística INE, 2013). Although in lower intensity, the public relations industry has also suffered the effects of the crisis. In this regard, the European Communication Monitor, an initiative organized by European Public Relations Education and Research Association (EUPRERA), describes an industry affected by budget cuts and practitioners overall satisfied with their work, while unhappy with the salary and difficulties in reconciling work and family life (Moreno, Zerfass, & Navarro, 2011, 2012). Either way, apart from the reduction of resources, PR practitioners face the current economic crisis from a proactive perspective, using different types of strategies: focusing on the most relevant issues and stakeholders, facing a growing demand to assess its performance and investing in new communication tools and channels.

At the same time, in its latest survey, Dircom (2010) reflected a booming sector in which practitioners assume greater responsibility for defining strategies, managing intangibles, and becoming part of the senior management of the company. In fact, the association (Dircom, 2010) reported an increase of the number of large organizations with their own communication department, from 75.4% in 2000 to 91.3% in 2010.

Although scholars usually study the domestic industry as a single market, it is worth noting that Spain is an asymmetrically federal country, with 17 autonomous regions, 50 provinces, two autonomous cities, and five official languages. Furthermore, in Spain we find two types of public relations practices: On one hand, a core of globally competitive companies that receive state support and have been able to develop some best practices and excellence in public relations and, on the other hand, a large group of small and mid-size companies practicing one-way models. Significant progress has been made in recent years, but the profession in Spain still has a long road ahead to overcome the obstacles imposed by excessive levels of government intervention, highly regulated markets, clientelist relationships[3] between the political and the business powers and an important number of businesses led by people who do not understand the role of public relations (C. García, 2013).

Leadership Research in Spain

Public relations research in Spain has on the whole been carried out in the academic sphere, which was only possible once the discipline was classified as a university subject in 1971, although it was not implemented into practice until 1974 (Xifra & Castillo, 2006). Despite a deeply rooted, historical delay in economic and social development caused by Franco's dictatorial regime (1939–1975), Spain has experienced an increasing influence of the public relations profession in recent decades, and, at the same time, academic development in both research and education has taken place (Moreno, Navarro, & Zerfass, 2011, 2012a). A comprehensive review of doctoral dissertations published between 1965 and 2004 has revealed the presence of an increasing volume of theoretical and empirical research; however, there is a lack of qualified and specialized PhD programs (Xifra & Castillo, 2006). Although these data are positive and the rise seen over the past few years is comparable to other countries, public relations research is still less productive than research in other core areas of the communication sciences (González, 2011; Martínez Nicolás & Saperas, 2011).

In regard to leadership in public relations and communication management, research published to date has focused on the leader's position in the company, participation in management levels, types of responsibilities assumed and their relative influence and leadership styles (ADECEC, 2004, 2008; Dircom, 2000, 2005, 2010; Gutiérrez-García, 2010; Matilla, 2010; Matilla & Marca, 2011; Morales & Enrique, 2007; Moreno, 2004; Moreno, Zerfass, & Navarro, 2011, 2012c; Mut, 2006; Top Comunicación & Burson-Marsteller, 2013). However, little work has been done regarding the skills, attitudes, and behaviors that promote excellent leadership or that examines leaders' perceptions or beliefs about the profession.

The Global Leadership Study in Spain

Spain was one of 23 countries that participated in the global study of leadership in public relations in 2012 that was carried out by the Plank Center for Leadership in Public Relations at the University of Alabama. In the qualitative phase, between March and June 2012, in-depth phone interviews were conducted with 12 corporate and agency PR leaders in Spain (seven women, five men), all of them high-level communication executives at their companies, nonprofits, or agencies. Participants' years of experience ranged from 12 to 38 years and represented a diverse mix of 12 organizations: public relations agencies (3), multinational companies (4), nonprofit organizations (4), and one theme park.

The interviews, which averaged 41.7 minutes in length, were recorded, transcribed, and coded using the constant comparative method of analysis. Details about the online survey implemented in Phase 1 of the study, and interview questions and objectives are covered in Chapter 3 in this book.

As there is no particular theoretical framework for public relations leadership in the Spanish literature in communication management, this research was based on Meng's (2012) theoretical model of leadership. Using this approach, interviews were conducted to discuss top issues in depth, how leaders manage them, the extent to which cultural and structural factors assist and constrain their work, qualities of excellent leadership in Spanish public relations, and the current state of leadership development. This chapter also provides qualitative analysis about leadership needs for the future.

Top Issues for PR Leaders in Spain

Overall, Spanish communication executives interviewed are concerned about the changes taking place in the profession after the breakthrough of social media and the related issues of how best to deal with the challenges related to online communication channels. These challenges include the increasing volume and speed of information flow, the difficulty in locating and having an impact on key targets, growing reputational risks, and the lack of development and implementation of assessment measures, which may harm the effectiveness of the public relations campaigns.

These results corroborated the previous findings of the Spanish survey, which indicated that the top issues in Spain for professionals are management of the digital revolution and the growth of social media, followed closely by the challenge of handling the speed and volume of the information flow. Two other issues, improving the measurement of communication efficacy rates and being prepared to deal effectively with crises that may arise, were tied for third (Table 16.1).

It is clear that "Revolution 2.0" has forced organizations to deal with the new challenges of a more open and connected society. In the light of rapid developments in economy and technology, the field of public relations has experienced dynamic and profound changes in recent years (Zerfass & Simon, 2012). The active participation of the audience in the communication process, the increasing exposure to reputational crisis, and the obligation to respond to the demands of transparency and dialogue are the main challenges for PR leaders in Spain.

Although some of these concerns have been noted in previous studies (Moreno, Zerfass, & Navarro, 2012b, 2012c; Top Communication & Burson-Marsteller, 2013), participants in this research emphasized the effects of social media blooming, highlighting the difficulty of disseminating the organization's message and reaching out to key publics. A PR executive summarized this position: "The Internet

TABLE 16.1 The Most Important Issue to the Communication Leader

Issues	Frequency	Percentage
Managing the digital revolution and the rise of social media	45	21.6
Dealing with the speed and volume of information flow	43	20.7
Improving the measurement of communication effectiveness to demonstrate value	26	12.5
Being prepared to deal effectively with crises that may arise	26	12.5
Dealing with growing demands for transparency of communications and operations	24	11.5
Finding, developing, and retaining highly talented communication professionals	12	5.8
Meeting communication needs in diverse cultures and globalizing markets	11	5.3
Improving employee engagement and commitment in the workplace	10	4.8
Meeting increasing demands for corporate social responsibility	6	2.9
Improving the image of the public relations/communication management profession	5	2.4
Total	208	100.0

has caused a total fragmentation of the key publics. Nowadays, trying to reach an audience that is even slightly representative means a big effort. We are doing some experiments and learning on the way."

The lack of effective control over messages is another consequence of the emergence and consolidation of the new digital channels. The PR leader at a nonprofit organization spoke about the obligation to respond quickly to the demands of the public, which has modified the working routines of practitioners: "Communication cannot be controlled and structured anymore; there is just no time. As a communication department, you need to have reactivity, but also as a whole organization."

An agency leader also described the shifts needed by communication departments to face the new demands of online communication:

> Work teams must readjust themselves in order to face this challenge, to change their routines and also react carefully to the speed and exponentiality that messages have. The training of the professionals that work in agencies and of course customer service has changed. We have introduced in communication plans a new channel, which is the Internet, and all the tools that it allows us to use.

In parallel to the economic recession faced by the country, Spanish media are experiencing their own crisis. This gloomy landscape translates into a decrease in advertising investment, reduction in the workforce, closures of media, decrease in print runs, adaptation to new formats and transitions from the press for payment to the free concentration of companies to reduce cost or employment regulation orders (Farias & Gómez, 2011).

The plight of the media industry is also affecting public relations practitioners, who expressed their concerns about the increasing difficulty of publishing the organizational message in the traditional media: "It is harder and harder to find traditional media whose approach is impartial," stated an agency leader, an opinion supported by an nongovernmental organization (NGO) communication executive who believes that is very difficult "to reach the media with a limited budget and make them show what we do in our organization." In order to overcome these obstacles and achieve media coverage, some practitioners suggested making a greater effort to define clear and direct messages: "We need to do more to create a common culture, define messages, and plan the communication strategy along with management so that everyone knows where we are going. The selection and training of new spokespersons has been essential," said one PR leader.

The Next Big Issue

When communication leaders were asked to forecast the next big issue, responses were wide ranging. However, some deep concerns about how to deal with the traditional media crisis were expressed. An executive at a nonprofit organization said,

> Social networking offers us the opportunity to reach the key public without intermediaries, but I think we lose the richness of traditional media, the analysis, and the ability of seen things from a different perspective. This loss is impoverishing us.

The importance that Spanish PR executives attach to printed media is closely related to the current status of the profession, where a majority of public relations professionals are trained journalists. Practitioners that have not received specific PR training have difficulty using public relations strategies, particularly the two-way-symmetrical model, which requires knowledge in research. In fact, prior studies have pointed out that media relations is still the main public relations activity in the Mediterranean countries, with Spain at the top (90%). In this spirit, C. García (2013) affirmed that the relevance of media relations, especially newspapers, is also linked to the strong interconnection between political and business powers.

On the other hand, two PR leaders explained that understanding communication management from a strategic perspective is a current and future challenge. "Practitioners should be ready for the 'big idea' costumers are asking for," said one of the interviewees. This position was further supported by a senior executive at a construction company: "We must move towards a much more strategic perspective, providing certainties, removing noise, establishing relationships and generating dialogues, both rational and emotional."

The economic crisis appears as a recurring issue among the Spanish communication leaders. The PR leader at a nonprofit organization spoke pessimistically about the ability of communication departments facing budget cuts:

> There is a love–hate relationship with the departments of communication. We are considered essential but when the budget must be reduced they always start with the communication department. The impact of communication is not seen immediately. It is work in the medium or long term and requires a person with specific knowledge.

Regarding the loss of power of communication departments, the PR leader at a technological multinational said, "At this time, communication departments have ceded the control of social media channels to marketing departments, which in many companies are managing the relations with stakeholders."

There is also the belief that the pervasive influence of digital technologies and social media will be a challenge for future leaders in the field. As one of the PR executives explained, "The evolution of online communication is unpredictable, and we will need to be prepared for new and profound changes. The new communication technologies have forced organizations to address reputational risks that until a few years ago were unexpected."

Cultural and Structural Influences on Leaders

The economic crisis and the significant budget cuts in communication departments are hindering the leadership of Spanish practitioners. This can be translated into understaffed departments and a dangerous demand for short-term results, adding pressure for strategic planning. "When organizations are forced to cut their budgets, they usually start with communication departments," said one of the leaders interviewed. "In Spain the greatest impediment we face is limited resources. As a result of the crisis, budgets have had to adjust, and cannot measure the results of many actions."

In addition to the difficulties related to the lack of economic resources, respondents named the following cultural and structural barriers to greater public relations leadership:

- Lack of transparency
- Short-term return
- Geographic dispersion
- Internal politics
- Complexity of the company

From a structural perspective, 11 of the 12 executives interviewed affirmed that the function they perform is respected by other leaders in the organization, and they felt that their work is recognized and useful. "The chief executive officer is a great media personality. He is always available to take part when we need him to do so, and he has encouraged public relations work in new markets as a vehicle to make the brand well known and also to accelerate the maturing process of the brand," said a leader at a multinational company. Just one of the interviewees said that the chief executive of their company did not understand or defend public relations: "There is no communication culture, and I do not think the strategic value of communication is really recognized."

The organizational cultures described by the executive communicators placed high value on creativity, work effort, integrity, flexibility, responsibility, work-team relationships, innovation, and dynamism as key factors for promotion. The importance of working in companies with an "open and horizontal culture" was seen to be a factor in helping the communication function: "Our structure makes communication easier. The company is very open and has a flat structure, everything flows. Everyone says their opinion, handles information, and shares their doubts," pointed out a technological communication leader.

Characteristics and Qualities of Excellent Leaders

According to Spanish PR executives, the most valued characteristics or qualities to exercise excellent leadership in Spain are good communication knowledge and skills (mentioned by 5 of the leaders interviewed), strategic vision (3), credibility (3), flexibility (3), team-building capabilities (2), and passion (2). Other characteristics mentioned were influence, self-confidence, patience, consistency, empathy, possessing a compelling vision for how communication can help the organization, and cross-disciplinary knowledge.

Overall, these results largely focus on individual traits and skills, which are consistent with three of the seven dimensions of leadership: communication knowledge management, visioning ability, and team leadership and collaboration. The other four leadership dimensions were notably absent, that is, strong ethical orientation, strategic decision-making capability, two-way communication culture, and ability to develop coalitions. These differences may reflect the diverse perspectives from leaders (selected for the qualitative) versus the larger population of practitioners (participants in the survey represented a cross section of hierarchical levels and years of experience).

The Future Leaders

The communication executives also addressed the development of future leaders primarily from the point of view of their skills, rather than focusing on personal attributes or other leadership capabilities or qualities. In this regard, most agreed that the next generation of practitioners will have to master the digital tools. One PR leader at a toy multinational summarized this position: "New generations will have to have a deep and total knowledge of new technologies. The goal will be the same, but the way to reach it will change."

Nevertheless, above all, they are required to be multitasking and multidisciplinary: "They will have to be open minded, with a variety of backgrounds, open to new disciplines, ways of working and thinking. In short, future leaders will need a more versatile and multidisciplinary education," explained one leader. Uncertainty about the development of the profession and the continuing changes to which the field would appear to be destined will compel further training, greater strategic thinking, global vision, and the ability to work in international markets.

Training must play a major role in the development of future leaders. As one agency senior executive said, "They will have to be much more 'Renaissance' than we are; they will need to have global knowledge, speak many languages and be able to understand the cultural differences in a global world."

Just two leaders spoke about personal attributes, stressing the importance of professional ethics: "Future leaders will also have to be multidisciplinary and flexible, but conserving the essence of a good public relations employee—transparency, credibility and ethics," one said. Another pointed out that "they will have to be very sensitive to their environment, very ethical, responsible and educated."

Survey participants in phase 1 also emphasized the importance of skills in improving the individual development of future leaders (Table 16.2). Respondents

TABLE 16.2 Actions That Might Be Taken to Improve the Development of Future Leaders

Actions	M	SD
Strengthen change management skills and capabilities	5.77	1.205
Improve the listening skills of professionals	5.67	1.077
Enhance conflict management skills	5.51	1.138
Increase cultural understanding and sensitivity	5.35	1.346
Impose tough penalties on ethical violators	5.33	1.461
Develop better measures to document the value and contributions of PR	5.30	1.348
Develop training to enhance the emotional intelligence of PR professionals	5.29	1.256
Strengthen the business/economic component of communication education	5.09	1.332
Develop a core global education curriculum	4.95	1.452
Enhance professional skills in coping with work-related stress	4.95	1.439
Urge professional associations to work together to develop leaders	4.81	1.254
Require professional accreditation or licensing	4.60	1.621

Note: SD = standard deviation. Items measured on a 7-point Likert-type scale from 1 = *a little bit* to 7 = *a great deal* of importance.

considered reinforcing change management, listening, and conflict management skills as especially beneficial for developing excellent leaders. They gave less weight to systemic development approaches, such as requiring professional accreditation or developing a core global education curriculum.

Current State of Leadership Development and Future Leadership Needs

As indicated earlier, public relations plays a secondary role in Spanish universities, where the degree is called "advertising and public relations" and tends to be linked to communication departments dominated mostly by journalists and advertisers (Hellín & García, 2011). One proof of the relatively minor status of the discipline is the small percentage of course subjects referred to public relations in the academic curriculum: Just 19.12% of the total course participants in the degree (Matilla & Hernández, 2010). Xifra (2007) summarized this position:

> The autonomy given to universities allowing them to set their own compulsory and elective contents has clearly undermined public relations, relegating public relations education to second place. Despite its name, the Degree in Advertising and Public Relations does not include two majors. It is an Advertising major with a Public Relations minor. (p. 212)

The adaptation of the traditional educational system to the convergence process of European Higher Education Area, based on training and oriented to skills and competencies, offered some hope for increasing the strength of the discipline in higher education. However, a recent study showed the absence of notable changes in the degrees with respect to the model prior to the implementation of the Bologna Process study (Matilla & Hernández, 2012).

Among the short offering of specific subjects about public relations at the university level, leadership does not receive any attention, nor does it appear to be sufficiently valued by practitioners. In fact, Spanish communication leaders believe that priority training topics are corporate communication, media relations, corporate image, and events planning. In addition, for the immediate future, they predicted specific training needs for digital environments, new Information and Communications Technology ICT methodology research, corporate social responsibility (CSR) and negotiation techniques. These topped the list for defining training objectives and informing communication strategies in this area (Dircom, 2010, p. 38). Leadership was not mentioned.

However, in a global sense, leadership studies have proliferated in recent years, mainly as a result of the unexpected interest that coaching courses have generated in Spain. According to e-magister web (one of the major search engines for academic degrees), different academic institutions, mostly business schools and training centers, offer 3,083 official and unofficial postgraduate courses on leadership. This offer includes a great variety of short- and long-term programs with both theoretical and practical orientation. However, the quality of such programs is unknown, though likely to vary considerably. It's also unknown to what extent such courses would be valuable for communication leaders.

The lack of interest in public relations leadership also could be related to some extent to the relatively recent implementation of communications departments in companies, with the existence of a wide array of different names and roles associated with public relations and also with the difficulty of determining, concisely, the practice areas of the profession. These circumstances suggest that the communication function has not yet been institutionalized in Spain, which directly influences the current lack of a clear definition of the functions for which the director of communications is responsible. The most telling evidence of this indifference to leadership among PR practitioners is the absence of specific training programs or workshops organized by professional associations in the field.

In a general sense, the tasks of chief communication officers (CCOs) are often recognized to include a diverse list of responsibilities: media relations; corporate and internal communication; design and evaluation of strategies for internal and external communication; management of business confidence in the presence of changes; strategic communication planning; the selection of partner companies and staff personnel; and, above all, management tasks (Dircom, 2010; Gutiérrez-García, 2010; Matilla & Marca, 2011; Morales & Enrique, 2007; Mut, 2011).

Therefore, a paradoxical situation exists: Although Spanish companies and institutions recognize the importance of communications (in creating communication departments and giving them, at least in organization charts, managerial responsibilities and weight in decision making), this acknowledgment is nominal in many companies, or at best purposeful in some companies, where communication tasks and responsibilities are largely tactical and procedural—technical roles. Thus, the following can be concluded: "The practice requires greater professionalism in order to be considered a function that adds value to good management in companies" (Gutiérrez-García, 2010, p. 154).

In conclusion, leadership development at both professional and academic levels is a task that remains pending for the profession in Spain, and may continue to be so for several reasons. First, to make progress on the path to excellent leadership would require eliminating the historically unequal status of the classes in public relations compared to those in advertising, to the clear detriment of the former. Second, Spanish universities and professional associations must first prepare communication leaders with specific postgraduate and development training programs.

However, these measures will be useless if organizations keep avoiding hiring professionals with public relations degrees and opt instead for journalists and marketing specialists. It is worth noting that, in this regard, Spain suffers from a universal irony: "Only a very small number of the nation's senior-level public relations executives and managers studied Public Relations at a university" (Wright & Turk, 2007, p. 582).

On the other hand, researchers should make an effort to deeply explore this subject, as it is the key to the success of organizations, and to analyze the cultural factors that determine the leadership in Spain. It should not be forgotten, following Berger and Reber (2006), that public relations leaders play a major role in the success, image, and future of their companies, while at the same time influencing employers' behaviors, attitudes, and beliefs and helping establish organizational culture and communication environment. In addition, their work helps increase the value of public relations and company efficiency and enhances decision making (Berger & Meng, 2010).

Finally, organizations themselves should provide career pathways for their communication leaders and support their professional development with training programs to advance their knowledge and skills in order to increase leadership capacity and capability. This will improve communication inside and outside the organization and help the company achieve its goals.

Notes

1. This cost is based on the euro to U.S. dollar exchange rate on August 26, 2013.
2. After nearly three decades of authoritarian rule with a systematically suppressed flow of information, a press law approved in 1966 provided a degree of liberalization for publications and eliminated prior censorship. However, a free press did not truly flourish until Spain moved toward democracy.
3. Following Hallin and Mancini (2004), clientelism refers to a particularistic form of social organization in which formal rules are less important relative to personal connections.

References

Association of Communication Directors. (2000). *El estado de la comunicación en España: empresas y organismos públicos e instituciones* [The state of communication in Spain: companies and public organizations and institutions]. Available online at www.dircom.org

Association of Communication Directors. (2005). *El estado de la Comunicación en España* [The state of communication in Spain.]. Available online at www.dircom.org

Association of Communication Directors. (2010). *El estado de la Comunicación en España* [The state of communication in Spain.]. Available online at http://mouriz.files.wordpress.com/2010/05/estado-comunicacic3b3n.pdf

Association of Public Relations and Communication Agencies. (2004). *La comunicación y las relaciones públicas en España. Radiografía de un sector* [Communication and Public Relations in Spain: A Sector Landscape.]. Available online at www.adecec.com

Association of Public Relations and Communication Agencies. (2008). *La comunicación y las relaciones públicas en España. Radiografía de un sector* [Communication and Public Relations in Spain: A Sector Landscape]. Available online at www.adecec.com

Berger, B. K., & Meng, J. (2010). Public relations practitioners and the leadership challenge. In R. L. Heath (Ed.), *The SAGE handbook of public relations* (pp. 421–434). Thousand Oaks, CA: Sage.

Berger, B. K., & Reber, B. H. (2006). *Gaining influence in public relations: The role of resistance in practice.* Mahwah, NJ: Erlbaum.

Farias, P., & Gómez, M. (2011). El estado de la profesión periodística y la crisis de los medios e España [The state of journalism and media crisis in Spain. *Razón y Palabra,* V (77). Available online at www.redalyc.org/articulo.oa?id=199520010096

Fundación EOI. (2010). *Nuevos modelos de gestión y función de los responsables de comunicación. Estudio sobre el modelo español de gestión y reporting de intangibles para un Dircom* [New management models and the role of CCOs. Study on the Spanish model of management and reporting of intangibles for Dircom.]. Madrid, Spain: Author. Available online at www.eoi.es/sc/webeoi/publicaciones/Nuevosmodelosgestioncomunicacion_2010.pdf

García, C. (2013). Clientelism, economic structure, and public relations in Southern Europe: An example of diversity in the Western World. *Public Relations Journal,* 7(2), 214–241.

González, S. (2011). El DirCom en el escenario de la convergencia: claves para una transformación [The Dircom in the Scenary of Convergence: Keys for a Transformation]. *Revista Internacional de Relaciones Públicas,* 2(1), 119–137.

Gutiérrez-García, E. (2010). Corporate governance and corporate communication: What is the role of communication managers in Spain? *Palabra clave,* 1(13), 147–160.

Hallin, D. C., & Mancini, P. (2004). *Comparing Media Systems: Three Models of Media and Politics.* New York: Cambridge University Press.

Hellín, P., & García, J. (2011): La integración de la publicidad y las relaciones públicas en el Espacio Europeo de Educación Superior. Fernández, A. B. y García, F: VI Congreso Internacional de Investigación y Relaciones Públicas [The integration of advertising and public relations in the European higher education area]. *Icono, 14,* 96–106.

Instituo Nacional de Estadistica (INF). (2013). *EPA. Resultados Trimestrales: 2° Trimestre 2013.* Available online at the INE website: www.ine.es/CDINEbase/consultar.do?mes=&operacion=EPA.+Resultados+trimestrales&id_oper=Ir

International Communications Consultancy Organization (2012). *ICCO world report: Global PR picks up the pace.* Available online at www.iccopr.com/knowledge-base/Worldreports.aspx

Martínez, N. M. & Saperas, E. (2011). Communication research in Spain, 1998–2007. An analysis of papers published in Spanish communication journals. *Revista Latina de Comunicación Social,* 66, 101–129.

Matilla, K. (2010). Pasado, presente y futuro del "Dircom" en España [The past, present, and future of the "Dircom" in Spain]. *FISEC-Estrategias—Facultad de Ciencias Sociales de la Universidad Nacional de Lomas de Zamora, 14*(4), 3–24.

Matilla, K. & Hernández, S. (2010). Las asignaturas de Relaciones Públicas en el marco del Espacio Europeo de Educación Superior [The subjects of Public Relations in the European Higher Education Area Context]. In J. Sierra (Coordinator), *Los estudios de Ciencias de la Comunicación en el EEES* (pp. 293–307). Madrid, Spain: Fragua.

Matilla, K. & Hernández, S. (2011): Bolonia primer año: los estudios universitarios de RRPP en Cataluña en el curso 2010–11 [Bologna 1st Year: The University Studies of Public Relations in Catalonia (Course 2010–2011)]. *Icono, 14,* 35–59. Available online at http://airrpp.org/wp-content/uploads/2012/12/actas_VIcongreso_AIRP.pdf

Matilla, K. & Hernández, S. (2012). Bolonia segundo año: Los estudios universitarios de Relaciones Públicas en Cataluña (curso 2011–12) [Bologna 2nd Year: The University Studies of Public Relations in Catalonia (Course 2011–2012). *Revista Internacional de*

Relaciones Públicas, 2(4), 247–276. Available online at http://revistarelacionespublicas. uma.es/index.php/revrrpp/article/view/117

Matilla, K. & Marca, G. (2011). La función estratégica del Dircom en España en 2010 [The Strategic Function of "Dircom" in Spain in 2010]. *Revista Internacional de Relaciones Públicas*, 2(1), 11–23.

Melida, A. (2013, June 30). After the bubble burst: What now for Spain in the age of austerity. Available online at the IPRA website: www.ipra.org/itl/01/2013/after-the-bubble-burst-what-now-for-spain-in-the-age-of-austerity

Meng, J. (2012). Public relations leadership: An integrated conceptual framework. *Public Relations Review*, 38, 336–338.

Morales, F., & Enrique, A.M. (2007). The concept of the Dircom. His importance in the model of integral communication. *Anàlisi, Quaderns de Comunicació i Cultura*, 35, 83–93.

Moreno, A. (2004). Spain. In B. van Ruler & D. Vercic (Eds.), *Public relations and communication management in Europe. A nation-by-nation introduction to public relations theory and practice* (pp. 393–412). Berlin, Germany: Mouton de Gruyter.

Moreno, Á., Zerfass, A., & Navarro, C. (2011). European Communication Monitor 2010: España en línea con los profesionales europeos [European Communication Monitor 2010: Spain in line with European professionals]. *Anuario de la Comunicación, 9*, 32–41.

Moreno, Á., Navarro, C. & Zerfass, A. (2012a). Relaciones Públicas, un término desacreditado en España y el resto de Europa: Conclusiones del European Communication Monitor 2011 [Public relations, a Discredited Term in Spain and in the Rest of Europe: Conclusions of the European Communication Monitor]. *Hologramática – Facultad de Ciencias Sociales, 17*(2), 115–140.

Moreno, Á., Zerfass, A., & Navarro, C. (2012b). *Tendencias de Comunicación en Europa* [Communication Trends in Europe]. *Anuario de la Communication, 10*, 29–34.

Moreno, Á., Zerfass, A. & Navarro, C. (2012c). La situación de los profesionales de relaciones públicas y comunicación estratégica en Europa y en España. Análisis comparado del European Communication Monitor 2009 [The situation of public relations and strategic communication practitioners in Europe and Spain. Comparison of European Communication monitor 2009]. *Trípodos, 5* (Suppl.), 299–313.

Mut, M. (2011). El director de comunicación del cambio [Communication Manager of Change]. *Revista Internacional de Relaciones Públicas*, 2(1), 107–118.

Navarro, C., Moreno. A., & Zerfass, A. (2012). Análisis longitudinal de la profesión de Relaciones Públicas en España en los últimos cinco años (2007–2001) [Longitudinal Analysis of Public Relations Practice in Spain during the Last Five Years]. *Anagramas, 10*(20), 53–66.

Organisation for Economic Co-operation and Development. (2010). *OECD Factbook 2007* [OECD Factbook Statistics database]. Paris, France: Author. doi:10.1787/data-00375-en

Puesto Base (2011). *El sector de las Relaciones Públicas en España. Análisis Económico* [Public Relations Sector in Spain, Economic Analysis]. Available online at www.torresycarrera. com/blog/puestobase/wp-content/uploads/2012/09/Informe-PR-Spain.pdf

Rodríguez Salcedo, N. (2008). Public relations before "public relations" in Spain: an early history (1881–1960). *Journal of Communication Management*, 12(4), 279–293.

Rodríguez Salcedo, N. (2012). Mapping public relations in Europe. Writing national histories against the USA paradigm. *Comunicación y Sociedad*, 25(2), 331–374.

Tilson, D., & Saura, P. (2003). Public relations and the new golden age of Spain: A confluence of democracy, economic development and the media. *Public Relations Review*, 29(2), 125–143.

Top Comunicación, & Burson Marsteller. (2013). *Informe el Dircom del futuro y el futuro del Dircom* [Report on the Dircon of the future and the future of Dircom]. Available online at http://burson-marsteller.es/wp-content/uploads/2013/03/Informe-Futuro-Dircom.pdf

Villoria, M., Van Ryzin, G. G., & Lavena, C. F. (2013). Social and political consequences of administrative corruption: A study of public perceptions in Spain. *Public Administration Review, 73,* 85–94. doi:10.1111/j.1540–6210.2012.02613.x

Wright, D. K., & Turk, J. V. (2007). Public relations knowledge and professionalism: Challenges to educators and practitioners. In E. L. Toth (Ed.), *The future of excellence in public relations and communication management: Challenges for the next generation* (pp. 571– 588). Mahwah, NJ: Erlbaum.

Xifra, J. (2007). Undergraduate public relations education in Spain: Endangered species? *Public Relations Review, 33,* 206–213.

Xifra, J., & Castillo, A. (2006). Forty years of doctoral public relations research in Spain: A quantitative study of dissertation contribution to theory development. *Public Relations Review, 32*(3), 302–308.

Zerfass, A., & Simon, K. (2012, October). *Mapping the future of public relations profession: Contrasting perceptions of next generation professionals and experienced PR practitioners across Europe.* Paper presented at the Annual Euprera Congress, Istanbul, Turkey.

17

TRANSCULTURAL STUDY ON LEADERSHIP IN PUBLIC RELATIONS AND COMMUNICATIONS MANAGEMENT

Results for Brazil

Andréia S. Athaydes, Gustavo Becker, Rodrigo Silveira Cogo, Mateus Furlanetto, and Paulo Nassar

The Global Study of Leadership in Public Relations and Communications Management was carried out in 23 countries under the scientific coordination of the Plank Center for Leadership in Public Relations at the University of Alabama. Specific results for Brazil are presented in this chapter. The results were gleaned from two data collection processes—15 in-depth interviews with recognized Brazilian communications directors at national and multinational companies headquartered in the country, and 303 responses to an online survey from various levels of communications managers in the country.

Profiles of Interviewees and Survey Participants

Interviewees

The professionals interviewed in the qualitative stage were found through intentional selection from a convenience list, with regional indications given by the directors at Aberje, the Brazilian Association for Business Communication. Aberje has been in existence for more than 45 years, has members in 21 economic segments, operates nationwide, and helped facilitate access to senior communication managers for the interviews. Fifteen individual recorded one-to-one interviews, lasting an average of 45 minutes and totaling 9.5 hours of audio, were completed between June and August 2012.

Eight women and seven men, with three different job titles but within an equal hierarchical level of management responsibilities (coordinators, managers, and executive officers), were selected and approached. They came from the mining, auto and cement industries; pharmaceutical and apparel sales; highway management, financial, and consulting services; agribusiness; the corporate trade industry; the federal government; and universities.

The title most used in their positions is "corporate communication." Overall, their duties cover both internal and external communications, and even advertising matters in some cases. They possess between 4 and 35 years of experience in the field, with most having more than 20 years of experience. They indicated that they began their careers in corporate communications because of life and market circumstances, rather than specifically because of a career plan or specific interest in this work.

Survey Participants

Regarding the online global survey, the main features of the 303 Brazilian professionals who took part in the study are as follows: 72.9% are women and 27.1%, men. A majority is younger than 35 years of age (53.1%), but a more senior profile of those older than 55 years of age also participated (8.6%). Based on this younger profile, professional experience in the area was fewer than 11 years (52.1%). The largest number of participants worked at private companies or organizations (30.3%). Employees of communication agencies represented about one sixth of participants (15.9%), whereas freelance professionals accounted for 10.2% of participants. In the context in which they work, about one third (32%) perform a leadership role in their workplace. The majority of participants (54.9%) worked in teams or units with fewer than five professionals.

The professional education of the participants is mostly in public relations and strategic communication (59.4%), followed by journalism. The highest degree held by 40.3% of participants is a bachelor's degree. Nearly 60 percent (58.8%) of participants have completed graduate studies (specialization, master's, and doctorate). This is some evidence of a trend that appears to be on the rise in Brazil for the last decade, that is, seeking greater qualification and education in corporate communications.

Main Questions for Brazilian Communications Managers

The in-depth interview script (see Appendix B) began with an indication of the most important issue in communications management that the interviewee happened to be dealing with at that time and that most involved him or her. This issue was then explored more fully regarding what made it so important and how it affected this person and his or her organization, in terms of selecting tactics and strategies, budget planning, personnel profiles for hiring, approaches to measurement, and even changes in work habits. Reflection was also encouraged regarding how the interviewee successfully managed the problem and whether the company's executives fully understood the implications of this issue.

The particularities of each business sector in Brazil covered in this study are a determining factor in establishing the communications manager's priority in issues management. The point of view is always significantly imbued with specific features of economic operation, as can be seen for example in the focus on the client for the auto industry and apparel retailers, the low profile of agribusiness representatives or business-to-business ventures, and the high importance of community relations to mining industries. At any rate, on the researchers' part, a wider understanding of the management of corporate communications was always sought in the questions raised.

The Key Issues in Brazil—the Interviews

Brazilian communications managers quite consistently described the top issue in their organizations as organizational culture—a working environment in which the communication function is not fully supported, nor is the value of communication and public relations fully understood. This issue manifested itself in several ways.

First, some participants spoke about the need to internally build a "culture of communication," given internal peers' lack of understanding of the importance of the communication function and how it works. This happens in relation to concepts and general operation as well as in relation to their interfaces with specific publics. This challenge has an impact on the size of budget received for training or expanding their teams, as well for as infrastructure equipment for communications programs and planned programs. The following comments from Interviewee 5 reflect this concern:

> Colleagues that we need day to day still have a different sense of timing in communication; they don't see that it is faster and faster. They have their own list of tasks to fulfill and their own list of priorities, and communication is not at the top of the list. So, the issue of being able to approve things, and detect the need for communication and implement this in a very short time, is still lacking.

Interviewee 9 also noted that "many people look at communication with a very simplistic vision, of the 'anyone can do it' kind of view. And when there's change, there are people who resist it; they remain stern and are annoyed." Interviewee 10 provided another example of this issue: "Organizations also do not fully see communication as a tool for business. There is still a cloud over all of the potential in the area and the changes that could be implemented that may positively impact image."

However, and given this internal perception problem, it is interesting to note that the CEOs are largely viewed by interviewees in an extremely positive light regarding their willingness to understand and invest in communication, leading to the belief that the communication understanding impasse occurs at other levels, as pointed out next.

Second, the work environment itself is unstable given demands to implement many processes of change of varying degrees, and to have to deal with imminent crises. Among the signs of change, for example, are the interconnectedness of society on the Internet and the demands to reconcile the international group's strategic vision with local demands and characteristics. This challenge directly influences reputation, according to Interviewee 3: "There will be a need to train those who will work with communications to adapt to such unstable scenarios. Later, there is the challenge of dealing with people from different generations, inside and outside of the communications function."

Third, other internal communications issues are related to creating both a harmonious workplace that guarantees productivity and engages employees as external spokespeople for the brand. This is important because there is also an awareness of the plurality of voices in society, where opinions and controversies are on open display, yet this development does not fully play out internally where communicators now need to learn and to decentralize control of narratives. Interviewee 1 described this reality:

> Today we live in a network model of society, connected 24/7. The idea that the internal public just stays inside of the company and gets information here, and doesn't have a voice beyond the walls of the organization, no longer holds. Today, these spaces are mixed, and the employee is also an actor and broadcaster of company communications. Before, you could think about exercising 100% control, and now you have no control.

This recurring point of view is exemplified in the opinion of Interviewee 2: "We see how important employee engagement is, because when they are involved, they embrace the idea and become cheerleaders for the brand."

A Cluster of Related Issues

Beyond this overriding concern for a culture that understands and supports communication, a cluster of interrelated issues was mentioned during the interviews, including working in unstable situations, the importance of relationships with the internal public, the need to position communication as a strategic area, the difficulty of overcoming the tendency of some organizations to want to keep a low profile, the conflicts between excessive internal and external demands and the current and perhaps outdated structure of teams, and the lack of internal clarity and understanding of how community relations and sustainability can leverage reputation.

TABLE 17.1 Participants' Assessment of the Most Important Issue in Brazil

Issues	M	SD
Being prepared to effectively deal with crises that may arise	6.50	0.92
Dealing with the speed and volume of the flow of information	6.46	0.93
Improving indicators of communication efficacy to show value	6.34	0.98
Dealing with growing demands for transparency in communications	6.25	1.06
Improving employee engagement and commitment in the workplace	6.21	1.11
Managing the digital revolution and the rise of social media	6.13	1.06
Finding, developing, and retaining talented communications professionals	6.02	1.17
Serving the growing demands of corporate social responsibility	5.91	1.22
Serving communications needs in diverse cultures and globalized markets	5.82	1.13
Improving the image of the public relations profession	5.64	1.55

Note: SD = standard deviation. Issues were assessed by 303 respondents on a 7-point Likert scale, with 1 = *a little bit* to 7 = *a great deal* of importance.

Top Issues in the Online Survey

The first question in the survey also investigated key issues (Appendix A). On a scale of 1 (*not very*) to 7 (*very*), participants expressed their opinion on how important they or their managers think the 10 predetermined issues are (Table 17.1). "Being ready to effectively deal with crises" came up as the most relevant topic, followed by "dealing with the speed and volume of the flow of information," and "improving indicators of efficacy in communication to show value." These concerns are pertinent to the profile of Brazilian leaders in the area, especially if we consider that in the last decade, many Brazilian organizations and/or multinationals headquartered in Brazil experienced institutional and financial crises, with significant repercussions in the media, which consequently shook their images and credibility.

Yet, concern with the speed and volume of the flow of information has an impact on all professions, although in the case of communications, the raw material is information. New technologies allow for faster access in real time to information, making citizens seeking fast and precise responses to their demands even more finicky. Therefore, communications professionals, who are responsible for managing information at their organizations, are looking for mechanisms that can facilitate the selection and dissemination of truly high-priority information.

In relation to indicators measuring efficacy, two situations explain these concerns: (a) an increased consensus between managers at Brazilian organizations that communications results are tangible, especially regarding the financial value of brands in the world, and (b) Brazilian professionals are increasingly held responsible by the organization's leaders in this respect, and they are themselves requesting greater participation in the decision-making process in their organizations. Hence, this achievement is possible once these professionals are able to provide adequate evidence of the result of their strategies and actions.

TABLE 17.2 Most Important Issue for the Communications Leader in Brazil ($n = 303$)

Most Important Issue for the Communications Leader	Frequency	Percentage
Improving indicators of communication efficacy to show value	65	21.5
Dealing with the speed and volume of the flow of information	53	17.5
Improving employee engagement, commitment in the workplace	49	16.2
Dealing with growing demands for transparency	31	10.2
Being prepared to effectively deal with crises that may arise	25	8.3
Serving communications needs in diverse cultures and markets	24	7.9
Finding, developing, and retaining talented professionals	22	7.3
Improving the image of the public relations profession	12	4.0
Managing the digital revolution and the rise of social media	11	3.6
Serving growing demands of corporate social responsibility (CSR)	11	3.6
Total	303	100.0

In the second survey question, participants selected which of the 10 issues was the most important issue to them or to their communication leaders (Table 17.2). When having to choose just one issue, the assumption is that the participants are still forming their opinion, considering the low percentage round in each of the response options offered. Nevertheless, the top three issues are "improving indicators of communication efficacy to show value" (21.5%), "dealing with the speed and volume of the flow of information" (17.5%), and "improving employee engagement and commitment in the workplace" (16.2%). These three issues account for more than half of the responses.

The first two themes prioritized were already justified earlier. The third, which regards the concern of PR and communications leaders with the participation and commitment of their teams, is due to the paradigm shift where organizations are beginning to see their employees as human capital, one of the main components in driving innovation and improving productivity and competitiveness in the market.

Digital social media does not show up among the top issues for Brazilian communications managers in either the qualitative interviews or the survey. Notwithstanding this, probing this question in the in-depth interview leads to an immediate response about its relevance. There seems to be other more pressing tasks in day-to-day work life, despite the significant penetration of social internet platforms in Brazil (the country is at the top of rankings on use of Facebook, Twitter, Pinterest, LinkedIn, and others). Based on the preferences for interaction coming from the organizations consulted, the face-to-face communication format is still preferred. Even so, these professionals see the growing importance of the virtual scenario, especially because it is a space for publishing opinions and ideas that should be monitored and responded to with agility, and the managers we interviewed stated their intentions to act more promptly and fully on this issue in the future.

Cultural and Structural Influences on Leaders

Interviewees also were asked to briefly describe the culture of their organizations, from the perspective of the most important cultural and structural values that help and/or hinder the success of communication efforts. Based on this, we asked whether the employing organization's top executive valued and invested in communications and public relations and for the respondent to provide practical examples.

The ideas of simplicity, transparency, and appreciation of people go far beyond the interviewee's manifestations regarding cultural factors in Brazilian organizations. They are tied up in the notion of collectivity and awareness of interrelationships and, therefore, impacts on sustainability. The workplace is characterized by the possibility of developing a kind and humane nature, facilitated by the existence of teams with long-lasting relationships and individual employees with long careers. These features support smaller or less vertical hierarchical structures to better meet the need for rapid responses to internal and external demands. Interviewee 3 captured this notion of culture: "The company works with simplicity and humbleness in recognizing that you don't know everything, that people are very open and the exchange of information is very fast. The ethical issue is also very important here."

For these leaders consulted, communication has become more and more successful because of factors such as the existence of dialogue and freedom in dealing with strategic publics, a direct line to the company's upper management and real involvement and influence in decision making. Regarding barriers, the leaders pointed to a lack of trust from internal peers who are unaware of the importance or potential of communication in the organizational dynamic, which causes problems in information moving down from leaders to their teams. Interviewee 7 summarized the idea as follows: "The lack of information and clarity in other areas geared towards communications is a problem. Because communication does not have the clarity of governance information, it will also not be clear enough to pass on."

In the insights gained in the interviews, what is most noticeable is the uniform positioning of the corporate communications function; it is directly connected to the top levels of the organizations, and the PR leaders regularly participate in committees and in internal decision-making forums. Brazilian communications managers with high-profile careers already have a presence within executive structures, as well as the trust of executives, although this does not always equal total understanding of their skills and processes among other executives in their organizations. An open-door policy allowing employees to speak freely, and permanent systems for consulting stakeholders, are practices mentioned as benefitting the fluidity of communications.

Overall, the vision of the CEOs at the organizations surveyed regarding communication as a fundamental factor in work is quite positive. The CEO is mentioned as a figure of permanent support for the function's points of view in internal and external processes. In addition, the CEOs are consistently available spokespersons, precisely because of their awareness of how reputation impacts all actions. As Interviewee 4 indicated,

> [The CEO] invests in and believes in 24 hour a day communication. This can be seen in the very demands that he makes of our area, in his rapid responses to our requests, and in his understanding of the timing of things.

This perception is similar to that expressed by Interviewee 12: "[The CEO] invests and invests quite a lot in communication, which can even be seen in the budget for it. And he is available to talk. He fully supports and understands the communication process."

However, the view is somewhat less encouraging in the results of the online survey, in which participants were asked to evaluate the performance of the top communication leader and to evaluate the extent to which the CEO understands and values communication in their organization. Again using a 1–7 scale, Brazilian practitioners rated the performance of their top communication leader about average ($M = 4.45$), and the level of CEO understanding and support for communication at about the same level ($M = 4.39$). Further, the presence of two-way communications in their organizations was rated even lower ($M = 4.25$). These findings confirm the importance of the top issue expressed earlier regarding the need to build stronger internal cultures for communications in Brazilian organizations.

Features and Qualities of Excellent Communications Leaders

The Brazilian communications managers consulted in the interviews agreed that being an excellent leader requires strategic vision of the business (not restricted to the auspices of communications); vast knowhow of management; the ability to relate well with others; and empathy, flexibility, and an exemplary and inspiring attitude. The leaders of the future will also need to be more open to a multitude of opinions and decentralization of the control of communication content for the organization; for this reason, future leaders must have a perfect understanding of online interactions and possess an attitude of absorption, processing and rapid action.

Overall, these leaders will see the communications area in a more integrated manner that is susceptible to constant changes, without centralized messages, while keeping an eye on the importance of humanism, even while mastering technological advances. This is how Interviewee 2 explained it: "There will be maturing on the issue of not being able to control what is said about companies. Communications professionals will understand that the role of organizations is to operate as facilitators of this process, and not just creators."

The inexistence of borders for the various modalities of communications is another insight, expressed by Interviewee #6: "Professionals will be less attached to matrices, traditions, segmentations. We do not think of communication, we think in parts, and future professionals should remove the fencing that separates areas." Interviewee 7 added, "They should be more integrated: even if they are focused on one degree area, they will have to have an overview of all of the areas of communication. The professional of the future is multidisciplinary." This vision also was expressed by Interviewee 11: "A multidisciplinary professional who understands communication as a process, and who is able to see communication at every step of the process and knows how to interpret the facts."

The third question in the survey (Table 17.3) examined the conditions and/or qualities that participants believe are important for them to manage key issues and exercise leadership of their area in the organizations in which they work. Respondents rated strategic decision making the highest: "participating in your organization to make strategic decisions in relation to the issue" ($M = 6.66$). Nevertheless, "having communications know-how to develop appropriate strategies, plans and messages" ($M = 6.65$) and "providing a convincing vision of how communication can help the organization" ($M = 6.59$) were also highly rated. The condition least valued by the respondents relates to "having the ability to develop alliances inside and outside of the organization to deal with the issue." However, it is worth noting that all seven leadership dimensions were highly rated, with means above 6.0.

This result probably shows that participants believe there is a need for balance between these conditions and personal competencies. For example, taking part in the organization's decision-making process will only be possible if the professional

TABLE 17.3 Participants' Assessment of Leadership Dimensions

Leadership Dimensions	M	SD
Participating in strategic decision making at your organization in relation to the issue	6.66	0.70
Having communications knowhow to develop appropriate strategies, plans, and messages	6.65	0.71
Provide a convincing vision of how communication can help the organization	6.59	0.78
Have a strong ethical stance and set of values to guide actions	6.58	0.76
Having the ability to build and manage professional work teams to address the issue	6.44	0.87
Work at an organization that supports two-way communication and shared power	6.22	1.05
Have the ability to develop alliances inside and outside of the organization to deal with the issue	6.21	0.93

has the technical and ethical knowhow to take on this role and, beyond this, if the professional knows how to show other managers the importance of communication to the success of strategic goals. Surely one condition triggers the other, or is related to the others. Based on these data, the assumption can be made that communications managers are still looking for recognition of their work and an understanding regarding their contribution to the development of organizations.

Current State of the Development of Communications Leaders in Brazil

In Brazil, public relations as a profession is regulated by federal law (Law no. 5.377, 1967), which resulted in a federal board being constituted, with regional boards under this federal board, as well as the Conferp System (Decree-Law no. 860, 1969), whose main duty is to ensure compliance with the code of ethics and the legal exercise of this profession. Today, under the auspices of Brazilian democracy, this regulation of the profession in the country—which requires that professionals working in the area must not only have proof of completion of a specific public relations undergraduate degree, but they must also apply for professional registration with the regional board where they are domiciled—raises ongoing questions among professionals and academics.

In the 1990s, the Conferp System organized a wide-ranging discussion with the profession, titled "National Public Relations Parliament" (1997), aimed at reviewing some aspects of the law, especially the requirement for professional registration. After 5 years of discussion (1992–1997), the final document was submitted to the industry during the Brazilian Public Relations Congress in the city of Salvador/Bahia. The main decisions were (a) continuing the requirement for professional registration to practice the profession and (b) accepting professional registration from practitioners who have undergraduate degrees other than public relations, such as business administration, journalism, advertising and so forth, but who have a specific graduate degree in public relations.

The debate on regulation of the profession is also discussed in academia, as evidenced in the final report issued by the Commission of Specialists, established in 2010, to draft the "Proposed National Curricular Guidelines for Public Relations Courses" (Kunsch, 2010). This report underscores that public relations professionals in the organizational communication area are articulators of corporate and institutional communications policies, working in an integrated manner, especially with professionals from other fields.

The Brazilian Association of Corporate Communication (Aberje), which plays a leading role in Brazil in the field of organizational communication and public relations, has proposed that an appropriate professional profile is one that is classified as a professional mix; in other words, professionals working in the area, will possess knowhow and experiences beyond communication, in fields such as the social sciences, administration, psychology, anthropology, history, law, architecture, and others. This organization believes that this broader character ensures good performance of activities in the long term.[1]

After a new public consultation of professionals, the Conferp System (2011), in turn, released its decision to take over approval of the professional expansion as proposed in line with the flexibilization program, with changes to Law no. 5.377. Therefore, faced with what professionals wanted and the current demands of the Brazilian markets, the respective trade associations in Brazil are leading initiatives, each within its own legal and institutional role, to change the profession in Brazil starting with the next decade.

Until the flexibilization proposal takes effect, current professional training occurs at the undergraduate level. About 120 higher learning institutions in Brazil offer programs in public relations, with courses that vary from 7 to 10 semesters in length. At the same time, graduate courses are offered in the area at three levels: specialization, master's, and doctoral, accounting for more than 100 programs in the biggest states in Brazil. Over the last two decades, the number of graduate-level courses has skyrocketed, at the master's and doctoral levels, especially in Brazil's southeastern and southern regions.

Regarding professional education, Brazilian law stipulates an approximate percentage of about 40% of the common subjects must be included in education in public relations, journalism, and advertising. Thus, professionals in these three areas share some common knowledge.

The study *Professional Profile of Corporate Communications in Brazil* (Aberje, 2013) was undertaken with the aim of contributing knowledge of aspects connected to the personal, academic, and professional lives of those working with Corporate Communications activities in Brazil. It was based on the relationship databases of Aberje and Abracom, the Brazilian Association of Communications Agencies, and it offers some insights into the area. The prevailing profile in the study is a woman, between 22 and 30 years old, who is single with no children and working in the state of São Paulo, the country's economic center. Having studied at private universities, she holds an undergraduate degree in journalism and a graduate degree at the specialization/MBA level. She also communicates well in English. She has worked in the communications area for 4 to 7 years and currently works at a private national company in the services sector with up to 500 employees, with an emphasis on communications agency work, where she has worked under the CLT[2] regime for 1 to 3 years. She currently holds an analyst level position.

This study (Aberje, 2013) helps to understand the directions for qualification of the Brazilian communicator. For example, the Aberje (2013) study indicates that graduate studies at the specialization/MBA level are preferred by 50% of professionals in terms of continuing studies, with 31% not studying further. Marketing, at 24%, and communications, at 16%, were the most frequently chosen areas to take extension courses and courses to supplement undergraduate studies. Also regarding the next item in this chapter, most participants (78.2%) believe that the corporate communications market will grow in the next 5 years, with 25.8% betting on major growth.

Leadership Needs for the Future

When interview participants were asked about the next challenge for communications managers in Brazil, they were almost unanimous: speed in interlocutions in real time is already causing profound changes in how communication is done at organizations. This speed tends to give communication greater power, but also to create information overload and diminish stakeholder capacity to retain message content. One example was provided by Interviewee 8: "It is increasingly complex when dealing with people. They are very stressed out by too much information."

Similar perceptions were captured in the survey, in which practitioners were asked to evaluate 12 approaches for preparing future leaders in communication (Table 17.4). Brazilian respondents' preferred training leaders in these areas: "strengthening competencies and skills in managing changes" (M = 6.24); improved "conflict management competencies" (M = 6.11); and enhancing "professionals' listening skills" (M = 6.04). It can therefore be assumed that respondents' interests lie in developing capabilities related to management, diplomacy, and negotiation, given the fragility of relationships and the speed of societal transformations.

In relation to formal professional education, participants were found to somewhat value "reinforcement of the business/economic component of educational

TABLE 17.4 Improving Development of Future Leaders

Leadership Development Approaches	M	SD
Strengthening of competencies and skills in managing change	6.24	1.01
Improvement of conflict management competencies	6.11	0.97
Improvement of professionals' listening skills	6.04	1.00
Development of better measures to document the value and contributions of public relations	6.02	1.14
Development of education to improve the emotional intelligence of PR professionals	5.93	1.16
Strengthening of the business/economic component of educational communications programs	5.87	1.09
Development of cultural understanding and sensitivity	5.77	1.14
Calling on professional associations to work together to develop leaders	5.71	1.16
Imposition of harsh penalties on ethical violations	5.62	1.57
Reinforcement of professional competencies in dealing with job-related stress	5.58	1.27
Development of a global educational curricular core	5.27	1.53
Requirement for professional registration	4.96	2.07

communications programs" ($M = 5.87$). However, from the perspective of these same participants, "development of a global educational curricular core" ($M = 5.27$) does not seem to be considered as important in training future leaders. Based on the supposition that strengthening the profession means thinking, planning, and acting jointly, and that the convergence of these efforts occurs through trade associations, it is noteworthy that actions connected to them were less valued by some participants. Both the "calling on professional associations to work together to develop leaders" ($M = 5.71$) and the "imposition of harsh penalties on ethical violations" (5.62), as well as the "requirement for professional registration" (4.96), were rated as less important than other approaches.

Professional registration, moreover, seems quite debatable, because it received the lowest score among the 12 actions proposed and was marked by the greatest disagreement or deviation ($SD = 2.07$) among respondents. If in some countries there is a certain interest in regulating the public relations profession, with the aim of qualifying or accrediting the function, in Brazil, where this already exists, professional opinions on this matter go back and forth. Also, we note that the survey respondents gave significant importance to the "development of better measures to document the value and contributions of public relations and communications" ($M = 6.02$). If thinking that professionals should document their contributions is in line with trade associations, then, based on previous responses, the respondents may not have a very clear idea of what this kind of organizational role is.

Finally, participants also highlighted the need to reinforce competencies and skills among new generations in managing change and conflict management, as well as improving listening skills. In contrast, the imposition of severe penalties on ethical violations, as well as required professional registration, was at the bottom of the respondents' ranking of importance. These findings may be interpreted as a trend toward something that has already been discussed many times in Brazil, which is deregulation of the public relations profession in the country.

Final Considerations

There are undeniable differences in development, understanding, and projection of the communications area or function at Brazilian organizations, compared to the overall global results. In Brazil, there is a fundamental need, expressed at the top of managers' concerns, regarding a lack of recognition from internal peers: Without approval from the other departments, this sector cannot advance, obtain an appropriate budget and teams, or participate meaningfully in decision making. What is noteworthy is that, nevertheless, the PR leaders we interviewed appreciate and defend their CEOs, and refer to them as visionary leaders who are aware of the important association among communication, reputation, and performance. However, the CEOs have not been able to break the stereotypes or reduce ignorance and instill a new attitude in the organization about the value of communication among managers at other levels and in other areas.

Although in the Brazilian economic area there is a perception of some stability in recent years, the communications sector is seen as facing continued movements of change, oftentimes leading to crises. Also, the skill of being transparent and, at the same time, protecting the organization from potential conflicts of image, is an unavoidable point of concern. With national organizations increasingly acting internationally, culture clashes have to an increasing degree become common and may contribute to this situation.

The emergence of employees as the main stakeholders in organizations in Brazil, regardless of their business segment, is another quite important finding in this study. From a market with a traditional focus on the consumer, a more balanced scenario is being uncovered among the various relationship groups. The contingent of people that have a closer relationship—and not just from a geographic perspective—end up taking a leading role due to their increased credibility as thought leaders in the public sphere. It is also possible to attribute this concern to the coexistence of different generations in the workplace, with multiple expectations to be met, which makes everything more complex.

Although the global research project may have begun with the supposition that digital media is predominant, this issue is not a priority for Brazilian managers. Its incursions into this area are just beginning. Nevertheless, practitioners recognize that it will become a requirement by 2015. Yet, there are other points to resolve first. This interface in Brazil is well known, although the very popular nature and use of interactive digital platforms is recognized among various classes of the population. The corporate world is still at an initial stage of planning digital strategies and tactics.

It is worth mentioning the maturity of the managers interviewed: Although they show less concern with this or that digital tool and with how to make it work for the organization, they understand the reality of the internet and increasing mobility as having the potential to create serious information overload. This does imply difficulties for communicating corporate messages to just one citizen, who is set on by so many simultaneous appeals from organizations. Respondents also reported they were aware they no longer are the main sources of content and information distribution. At a time of multi-protagonism and fluid confidence, being a leader means sharing, above all.

Notes

1. The understanding of this mix is explained in the "Aberje 40 anos" document (Aberje, 2007), available at http://issuu.com/aberje/docs/aberje40anos?e = 1148821/2994319.
2. CLT means Consolidation of Labor Laws. CLT is a legislative standard for regulatory laws relating to labor law and procedural law Labour in Brazil. The CLT was approved by Decree-Law No. 5.452, of May 1, 1943, and sanctioned by Getulio Vargas, Brazil's president at the time. It is the main instrument for regulating the relations of the individual and collective work.

References

Aberje. (2007). *Aberje 40 Anos*. [Aberje at 40 years]. Available online at http://issuu. com/aberje/docs/aberje40anos?e=1148821/2994319.

Aberje. (2013). *Perfil do Profissional de Comunicação Organizacional no Brasil*. [Profile of the Organizational Communication Professional in Brazil]. São Paulo, Brazil: Aberje. Available online at www.aberje.com.br/pesquisa/PerfilProfComunicacao2013.pdf

Conferp. (1997, October). *Parlamento Nacional: conclusões do Parlamento Nacional de Relações Públicas* [National Parliament: Findings of the National Public Relations Parliament]. Atibaia, São Paulo, Brazil: Conferp. Available online at www.conferp.org.br/consulta/?p=576

Conferp. (2011, December). *Consulta Pública aos Profissionais de Relações Públicas: resultados, diagnóstico, plano de ação* [Public Consultation on Public Relations Professionals: Results, Diagnosis, Plan of Action]. Brasília, Brazil: Conferp. Available online at http://conferp. org.br/consulta/?p=704

Decree-Law no. 860, September 11 (1969). Available online at www.conferp.org. br/?p=204

Kunsch, M. M. K (2010, October 20). *Proposta de Diretrizes Curriculares Nacionais para os Cursos de Relações Públicas* [Guidelines proposal of a National Curriculum for Public Relations Courses. Brasília, Brazil: Experts Committee Established by the Ministry of Education. Available online at www.aberje.com.br/userfiles/file/Relatrio%20 Diretrizes%20Curriculares%20Relaes%20Pblicas.pdf

Law no. 5.377, December 11 (1967). Available online at www.conferp.org.br/?p=179

18

KEY LEADERSHIP CHALLENGES AND FACTORS IN PUBLIC RELATIONS AND COMMUNICATIONS IN MEXICO

Marco V. Herrera and Rebeca I. Arévalo Martínez

The world is facing major challenges as a result of technological progress. Humankind now possesses the power that comes with social networks, whose very existence—when added to the power of communications—is generating new lines of ongoing information, connecting the entire world, and doing so free of time constraints. Consequently, the world is producing new dynamics that position the economy, politics, and social change under a new world mind-set. Events and information formerly not divulged for hours or even days because of the time elapsed from their leaving the communities where they were generated and reaching beyond now take less than a minute to make it to the farthest reaches of every continent. Thus, they become world news as a result of the globalization process and technological developments that humans have produced in the name of communications, including the Internet, cellular phones, and social networks.

From the standpoint of communications and public relations, this situation drives two major challenges for the profession and for present and future leaders in charge of managing communications in every kind of national or multinational organization. The first challenge consists in learning the type of leadership skills that will be required for dealing with the empowerment of citizens and new consumers; the second entails the need to identify those cultural factors within companies that need to be strengthened if the latter are to better face the challenges posed by social networks in future.

Theoretical Perspective of the Relationship Among Communications, Public Relations, and Leadership

When researching the topic of leadership in communications and public relations in Mexico, we are compelled to first look at the concepts of company, communications, public relations, and leadership. The definition of company that we deemed most appropriate for this investigation is the systemic perspective that makes it possible to outline its relationship to communications. For Alfred Hall and R. Fagan (1962), a system is a set of objectives and the relations between these and their attributes. Within this context, the objectives are called system components; the attributes correspond to the properties of the objectives, and the relations keep the system together.

In this approach, the concept is that there are interactional objectives—namely, the people that communicate—and these, in turn, compose systems that interact. This is why Watzlawick, Beavin, and Jackson (2002) consider that interaction among people entails an exchange of messages and is always developed within the context of certain interactional lines, those that each company establishes. In sum, from this standpoint all conduct is then communication, hence the importance of studying interpersonal communications. Watzlawick et al. (2002) define human interaction as

> A communications system characterized by the properties of general systems: time, as a variable, system and sub-system relations, totality, feedback and equifinality. Interactional systems are considered the natural focal point for a pragmatic long-term impact assessment on communicational phenomena. (p. 139)

Thus, in organizations, communications becomes a specialty department that has witnessed multiple variations throughout its development, ranging from communications (whose purpose deals exclusively with the company's operations) to strategic communications that plays a preponderant role in the attainment of results. The latter approach has been given different meanings, ranging from internal communications, organizational communications, and corporate communications all the way through business communications, productive communications, and integrated communications for organizations. Conversely, public relations has been developed and is differentiated from communications by virtue of being intrinsically linked to seeking the good will of external audiences toward the company.

Because this research study picks up on the concept of the company understood from the overall point of view, it consequently demands that communications be considered a strategic element that permits encompassing messages addressed to different audiences under one single cultural umbrella that is geared specifically to the attainment of results. Thus, the definition of organizational communications aptly underscores that it takes place within an economic, a political, a social, or a cultural system, seeking collective solutions to make it more productive on three fronts: institutional or corporate communications; internal communications, integrated communications, or marketing; and advertising (Rebeil & Ruíz Sandoval, 1998).

Communications has become an integral part of strategic planning in organizations given the crucial role it plays in linking productive processes to the company's mission (Rebeil & Nosnik, 2011), led by communications professionals who contribute to the equation by proposing appropriate solutions for given circumstances and company contexts (Narvaez & Campillo, 2011).

As a result of the foregoing, even while internal communications continues to be an important factor to create and maintain good relations among members of the organization, in addition to integrating them and encouraging them to attain their organizational objectives (Andrade, cited in Fernández, 2002), leadership among the executives in charge of communications within companies becomes of the utmost importance, for they drive and support programs and, in essence, become the face of the company to the interest groups.

Leadership is related to the highest levels of performance on behalf of collaborators given that their attitude and enthusiasm help create a good job environment. A leader with good personal skills and relations and the ability to direct groups can foster a climate (a culture of productivity) that invites participants to better performance and harder work. Among this leader's outstanding skills will be that of communication, given that this favors human relations, the work environment, and the attainment of results (Siliceo, 1995).

Hence, leadership is building a more productive organizational culture—namely, an equitable, meaningful, and transcendent approach to the contributions of the workers. Regardless of their hierarchical standing within the organization, all personnel must have a clear and in-depth knowledge of what real productivity is as the basis of organizational competitiveness (Siliceo, Casares, & González, 1999). It stands to reason, then, that the role of leaders is not restricted to directing or guiding employees in operational terms, for they will exert a direct influence on the performance of employees through the bond that results from diverse communications and public relations endeavors implanted in the company. For this reason, the impact and relevance of these endeavors are so complete.

In specific terms, in Mexico, the development and evolution of this discipline, interestingly enough born from professional need and spheres even before being present in academia, "has been determined by the educational, economic and social factors of the environment and not only by its ability to evolve in discipline, practice and representatives" (Rebeil, Arévalo, & Lemus, 2011, p. 106). Therefore, step by step, communications and public relations have proved their contribution as a key success factor for organizations and, therefore, have attained better understanding on behalf of the types of institutions, organizations, and companies that they handle and from their clients, consumers, and citizens as a whole as well (Rebeil & Herrera, 2012).

Last, it is important to mention that we are dealing with a function that has grown and evolved through generating solutions for the needs expressed in the practice. Communications and public relations management has enjoyed the guidance of its leaders throughout its growth, which serves to underscore the importance of its contribution.

Guidelines and Methodology

The research project on communications leadership and culture in Mexico is part of a global study of leadership in public relations and communications management in 23 countries, undertaken by the University of Alabama and the Plank Center for Leadership in Public Relations. The study was developed in two phases: quantitative, through an online questionnaire targeted to leaders and their collaborators, and qualitative, through in-depth interviews of selected leaders.

The process began with the design of a questionnaire to be applied through interviews at the global level, which was translated into nine languages. A list was drawn up of public relations leaders in Mexico, ensuring it would be balanced, representative, and inclusive of the most important leaders in the field in the country. Total length of the research project process was 8 months, from October 2011 through May 2012.

The 16 interviews in Mexico included the following company hierarchies: 11 directors, one assistant director, three managers, and one coordinator, representing major private companies. Of the interviewees, 25% worked for Mexican firms, and the remaining 75% worked at multinational corporations with operations in Mexico. The sampling of executives interviewed was equally divided: 50% women and 50% men.

The interviews were structured to capture the perceptions of communication leaders regarding three major themes: (a) the issues of most pressing concern to communications and public relations leaders, (b) organizational cultural and structural factors that influence communication practice, and (c) the main leadership qualities and dimensions required for communications and public relations (Appendix B).

The global online survey (Appendix A) was completed in Mexico by 210 people with experience in the field of corporate communications or public relations. The sample includes both men (48%) and women (52%). Various sectors of the economy were taken into consideration, and a nice balance of organizational types was achieved—public-sector companies, not-for-profit organizations, communication agencies, and self-employed. The survey sought to learn what the most important issues that leaders confront are, the strategies and tactics leaders use to manage the issues, how the issues affect leaders' roles and practices, and what approaches might be used to improve the development of future leaders. In the following sections, the results of the interviews with 16 public relations leaders are first presented, followed by some findings from the survey of 210 communicators in Mexican organizations.

Vision of Communications and Public Relations Leaders—the Interviews

The Most Important Issue

Results from the interviews highlighted three important issues for executives: (1) the need to have good, reliable internal communications to engage employees and align them to the company's business objectives, values and philosophy; (2) performance results that will convince top management of the value and important contribution of communications endeavors; and (3) actions and approaches required to better understand target audiences. Other issues that were mentioned once included social networks, culture, professionalization of the field and advertising.

Initial results lead us to infer that in Mexico large corporations and their top management still under estimate the importance of communications as a business process, given that, based on quotations taken from interviews, the internal communication process holds its own natural place in the understanding of executives; they understand the importance of employees. On being closer and more exposed to the pressures exerted by external stakeholders, however, communication executives first try to help top management understand the importance of communications in daily business processes, and subsequently, they attempt to grasp who the key stakeholders are and how they are responding. One communication assistant director said,

> I'm betting that in the mid-term, when we begin to see the fruit of communications, when we begin to have a more effective media platform, when the campaign begins to release messages and when stakeholders begin to realize the value of communications, directors will realize that it is in their benefit to begin opening doors and listening.

The foregoing is related to the budget and financial resources invested in communications, given that in those cases where executives handle the advertising budget they believe that money earmarked for advertising strategies is more important and has greater influence than does money assigned to internal and corporate communications, precisely because of the pressure placed on their audiences. In this regard, an internal communications executive with 18 years' experience said,

> For a company, the communications department represents a cost and must have a return on investment; then, the metrics show how we are doing with this return on investment . . . in the organization where I work, the communications department has no budget, other than salaries. Any communications campaign we want to do has to be in house.

On the other hand, it is important to mention that the experience gained by the executives allows them to be sensitive to the movements of society and their effects on perception, opinion, and conduct as concerns the various audiences. For this reason, it is so important to them to understand the different audiences and constantly monitor them, as expressed by an executive of corporate communications and public affairs with 28 years of experience: "You need to answer, constantly engage in networking, monitoring what is said of the company and someone dedicated to it that can respond to public concerns and to the clients of the company's key audiences."

As concerns reputation management, we think this is where the need to understand the audiences and their perception of the company comes from. This is particularly true in today's social context where more than ever we are subject to the speed with which news travels and to the impact of the media on business and social contexts in the contemporary world. According to the corporate communications director for Mexico and Central America of a multinational company with 12 years of experience, "What worries me most is social media, the speed at which information travels, and today this is an area that has to be well-covered . . . if you do not pay attention, it may damage the reputation of your brand."

The Influences of Cultural and Structural Factors in Organizations

The interviewees were asked to speak about the culture and values of their organizations, especially the cultural or structural factors that facilitate or impede communication practice. The organizational values most mentioned by communications leaders were the following: first, the honesty of the company; second, customer service; and, third, with an equal number of mentions, professionalism, social responsibility, ethics, and innovation. A good example of the value of innovation was expressed by an officer of internal and external communications of a multinational company, who has 16 years of experience:

> The company is consistent with their values—among which are commitment, leadership, innovation and closeness—and it is consistent in practice because, from what I've experienced, it is a company that has made me experience and apply everything, or almost everything, I wanted.

On the other hand, regarding the factors that the executives interviewed consider fundamental to the success of communications management, three were mentioned most often: (a) the extent to which communications leaders take part in executive decisions; (b) the position that the function holds within corporate structure, and this specifically refers to the fact that ideally communications should be placed in the top tier of organizational structure; and (c) the extent to which cultural or structural factors may hinder their success. Being part of the organizational structure becomes a success factor, as noted by one manager of corporate communications and public relations in Mexico for a multinational firm:

> There are global elements for communications, to which I have access. I am part of a council of a global group from which we can study best practices, ways of working that can be shared and do what is called *glocalizing*.

Leadership in Communications and Public Relations

The heads of communications departments we interviewed felt that organizational leaders and top management largely value and thereby defend their work. The importance given by managers is essential, as was expressed by a director of corporate affairs in Mexico who works for a multinational company: "We are seen as strategic advisors, and the corporate affairs department is understood to be one of the most important areas of the business, along with the marketing and finance departments, in addition to adding value and key responsibilities."

Concerning the manner in which communication leaders prove the value and effectiveness of communications and public relations, four approaches were mentioned: the implementation of specific metrics, the use and application of surveys, the measurement of the recall of messages disseminated among company collaborators, and the carrying out of communications audits. An example of measurement was described by the director of corporate communications for Mexico and Central America of a multinational company, who said that the main measure is the rate or level of reputation: "To achieve this we have to improve aspects in a specific topic, such as generating stories about suppliers, spreading the word of our sustainability and achieving media coverage. All this will affect the recognition rate."

Regarding the most important characteristics and qualities needed to produce excellent leadership, the most frequent answers included the need to be strategists, coordinators of group efforts, good communicators and visionaries, good team leaders, and the crucial need to be well informed. To a lesser degree, other qualities mentioned were being good planners, showing a spirit of service, and the ability to relate to others. A corporate communications executive with 12 years of experience said that some of the main characteristics of excellence in communications leadership are "a very open mind with a vision and sensitivity to listen to people, and a positive mind, in addition to being a planner and administrator." A few interviewees also mentioned such characteristics as consistency, pursuit of the common good, tolerance of frustration, emotional intelligence, passion, competitiveness, assertiveness, open-mindedness, sensitivity, and positivity.

Respondents also mentioned the turning points that drove their career path upward; these included staying up to date and pursuing continuing education, as well as creating value for the company and ensuring that said value becomes visible. According to one director of corporate affairs for Mexico and the Caribbean in a multinational company, it is important

> to be a strategic partner of customers, to be very close to high command, near the CEO, to be a consultant . . . position oneself in the service department, offering opinions and making important calls for decision making, all as a consultant to top management.

To a lesser degree, other tipping points included making mistakes and learning from them, learning from others, becoming a strategic company partner, being tenacious, maintaining enthusiasm on the job, being reliable, serving as a support department for other functions, working at a large company and taking on challenges and maximizing opportunities as they arise. In short, Mexican communication leaders described a wide range of desirable leadership traits and qualities and a diverse number of career tipping points.

The Future of Leadership in Communications and Public Relations in Mexico

The leaders we interviewed also were asked to identify the most important challenges that the communications discipline and its leaders will face in the country over the coming three to five years. The most frequently cited challenges included digital communication, matters related to technology and management of social networks. Other topics or issues included strategic communications, sustainability, specialized segmentation of audiences, and more effective leadership on behalf of communicators.

Among the main characteristics and qualities that future communications leaders need to exhibit are becoming experts in social networks and having the capacity to coordinate teams focused on the common good. Mentioned less often was the importance of developing greater learning ability, knowing how to create and offer demonstrable value, and possessing the capability to analyze and anticipate challenges for the work performed. A somewhat recurring trend was that of promoting ethics and transparency, as well as the capacity to better understand globalization.

Opinions of Communications and Public Relations Professionals—the Survey

The Most Important Issues

Survey participants said the issue of most concern is "Improving the measurement of communication effectiveness to demonstrate value." This confirms that in Mexico—despite good development attained in the field of communications—today's professionals are still lacking real measurement tools to demonstrate the results of their work to management. This refers to both the value and the reach of the results. For the market, this poses the dilemma of establishing goals versus measurement mechanisms, yet no appropriate formula has been found to convince corporate management of the value of communication results.

All of the top five issues, as measured on a 1–7 scale, were deemed very important by the survey participants, as follows:

1. Improving the measurement of communications effectiveness to demonstrate value ($M = 6.27$)
2. Managing the digital revolution and rise of social media (6.19)
3. Dealing with the speed and volume of information flow (6.13)
4. Being prepared to deal effectively with crises that may arise (6.13)
5. Improving employee engagement and commitment in the workplace (6.12)

The second, third, and fourth most important issues are all linked to new technologies and the digital revolution. This suggests that once the concern of proving the value of communications and its scope is handled, then the rise of social media and information flow and management become priorities. Perhaps Mexican practitioners can use new technologies and tools to assist measurement efforts. This also may be an opportunity to implement studies to learn of the asymmetries in these fields and employ measurement techniques to determine their impact and assess possible solutions.

Leadership Skills and Dimensions

The global survey also examined the skills and qualities that communication leaders must possess in order to be successful in facing the main issues and challenges confronting the profession. The seven skills or qualities of leadership in the survey are based on the seven dimensions of excellent leadership in public relations developed by Meng and Berger (2013). Mexican communication leaders rated all seven of the dimensions very highly ($M = 6.05$–6.36 on a 1–7 scale), which is quite consistent with the results in other countries in the global study. The ranking in Mexico is as follows:

1. Providing a compelling vision for how communications can help the organization ($M = 6.36$)
2. Possessing communications knowledge to develop appropriate strategies, plans, and messages ($M = 6.31$)
3. Participating in your organization's strategic decision-making regarding the issue ($M = 6.30$)
4. Possessing a strong ethical orientation and set of values to guide actions ($M = 6.25$)
5. Having the ability to build and manage professional work teams to address the issue ($M = 6.22$)

6. Having the ability to develop coalitions in and outside the organization to deal with the issue ($M = 6.22$)
7. Working in an organization that supports 2-way communications and shared power ($M = 6.05$)

"Providing a compelling vision for how communications can help the organization" is rated highest ($M = 6.36$). We believe this is closely linked to what is considered the most important issue among survey participants, namely, "Improving the measurement of communications effectiveness to demonstrate value." This reaffirms that the measurement issue is the primary concern for communications and public relations professionals in the country.

Two other highly rated skills and capabilities were "Possessing communications knowledge to develop appropriate strategies, plans and messages" ($M = 6.31$) and "Participating in your organization's strategic decision-making regarding the issue" ($M = 6.30$). In our view this supports two prevailing paradigms still affecting the communications environment in Mexico. On one hand, regarding communication skills and knowledge, some organizations still hire personnel hailing from other professions, and they often lack skills for managing communications. On the other hand, public relations leaders have not been granted a fully strategic role in decision-making processes by management of companies and organizations.

One might even say that in today's Mexico, communications is still undervalued, still understood perhaps as something anyone can do naturally. There is little understanding regarding communications in general, and even less understanding regarding the complexity of the business, political, and social changes that have made effectively managing communications increasingly critical.

Some Demographic Variations

The survey results also provided some interesting demographic variations, and we highlight a few of them in this section.

Leadership Skills by Years of Experience

- Respondents with fewer than 11 years of experience in public relations and communications believe that the most important leadership skill in the field of communications is "Providing a compelling vision for how communications can help the organization." They rate this dimension significantly higher ($M = 6.46$) than the other two experience groups: 11 to 20 years ($M = 6.31$) and more than 20 years ($M = 6.28$). This could mean that less experienced professionals want to ensure that communications is granted the importance it deserves within the organization.
- Those whose experience ranges from 11 to 20 years declare that the most important leadership quality is "Having the ability to develop coalitions in

and outside the organization to deal with the issue." They rate it significantly higher ($M = 6.34$) than the other two groups. One might infer that this group understands communication to be a tool with the power to reconcile the interests of an organization in both the internal and external spheres.

- Those with more than 20 years of experience rate two leadership dimensions significantly higher than the less experienced groups: "Possessing communications knowledge to develop appropriate strategies, plans, and messages" ($M = 6.51$) and "Possessing a strong ethical orientation and set of values to guide actions" ($M = 6.52$). Perhaps those with greater experience believe the need in Mexico is most acute for skilled professionals who can help the organization embrace communications as a strategic tool to attain key objectives, and who can demonstrate strong professional ethics and behaviors.

Leadership Capabilities by Type of Organization

Survey respondents represented five sectors according to their sphere of activity in the field of communications at large: public companies, private companies, not-for-profits, communication agencies, and self-employed:

- Practitioners in four of the five sectors (public companies excluded) said the most important dimension of leadership is "Providing a compelling vision for how communications can help the organization." This is consistent with earlier comments regarding communications still being in the process of proving its importance to top management. Survey participants from these four sectors rated all but one of the seven leadership dimensions higher, and usually significantly higher that the public company sector.
- Those in the public company sector said the most important leadership dimension is "Having the ability to develop coalitions in and outside the organization to deal with the issue." This speaks to the need for public organizations to overcome internal bureaucratic inertia first of all, and then to understand that communications is a powerful tool to negotiate with the various social layers in the country's fabric.

Leadership Capabilities by Gender

- Professional women (109) and men (101) in the survey viewed leadership dimensions quite differently. Women said that "Providing a compelling vision for how communication can help the organization" ($M = 6.56$) was the most important capability. Men stated the most important capability was "Participating in your organization's strategic decision-making regarding the issue" ($M = 6.20$). More important, women rated six of the seven leadership dimensions significantly higher than did men. Men rated significantly higher than did women the organizational culture dimension: "Working in an organization that supports 2-way communication and shared power." The high rating ($M = 6.82$ on a 7.0 scale) suggests that men place the greatest importance on internal culture, or that they are extremely satisfied with their own organizational culture.

- The Mexican industry is dominated by women, according to the most recent study published by the Mexican Association of Public Relations Professionals (PRORP; 2012), which found that women make up 59% of the industry. In this regard, the results of our survey may indicate that women still feel they have to prove themselves through excellent communication knowledge and skills in order to hold management or executive positions, whereas men (owing to diverse factors, including cultural) already hold decision-making positions and are comfortable with their existing organizational cultures.

Leadership Capabilities by Age

Respondents were divided into four age groups. The youngest groups (<36 and 36–45) and the older groups (46–55 and >55) rated leadership capabilities somewhat differently, although they rated all dimensions highly.

- Respondents in the under 36 age group ($M = 6.46$) and the 36–45 age group ($M = 6.36$) indicated that the most important leadership capability was "Providing a compelling vision for how communications can help the organization" deal with key issues.
- On the other hand, the 46–55 ($M = 6.34$) and over-55 age groups ($M = 6.38$) rated the most important leadership capability as "Participating in your organization's strategic decision-making regarding the issue." This may be a reflection of the fact that these individuals may be more likely to actually be involved in strategic decision-making.

Developing Future Leaders

The survey also examined what respondents think about the development of communications leaders in the future and what's needed to strengthen the profession; 12 development approaches were listed, and survey participants rated them on a 1–7 scale.

Respondents gave the highest rating to the approach, "Strengthen change management skills and capabilities" ($M = 6.23$), and the lowest rating to "Require professional accreditation or licensing" ($M = 4.91$). Two other soft skills were also rated highly: "Enhance conflict management skills" ($M = 6.01$), and "Improve the listening skills of professionals" ($M = 6.07$). These results are quite consistent with the global findings, and they also reflect the need to attain leadership without limitations, which means that communications professionals must be able to sensitize and adapt strategies and tactics for the different cultures that this globalized world encompasses, as well as the need for immediacy in conveying messages.

Conclusions Regarding Professionals in Communications and Public Relations

When comparing results from the Mexico study to the worldwide results, Mexico shows some similarities and some important differences. At the global study level, professionals chose "Dealing with the speed and volume of information flow" as the most important issue. Mexican professionals instead named "Improving the measurement of communications effectiveness to demonstrate value." Only Mexico ($M = 6.28$) and Brazil ($M = 6.34$) rated this issue highest among all countries, and they rated it significantly higher than all other countries.

Regarding the second most important issue, Mexico and the global results were the same: "Managing the digital revolution and rise of social media." Professionals worldwide named "Improving the measurement of communications effectiveness to demonstrate value" as the third issue. Mexican communicators, however, selected "Being prepared to deal effectively with crises that may arise" as the third most important issue.

Our first observation is that concern over the digital revolution underway holds equal importance worldwide and in Mexico; thus, penetration of technology and its effects is linear across the world, and organizations are increasingly interconnected across the board, either because they belong to large multinational corporations or because they have operations with strategic partners in other regions.

Regarding Mexico's choice of improving the measurement of communications effectiveness as the priority, this is a result of professionals still needing to drive communication as a business strategy and to convince management of its importance, as opposed to more developed nations, where this statement holds third place. Precisely in this regard, differences regarding the third most important issue lead us to infer that countries with higher levels of business development, and more stable and equitable economic conditions, grant more importance to "Improving the measurement of communications effectiveness" from a value-added standpoint, whereas preparing for crisis is a professional practice and is, therefore, already standardized.

Mexican communicators, however, still struggle within their organizations to carry out professional crisis management. Also, the Mexican market considers crisis management to be a specialty field, thereby leading us to infer that this area exerts influence on the structure and development of the media in Mexico, including major monopolies, as well as complex social and democratic procedures.

As regards leadership capabilities, similar differences are found between results in Mexico and the global results. "Participating in your organization's strategic decision-making regarding the issue" ($M = 6.30$) is the highest rated capability in the global study; it is only the third highest rated leadership capability in Mexico. The highest rated in Mexico is "Providing a compelling vision for how communications can help the organization" ($M = 6.37$). It is intriguing that vision is rated significantly higher in the three Latin American countries—Brazil, Chile, and Mexico—than in all other countries. On the other hand, Mexico was similar to most other countries in rating as the second most important capability that of "Possessing communications knowledge to develop appropriate strategies, plans and messages."

Next Steps in Leadership in Communications and Public Relations

By way of conclusions for this investigation, we offer three insights. First, we found that the way of structuring, operating, and managing communications and public relations in different private organizations in Mexico is determined by the social, economic, and political circumstances of the country; with multinational companies, this has induced them to adapt some of their global policies and vision to the context of Mexico. In the foregoing cases, communications has played a crucial role. The study also made it clear that business communications is geared to the attainment of company objectives, regardless of the type of organization in question; therefore, the results must be measurable.

Second, the ever-changing environment demands continuous adjustments on behalf of the organizations in their communications and public relations systems. This ensures their permanence, and thus they become the choice of millions of consumers globally who not only take into account the characteristics of a product or service in their purchase decision, but also the attributes of the company that provides them. Therefore, image, reputation, presence, and corporate social responsibility are matters of increasing importance to consumers. This underscores the importance of the role of communications and public relations in the daily operations of any given company, as well as the relevance of creating and implementing strategies that are increasingly tailored to target these themes.

In this context, management of communications and public relations in the organization becomes a crucial success factor that determines the generation of more links between the company and its interest groups, while at the same time increasing the possibility of attaining business objectives. This makes the role of communications and public relations a strategic element that progressively determines the success of companies.

Third, we noted that companies in Mexico, concerned about increasing global competitiveness, seek communications leaders with expertise and knowledge of key corporate functions that will assist in securing the desired objectives. Leadership that generates productive culture and is geared toward the attainment of results (Siliceo, 1995) today translates as multitasking management with greater strategic influence to match the structural and cultural environment needed for further development, just as the study shows. Communications understood as a system (Watzlawick et al., 2002) continues being the current, valid, and representative approach for the communications function within companies, even in light of the difficulties that globalization and intercultural management add, given their effect on both internal and external audiences through digital communications.

The results of the study show that the function of communications and public relations is increasingly complex. Leaders must not only perfect their skills but acquire new ones as well, given that both communications executives and their work teams need to reach increasingly specific audiences that are micro-segmented and display the complexity of maintaining the essence of the message in multiple channels and diverse languages simultaneously.

The study allows us to visualize both the form and the function, thereby detecting the need to build a new educational model for the development of effective leadership for communications and public relations. This model should be based on the development of competencies founded on traditional knowledge of communications, while integrating a series of new disciplines that are necessary to face the future development of business, the needs of the population, and the cultural challenges of the new multicultural societal group of our times.

References

Asociación Mexicana de Profesionales de Relaciones Públicas. (2012). *Estudio Anual 2011 de la Industria de Relaciones Públicas en México* [2011 Annual Study of the Public Relations Industry in Mexico.Mexico City, México: PRORP.

Fernández, C. (2002) *La comunicación en las organizaciones* [Communication in organizations]. Mexico City, Mexico: Trillas.

Hall, A., & Fagan, R. (1956). Definition of system. In *General systems, yearbook for the Society for the Advancement of General Systems Theory* (Vol 1., p. 18-28). Stanford, CA: International Society for the Systems Sciences.

Meng, J., & Berger, B.K. (2013). An Integrated Model of Excellent Leadership in Public Relations: Dimensions, Measurement, and Validation. *Journal of Public Relations Research, 25*(2), 141-167.

Narvaez, L., & Campillo, I. (2011) Transformación de las organizaciones. El papel estratégico de la comunicación [Transforming organizations. The strategic role of communication]. In M. A. Rebeil (Ed.), *Comunicación estratégica en las organizaciones* (pp. 47–66). Mexico City, Mexico: Trillas.

Rebeil, M. A., Arévalo, R., & Lemus, G. (2011). El ejercicio de las Relaciones Públicas en México [The public relations performance in Mexico]. *Revista Internacional de Relaciones Públicas, 1*(1), 97–110.

Rebeil, M. A., & Herrera, M. (2012). Public relations in Mexico. Culture and challenges vis-à-vis globalization. In K. Sriramesh & D. Verčič, *Culture and public relations. Links and implications* (pp. 163–181). New York, NY: Routledge.

Rebeil, M. A., & Nosnik, A. (2011) Introducción [Introduction]. In M. A. Rebeil (Ed.), *Comunicación estratégica en las organizaciones* (pp. 11–23). Mexico City, Mexico: Trillas.

Rebeil, M. A., & Ruíz Sandoval, C. (1998) *El poder de la comunicación en las organizaciones* [The power of communication in organizations]. Mexico City, Mexico: Plaza y Valdés Editores/Universidad Iberoamericana.

Siliceo, A. (1995) *Liderazgo para la productividad en México* [Leadership for productivity in Mexico]. Mexico City, Mexico: Limusa.

Siliceo, A., Casares, D., & González, J. L. (1999) *Liderazgo, Valores y Cultura Organizacional: Hacia una organización competitiva* [Leadership, Values and Organizational Culture: Towards a competitive organization. Mexico City, Mexico: McGraw-Hill.

Watzlawick, P., Beavin, J., & Jackson, D. (2002) *Teoría de la comunicación humana: Interacciones, patologías y paradojas* [Theory of human communication: Interactions, pathologies and paradoxes] (12 ed.). Barcelona, Spain: Herder.

19

U.S. PUBLIC RELATIONS LEADERS PURSUE TALENT, DIGITAL MASTERY, AND STRONG CULTURES

Bruce K. Berger, Juan Meng, William Heyman, Mark Harris, and Mark Bain

Public relations has a long history in the United States and is today a growing, mega billion-dollar industry (Holmes, 2012). A decade ago Manekin (2001) estimated that corporations, government agencies, and special interest groups spent $30 billion on public relations activities. Although capitalism and democracy don't require organizations to practice public relations, these economic and political systems have served as fertile grounds for the growth of the profession in the commercial, political, and social arenas in the United States.

The profession also has long enjoyed a network of professional groups and associations, and university undergraduate and graduate education programs have spread rapidly in the past 30 years. More than 300 colleges and universities now offer degrees or courses in public relations, and 10,000 college students are members of the Public Relations Student Society of America (2013).

Part of this growth and success is due to the hard and visionary work of public relations leaders, who play key roles in their organizations. They lead change programs, make strategic decisions, advise organizational executives, model ethical behaviors and two-way communication, and carry out diverse communication programs. Effective leadership in public relations can increase the value of communication management and help organizations make good decisions, build reputation, enhance organizational culture, and achieve specific goals (Berger & Meng, 2010).

Despite the growth of the profession and the documented value of excellent leaders in the field, however, little empirical research about leadership in public relations has been conducted until quite recently. Yet, something as vital as leadership in the field should be closely examined to help us learn what constitutes excellent leadership in the field and to determine how to create even better leaders for an uncertain future. If we believe that it's possible to systematically improve public relations leadership over time (Townsend, 2006), then we need to research it thoroughly, develop relevant theories, and articulate the developmental steps and educational requirements for building better leaders.

This kind of thinking led the Plank Center for Leadership in Public Relations at the University of Alabama to conduct a 23-country study of public relations leadership in 2012 (Berger, 2012). In the first phase of the study, nearly 4,500 global professionals shared their insights about key issues in the field, how those issues influence practice and leadership roles, what are the key dimensions of leadership, and what can be done to better prepare leaders. More than 800 professionals in the United States participated in this survey. In the second phase, in-depth interviews were conducted with 137 communication leaders in 15 countries.

This chapter provides a qualitative assessment of several key questions in the global survey. Sixteen U.S. communication executives participated in in-depth interviews to discuss how key issues affect their leadership roles, cultural and structural influences that shape their work, and crucial requirements for future leaders, among other topics. We first present the qualitative findings from the interviews. Then we discuss the current state of leadership development and conclude with an analysis of leadership needs for the future of the profession.

In the global survey, U.S. professionals said the top three issues that affect public relations practice today are dealing with the speed and volume of information flow (24.6% of survey participants), being prepared to deal with crises (16.4%), and managing the digital revolution (15.1%). Overall, in their interviews the 16 executives confirmed the pervasive power of the digital revolution, but said the quest to find top talent and to develop strong cultures in their organizations were equally pressing concerns. They also emphasized that future communication leaders must "first think like a business leader" and said their direct reporting relationship to the CEO or president was their strongest form of structural power—their passport to strategic decision making for the business. Their willingness to take risks or deal with difficult crises was the key tipping point in the careers of many of them.

Sample and Method

A list of 28 high-level corporate and agency public relations executives was constructed to provide a range of industry types and a balance of male and female leaders. All 28 leaders were invited to participate in phone interviews. Ten declined, and interviews were scheduled with the other 18 leaders. Using a 17-question guide (Appendix B), depth interviews were completed with 16 public relations executives (nine men, seven women), in the summer and fall of 2012; two other executives began but were unable to complete their interviews.

Of the 16 leaders, 12 were members of the Arthur W. Page Society (AWPS), which is a professional association for senior communications executives who are chief communications officers of *Fortune* 500 corporations, CEOs of the world's largest public relations agencies, and leading academics from top business and communications schools. The other four participants were high-level communication officers at their company or agency. Participants' years of experience ranged from 22 to 40 years, averaging 29 years. Interviewees represented a diverse mix of nine organization types: agencies (2), energy/utilities (3), financial services (2), food manufacturing and industrial manufacturing (2), information technology (3), insurance (2), medical instruments (1), and pharmaceutical (1).

The telephone interviews ranged from 42 to 58 minutes in length, averaging 48.2 minutes per interview. The interviews consisted of mostly directed questions and were recorded, transcribed, numbered, and then first coded and subsequently analyzed by two trained coders who used the constant comparative method of analysis. The collective transcripts yielded a 340-page document for analysis.

Top Issues for Leaders

Participants were first asked to name the top two issues they deal with on the job and explain how each issue affected their work and leadership role. Understanding key issues is important because they provide the context for practice and shape what leaders do (Rosebush, 2012). Three issues dominated: professional talent, organizational culture, and the digital revolution. Nine executives said the ongoing quest to find, develop, and retain top talent at all levels was a crucial concern. Seven executives said the challenge to build a transparent, participative, and information rich organizational culture was a major issue. Seven executives also said learning to manage the game-changing digital revolution was a top issue. Collectively, these three issues accounted for about three quarters of all issues mentioned.

Issue 1: The Hunt for Talent

The talent issue isn't new, but the public relations executives said globalization, changing stakeholders, growing transparency requirements, and the digital revolution and corresponding information flow have exacerbated it. Five women and four men (eight of nine organizational types) said the talent issue consumed a majority of their time and was the most crucial part of their leadership role because it affects not only hiring and training, but also strategizing, planning, structuring the function, project team assignments, and other practice elements. An energy company communication leader summarized this position: "Having the right team is more crucial than ever in our hyper work world today. The majority of my time is spent finding, developing, retaining and managing people."

Regarding hiring talent, an agency leader echoed the sentiments of many in highlighting the great need for digital and research specialists:

> We're looking for specialists now. We used to be all generalists and everybody knew a little bit about everything, but that's no longer working. So

we're looking for people with deep specialties in research, design, software development, social networking. We have an increased focus on people strategists who understand research and measurement.

However, hiring entry-level specialists is only part of the talent issue. The public relations leader at an insurance company emphasized the need for developing professionals already in the function, as well as hiring new skill sets at higher levels:

> I purposefully look outside to bring in change agents, people who have a different set of skills and who see the vision. We also are training people; I've sent folks through the Future Leaders program at Arthur Page so they can be exposed to the changing landscape we're facing. Sometimes it's very specific skills, and we do our own training. We don't have enough people who understand social media, for example. And what's amazing to me is within my staff, whenever a position has opened up in that area, the traditional communication folks are not gravitating to that. It just blows my mind. People, this is the future, you know? If you're not engaged in this, you're gonna become irrelevant.

A leader in an industrial manufacturing company described why finding the right people at all levels is so crucial:

> If you don't get the right people in the right jobs, it takes more people to get the work done. The budgets and the downsizings over the last five years are just not forgiving. When you have people who aren't carrying their full load, it puts stress on the people who are high performing. The organization I came from had so many weak links that I put really hard stress on two or three people while the others just came in, did their thing, and left. I just didn't have time to develop people. I inherited people, and now I have zero patience for those who don't perform at a high level.

This communication leader also spoke to another dimension of the talent issue—the challenge of preparing leaders and frontline managers to be more effective internal communicators and listeners:

> The lack of accountability of mid-level managers and supervisors for effective communication is frustrating. Most top leaders get it. But you get into that middle layer where most people have come up through the organization, and where their jobs are more tactical, less strategic, and they don't have a clue how to get the information out there. Nobody has taken the time to explain the communication needs of people, or they don't have the skills, and so the information goes into a black hole.

An information technology communication leader said the best teams blend old and new skills, and both new and longtime professionals require training:

> I need both traditionalists and millennials. The more traditional PR folks— they're great writers, great storytellers, and those skills are always going to be in high demand. However, the challenge is to get them to change how they look at news cycles, and faster ways to tell the story. So, there's a huge training need for them. The millennials are incredibly advanced with the channels, very open, very keen to tell that story. But the challenge with them is their writing skills aren't as strong, and their understanding of the business is still wanting.

A food manufacturing company leader best summarized the encompassing power of this ongoing issue for the communication leaders we interviewed:

> The talent issue touches virtually all aspects of my work: hiring and development, formation of teams, budgeting, strategic planning, resource allocations and so forth. Getting the right people in the right places to do the right things in the best way is the ongoing challenge in leadership. Isn't that what leadership's all about?

Issue 2: The Cultural Challenge

Three female and four male executives (six of nine organizational types) said the challenge to create a strong organizational culture was a top issue. Most described their work to help the organization become more transparent, reflect its values in decisions and actions, engage employees, and strengthen internal communications. A financial services communication leader described the competitive advantage that a strong culture can produce:

> I really believe in the authentic organization. Aligning people behind values and strategy so that we're all moving forward, making the right decisions, is absolutely related to maintaining reputation. When you have a strong organizational culture, when your values are exhibited, frankly that's the only way we're going to get there. The *how* is just as important as the *what*.

A pharmaceutical communication leader said her company's culture was strong because it's grounded thoroughly in their customers and communities:

> Culture is the huge piece that influences the agenda from the inside out. Our culture is one way to set our company apart. Getting people to engage in our culture internally in order to live in it externally is a very important

piece of who we are. We've found that by engaging in our patient communities, engaging with our physician thought leaders and patients and families, and engaging with the advocacy organizations—we can demonstrate that we are a different kind of company and show that we are living and breathing their experience, we are making it very personal.

Several public relations leaders, however, spoke about the cultural issue as a kind of barrier to more effective communications and shared practices. For example, a public relations leader in the manufacturing arena described the pressures of a results-driven culture:

> Our company culture is very unforgiving, very intense. It's high performing. It's all about results. It's a very, very difficult place for new people. It's a very closed organization. It's very siloed. Which means little centralized business strategy, little practice sharing, no talent sharing.

Another leader in an industrial manufacturing company described a communication culture that is tightly controlled, even in a complex global world:

> What we've learned over the years is frankly to be pretty prescriptive. This place has an incredibly disciplined and centered base of power and direction. That is reflected in large part by how we get work done. To give you a practical example—I clear every news release that's issued in the company. I clear and then get my CEO's agreement on any media relations opportunities for the top 50 people in the company. So, holy cow! That's pretty tight!

Issue 3: The Digital Revolution

Four male and three female executives (five organizational types) described the critical need to understand, strategically use, and fully evaluate the pervasive influence of digital technologies and social media. Most of the executives interviewed said that digital media was a game changer that touched the profession and the work of leaders in many ways—hiring, strategizing, measuring, counseling, and so forth.

A financial services communication executive said the flood of data was changing their company and providing the communication function with a real opportunity to lead:

> This is the way for us to connect with the business and to lead. We are using data to change the organization, not just the go-to-market approach, but also to drive process improvement on the total customer experience and to inform business decision making.

An energy company communication leader explained how social media affects what the communication team does and the time required to acquire, process, and distribute information:

> Social media has redefined everything we do, and here's how we are managing now. We outsourced some information gathering and preparation of briefing documents. They troll information all the time. We have a really solid briefing first thing every morning. I have a team that has a pretty good sense of what to bubble up, and I have a sense of what to bubble out, down, up, which means we are tethered 24/7. I've had to manage when to focus on information and when to be thoughtful about what to do with it. How we changed from three years ago is there are a lot more face-to-face meetings—a lot more communication among executives to make sure that everybody is fully informed and participating in problem solving.

Most agreed that the digital revolution was work altering in nature, but one information technology leader expressed concern about the growing lack of human touch:

> The art form of the relationship is looking like it will diminish as we increasingly change our work environment. A lot of my teams work virtually, from home. I came from the environment where you worked within a group, face to face, and so we learned the art form of relationship-based communications. We worked with journalists. We worked with analysts. So, one of the things that I'm constantly reminding my teams is a lot of what we do still, apart from being storytellers, is relationship based. And it's more important than ever as we move into the social digital world that sitting behind these channels are people, organizations that still have a real human need for connection and understanding.

Two communication leaders were more cautionary about digital and social media, though both cited many examples of their use in their organizations. An executive in a medical equipment company said,

> I always bristle a little bit when I hear social media being the biggest challenge. Social media is a channel. It's like many other channels, and we all need to be smart about the various channels and how to embrace them. But I always think that focusing on the channels is thinking like a communications person. Focusing on the issues is thinking like a business person. We're definitely using social media, but let's evaluate it critically. Let's think about what we want to accomplish with the channel first.

The Next Big Issue?

The communication leaders were preoccupied with talent, culture and the digital revolution. However, they mentioned several other issues, including managing corporate reputation, leading change of all kinds, engaging employees more fully, and transforming the function into a high-speed information processing, interpreting, and storytelling center.

When asked to forecast the next big issue, responses were wide ranging. Several leaders said that managing the digital revolution and the challenge of organizational culture were current and future challenges. Others said that producing more creative content, measuring the return on communication work, and redefining the roles of the profession and the professionals were looming as ever larger issues.

Six executives, however, said the next big issue was how communication leaders could become better and more capable business leaders. One financial services leader said, "We must take the time to truly learn the business and be able to talk it—I mean the numbers, the data, which get to the highest priorities of any business." Another put it more directly: "My responsibility is to help manage the company. In addition, I have specific responsibilities for communications. But it's the business first." This leader argued that it's not just about having a social media strategy; rather it is a social business strategy—how organizations adapt products and services and then sell them in a new social world.

The communication leader at a manufacturing company said thoughts about the future keep them awake on many nights:

> I don't look ahead as a thought leader in my profession; I look ahead as a business person who is trying to support the company's growth and strategy. I worry about things like the organizational structure in the Middle East, and how am I going to staff to support the business? What am I going to do in Russia when we finally acquire a business there? How do I learn the culture? I think it's less around thought leadership; the big issue for communication leaders is to understand the business and to align your team to support the business.

The importance of possessing business and financial knowledge, and seeing ones' self as a business leader resonates sharply with a depth study of employee communication leaders in 10 global companies (Burton, Grates, & Learch, 2013). In-depth interviews these leaders said it was business first, communication second. Having business acumen greatly added to their credibility and influence.

Cultural and Structural Influences on Leaders

Facilitators of Leadership Effectiveness

More than half (nine) of the executives said that reporting to the CEO had the greatest influence on their leadership effectiveness. Being part of the structure of the most powerful senior management team helped them be more effective functional leaders and more involved in the company's strategic decision making. This is consistent with the global leadership survey findings, in which participants in every country rated highest of seven leadership dimensions the strategic decision-making component (Berger, 2012). As one public relations leader in the insurance industry said,

> Number one, I report to the CEO. I'm seated at the management table, and I can't overestimate the importance of that. It's where all the big decisions happen, and all those decisions have crucial communication implications. I need to be there to lead that discussion.

Four executives said the best facilitator of their leadership role was the overall culture of their organizations, variously described as "collaborative," "consensus-oriented," and "cohesive" in nature. These leaders indicated that communication and public relations have long been a valued part of the organization.

Three leaders said their function's strong performance record over the years had earned the trust and respect of other leaders in the organization, and they felt pressure to continue that legacy. An executive in the information technology industry said,

> The reputation we've developed over the years has allowed us an extraordinary amount of autonomy, and we take that responsibility really seriously. We get a lot of credibility from the very top. They give us a lot of permission and latitude to pursue excellent communications.

Barriers to Leadership Effectiveness

Interview participants collectively named the following well-known cultural and structural barriers to greater public relations leadership and functional success (none mentioned more than three times):

- Internal politics (competing agendas, turf fights)
- Functional silos
- Limited resources
- History of public relations as a weak function
- Lack of empowerment versus other functions
- A "slow" culture of decision making

- Jargon-filled corporate communications that affect credibility
- CEOs who were too hands-on and controlling
- Too much time invested in endless reports and questionable measures
- Lack of understanding of the role of public relations

Three leaders mentioned functional silos and their negative impact. "Our organization is and always has been siloed," one said.

> All of our businesses have presidents and their own communications people. Thus, there is no overall central strategy, no best practices sharing, no talent sharing, no opportunity for people to move across the organization. We can't be as successful as we need to be.

The old issue of *they don't understand what we do* was named by two executives, who pointed to prior poor performance or inadequate functional leadership as the rationale for this issue. Two executives also said a big impediment was the "slow" cultures in which decisions were taken and enacted. "Everyone and I mean everyone gets a say in our company, and thus it takes so much time to move ahead," one said. "I like the idea of consensus, but we are moving too slowly in our industry. We need to run, not walk."

Characteristics and Qualities of Excellent Leaders

When asked to name two or three of most important qualities or characteristics of excellent leaders in the field, the 16 public relations executives named 14 of them, shown in the following list. These are quite consistent with the leadership qualities and dimensions in the integrated model of excellent leadership in public relations developed by Meng and Berger (2013):

- Business knowledge (7)
- Team-building capabilities (7)
- Visionary (6)
- Relationship-building skills (4)
- Listening skills (4)
- Communication knowledge and skills (4)
- Critical-thinking capabilities (3)

Others mentioned were authenticity, courage, passion, reflective-thinking skills, patience, visibility, and writing capabilities.

Being a business leader as well as a functional leader was again emphasized. As one executive pointedly stated, "Be a business person first—understand how the organization makes money." Possessing team-building skills and being visionary were often linked as the top two qualities. A communication leader in the insurance industry put it most succinctly: "The first thing is having the ability to set an agenda, or hold a vision. Then, to sell and communicate that vision to others and to build high-performing teams to execute to the vision." Another said, "The best leaders have a clear and compelling vision and can communicate it effectively. They can do that because they understand people. And they come to understand people by listening to them."

Will Future Leaders Be Different?

The communication executives answered this question with no and yes. A handful said that certain primary traits or characteristics of great leaders would remain vital, for example, honesty, visionary, ethical, motivational, good listener, and so forth. One financial services executive summarized this bundle of key traits and skills:

> The primary leadership traits shouldn't change. I think it's how you interact with people, how you motivate, how you communicate and engage with people. It's about empathy and enabling employees. I don't see those things disappearing. I think some of the great leaders of the past would still be great leaders today, and great leaders tomorrow.

On the other hand, most indicated future leaders would be different given the digital revolution, globalization, newly empowered stakeholders, and other dramatic changes sweeping the profession and world today. We grouped these changes into four themes.

First, future leaders will be better educated, will come from more diverse economic backgrounds, and will be more business savvy. As one financial service executive said,

> They'll understand how the organization works. They'll speak like the CEO about how the business runs. They'll understand the financials. It won't be enough to be a good communicator; you will have to be a good businessperson, too. That's the direction of our evolution.

Second, future leaders will be more knowledgeable of, and reliant on research, data, and measurement. A leader in the information industry said, "They will be heavy data users and analyzers. And they will have grown up thinking digital first."

Third, hope was expressed that future leaders will be bolder, more culturally aware. An agency leader said,

> People in communications positions are often too timid. They always try to be politically correct. I don't think we do ourselves any favors by allowing other people to be the ones driving the business and coming up with the big ideas. That's a missed opportunity.

Fourth, the leadership role is constantly evolving, it will be more important than ever, and the work of public relations will be more diffused in the organization. "Here's the thing," an energy company leader said,

> We cannot carry the weight of our corporate reputations in our department. It's as much about influence within our organizations to influence their behaviors, their decisions, so we don't disconnect from society. We have to sensitize our organizations, educate them so they are as much stewards of our reputation as we are.

Tipping Points for Success

We asked the communication leaders to talk about their careers and identify what events or experiences were "tipping points" for them—key moments or experiences that helped their careers take off. They mentioned 18 tipping points: successfully dealing with challenging crises (5) and taking risks on the job (4) were cited most often. "Risk taking" here refers to seeking out or volunteering for difficult assignments. One insurance communication leader said, "I always looked for opportunities that scared me because learning drives me, and tough challenges are great teachers. I took assignments nobody else wanted." An executive in the information technology industry also equated risk taking with learning: "Taking risks helped me enormously. I moved out of my comfort zone, learned new skills and discovered new ideas."

Other tipping points included international work assignments, experience in "rough and tumble" politics at a young age, working in a "do everything" first job, initiating and leading a major change initiative, acquiring an MBA and gaining business knowledge, and having a great mentor who opened doors.

Tipping points are diverse and can involve other life experiences, too. For the majority of this sample of executives, however, taking risks and performing well under fire in crises were experiences that spurred professional growth and development. As several executives explained, these experiences increased self-confidence, enriched critical thinking capabilities, expanded networks of contacts, and sharply raised awareness and recognition of performance. These findings are consistent with those of Berger, Reber, and Heyman (2007), who found that 40% of the 97 communication executives they interviewed said their tipping points involved crisis management or risk taking.

Current State of Leadership Development

The landscape of leadership development opportunities in the United States is populated with diverse but disconnected structures and approaches (Berger & Meng, 2010). Adolescents can develop leadership skills and knowledge in school projects and in social, religious, and community clubs and organizations. At the university level, students can develop leadership skills, style and capabilities in their course work and through club activities, mentors, internships, campaigns, and service learning projects. In addition, "leadership studies" programs, often linked to business schools or honors colleges, have grown steadily in higher education in the past 20 years (Greenwald, 2010).

Erzikova and Berger (2012) found that university public relations educators believe they help develop leaders. Few offer specific leadership courses, but elements of leadership are integrated throughout public relations classes. Educators said the most important leadership qualities they help students develop are a strong ethical orientation, problem-solving abilities, and communication knowledge and expertise. Rogers (2012) found that faculty advisors for Public Relations Student Society of America chapters demonstrated, taught, or modeled excellent leadership in their roles with students. Indeed, role models in the field can have a powerful impact on perceptions of excellent leadership, as well as spur interest in becoming a leader (Berger, Meng, & Heyman, 2009).

Three broad approaches to leadership development are possible at the professional level. First, some organizations provide their own educational programs and activities for rising managers and directors. GE, IBM, Southwest, and 3M are examples of companies with excellent internal development programs (O'Connell, 2010). Many companies and agencies offer some form of in-house development for those identified as rising stars, but the best share certain common approaches. "They address leadership development on multiple fronts, from articulating how leadership behavior needs to change to meet the challenges of the future to managing their pools of successors for mission-critical roles" (O'Connell, 2010, para. 5). Ultimately, perhaps it's up to communications leaders to be assertive in creating individual/team development plans. Leaders who do will optimize their existing talent and raise performance, whereas leaders who don't or delay will be at risk because management expectations for high (and immediate) performance continue to rise.

Second, professional associations like the Public Relations Society of America, the Arthur W. Page Society, and the Institute for Public Relations also help prepare communication leaders. They do so by providing opportunities for members to lead teams, committees, and initiatives in the organizations; build social networks; and participate in specific leadership development programs or tracks. The Page Society's Future Leaders Experience is one of the most comprehensive approaches. This 2-year program consists of six 3-day learning modules and is "designed to prepare high-performing communication executives for the role of the chief communication officer" (Future Leaders Experience, 2012). Communication leaders from companies and agencies "teach" the modules, which rely heavily on in-class simulations, case studies, and extensive networking opportunities.

Third, numerous leadership suppliers and trainers offer a vast array of programs and workshops; the Center for Creative Leadership is one of the better known. A growing number of university business schools offer intensive management and executive development programs. In fact, businesses invest heavily in leadership training programs for their employees—more than $170 billion annually (Myatt, 2012). Overall, a plethora of training and development opportunities are available to those interested in advancing their knowledge and skills or those selected for leadership development, at many stages in life. Still, it's debatable whether leadership in public relations today is any better than in the past; we have no way of knowing because the outcomes are not measured in any systematic manner.

Leadership Needs for the Future

This book opened with the question, How much better would PR leaders be if they had intentional preparation for leadership positions (Townsend, 2006)? We imagine many would agree that leaders might be better, though gaining consensus around what those preparations should entail would be difficult. Myatt (2012), for example, bemoans the money and time spent on rote leadership *training*. He argues for focusing on personal leadership *development*. "Don't train leaders—coach them, mentor them, disciple them, and develop them. Training is transactional—development is transformational" (Myatt, 2012, p. 2).

A number of issues associated with existing public relations development programs in the United States have been identified. These include limited access to formal programs for many professionals, high costs of participation, varying content and teaching approaches, and the absence of metrics to assess either short- or long-term outcomes of the training (Berger & Meng, 2010). Middlebrooks and Allen (2008) raised these and other issues, too. They described the field of leadership education as a "dizzyingly complex landscape" (Middlebrooks & Allen, 2008, p. 77) in a world marked by new realities that will require some changes in leadership competencies and possibly even new conceptualizations of what leaders are. We have adapted some of their issues and questions to our discussion here of leadership in public relations.

Drawing from their work, for example, what is the appropriate content for leadership development programs in our field, and how should it be taught? What is an appropriate development continuum for future leaders? How do we incorporate real world context, organizational culture, and political structures into development programs? Many leader training programs or workshops are brief and intense: Are these sufficient given the time it takes to develop relevant skills, capabilities, and behaviors?

How do we gauge the effectiveness of leadership education and development programs? What measures should be used? We know that some who are trained become successful leaders while others do not. Why? Malcolm Goldsmith (2007), personal coach for many *Fortune* 100 CEOs and provider of leadership development for many executives, reports that fully 30% of the executives who undergo his intensive training programs go back to work and do absolutely nothing differently. How much learning and development actually travel back to the job and become translated into meaningful improvements?

Through the work of the Plank Center and other research initiatives, we're beginning to better understand the qualities, dimensions, and characteristics of excellent leadership in public relations. These findings are providing the basis for constructing a theory of excellent leadership. The communication executives we interviewed spoke at length about how the search for talent, organizational culture, and the digital revolution have an impact on their work. Yet, these are but a few of the many issues with which they deal in our dynamic and complex world.

We need to expand our conversation about this crucial topic and create a national agenda for the research and preparation of the next generation of leaders. So much of our work in public relations is grounded on the need for research and for informed and strategic decision making. Is the development of future leaders any different? Shouldn't the same approaches be applied to help prepare them to successfully navigate the new hyper-realities of urgency, transparency, globality, and complexity?

References

Berger, B. (2012). *Key themes and findings: The cross-cultural study of leadership in public relations and communication management.* Tuscaloosa, AL: Plank Center for Leadership in Public Relations. Available online at http://plankcenter.ua.edu/wp-contentuploads/2012/10/Summary-of-Themes-and-Findings-Leader-Survey.pdf

Berger, B., & Meng, J. (2010). Public relations practitioners and the leadership challenge. In. R. L. Heath (Ed.), *The SAGE handbook of public relations* (pp. 421–434). Thousand Oaks, CA: Sage.

Berger, B., Meng, J., & Heyman, W. (2009, March). *Role modeling in public relations: The influence of role models and mentors on leadership beliefs and qualities.* Paper presented at the 12th International Public Relations Conference in Miami, FL.

Berger, B., Reber, B., & Heyman, W. (2007). You can't homogenize success in communication management. PR leaders take diverse paths to the top. *International Journal of Strategic Communication, 1*(1), 53–71.

Burton, K., Grates, G., & Learch, D. (2013). *Best in class practices in employee communication.* Gainsville, FL: Institute for Public Relations. Available online at www.instituteforpr.org/iprwp/wp-content/uploads/IPR_Best_in_Class_White_Paper_Final_04_2013.pdf

Erzikova, E., & Berger, B. (2012). Leadership education in the PR curriculum: Reality, opportunities, and benefits. *Public Relations Journal, 6*(3). Available online at www.prsa.org/Intelligence/PRJournal/Documents/2012ErzikovaBerger.pdf

Future Leaders Experience. (2012). Arthur A. Page Society [Brochure]. Available online at www.awpagesociety.com/wp-content/uploads/2012/12/AWPS_Future-Leaders-Brochure-2012.pdf

Goldsmith, M. (2007). *What got you here won't get you there.* New York, NY: Hyperion Press.

Greenwald, R. (2010, December 5). Today's students need leadership training like never before. *The Chronicle of Higher Education.* Available online at http://chronicle.com/article/Todays-Students-Need/1256041/

Holmes, P. (2012, July 23). Global PR industry up eight percent to $10bn. Available online at http://globalpragencies.com/analysis/2012-global-pr-industry-eight-percent-10bn

Manekin, M. (2001, August 16). PR nation. *Valley Advocate.* Available online at www.ratical.org/ratville/PRnation.html

Meng, J., & Berger, B. (2013). An integrated model of excellent leadership in public relations: Dimensions, measurement, and validation. *Journal of Public Relations Research*, 25(2), 141–167.

Middlebrooks, A., & Allen, S. J. (2008). Leadership education: New challenges, continuing issues. *International Leadership Journal*, 1(1), 77–85.

Myatt, M. (2012, December 19). The reason leadership development fails. *Forbes*. Available online at www.forbes.com/sites/mikewyatt/2012/12/19/the-1-reason-leadership-development-fails/

O'Connell, P. (2010, February 16). How companies develop great leaders. *Bloomberg BusinessWeek*. Available online at www.businessweek.com/stories/2010-02-16/how-companies-develop-great-leadersbusinessweek-business-news-stock-market-and-financial-advice

Public Relations Society of America. (2013). PRSA—advancing the profession and the professional. Available online at www.prsa.org/

Rogers, C. (2012). *Leadership development: Where do PRSSA faculty advisors stand?* Unpublished research paper prepared for the Plank Center for Leadership in Public Relations, University of Alabama, Tuscaloosa.

Rosebush, J. S. (2012, March 30). Why great leaders are in short supply [Blog entry]. Available online at http://blogs.hbr.org/cs/2012/03/why_great_leaders_are_in_short.html

Townsend, D. (2006). From the editors' clipboard. *Journal of Leadership Education*, 5(3), viii–ix.

SECTION IV
Creating the Future

This concluding section summarizes the research, examines key themes in the findings, and looks to the future of leadership in public relations with respect to practice, education, and additional research. We argue that the profession needs to intentionally and systemically address leadership development and assessment. We hope scholars and practitioners of public relations and communication management will benefit from this deep exploration of the crucial concept of leadership.

20

THE GLOBAL STUDY AND LEADERSHIP IN THE FUTURE

Bruce K. Berger and Juan Meng

The global leadership study underscores the profound transition underway in the profession and brings into focus the challenges and complexities that leaders in public relations confront. Although they play many roles, public relations leaders are above all sensemakers—they gather, process, interpret, and distill vast amounts of information in order to determine what's happening, what it means, what's relevant to their organization, how it's relevant, and what needs to be done about it. They then interpret and explain to others what the information or issue means to the organization. In doing so they attempt to influence meaning and help the organization reach collective understanding as the basis for appropriate decisions and actions.

This sensemaking role has always been essential, but our study suggests that the role today and in the future grows ever more vital and difficult due to a rapidly altering world and profession in which information is both raw material and final product. Our study examined this dynamic world, and through the interviews and survey results, we identified a number of themes and storylines about leadership in the field. In this concluding chapter we first discuss these themes and their implications, and then take a look at future leaders in public relations. Finally, we present implications of the study for practice, education, and future research.

10 Themes in the Findings

Each of the 10 themes or patterns discussed in the following grows out of analysis of the survey data and the interview transcripts by members of the international research team. We observed many patterns in the data, but here we discuss 10 of the most significant themes, each of which requires attention and consideration from organizations and professional associations.

1. The digital revolution transforms practice and leaders worldwide. The first part is old news, but the emerging story is how this transformation affects the roles, vision, and strategic decisions of public relations leaders. Nearly two thirds of survey participants rated four issues as most important, all linked to the digital revolution: (a) managing the speed and flow of information, (b) managing the digital revolution and rise of social media, (c) being prepared to deal with fast-moving crises, and (d) improving the measurement of communication effectiveness.

This theme was equally prominent in the interviews, where many executives said the digital revolution was a game changer that touched numerous aspects of their daily practice. These included hiring new employees with relevant skill sets, the structure of the communication function, strategic and tactical plans and choices, crisis planning and response, employee training programs, meeting venues, flexible work programs, new platforms for sharing best practices, environmental scanning, and the round-the-clock need to converse with external groups and individuals. A few of the executives said they were "on top" of digital media, a few admitted they were far behind, but most said it was an intense daily challenge and would likely remain so into the future; they were constantly learning and applying on the fly.

2. Soft skills and self-insights are the Holy Grail of future leaders. Digital media skills and enhanced measurement skills are vital for future leaders. But global practitioners consistently said that mastery of the so-called soft people skills—better listening, cultural sensitivity, emotional intelligence, conflict resolution capabilities, and change management skills—is essential for improving PR leaders for an uncertain future. More widely publicized systemic changes in the profession such as accreditation, a core global education curriculum, measurement standards, and enforcement of ethical codes, are also important, but survey results suggest systemic changes run second to soft skills.

These results yield a number of questions: Who, for example, is responsible for developing and providing training in soft skills? Should individuals or individual organizations tackle the issue? What's been done in the past, and is there anything we can apply from past experiences? Do university education programs need to be restructured to include more such training? What's the role of professional associations? Should leadership training and development initiatives be more planned and systematic for the profession globally?

3. Leaders and followers see the practice differently. The survey revealed that leaders and followers hold sharply different views about (a) the most important issues, (b) how future leaders should be developed, (c) the extent to which their organizations support two-way communication and shared power, and (d) the quality of current leadership performance. We imagine that leaders often rate their own performance higher than do their followers, but the divide between the two in this study is Grand Canyon sized.

The Summated Leadership Index also suggests there is a great deal of room for improvement in leadership in the field, everywhere. Closing this leadership gap first requires acknowledging that it exists, then preparing and executing programs to address the issue, and finally assessing results and acting on them. Does the collective will to address the gap exist? For us, the answer to this question is one of the keys to what happens next in terms of leadership development.

4. Measurement remains an 800-pound gorilla in public relations units in many organizations. Survey results indicated that the salience and valence of media coverage still rules measurement approaches in most surveyed countries. Yet, the measurement issue ranked as the third issue among 10 big issues in the field. What's going on here? The lack of meaningful measures of communication outcomes also was a central topic in executive interviews in several countries, notably Brazil, Mexico, and Russia. In Brazil, for example, the interviewed communication leaders argued that solving the measurement conundrum was a great way to build credibility into the function internally and to elevate the profession's image externally.

Given the sharply increased focus on measurement standards by several groups and organizations today, it seems likely that better and more reliable and meaningful measurement approaches and standards—and the moment of truth—are close at hand. Who will embrace these approaches, and who gets left behind? It seems clear to us that measurement leaders at the individual, functional and organizational levels will capture competitive advantage through such expertise.

5. Excellent leadership in public relations is multidimensional, complex, and . . . global? Everyone has an opinion and a personal mental model regarding what constitutes excellent leadership in public relations, based largely on personal experiences and observations. This study tested a previously developed, seven-dimension public relations leadership model that integrates individual skills, traits, behaviors, and cultural and structural factors. Factor analysis of the dimensions suggests the model is a reliable PR leadership scale in the countries studied.

More work needs to be done to refine and test the model, but it nevertheless provides an intriguing framework for examining leadership development, planning and evaluation in the field and classroom. Could a refined model and corresponding theory help guide preparation of an assessment tool or set of tools for evaluating leadership performance and identifying areas for attention on a national or even international scale?

6. For men and women, it's the same destination, but a different journey. When Betsy Plank entered the profession in the 1940s, the field was more than 95% male. Today, the practice is as much as 70% female, or more, in Brazil, Hong Kong, Latvia, the United States, and elsewhere, and women are ascending in greater numbers to leadership positions. Our survey provides evidence that women and men view leadership, and the possibilities and processes of becoming a leader, somewhat differently. In the study, women rated the following significantly higher than did men: 8 of the 10 top issues, all seven leadership dimensions, and all 12 approaches to future leader development. On the other hand, men perceived themselves significantly more often than did women to be leaders in the profession. Men also rated significantly higher than did women the performance of the top communication leader, the presence of two-way communication in their organizations, and the extent to which the CEO understood the value of public relations. Some possible reasons for these variations were discussed in Chapter 9.

The interviews with senior PR executives provided a somewhat different perspective—gender was not raised as an issue in the context of finding and retaining top talent, one of the pivotal issues for the executives, according to interview participants. Leaders in China, India, Latvia, Russia, and the United States said they were constantly on the lookout for individuals—age, gender, and organizational type didn't matter—who combined a multidimensional set of capabilities and a portfolio of diverse experiences which prepared them to be successful in capitalizing on opportunities and solving problems wherever they worked. They also felt that increasing the number of leaders at all levels with such capabilities would advance the profession and elevate credibility with a variety of audiences.

7. Some cultural and regional patterns are intriguing, but meaning is elusive.
Comparative studies can enrich our understanding of cultural similarities and differences, and some of which were highlighted in our global survey. As noted in Chapter 1, however, national and cultural comparisons are fraught with problems, which we explore in more detail later in this chapter. Nevertheless, here is one intriguing example from our study. Practitioners in the three Latin American countries (Brazil, Chile, and Mexico) gave the highest mean ratings, of all countries, to all seven of the leadership dimensions and to 7 of the 12 approaches to leader development. On the other hand, professionals in the German-speaking countries and the United Kingdom generally assigned the lowest mean scores to many issues, the leadership dimensions, and the development approaches.

Is this a reflection of cultural differences? Is it the product of other demographic variations among survey participants? Latin American participants, for example, were more often women, younger, and working in lower levels of the communication structure than were German and English professionals. Or does the unique history and state of practice for the profession in each of these regions come into play and drive these differences? Other factors also are possible, such as varying educational backgrounds, the extent to which practitioners are experienced survey participants, or differing views about the relative numerical rankings for answers. The other questions are difficult to answer, but we believe that possessing cultural knowledge helps leaders at all levels to better manage change and conflict, inspire followers, and build trust in their global organizations.

8. Lack of understanding of the role and value of public relations still constrains practice. The interviews with 137 leaders provided insights into some of the organizational cultural and structural factors that facilitate or impede practice. One of the most mentioned constraints is the perceived longtime lack of understanding and support for public relations by other executives and managers in organizations. This issue may be receding into the background in some countries and regions, but it looms large in the foreground in others, and it was discussed at length in interviews in Brazil, India, Latvia, Mexico, Spain, and Russia. Leaders in those countries said that lack of understanding of the practice, or misperceptions of it are reflected in low-level hierarchical positions, a focus on technical production rather than strategic management, limited resources, lack of participation in crucial decision-making arenas, internal politics, and so forth.

On the other hand, a strong reporting relationship with the CEO and other organizational leaders, along with clear recognition of the value of public relations, was linked in the German-speaking countries and the United States to participation in strategic decision making, an emerging role as organizational manager, and creation of a supportive organizational culture. Strong relationships with other organizational executives were the greatest form of structural support for public relations practice.

This support seemed to be a result of (a) the excellent work of one or several communication leaders who imbued the function with legitimacy based on their performance or (b) the product of an accumulated track record of excellent performance of the communication function as measured in results and outcomes. This supports the claims of communication leaders in the other countries, especially in Latin America, that measurement is the answer to many problems, including demonstrating the value of the function and elevating its reputation.

9. The potential power of individual leaders and of professional and educational systems to affect practice should not be underestimated or marginalized. During interviews in Germany, India, Latvia, Russia, and the United States, among others, a recurring point was that an individual leader, or an association of excellent leaders in the field, can have a dramatic and positive impact on what the profession does, what is accomplished, and how it is viewed. The power of one to make a difference, and the power of systems to formalize and drive change at scale, was expressed in a number of ways.

For example, a great leader can set the tone for communications in an organization and generate strong understanding of, and support for the work. A great leader can help build a culture for communication. A great leader can implant measurement standards and research practices into the communication mental model and planning and implementation in their organization. A great communication leader can motivate and inspire performance to unimagined levels. And great educational and professional systems can dramatically multiply knowledge and the effects of leadership in the field.

At the same time, some of those we interviewed pointed to a lack of great leaders across the profession, as well as to newer, less productive professional associations that contribute little to strengthening and elevating the practice. Interviewees in the Chinese-speaking countries, India, Latvia, and Russia, for example, described an absence of excellent leaders and role models in the profession. Others spoke about an uneven quality of education in public relations in their country or the limited scope or questionable quality of leadership development programs offered by their communication associations. In fact, leadership development programs for public relations professionals are limited or unavailable in many countries in the global study. As one communication executive put it, "We lack a leadership culture in public relations that supports and nourishes those who will take us into the future."

10. The transformation in public relations reaches beyond the digital dimension. The transformation driven by digital media has attracted great attention. Our survey confirms the significance of this change globally. But other profound changes are occurring, or seem likely to occur, and they will affect who leads in the future, how they are prepared to lead, and where the profession goes. Our survey captured the growing need for professionals to cultivate stronger "soft skills." Meeting this challenge may entail significant changes in education and professional development programs that have focused on boosting core technical and analytical skills.

The continued feminization of the profession, the somewhat different views of leadership held by men and women, the generational differences, and the sharp divide between leaders and followers underscore a transformation in public relations that goes beyond the digital and reflects an interrelated set of deep changes that infuses practice today and shapes it for tomorrow, everywhere. Excellent leaders in the future will make sense of these changes: they will understand them and their corresponding implications and will act on them. To encourage that development, more leadership research needs to be done, and the taken-for-granted considerations of leadership in the field need to be dropped in favor or some rich and ongoing dialogue on the topic and some important systemic changes that will focus on the future and those who will lead in the future.

A Profile of Future Leaders in Public Relations

During the interviews, we asked the communication leaders to look ahead 10 to 15 years and describe how future leaders might differ from current leaders, given the rapidly evolving world and practice. Many said some qualities, skills, and characteristics would remain the same, but future leaders would be significantly different in other respects. One U.S. financial services vice president best captured the notion of enduring traits or qualities:

> The primary leadership traits shouldn't change. I think it's how you interact with people, how you motivate, how you communicate and engage with people. It's about empathy and enabling employees. I don't see those things disappearing. I think some of the great leaders in the past would still be great leaders today, and great leaders tomorrow.

On the other hand, the communication executives described a number of changes and new requirements for future leaders, and their comments were fairly consistent across the sample. We used their most frequent comments to create the following composite of hypothetical future leaders in public relations:

> *More public relations leaders in the future will be women, given the high percentages of females in the profession, especially in emerging countries and economies.*
>
> *Future leaders will be better educated and armed with more specialist information and multidisciplinary education. A growing percentage of leaders will possess degrees in public relations or strategic communication, but they will also have a better understanding of advertising, marketing, technology, economics and business. Continuous education and training will be required to keep up with an ever expanding pool of knowledge and seismic changes in a world where the half-life of any acquired knowledge set is sharply reduced. In these and other ways future public relations leaders will increasingly be seen as business and organization leaders, as well as communication leaders.*
>
> *Having grown up wired, future leaders will think digital first, though hopefully not to the exclusion of human touch and interaction. Decision-making will grow out of analysis of mountains of data and carefully targeted research, rather than intuition, past experience, or gut-instinct. Measurement will be refined, routine and demanding. Transparency will be a practice, not an objective. Future leaders will possess extraordinary communication competence and knowledge, they will have a stronger internal and team focus, and they will combine great organizational clarity and a compelling vision for how communication connects the organization with others in the world.*
>
> *Future public relations leaders will have a global view and a work passport rich with global working assignments and diverse projects. They will be generalists of the world rather than media specialists. They will be motivational and inclusive—more given to hands on engagement and role modeling than to speeches and canned presentations. To lead will increasingly mean to go live, in person; a glut of social and digital media connections and conversations will drive people to seek out live leaders and activities. Future leaders will be risk-takers, fire fighters and formidable change agents who professionally and persistently push to create cultures for communication by knocking down internal barriers and driving engagement.*

Above all, they will be ethically branded, and they will be courageous—willing to speak truth to power and to challenge those who abuse or misuse power.

Implications of the Global Study

Drawing from the results of the quantitative and qualitative studies, and mindful of the vision for future leaders in the field, we discuss implications for practice, education, and research in this section. If the profession is serious about trying to improve overall leadership in public relations and communication management, then we believe there are some important considerations and steps to take in each of these arenas.

Communication Practice and the Development of Leaders

The most successful public relations programs and campaigns are often those grounded in research, guided by clear and measureable goals, shaped by appropriate strategies, carried out with the best tactics, and measured or assessed for results. National or international efforts to enhance leadership in the field should follow the same formula. Although many seem to agree that we should improve leadership in public relations, there appears to be little will power, wherewithal, or collective interest in doing so. Thus, the major implication of the global study for practice is the answer to this question: What if anything will be done to advance leadership in the field on a national or international level?

This is not to suggest that we don't have some great leaders in the field, or that development efforts are totally absent. We are blessed with some great leaders; some individuals and organizations are serious about developing leadership capabilities and capacities, and they do so steadfastly. Who knows, perhaps therein lies some of their individual or organizational competitive advantage. But there is little research, no compelling urgency, no systematic plan or approach for strengthening leadership in the field.

Everyone is busy, of course, and racing 24/7 just to keep up. New priorities emerge with frightening speed in organizations, and changes pile up on top of changes. Organizational and professional association agendas are packed with other urgent matters—Revolution 2.0, branding, best practices, content strategies, employee engagement, trust issues, organizational alignment, crisis communications, and so forth. The need to learn and adopt new tools and technologies seems relentless. So although leadership is considered of great importance, it nevertheless is somewhat taken for granted and is not an urgent priority.

So making leadership in public relations a priority is that most difficult first step. How might we begin? As we noted in earlier research (Berger & Meng, 2010), a national or international forum, consisting of key individuals from a number of associations and bodies, seems the best route to prioritizing leadership. Such a forum would drive dialogue about the topic and begin to build some shared understanding and consensus regarding the nature of leadership and its crucial dimensions. Current forums devoted to creating measurement standards might be a good model.

This would also provide a mechanism for beginning to review and take stock of what already exists—current development programs, the content of such programs, delivery mechanisms, best practices, and any corresponding metrics for examining success. Communication leaders who were interviewed in the global study indicated great interest in leadership development, but indicated that little formal development or training was available in their countries, apart from the United States. Other issues were simply more important.

On the other hand, a large number of national and international professional associations and centers exist and provide a framework for coordinated action at scale. In addition, a small but growing body of research about leaders and leadership in communication management provides important insights about the shape or content of leadership development. The integrated model of excellent leadership and the research findings regarding future development needs in the global study highlight a number of areas for consideration. Nevertheless, some kind of spark seems needed to ignite interest and spur action in leadership development in the field.

Implications for University Education

The interviews confirmed that university public relations education programs are a growth industry, though program contents and requirements range widely from technical-practical concentrations to theory-heavy orientations. Previous research (Erzikova & Berger, 2012) has shown that few educational programs include specific courses in leadership. However, leadership components and experiences are incorporated in some education programs through case studies, visiting professional lectures, campaign projects, shadowing exercises, and other approaches.

Educators have said they are advocates for leadership, and they help develop leadership awareness and skills among students by developing critical-thinking skills, focusing on codes of ethics and ethical problem solving, and modeling leadership behaviors in their classes (Erzikova & Berger, 2012). In addition, leadership development opportunities are available through team leadership assignments in classes, as well as leadership roles in the Public Relations Student Society of America chapters or other campus and community organizations. Internships and campaign projects provide access to potential role models and mentors on the job.

Most undergraduate programs apparently don't emphasize the kinds of soft skills highlighted in the survey—listening skills, conflict resolution, change management, emotional intelligence and so forth. Far more time and attention in classes are devoted to honing technical skills (e.g., writing and design for diverse media) and analytical skills (e.g., audience segmentation and case study analysis).

In looking toward the future, it seems worthwhile for educators to consider adding courses in listening and conflict resolution, for example, to their curricula. Given the difficulties associated with adding new courses to such curricula, an alternative is to restructure existing classes to incorporate parallel development of soft skills. Listening skills and exercises might be built into PR management classes, for example, while some change management principles and requirements can be addressed in case analysis in a variety of courses.

Other elements of leadership that can be incorporated are available from rich resource centers at the Plank Center for Leadership in Public Relations at the University of Alabama and/or the Page Center for Public Communication at Pennsylvania State University. Both centers provide rich leader resources including video interviews, speeches, print and electronic publications, and other materials that can be used in a variety of assignments in many PR classes to sharpen focus on leaders and leadership in the field.

A radical third alternative would be for educators to adopt a new mind-set about public relations education, one in which they no longer see their programs responding to marketplace needs, but rather in which *they* lead—they lead the profession based on a vision for the future that sees *every student as a potential leader who requires essential leadership skills.* Curricula are then designed around the future, and regarding this, the soft skills identified in the survey, along with the seven leadership dimensions in the integrated model for leadership in public relations, provide a sturdy framework for thinking and planning.

We can do far worse than to orient our public relations education programs around the seven dimensions of leadership examined in our study: self-dynamics (attributes, vision, reflection), ethical orientation, team collaboration/building, relationship building, strategic decision-making capability, communication knowledge management, and organizational culture and structure (power). Such an approach shifts our focus from a heavy communication knowledge management and media concentration to a more holistic approach that draws in the value of self-reflection, greater cultural sensitivity and awareness, and elements of power and strategic decision making.

Future Research Directions

The global study provides a baseline of data regarding leadership dimensions, development needs, key issues and strategies in the field, self-perceptions about a variety of topics, insights about future leaders, and the influences of culture and structure on leaders' roles and responsibilities. Like all studies, it reflects some weaknesses, notably different sample sizes and concerns with national comparisons, as discussed in Chapters 1 and 3. We also were disappointed that efforts to include practitioners in the Middle East region were largely unsuccessful. Despite these shortcomings, the study represents an important step in expanding our knowledge of leadership in the field from a global perspective. The study also points us in some future research directions, which we discuss in this section.

A number of intriguing research questions arise from the findings. On a smaller scale, some countries appear to be more advanced or successful in managing key issues. South Korean practitioners, for example, seemed to be quite advanced in their use of, or their confidence in communication technologies to help deal with the speed and flow of information. Why? What can we learn from South Korea? Differences also exist at the organizational level: Public relations leaders we interviewed from a handful of companies claimed they were "on top" of digital media or the transparency issue and were now focused on other matters. Could case studies or more depth interviews provide valuable insights into issue management strategies and tactics in diverse organizations and countries?

Leadership development programs represent another rich area for attention. Analysis of development approaches, and especially the use of metrics for assessing leadership improvement within the context of differing cultures, might provide the basis for a more consistent and systemic approach to developing our leaders. One valuable project would entail inventorying existing leadership development programs—their content, approaches, and associated metrics—now offered through university education offerings, professional association programs, or for-profit suppliers of development programs. Such an inventory could be the basis for formulating best approaches to development, or identifying crucial gaps in development.

These are just a few of many research possibilities. The Plank Center is interested in these and other efforts, but especially in two larger areas that are central to our global study: (a) the challenges inherent in multigroup or multi-country assessments and (b) development and extension of the integrated model of excellent leadership in public relations. We conclude the chapter with discussion of each area.

Multiple-Group Assessment in Measurement Invariance

In our global study we attempted to advance international public relations research by retesting the integrated leadership model of public relations (Meng & Berger, 2013) to determine if members of different backgrounds, regions, and cultures ascribe the same meanings to the seven leadership dimensions. More important, we advanced our test by integrating some other key constructs such as *issue management* and *leadership development* to enrich leadership theory development.

This is important because globalization continues to drive rapid growth of international promotional and communication strategies (Cui, Griffith, Cavusgil, & Dabic, 2006) and nonlocal consumption alternatives (Alden, Steenkamp, & Batra, 2006). The success of global corporations increasingly relies on their ability to transfer competitive communication strategies to local subsidiaries (Chung, 2001). Therefore, it is not surprising that the number of studies examining cross-national communication strategies is growing (e.g., Chen, 1996; Singh, 1995). Although such research provides valuable insights, few of the studies have emphasized the importance of minimizing the possibility of underlying biases in cross-national or multiple-group empirical research due to faulty data collection and/or analysis.

Demographic, ethnic, cultural, and psychological heterogeneity within certain regions has led researchers to question the standardization of promotional strategies in the international environment. Though some recommended approaches to avoid such problems have been addressed, for example, controlling for biases before or during data collection (e.g., Griffith & Schuster, 2002), the assessment of measurement invariance (MI) of data already collected has not been applied by public relations and communication scholars.

Multiple-group and cross-national comparative research has been conducted in marketing, organizational behavior, and communication studies, among others, and the importance of minimizing underlying biases in cross-national empirical research cannot be disputed. Such cross-cultural or cross-group data are frequently collected at the individual level using surveys. Before the research results can be compared across cultures or groups, it must be shown that subjects from different cultures or groups ascribed to essentially the same meanings for the measurement items. This draws attention to a potential source of bias: If results from cross-national or cross-group analyses are different from what was expected, researchers must question "whether the results are measurement and scaling artifacts or true cultural differences" (Mullen, 1995, p. 574). Observed differences in the results may not be due to the manipulations or relationships of interest, but rather to systematic cultural or group differences in interpretation and/or responses.

Therefore, the assessment of measurement invariance has been addressed by scholars in order to ensure comparability (e.g., Cheung & Rensvold, 2002; Mullen, 1995; Myers, Calantone, Page, & Taylor, 2000; Steenkamp & Baumgartner, 1998; Vandenberg & Lance, 2000). As a technique widely used by social science researchers, measurement invariance addresses the question of whether the same models "hold" across different populations (Mullen, 1995), that is, whether items used in survey-type instruments mean the same thing to members of different groups (Cheung & Rensvold, 2002). Meaning may be confounded, for example, when consumers' interpretations of a given construct and responses to certain scale items vary across cultures in which different languages are used and when researchers use translated versions of a survey instrument (Cheung & Rensvold, 1999, 2002).

As a consequence, if evidence supporting a measure's invariance is lacking, conclusions based on that measurement scale can be ambiguously or erroneously interpreted so that one doesn't know if the conclusions are due to a true attitudinal difference, or to different psychometric responses to the measurement scale. Failing to establish consistent and equivalent scales present the major threats to metric equivalence in multiple-group research (Myers et al., 2000).

Scholars in international marketing and management have argued that the validity of cross-national data analyses could be questioned if MI is not established and reported in the study (e.g., Singh, 1995; Steenkamp & Baumgartner, 1998; Van de Vijver & Leung, 1997). Therefore, our global project used a complex construct, *public relations leadership* and its seven critical dimensions, to address the importance of such assessment. We used the same measurement instruments across different countries and regions, as well as other important demographics (i.e., gender, years of experience, reporting level, and so forth). A key concern in doing so was our belief that comprehensive understanding and advancement of public relations leadership research requires that the validity of the scales and models developed in the United States or in any other single country be examined in other groups or regions as well. If evidence supporting a measure's invariance is lacking, conclusions based on that scale are ambiguous and weak. Thus, our research efforts sought an answer to this major question: Are the seven key dimensions of public relations leadership universally relevant?

Assessing the applicability of the theoretical framework of public relations leadership to different groups and other countries is an important step in establishing the generalizability and universality of a leadership theory in public relations, especially when research in the area is not fully explored. As suggested by Steenkamp and Baumgartner (1998), to achieve meaningful comparisons across groups or countries, the instruments used to measure the theoretical constructs of interest must exhibit adequate cross-group and cross-national equivalence.

Based on the results of our global online survey, we confirmed the universality of the seven dimensions of the public relations leadership construct by using multiple samples. All seven dimensions were confirmed to be critical in managing issues and selecting effective issue responsive strategies. The seven dimensions also were confirmed to be important in supporting the development of future leaders. Although the assessment of those key constructs indicated minor variances across different geographic groups, we believe the variance stemmed less from respondents' understanding and interpretation of the constructs than from the influence of other factors, such as the various stages of industry development in countries, varying organizational cultures, and varying cultural values at the societal level.

Unbalanced sample size also might be a major threat to the test itself. Although multiple-group assessment has been identified as a quality diagnostic tool for evaluating measurement equivalence, sample size requirements often limit the application of this method in certain studies (e.g., Bagozzi & Yi, 1989; Bollen, 1989). To avoid potential sample-size-related risks, we would recommend future research be designed to enlarge the sample size to generate adequate observations to match the number of parameters in the assessment. But, of course, we fully recognize the difficulty in recruiting good quality samples in global research today.

Despite repeated calls to report MI assessment in international research using a survey method, the research efforts presented in this global project also call for establishing methodological standards for all cross-national or cross-group empirical research in public relations. Although limited reports of MI in empirical cross-national or cross-group communication research have been identified, we believe that the attempt to conduct MI assessment would increase confidence in and respect for the field, especially when presented with a strong theoretical justification in the study. We hope that our study will help convince researchers who are interested in international public relations, communication, and multiple sample research to follow such standards and procedures, which can increase the rigor of multiple-sample and cross-cultural research in communication. Our own continuing research efforts will seek to advance understanding and usage of these procedures.

Advancing New Theory Development in Public Relations Leadership

Two important steps are required to accumulate knowledge to assist in theory construction: (a) the accumulation of results across relevant studies to establish facts and (b) the organization of facts into a coherent and useful form in building theories. Through this global project we have achieved both and articulated the importance of an integrated approach to leadership theory in our field. Moreover, we have confirmed the likely applicability of the integrated model of public relations leadership (Meng, 2012; Meng & Berger, 2013) in diverse nations and cultures, as well as with different issue management processes in practice.

Central to the mission of this global project is the generation of new knowledge to advance understanding of the critical role of leadership in public relations and to inform effective practice. We hope the results we collected will engage public relations scholars in advancing leadership as a vibrant and relevant field of scholarly research in public relations. We also hope the integrated model of public relations leadership and the seven critical dimensions can be used as the foundation for theory development and for stimulating other studies that aim to discover breakthrough knowledge for major advancement in our field.

We have achieved several significant steps in new theory development, such as theory conception and articulation, empirical testing and refinement, and further testing across different settings. Therefore, we suggest that efforts in theory affirmation and extension need to be addressed in future research to enrich theory-based knowledge and generate value-added contributions to the leadership concept. A variety of research topics and emerging worldwide phenomena can be used as possible topics for future leadership research that aims at advancing theory development.

For instance, the economic exchange relationship between developed and developing countries can provide valuable research openings to explore leadership development theories as effective communication strategies in a globalizing world. The growing influence of nonfinance indicators in business performance provides opportunities to examine the leadership role of public relations practitioners in improving organizational behaviors in social, political, and cultural sectors. The global competitive landscape of the next decade will likely be very different with the intervention of social media and digital revolution. Therefore, special effort is needed to investigate the role of public relations in leading such digital transformation for increased confidence and capability at the organizational level.

In addition, the frequency and the intensity of crises at various levels present challenges and opportunities to study leadership as a form of competitive advantage in searching for effective and efficient solutions. Such a phenomenon-motivated research agenda can help us advance knowledge of the integrated model of public relations leadership and explore valuable opportunities for new theory development. We invite interested colleagues to join us in this important effort.

Conclusion

Our study explored the concept of leadership in public relations and communication management through quantitative and qualitative data collected in 23 countries. As we noted in the first chapter, communication leaders at all levels are the profession's greatest asset, its richest form of human capital. The quality and performance of leaders have a great deal to do with the current and future success and legitimacy of the profession.

Whether you agree with our depiction of communication leaders as sense-makers or prefer an alternate metaphor, our research demonstrates that leadership in the field is complex, demanding, and insistent. Leaders don't get much time off or time alone backstage; they are electronically tethered to others in their organizations and to the constant *tick–tick–tick* of multiple events and conversations occurring in our around-the-clock world. They also are live, they are onstage, and they are watched, scrutinized, and continuously assessed in all they do. No wonder some professionals indicated they do not want to be leaders.

The practice of communication leadership, of sensemaking, is further complicated due to the presence of a divided consciousness that seems to go with the job—what novelist Jhumpa Lahiri (2013) refers to as "the intense pressure to be two things" simultaneously. Communication leaders, for example, must be convincing representatives of their organizations with individuals and groups outside the organization, while at the same time convincingly representing the interests of those outside groups and individuals to executives inside their organization. They must process vast flows of information and opportunities while at the same time converting this "bigness" of information to the "smallness" of messages—140-character expressions and 6-second-video brand messages. They must be authentic as individuals even as they serve as proxies for the values and practices of their organizations. Managing such intense pressure—so much cognitive dissonance—seems a crucial part of being a communication leader, but it is seldom investigated.

So there is much more to research and to learn about leadership in public relations, and we need to get on with it because the stakes are high. We believe that our integrated model of excellent leadership in public relations is a firm step in this direction. It provides (a) a useful framework to "see" the dimensions and requirements of leadership, (b) a thoughtful blue print for considering the development of future leaders, and (c) a basis for discussing assessment measures that might help us better evaluate the performance of our leaders. We hope that practitioners and scholars of public relations and communication management will benefit from our comprehensive exploration of the concept of leadership in the field.

References

Alden, D. L., Steenkamp, E. M., & Batra, R. (2006). Consumer attitudes toward marketing globalization: Antecedent, consequent and structural factors. *International Journal of Research in Marketing, 23*, 227–239.

Bagozzi, R. P., & Yi, Y. (1989). On the use of structural equation models in experimental designs. *Journal of Marketing Research, 26*, 271–284.

Berger, B., & Meng, J. (2010). Public relations practitioners and the leadership challenge. In. R. L. Heath (Ed.), *The SAGE handbook of public relations* (pp. 421–434). Thousand Oaks, CA: Sage.

Bollen, K. A. (1989). *Structural equations with latent variables.* New York, NY: Wiley.

Chen, E. (1996). *Transnational corporations and technology transfer to developing countries, UNCTAD, transnational corporations & world development.* London, England: Thomson Business Press.

Cheung, G. W., & Rensvold, R. B. (1999). Testing factorial invariance across groups: A reconceptualization and proposed new method. *Journal of Management, 25*, 1–27.

Cheung, G. W., & Rensvold, R. B. (2002). Evaluating good-of-fit indexes for testing measurement invariance. *Structural Equation Modeling, 9*, 233–255.

Chung, W. (2001). Identifying technology transfer in foreign direct investment: Influence of industry conditions and investing firm motives. *Journal of International Business Studies, 32*, 211–229.

Cui, A. S., Griffith, D. A., Cavusgil, S. T., & Dabic, M. (2006). The influence of market and cultural environmental factors on technology transfer between foreign MNCs and local subsidiaries: A Croatian illustration. *Journal of World Business, 41*, 100–111.

Erzikova, E., & Berger, B. (2012). Leadership education in the public relations curriculum: Reality, opportunities, and benefits. *Public Relations Journal, 6*(3), 1–24. Available online at www.prsa.org/Intelligence/PRJournal/Documents/2011ErzikovaBerger.pdf

Griffith, D. A., & Schuster, C. (2002). Before measurement equivalence: Ensuring conceptual equivalence. *Proceedings of the 2002 AMA Educators' Conference, USA, V*, 315–316.

Lahiri, J. (2013). *The lowland*. New York, NY: Knopf.

Meng, J. (2012). Strategic leadership in public relations: An integrated conceptual framework. *Public Relations Review, 38*, 336–338.

Meng, J., & Berger, B. K. (2013). An integrated model of excellent leadership in public relations: Dimensions, measurement, and validation. *Journal of Public Relations Research, 25*, 141–167.

Mullen, M. R. (1995). Diagnosing measurement equivalence in cross-national research. *Journal of International Business Studies, 25*, 573–596.

Myers, M. B., Calantone, R. J., Page, T. J., & Taylor, C. R. (2000). An application of multiple-group causal models in assessing cross-national measurement equivalence. *Journal of International Marketing, 8*(4), 108–121.

Singh, J. (1995). Measurement issues in cross-national research. *Journal of International Business Studies, 26*, 597–619.

Steenkamp, E. M., & Baumgartner, H. (1998). Assessing measurement invariance in cross-national consumer research. *Journal of Consumer Research, 25*, 78–90.

Vandenberg, R. J., & Lance, C. E. (2000). A review and synthesis of the measurement invariance literature: Suggestions, practices, and recommendations for organizational research. *Organizational Research Methods, 3*, 4–70.

Van der Vijver, F., & Leung, K. (1997). *Methods and data analysis for cross-cultural research.* London, England: Sage.

APPENDIX A

Online Survey: Global Study of Leadership in Public Relations and Communication Management

Introductions and Definitions: We are interested in your ideas and perceptions about leadership in *public relations* and *communication management*; these two terms mean the same thing in this study. We also use the term *leader* to refer to an individual(s) who is responsible for organizing and leading a communication group, unit or entire function to help an organization achieve its objectives. When we refer to *your communication leader*, we mean the highest-ranking public relations or communication professional in your work group, unit or function.

Section 1: Issues in the Field

In this section, we explore important issues in public relations and communication management. Please indicate to what extent you agree that each of the following issues is important to your communication leader (or you, if you are the leader) in your organization today. Use a scale of 1–7 for your answer, where "1" equals "a little bit" important and "7" equals "a great deal" of importance.

A little bit   1   2   3   4   5   6   7   A great deal

1. Dealing with the speed and volume of information flow
2. Meeting increasing demands for corporate social responsibility
3. Managing the digital revolution and rise of social media
4. Improving the measurement of communication effectiveness to demonstrate value
5. Being prepared to deal effectively with crises that may arise
6. Dealing with growing demands for transparency of communications and operations

7. Meeting communication needs in diverse cultures and globalizing markets
8. Improving the image of the public relations/communication management profession
9. Finding, developing and retaining highly talented communication professionals
10. Improving employee engagement and commitment in the workplace

Other issue (write it in)

Please indicate which one of these 10 issues, in your opinion, is the most important issue for your communication leader (or you, if you are the leader). Just click on the circle next to your top choice issue.

1. Dealing with the speed and volume of information flow
2. Meeting increasing demands for corporate social responsibility
3. Managing the digital revolution and rise of social media
4. Improving the measurement of communication effectiveness to demonstrate value
5. Being prepared to deal effectively with crises that may arise
6. Dealing with growing demands for transparency of communications and operations
7. Meeting communication needs in diverse cultures and globalizing markets
8. Improving the image of the public relations/communication management profession
9. Finding, developing and retaining highly talented communication professionals
10. Improving employee engagement and commitment in the workplace

Other issue (write it in)

For this most important issue you just selected, please indicate to what extent you agree that each of the seven following conditions or leadership personal abilities or qualities is important in helping your communication leader deal successfully with this specific issue:

A little bit   1   2   3   4   5   6   7   A great deal

12. Possessing communication knowledge to develop appropriate strategies, plans and messages
13. Participating in your organization's strategic decision-making regarding the issue
14. Possessing a strong ethical orientation and set of values to guide actions
15. Having the ability to build and manage professional work teams to address the issue

16. Providing a compelling vision for how communication can help the organization
17. Having the ability to develop coalitions in and outside the organization to deal with the issue
18. Working in an organization that supports two-way communication and shared power

Other quality/capability (write it in)

Continuing with the most important issue you selected, please indicate to what extent your communication team or unit is implementing each of the five strategies or actions listed below to help your organization deal with this most important issue. Your response can range from "1" for just "a little bit" of implementation, to "7" for "a great deal" of implementation.

A little bit   1   2   3   4   5   6   7   A great deal

#1 Dealing with the Speed and Volume of Information Flow

19. Developing new skills and/or improving work processes in your unit
20. Using new technologies to collect, analyze and distribute news and information faster
21. Hiring additional permanent or part-time employees
22. Assigning additional work and responsibilities to existing employees in the unit
23. Increasing the use of external consultants or agencies

Other strategy/action (write it in)

#2 Meeting Increasing Demands for Corporate Social Responsibility (CSR)

19. Generating public attention for the organization's CSR activities
20. Involving more employees in community projects and activities
21. Showcasing CSR achievements and employee accomplishments
22. Interacting directly with publics or groups who make demands for CSR activities
23. Convincing organizational leaders of the importance of CSR

Other strategy/action (write it in)

#3 Managing the Digital Revolution and the Rise of Social Media

19. Hiring employees with specialized digital media skills
20. Training team members and/or other employees in social media use and strategies
21. Creating key performance indicators for measuring social media activities
22. Monitoring stakeholder communications on the social web
23. Revising communication strategies to incorporate greater use of social media

Other strategy/action (write it in)

#4 Improving the Measurement of Communication Effectiveness to Demonstrate Value

19. Using business outcome metrics to measure effectiveness at the performance level
20. Monitoring and analyzing media coverage of the organization and its competitors or clients
21. Hiring external experts to provide measurement skills and develop metrics
22. Attending workshops on measurement to learn and adopt best practices
23. Focusing more on nonfinancial performance indicators than financial measures

Other strategy/action (write it in)

#5 Being Prepared to Deal Effectively With Crises That May Arise

19. Developing effective crisis communication plans for action
20. Using issue scanning and monitoring technologies to identify and track potential problems
21. Providing employees with training for crisis management procedures
22. Educating stakeholders about emergency communications and related response systems
23. Implementing effective issues management programs to reduce the risk of crises

Other strategy/action (write it in)

#6 Meeting Demands for More Transparency of Communications and Operations

19. Posting more company information on the Internet and/or Intranet
20. Monitoring stakeholder communications to identify transparency concerns

21. Communicating directly with external groups to address transparency issues
22. Providing more opportunities for 2-way communication between employees and leaders
23. Implementing an overall strategy to increase transparency throughout the organization

Other strategy/action (write it in)

#7 Meeting Communication Needs in Diverse Cultures and Globalizing Markets

19. Hiring more employees with international experience or language abilities
20. Providing cultural training programs for employees
21. Using national experts to guide communication programs in each country of operation
22. Monitoring and analyzing media coverage and developments in global markets
23. Implementing a global communication strategy for the organization

Other strategy/action (write it in)

#8 Improving the Image of the Public Relations/Communication Management Profession

19. Providing ethics training for team members and/or others in the organization
20. Supporting the education of future professionals at universities
21. Supporting research to advance knowledge of the value of communication management
22. Participating actively in professional association programs and activities
23. Modeling professional standards and ethical behaviors in your organization

Other strategy/action (write it in)

#9 Finding, Developing and Retaining Highly Talented Communication Professionals

19. Using search firms to help locate and evaluate talent
20. Providing superior financial incentives and benefits to top talent
21. Supporting the education of future professionals at universities
22. Designing individualized development plans for high potential professionals
23. Providing greater autonomy on the job to highly talented individuals

Other strategy/action (write it in)

#10 Increasing Employee Engagement and Commitment in the Workplace

19. Using reward and recognition programs to honor employees
20. Creating a positive communication climate to increase employee commitment
21. Increasing accessibility to, and visibility of senior organizational leaders
22. Facilitating the transfer of knowledge and best practices across units in the organization
23. Training front-line supervisors to improve their listening and communication skills

Other strategy/action (write it in)

Section 2: The Development of Future Leaders

In this section, we seek your thoughts about developing communication leaders for the future and strengthening the profession, in light of important issues in practice today. Please indicate to what extent you agree with the relative importance of each action below that might be taken to improve the development of future leaders in the field and enhance the communication profession. Use a scale of 1–7 for your answer, where "1" equals "a little bit" important, and "7" equals "a great deal" of importance.

A little bit   1   2   3   4   5   6   7   A great deal

1. Increase cultural understanding and sensitivity
2. Improve the listening skills of professionals
3. Develop training to enhance the emotional intelligence of public relations professionals
4. Urge professional associations to work together to develop leaders
5. Strengthen the business/economic component of communication education programs
6. Enhance conflict management skills
7. Develop better measures to document the value and contributions of public relations
8. Require professional accreditation or licensing
9. Impose tough penalties on ethical violators
10. Develop a core global education curriculum
11. Enhance professional skills in coping with work-related stress
12. Strengthen change management skills and capabilities

Other action (write it in)

Section 3: Your Perceptions About Leadership

We also are interested in your personal beliefs and perceptions about leadership. In this section, please indicate the extent to which you agree with the following statements. Use a scale of 1–7 for your answer, where "1" equals "strongly disagree" with and "7" equals "strongly agree" with.

Strongly disagree 1   2   3   4   5   6   7 Strongly agree

1. I consider myself to be a leader in communication management.
2. I don't want to be a leader in communication management.
3. I learn more about excellent leadership from role models and/or mentors on the job than from university education or management development programs.
4. Males or females can be equally capable leaders in public relations.
5. I prefer to work for a male leader on the job.
6. Females have better interpersonal communication skills than males.
7. The highest ranking communication professional in my organization is an excellent leader.
8. My organization encourages and practices two-way communication among members.
9. The CEO or top executive in my organization does not understand the value of public relations.
10. Leadership in communication management is different from leadership in other fields.
11. Leadership skills are more important than communication skills in leading a public relations unit or department.
12. I am optimistic about the future of the public relations profession in my country.

Section 4: Demographics

Please complete the following questions, which capture demographic information that will be used for categorizing the data. All information will be completely confidential.

1. Your total years of professional experience in communication management or public relations:

   Less than 5 years
   5–10 years
   11–15 years
   16–20 years
   More than 20 years

2. Type of organization for which you work:

   Publicly held corporation (stock ownership)
   Private or state-owned company

Communication or public relations agency
Nonprofit organization
Government organization
Educational institution
Political organization
Self-employed
Other, please specify:

3. Levels between your position and the highest ranked communication leader in your organization:

0 (I'm the top leader in public relations)
1
2
3
4 or more

4. You work in a communication unit or function that includes:

Fewer than 5 professionals
5–15 professionals
16–25 professionals
More than 25 professionals

5. Your gender

Female
Male

6. Your age:

Less than 25 years
25–35
36–45
46–55
56–65
More than 65

7. Your level of education:

High school graduation or equivalent
Bachelor's (or formal university) degree
Master's degree (formal graduate school degree)
Doctoral degree (highest graduate school academic degree)
Other, please specify:

8. If you earned a degree from a college or university, what was your major or primary area of study?

Advertising or marketing
Business administration, general business, or management
Computer science
Communication and media studies
Humanities (history, linguistics, literature, philosophy, speech, etc.)
Journalism studies
Mathematics or natural sciences (biology, chemistry, physics, etc.)
Public relations, communication management, strategic communication, corporate
communication, organizational communication, or public relations *and* advertising
Social sciences (anthropology, political studies, psychology, sociology, etc.)
Other, please specify:

9. Country in which you work:

Austria
Brazil
Canada
Chile
China (mainland)
Egypt
Estonia
Germany
Hong Kong
India
Jordan
Kuwait
Latvia
Lebanon
Mexico
Russia
Singapore
South Korea
Spain
Switzerland
Taiwan
United Arab Emirates
United Kingdom
United States
Other country, please specify:

NOTE: The following question will only appear for those respondents who have indicated above that they work in the U.S.

10. Which of the following best describes your ethnicity?

Asian
Asian American
Black/African American
Caucasian or white
Native American
Pacific Islander
Latino/Hispanic
Other, please specify:

APPENDIX B

Interview Guide: Global Study of Leadership in Public Relations and Communication Management

Opening Questions

1. Please tell me your current job title and your primary area of job responsibilities.
2. How many years have you worked in communications, and what drew you to this profession?

Thank you for that background. Our broad topic is leadership in public relations and communication management. In this study, I am using the terms "leaders" and "leadership" to refer to an individual(s) who is responsible for organizing and leading a communication group, unit or function to help an organization achieve its objectives. In this regard, I have two sets of questions to discuss with you today.

First, I will ask you to identify what are the two most important issues you confront as a leader in your organization. We live in a dynamic, rapidly changing world with many issues in communication management, of course. So I want you to identify two top issues you must deal with, and then I will ask you to explain how each issue directly affects your work and your leadership role. The second set of questions deals more with cultural and structural factors that affect your work. Let's start with the two top issues in the field.

Top Issue Questions

1. Please identify the most important issue in communication management that you are dealing with today—the one with which you are most concerned.
2. Why is this the most important issue or what makes it so important?
3. Important issues can affect many aspects of what you do on the job and how you do it, including the selection of tactics and strategies, the budgeting process, the kind of people hired, measurement approaches and many other

things. Please tell me as specifically as you can how this most important issue affects you and your work in the organization.

4. Thank you. Now please identify the second most important issue in public relations that you are dealing with today in your organization.

5. Why is this issue so important for you and your work?

6. As before, please describe to me how this issue specifically affects you and your work in the organization?

7. (*Note: Ask this question only if the person you are interviewing did not list digital or social media as a top #1 or #2 issues above.*) In our earlier survey, many leaders said that managing rapidly changing digital and social media was a top issue. Some suggested that digital media are revolutionizing the communication management field. Could you please comment on that by describing how digital and social media are affecting your own work and your vision for our profession in the future?

8. Thank you for sharing those insights. I have one last question about important issues in the field. In your view, and looking ahead 2–3 years, what do you see looming on the horizon as a potentially significant issue for you and other public relations leaders?

Cultural and Structural Factors

In this second part of the interview, I will ask you to respond to some questions about organizational culture and structure and how they influence your work, and the practice and perceptions of public relations in your company.

1. How would you describe the culture of your organization?

2. What cultural or structural factors in your organization help the communications function to be successful in its work?

3. Conversely, what cultural or structural factors in your organization impede or prevent the communications function from being more successful?

4. How would you describe your own leadership style?

5. Do you think some leadership behaviors or styles are universally accepted and effective across different cultures?

6. Do the senior leaders in your company value and champion public relations and communication management? Can you provide an example of how they do or don't?

7. What are the 2–3 key characteristics or qualities of excellent leaders in communication management?

8. What are the most important measures you use to demonstrate the value and effectiveness of your work to the organization?

9. Looking ahead, will communication leaders be different in the future than they are today? If so, how or in what ways?

INDEX